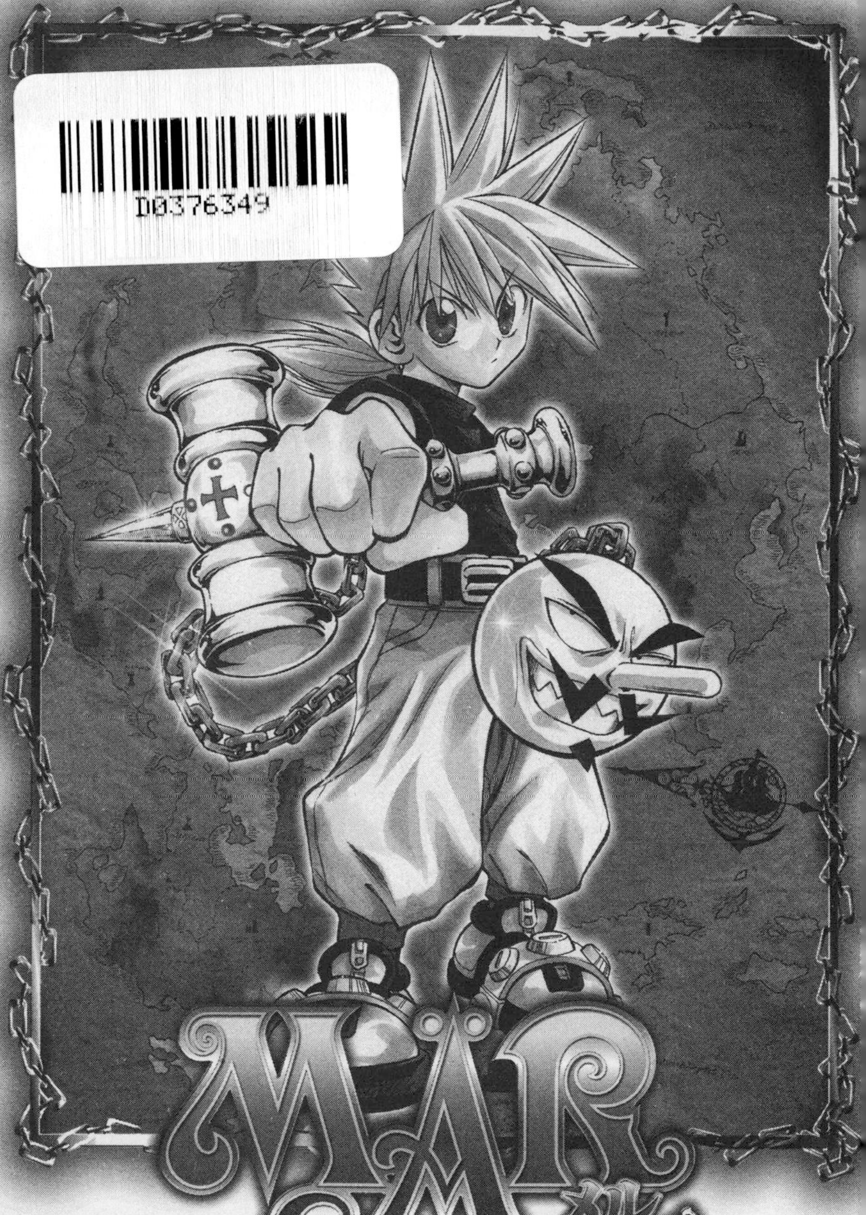
MÄR
MÄRCHEN AWAKENS ROMANCE

Vol.3

Nobuyuki Anzai

Characters

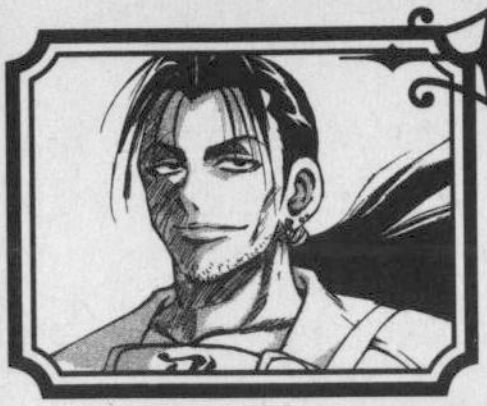

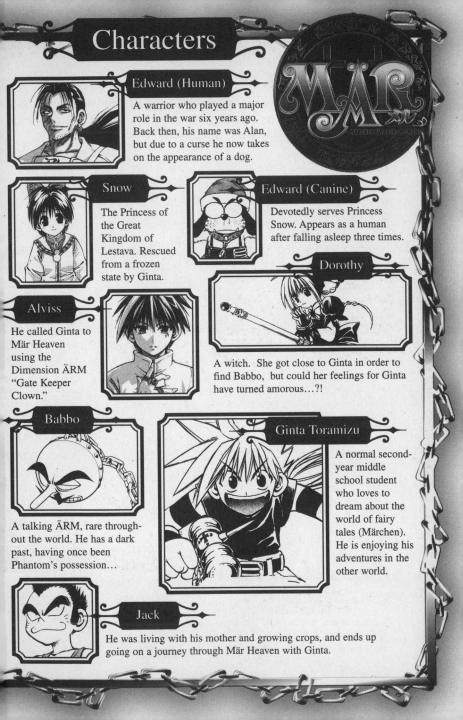

Edward (Human)

A warrior who played a major role in the war six years ago. Back then, his name was Alan, but due to a curse he now takes on the appearance of a dog.

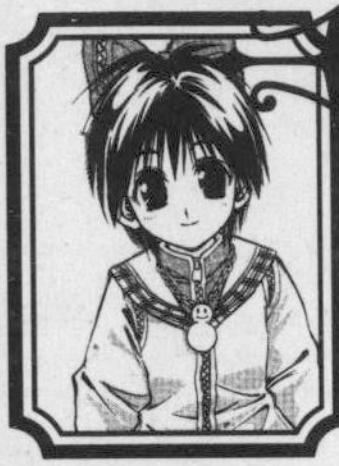

Snow

The Princess of the Great Kingdom of Lestava. Rescued from a frozen state by Ginta.

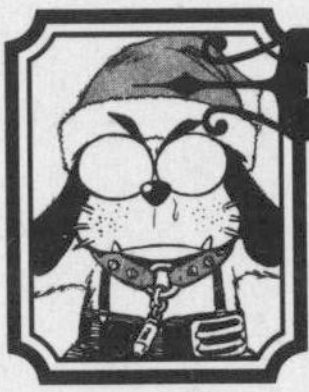

Edward (Canine)

Devotedly serves Princess Snow. Appears as a human after falling asleep three times.

Dorothy

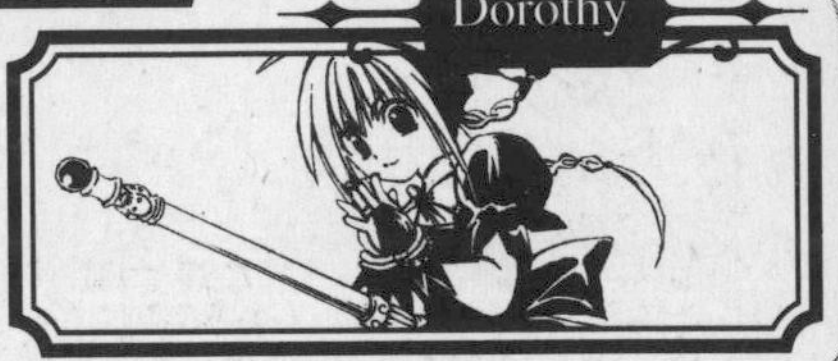

A witch. She got close to Ginta in order to find Babbo, but could her feelings for Ginta have turned amorous…?!

Alviss

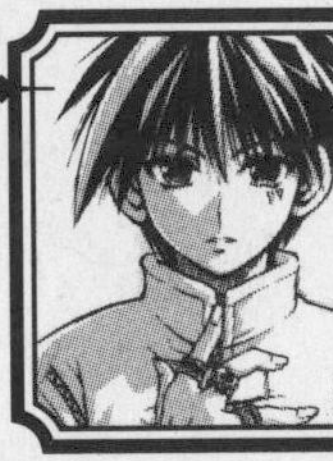

He called Ginta to Mär Heaven using the Dimension ÄRM "Gate Keeper Clown."

Babbo

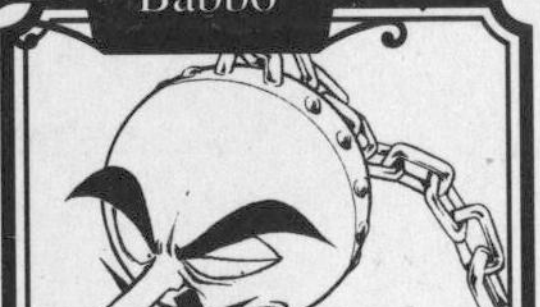

A talking ÄRM, rare throughout the world. He has a dark past, having once been Phantom's possession…

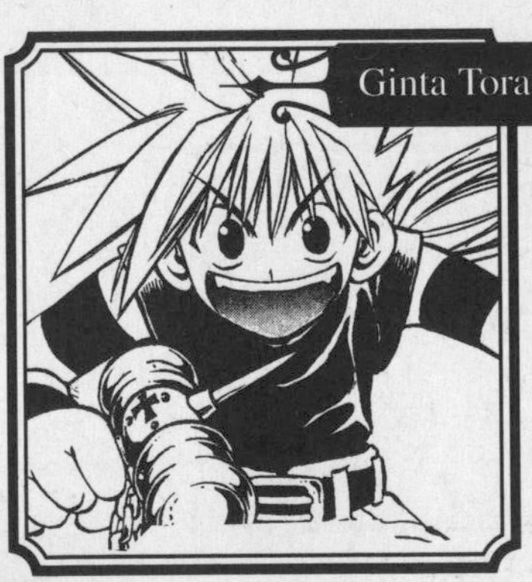

Ginta Toramizu

A normal second-year middle school student who loves to dream about the world of fairy tales (Märchen). He is enjoying his adventures in the other world.

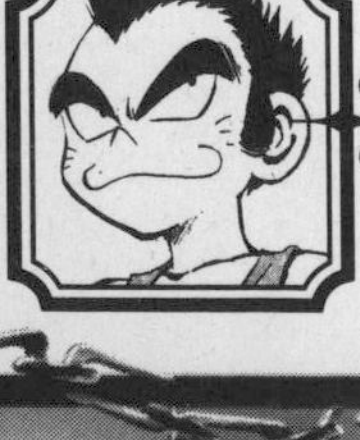

Jack

He was living with his mother and growing crops, and ends up going on a journey through Mär Heaven with Ginta.

AKT.20/New Strength

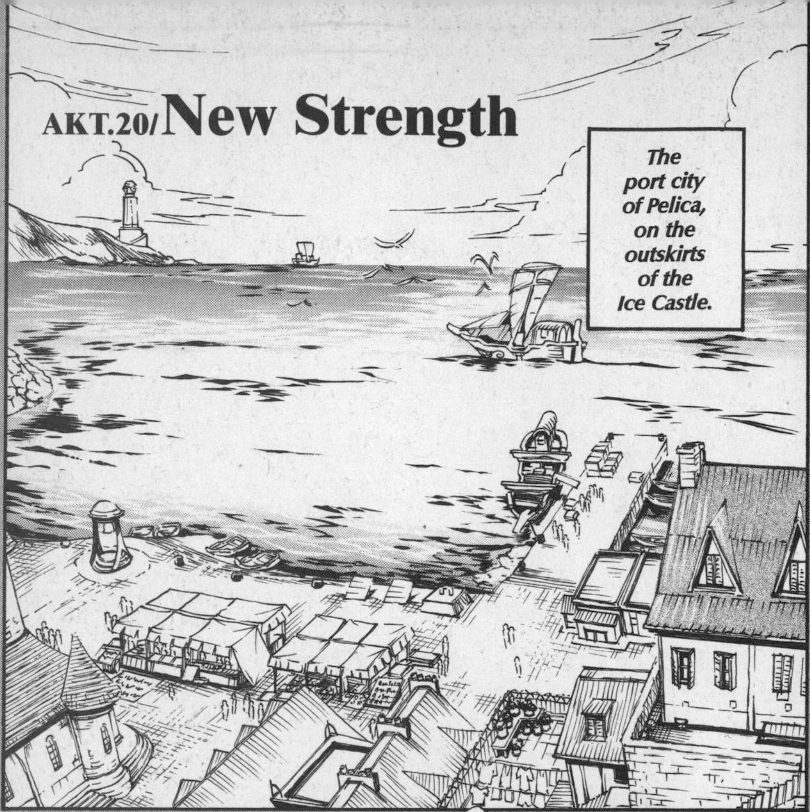
The port city of Pelica, on the outskirts of the Ice Castle.

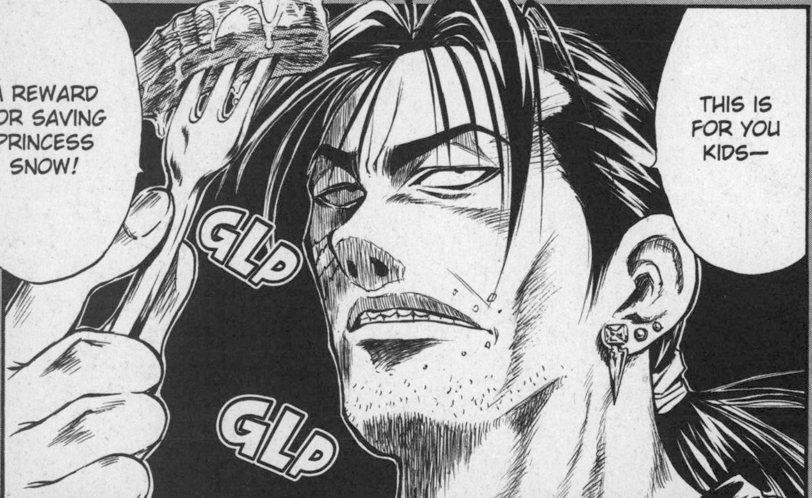
THIS IS FOR YOU KIDS—
A REWARD FOR SAVING PRINCESS SNOW!
GLP
GLP

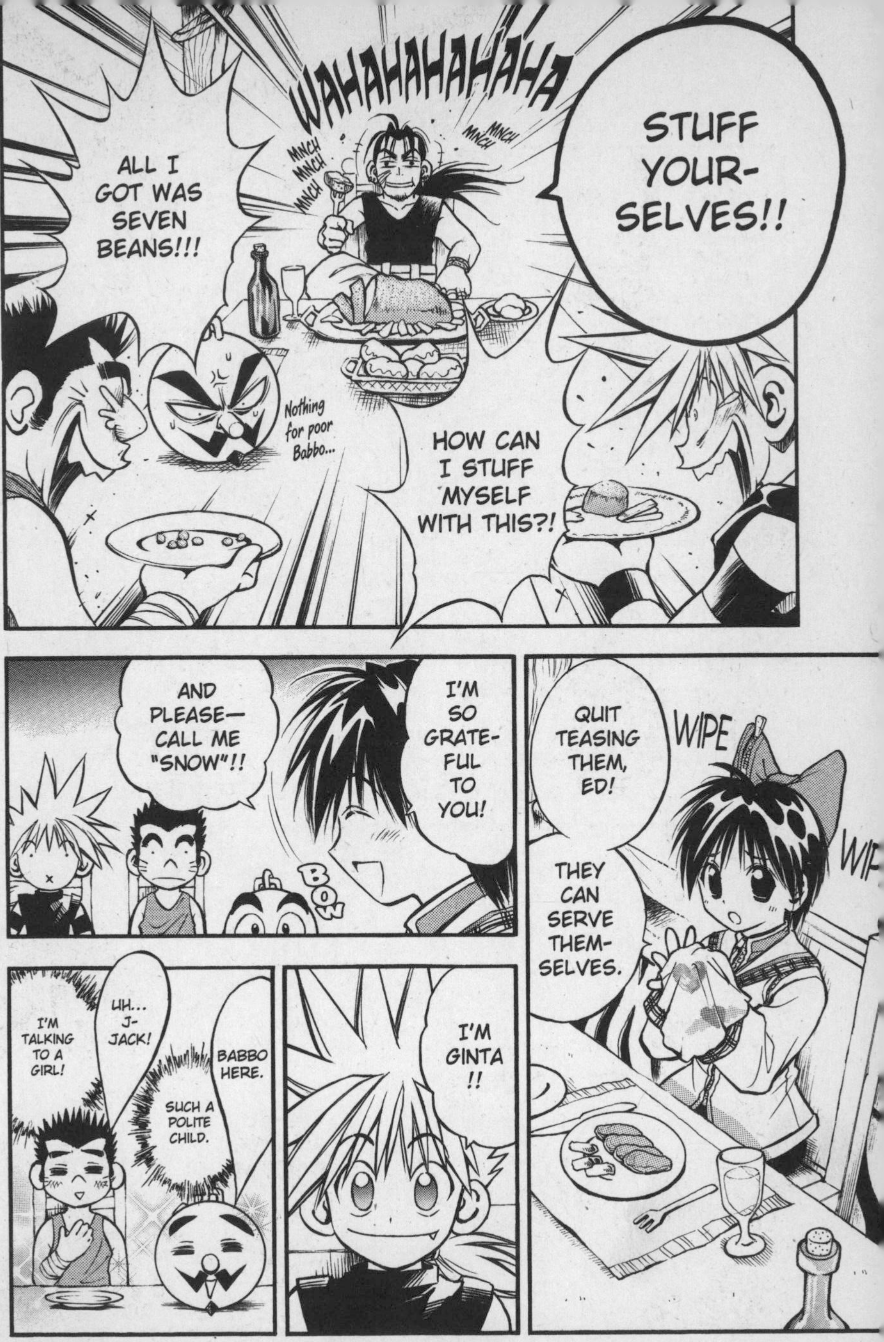
STUFF YOUR-SELVES!!
WAHAHAHAHAHAHA
MNCH MNCH
MNCH MNCH MNCH
HOW CAN I STUFF MYSELF WITH THIS?!
ALL I GOT WAS SEVEN BEANS!!!
Nothing for poor Babbo...
WIPE
QUIT TEASING THEM, ED!
THEY CAN SERVE THEM-SELVES.
I'M SO GRATE-FUL TO YOU!
AND PLEASE— CALL ME "SNOW"!!
BOW
I'M GINTA !!
BABBO HERE.
SUCH A POLITE CHILD.
UH... J-JACK!
I'M TALKING TO A GIRL!

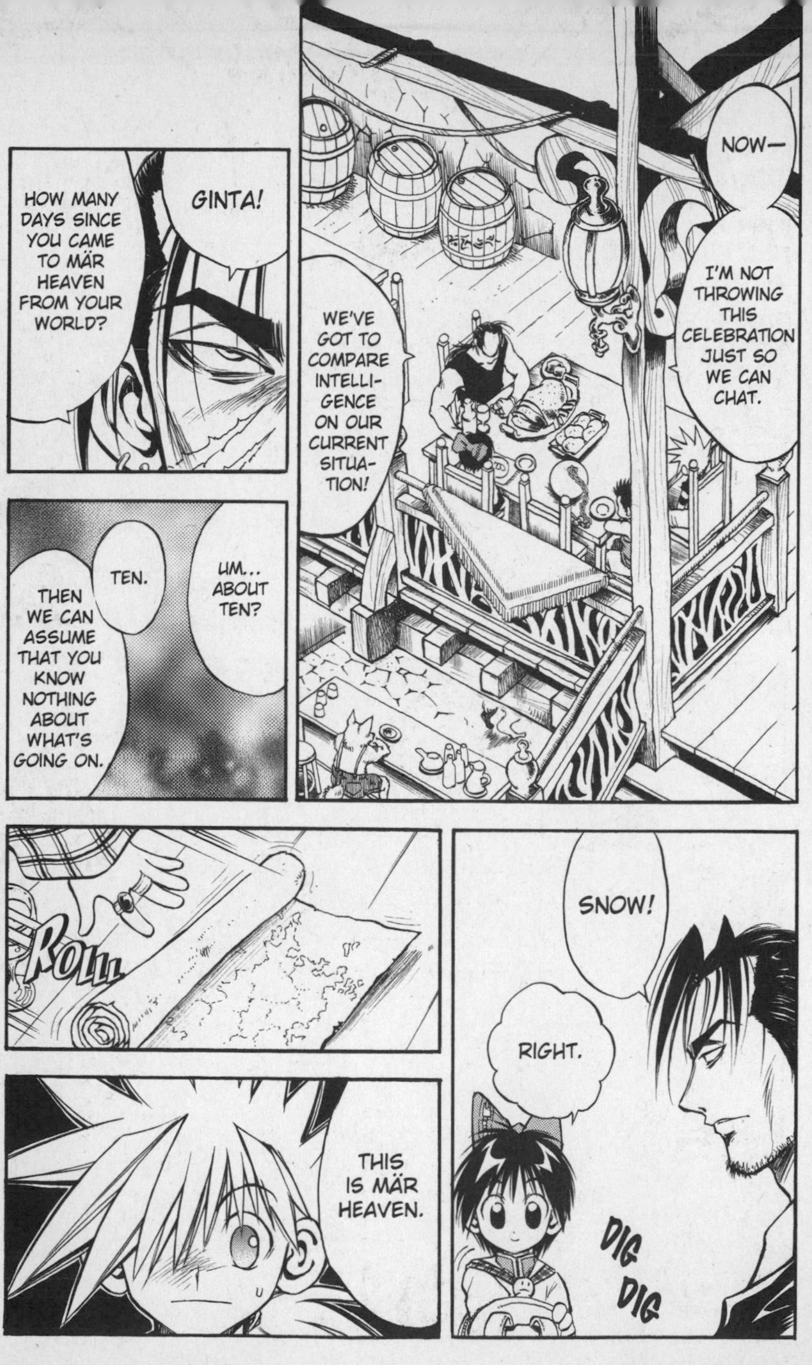
NOW—
I'M NOT THROWING THIS CELEBRATION JUST SO WE CAN CHAT.
WE'VE GOT TO COMPARE INTELLIGENCE ON OUR CURRENT SITUATION!
GINTA!
HOW MANY DAYS SINCE YOU CAME TO MÄR HEAVEN FROM YOUR WORLD?
UM... ABOUT TEN?
TEN.
THEN WE CAN ASSUME THAT YOU KNOW NOTHING ABOUT WHAT'S GOING ON.
SNOW!
RIGHT.
DIG
DIG
ROLLL
THIS IS MÄR HEAVEN.

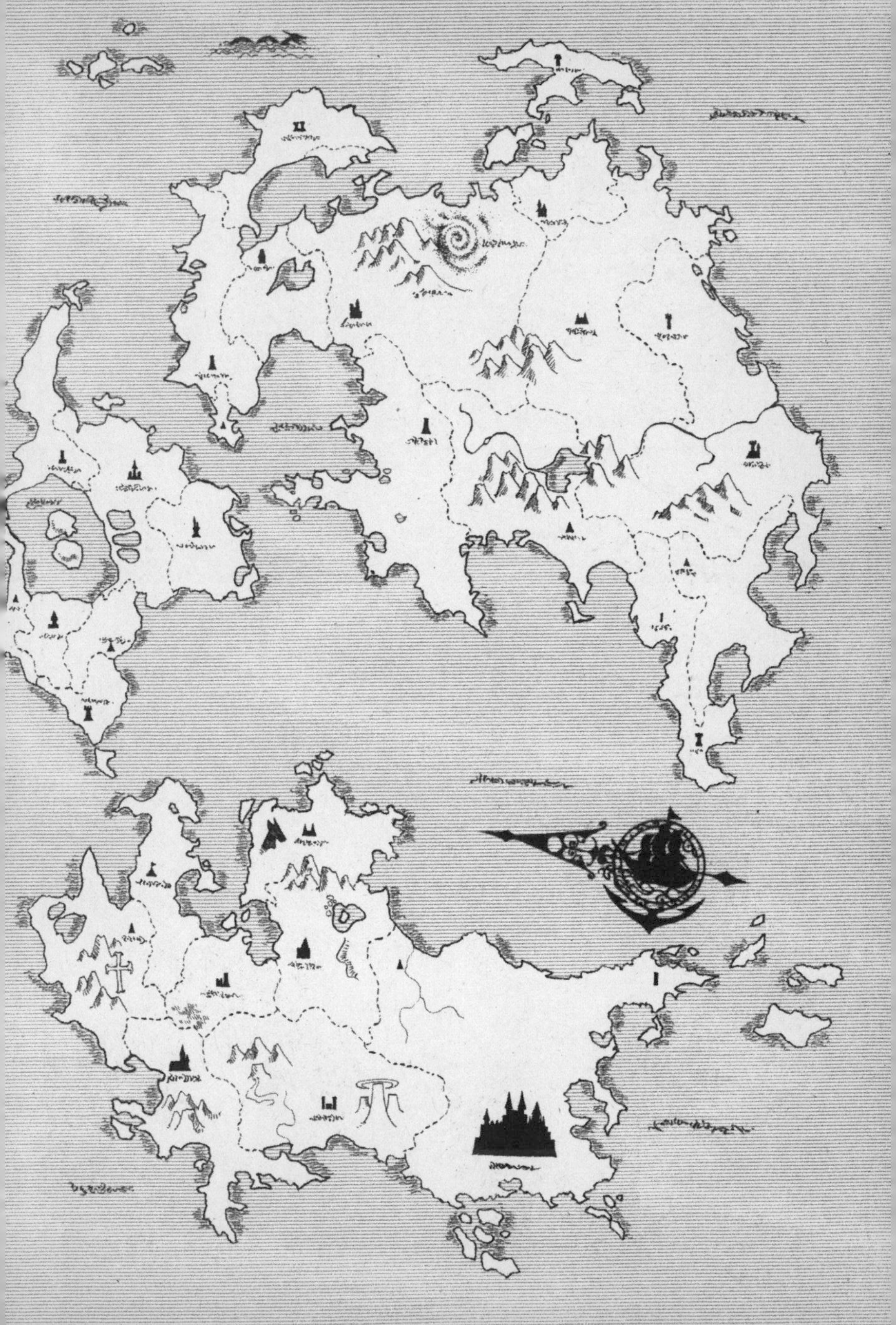

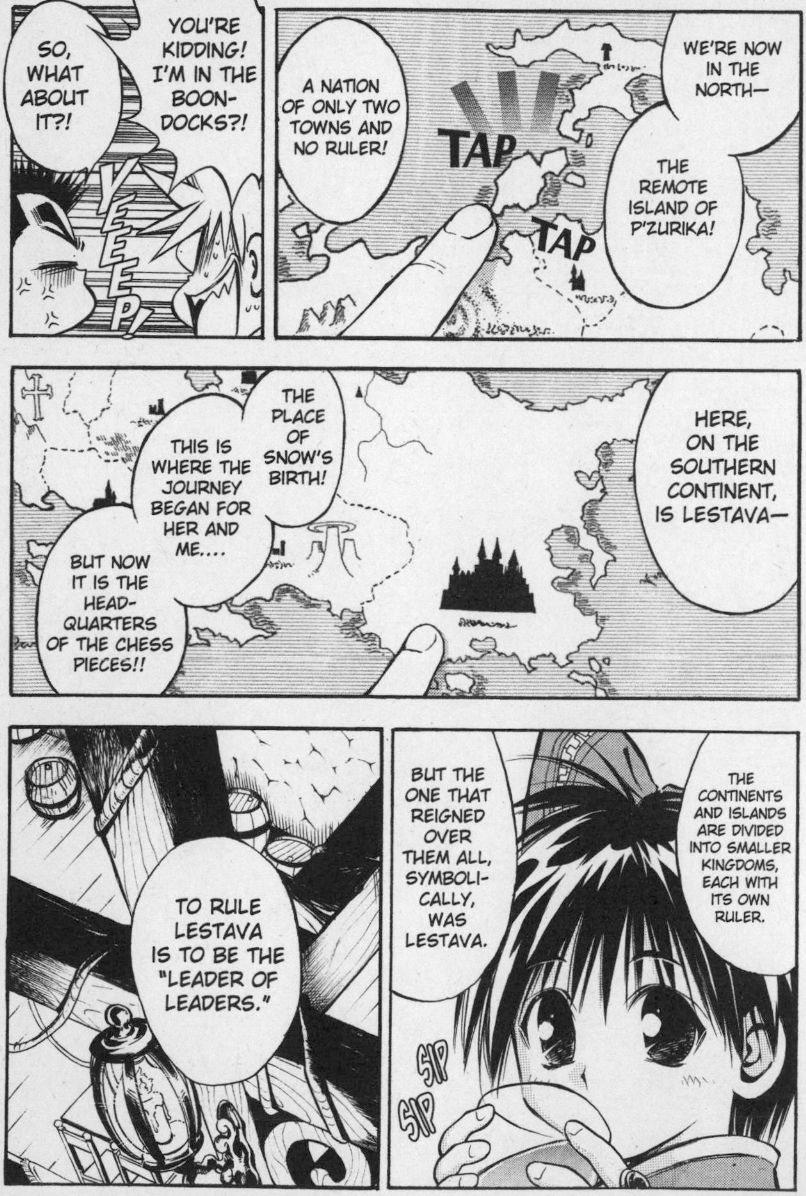
WE'RE NOW IN THE NORTH—
THE REMOTE ISLAND OF P'ZURIKA!
TAP
TAP
A NATION OF ONLY TWO TOWNS AND NO RULER!
YOU'RE KIDDING! I'M IN THE BOONDOCKS?!
YEEEP!
SO, WHAT ABOUT IT?!
HERE, ON THE SOUTHERN CONTINENT, IS LESTAVA—
THE PLACE OF SNOW'S BIRTH!
THIS IS WHERE THE JOURNEY BEGAN FOR HER AND ME....
BUT NOW IT IS THE HEADQUARTERS OF THE CHESS PIECES!!
THE CONTINENTS AND ISLANDS ARE DIVIDED INTO SMALLER KINGDOMS, EACH WITH ITS OWN RULER.
BUT THE ONE THAT REIGNED OVER THEM ALL, SYMBOLICALLY, WAS LESTAVA.
SIP
SIP
TO RULE LESTAVA IS TO BE THE "LEADER OF LEADERS."

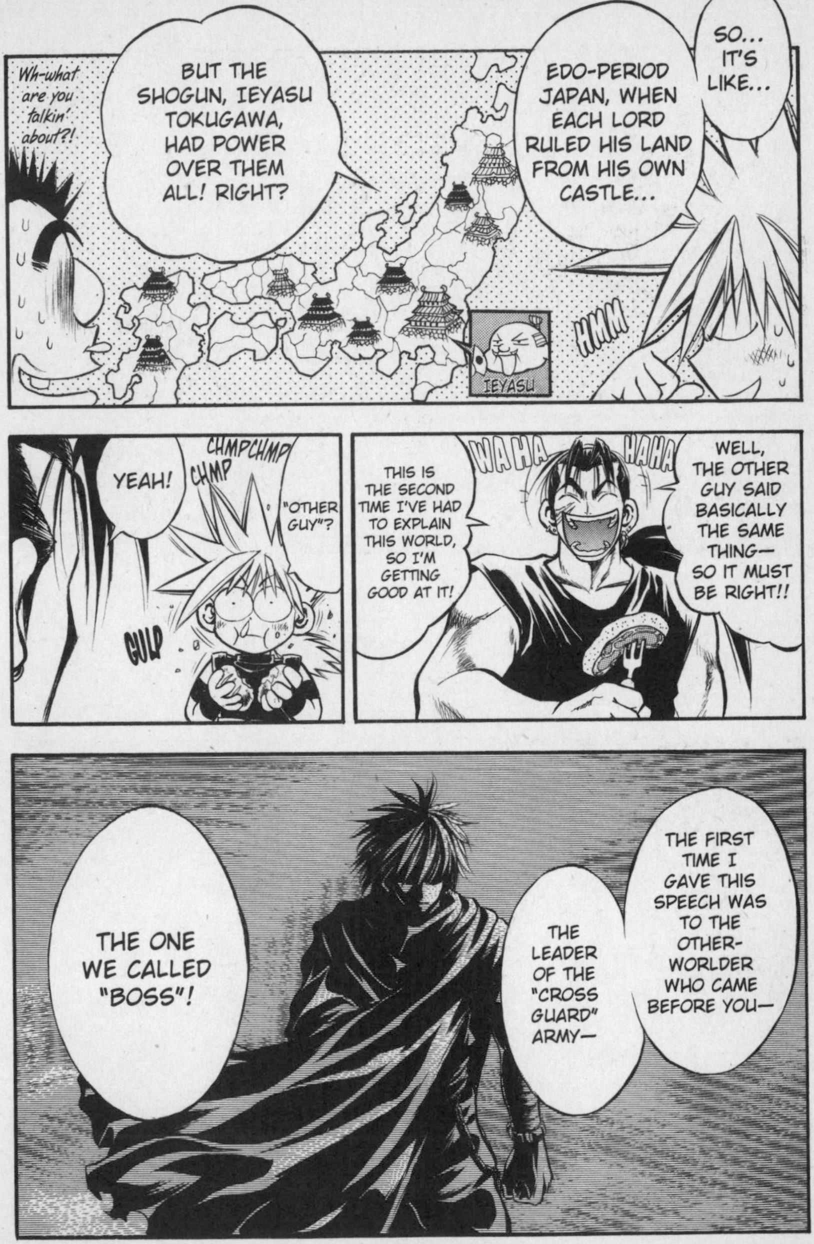
SO... IT'S LIKE...
EDO-PERIOD JAPAN, WHEN EACH LORD RULED HIS LAND FROM HIS OWN CASTLE...
HMM
IEYASU
BUT THE SHOGUN, IEYASU TOKUGAWA, HAD POWER OVER THEM ALL! RIGHT?
Wh-what are you talkin' about?!
WELL, THE OTHER GUY SAID BASICALLY THE SAME THING— SO IT MUST BE RIGHT!!
HAHA
WAHA
THIS IS THE SECOND TIME I'VE HAD TO EXPLAIN THIS WORLD, SO I'M GETTING GOOD AT IT!
"OTHER GUY"?
CHMPCHMP
CHMP
YEAH!
GULP
THE FIRST TIME I GAVE THIS SPEECH WAS TO THE OTHER-WORLDER WHO CAME BEFORE YOU—
THE LEADER OF THE "CROSS GUARD" ARMY—
THE ONE WE CALLED "BOSS"!

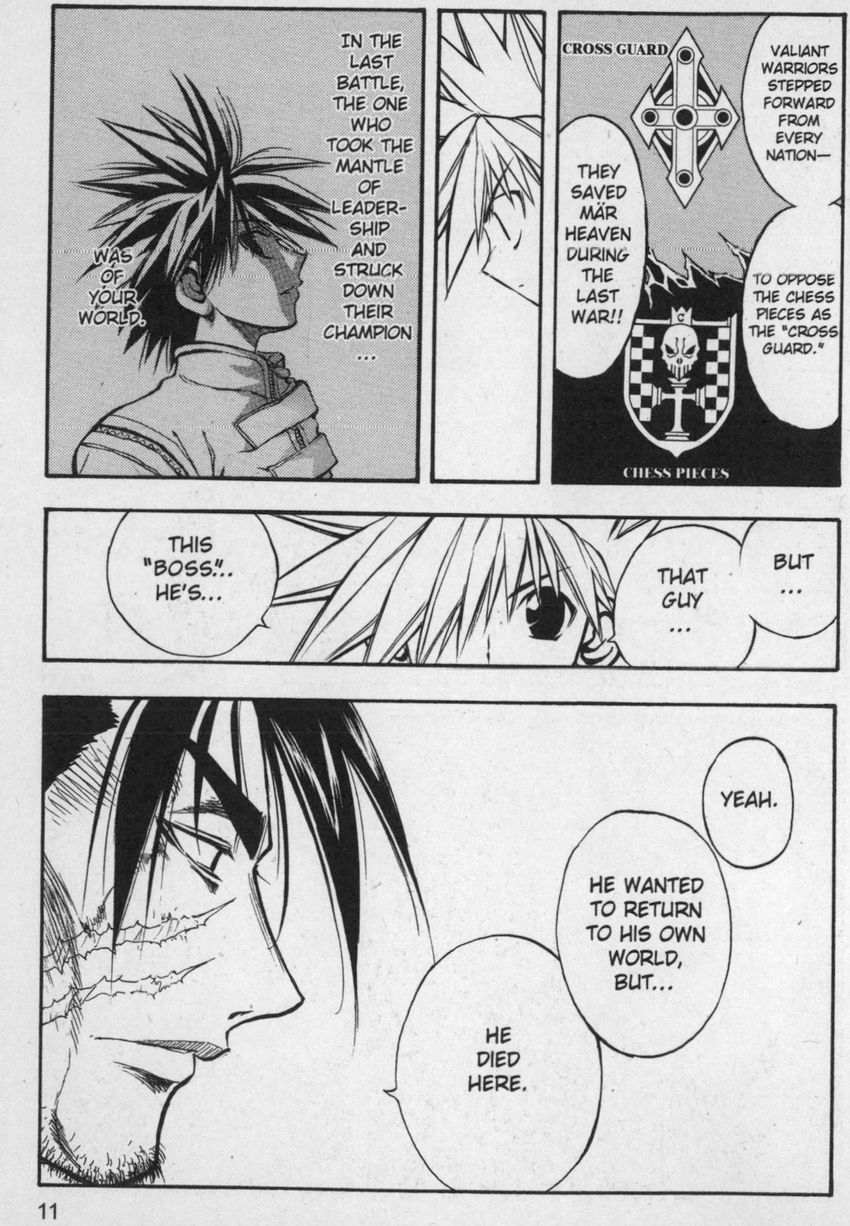
VALIANT WARRIORS STEPPED FORWARD FROM EVERY NATION—
CROSS GUARD
TO OPPOSE THE CHESS PIECES AS THE "CROSS GUARD."
THEY SAVED MÄR HEAVEN DURING THE LAST WAR!!
CHESS PIECES
IN THE LAST BATTLE, THE ONE WHO TOOK THE MANTLE OF LEADER-SHIP AND STRUCK DOWN THEIR CHAMPION...
WAS OF YOUR WORLD.
BUT...
THAT GUY...
THIS "BOSS"... HE'S...
YEAH.
HE WANTED TO RETURN TO HIS OWN WORLD, BUT...
HE DIED HERE.

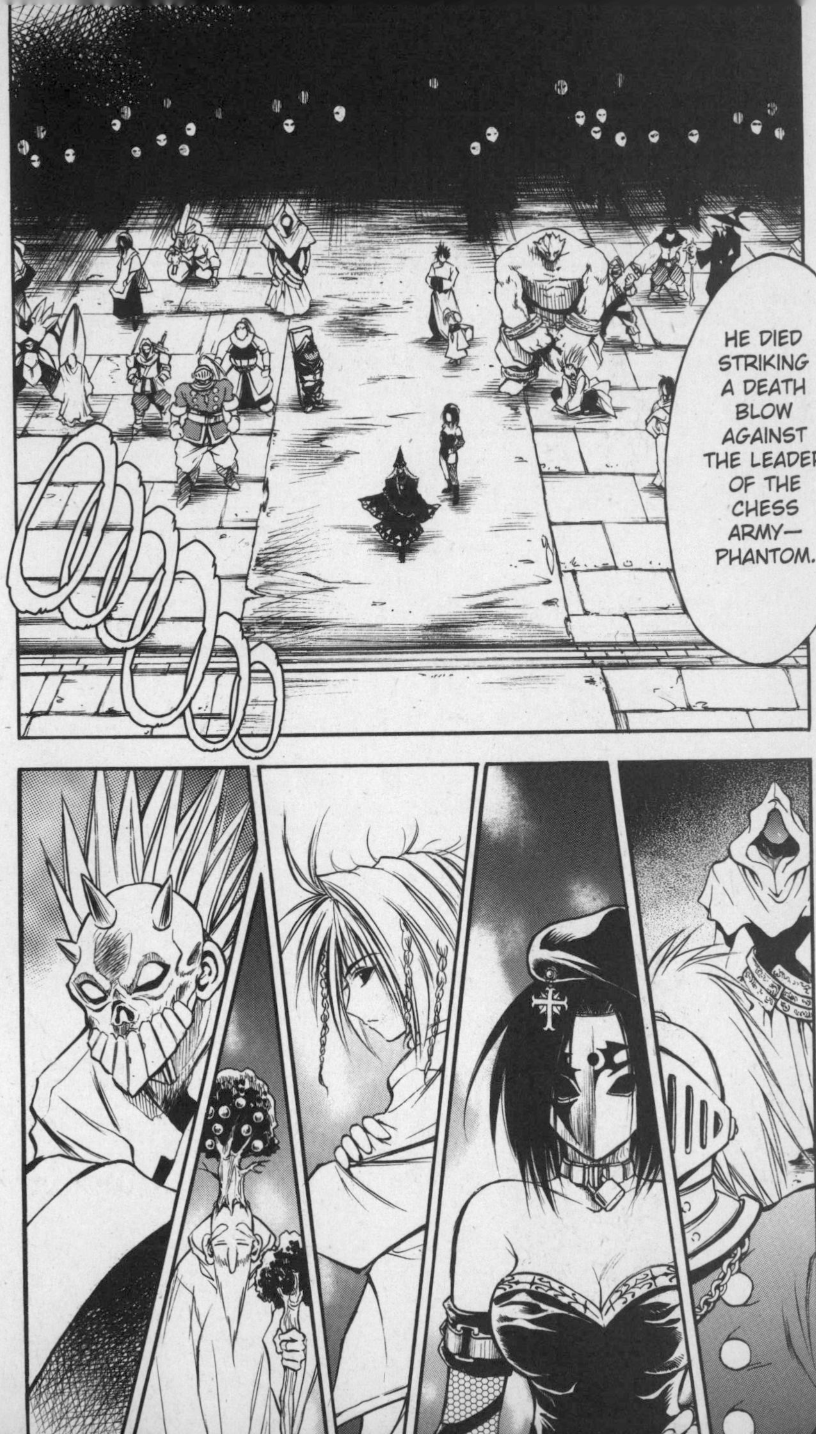
HE DIED STRIKING A DEATH BLOW AGAINST THE LEADER OF THE CHESS ARMY—PHANTOM.

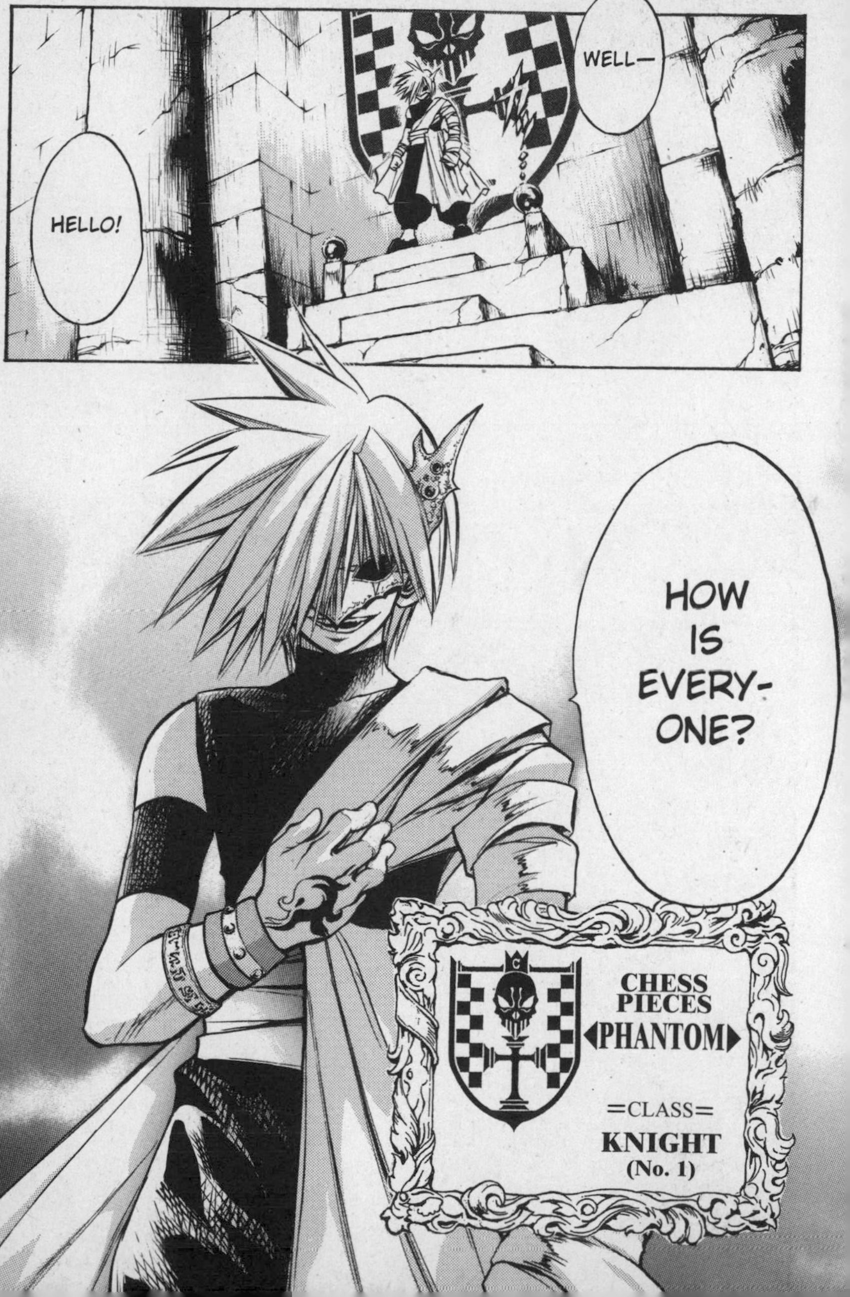
WELL—
HELLO!
HOW IS EVERY-ONE?
CHESS PIECES
◀PHANTOM▶
=CLASS=
KNIGHT
(No. 1)

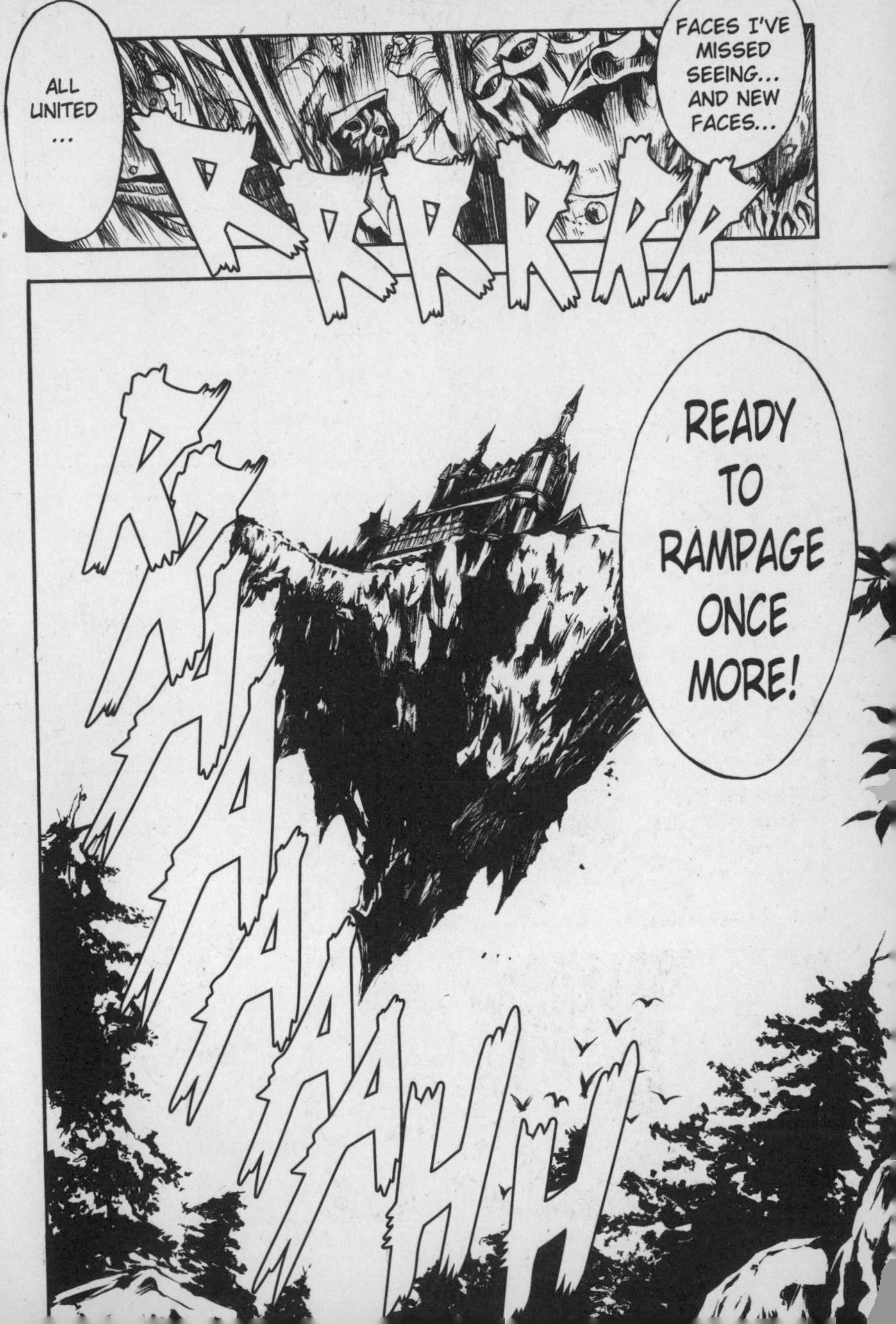
FACES I'VE MISSED SEEING... AND NEW FACES...
ALL UNITED ...
RRRRRR
READY TO RAMPAGE ONCE MORE!
RAAAAHH

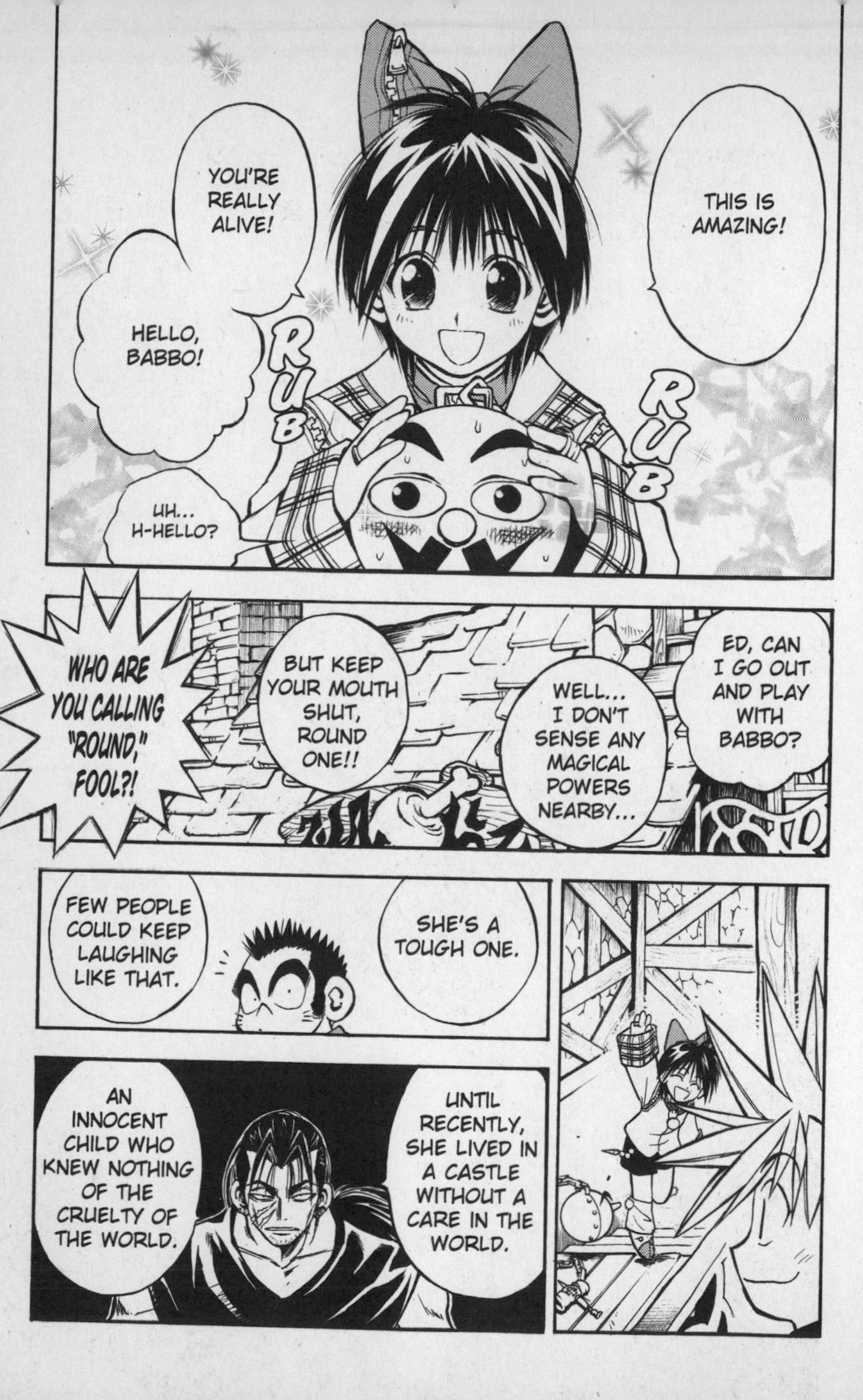
THIS IS AMAZING!
RUB
YOU'RE REALLY ALIVE!
HELLO, BABBO!
RUB
UH... H-HELLO?
ED, CAN I GO OUT AND PLAY WITH BABBO?
WELL... I DON'T SENSE ANY MAGICAL POWERS NEARBY...
BUT KEEP YOUR MOUTH SHUT, ROUND ONE!!
WHO ARE YOU CALLING "ROUND," FOOL?!
SHE'S A TOUGH ONE.
FEW PEOPLE COULD KEEP LAUGHING LIKE THAT.
UNTIL RECENTLY, SHE LIVED IN A CASTLE WITHOUT A CARE IN THE WORLD.
AN INNOCENT CHILD WHO KNEW NOTHING OF THE CRUELTY OF THE WORLD.

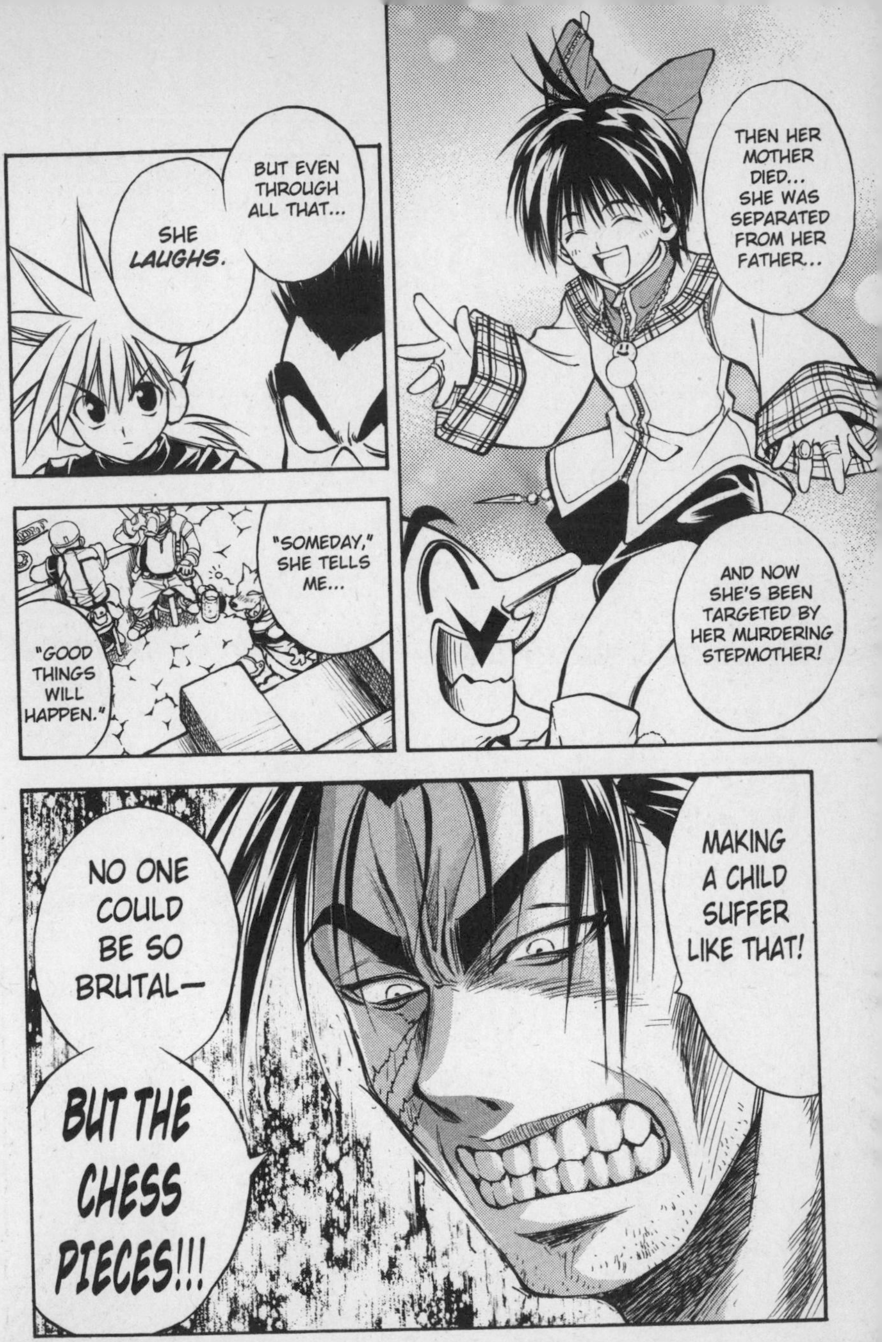
THEN HER MOTHER DIED... SHE WAS SEPARATED FROM HER FATHER...
AND NOW SHE'S BEEN TARGETED BY HER MURDERING STEPMOTHER!
BUT EVEN THROUGH ALL THAT...
SHE *LAUGHS.*
"SOMEDAY," SHE TELLS ME...
"GOOD THINGS WILL HAPPEN."
MAKING A CHILD SUFFER LIKE THAT!
NO ONE COULD BE SO BRUTAL—
BUT THE CHESS PIECES!!!

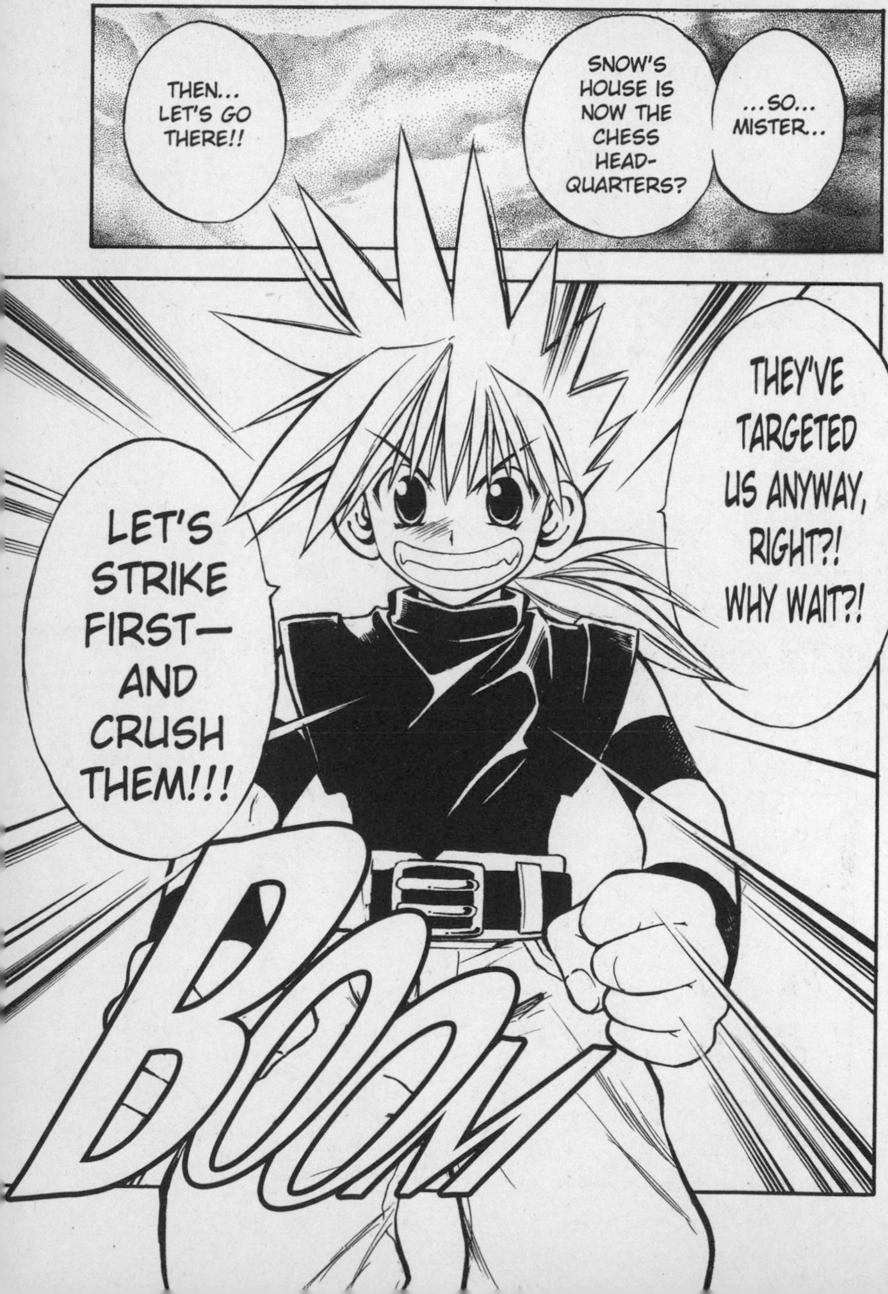
...SO... MISTER..
SNOW'S HOUSE IS NOW THE CHESS HEAD-QUARTERS?
THEN... LET'S GO THERE!!
THEY'VE TARGETED US ANYWAY, RIGHT?! WHY WAIT?!
LET'S STRIKE FIRST— AND CRUSH THEM!!!

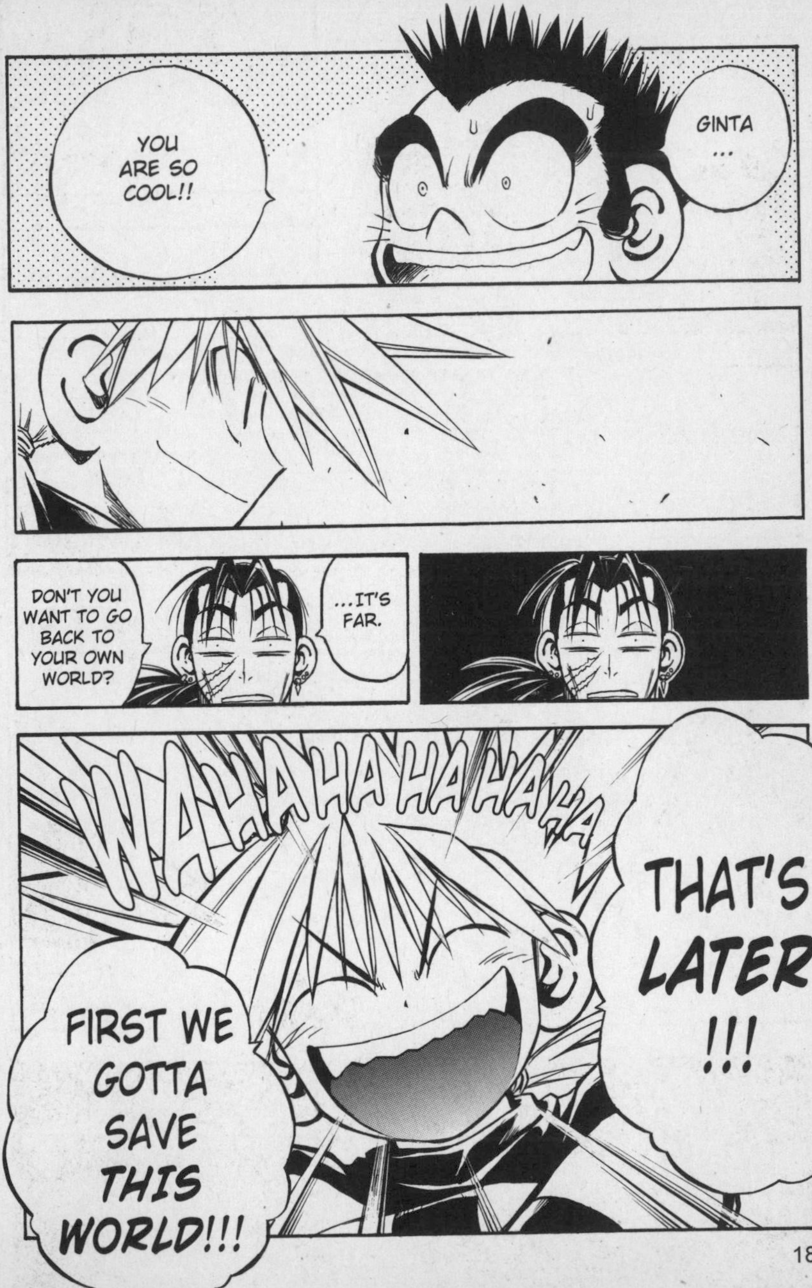
GINTA ...
YOU ARE SO COOL!!
...IT'S FAR.
DON'T YOU WANT TO GO BACK TO YOUR OWN WORLD?
WAHAHAHAHAHAHA
THAT'S LATER!!!
FIRST WE GOTTA SAVE THIS WORLD!!!

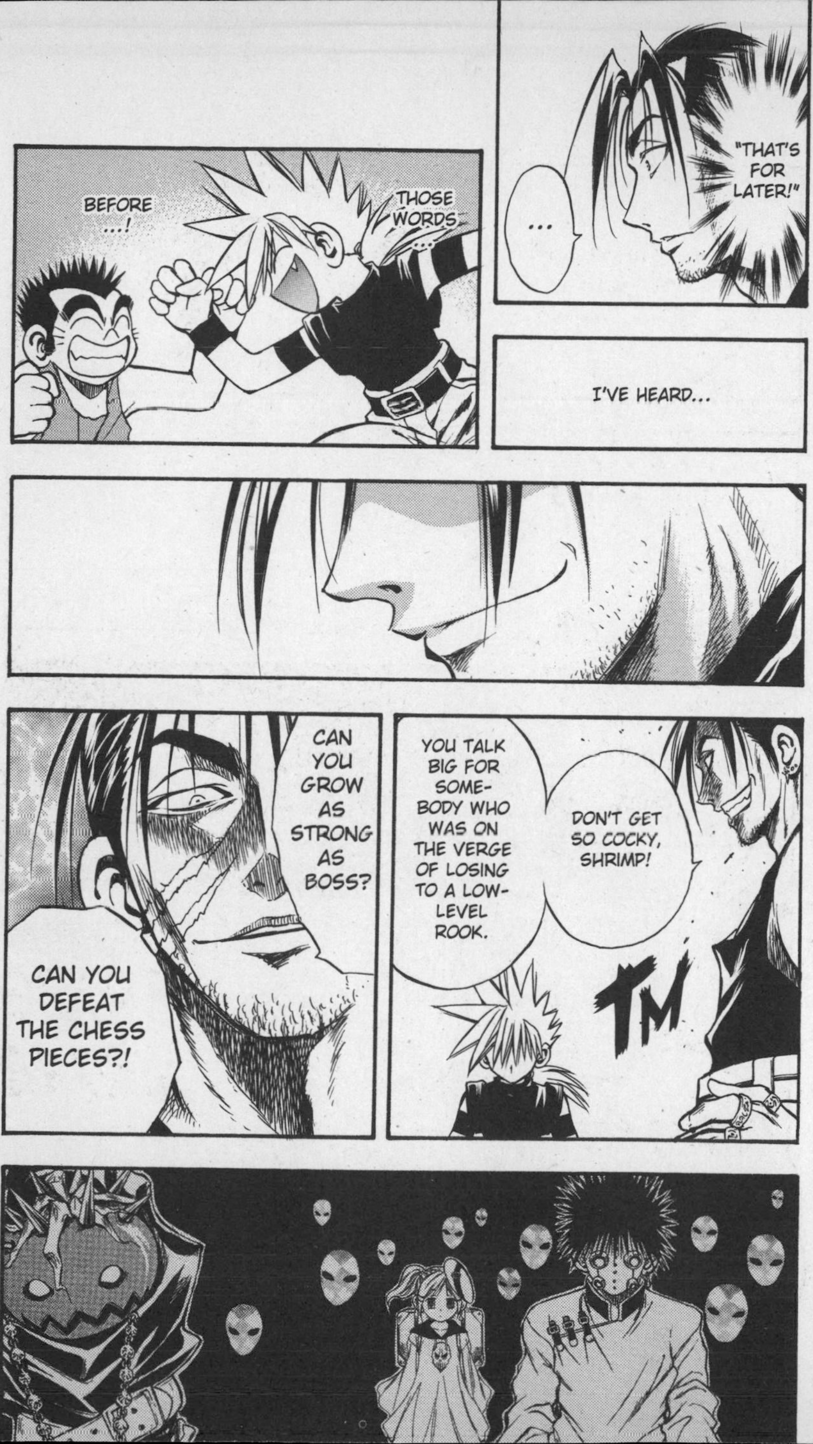
"THAT'S FOR LATER!"
...
THOSE WORDS
BEFORE ...!
I'VE HEARD...
DON'T GET SO COCKY, SHRIMP!
YOU TALK BIG FOR SOME-BODY WHO WAS ON THE VERGE OF LOSING TO A LOW-LEVEL ROOK.
TM
CAN YOU GROW AS STRONG AS BOSS?
CAN YOU DEFEAT THE CHESS PIECES?!

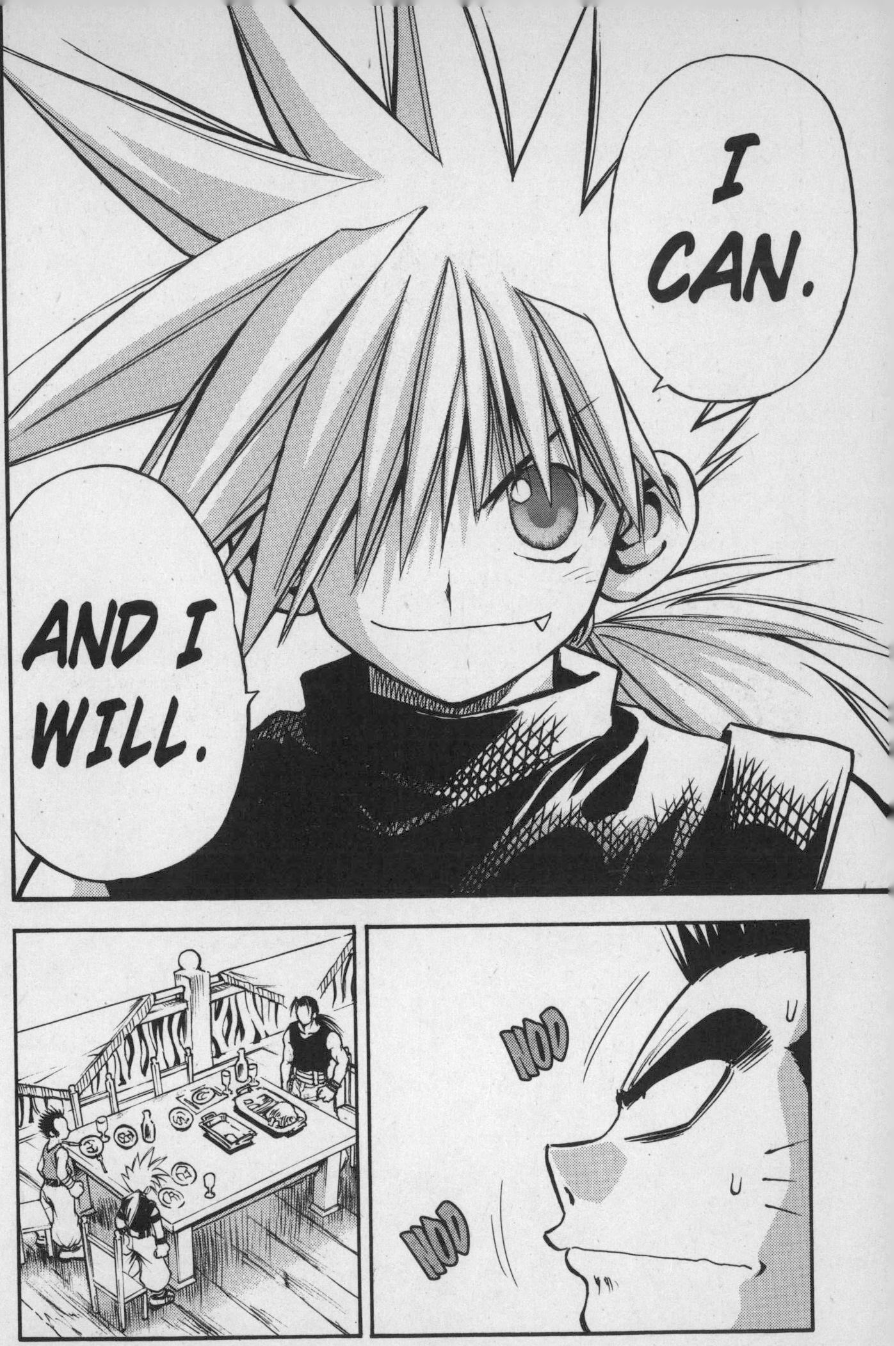
I CAN.
AND I WILL.
NOD
NOD

I KNEW IT.

BOSS...

ARE ALL YOU OTHER-WORLDERS THIS FOOLISH?

HE'S SAYING THE SAME THINGS ...

THAT YOU DID WHEN WE FIRST MET.

FINE, THEN ...

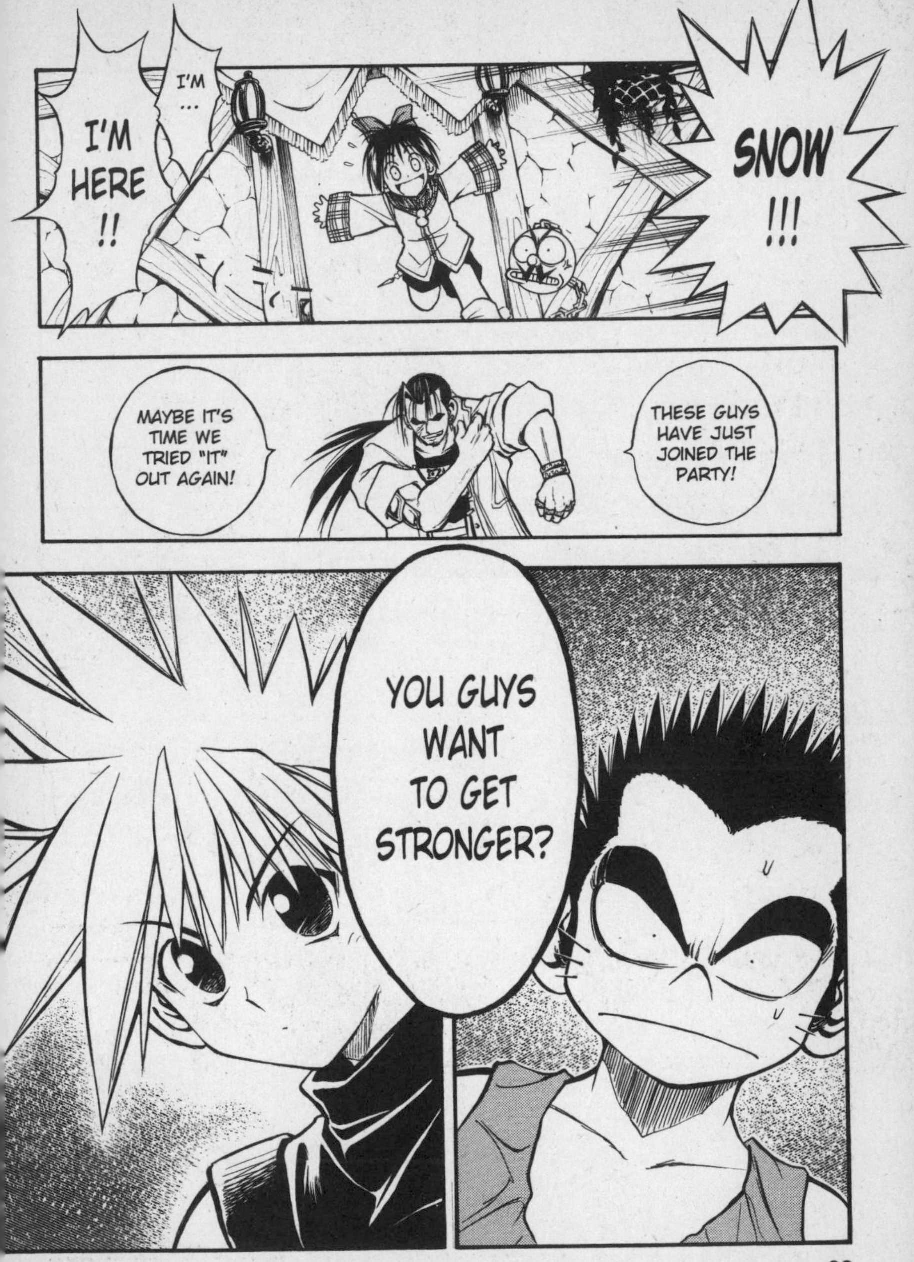
SNOW!!!
I'M ...
I'M HERE!!
THESE GUYS HAVE JUST JOINED THE PARTY!
MAYBE IT'S TIME WE TRIED "IT" OUT AGAIN!
YOU GUYS WANT TO GET STRONGER?

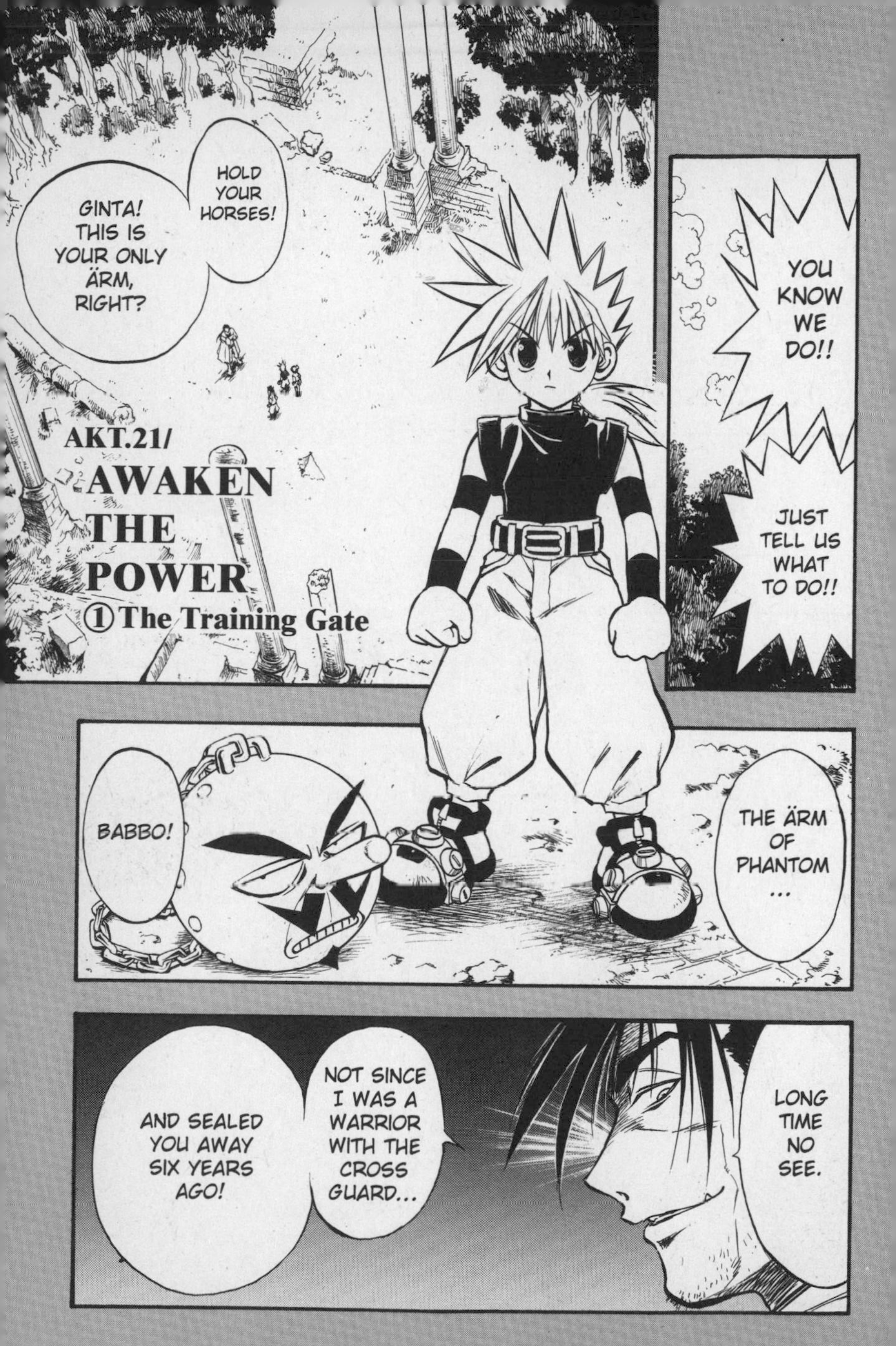
YOU KNOW WE DO!!
JUST TELL US WHAT TO DO!!
HOLD YOUR HORSES!
GINTA! THIS IS YOUR ONLY ÄRM, RIGHT?
AKT.21/
AWAKEN THE POWER
① The Training Gate
THE ÄRM OF PHANTOM...
BABBO!
LONG TIME NO SEE.
NOT SINCE I WAS A WARRIOR WITH THE CROSS GUARD...
AND SEALED YOU AWAY SIX YEARS AGO!

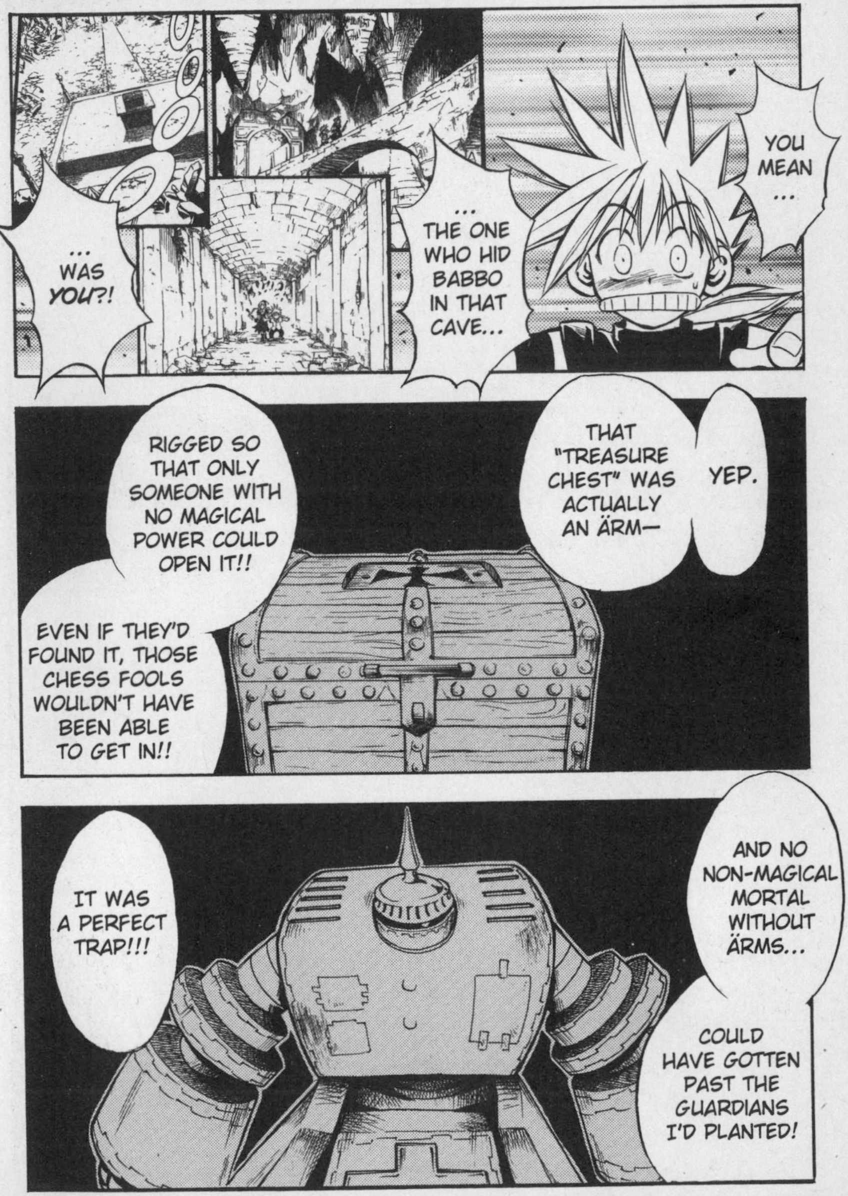
YOU MEAN ...
... THE ONE WHO HID BABBO IN THAT CAVE...
... WAS *YOU*?!
YEP.
THAT "TREASURE CHEST" WAS ACTUALLY AN ÄRM—
RIGGED SO THAT ONLY SOMEONE WITH NO MAGICAL POWER COULD OPEN IT!!
EVEN IF THEY'D FOUND IT, THOSE CHESS FOOLS WOULDN'T HAVE BEEN ABLE TO GET IN!!
AND NO NON-MAGICAL MORTAL WITHOUT ÄRMS...
COULD HAVE GOTTEN PAST THE GUARDIANS I'D PLANTED!
IT WAS A PERFECT TRAP!!!

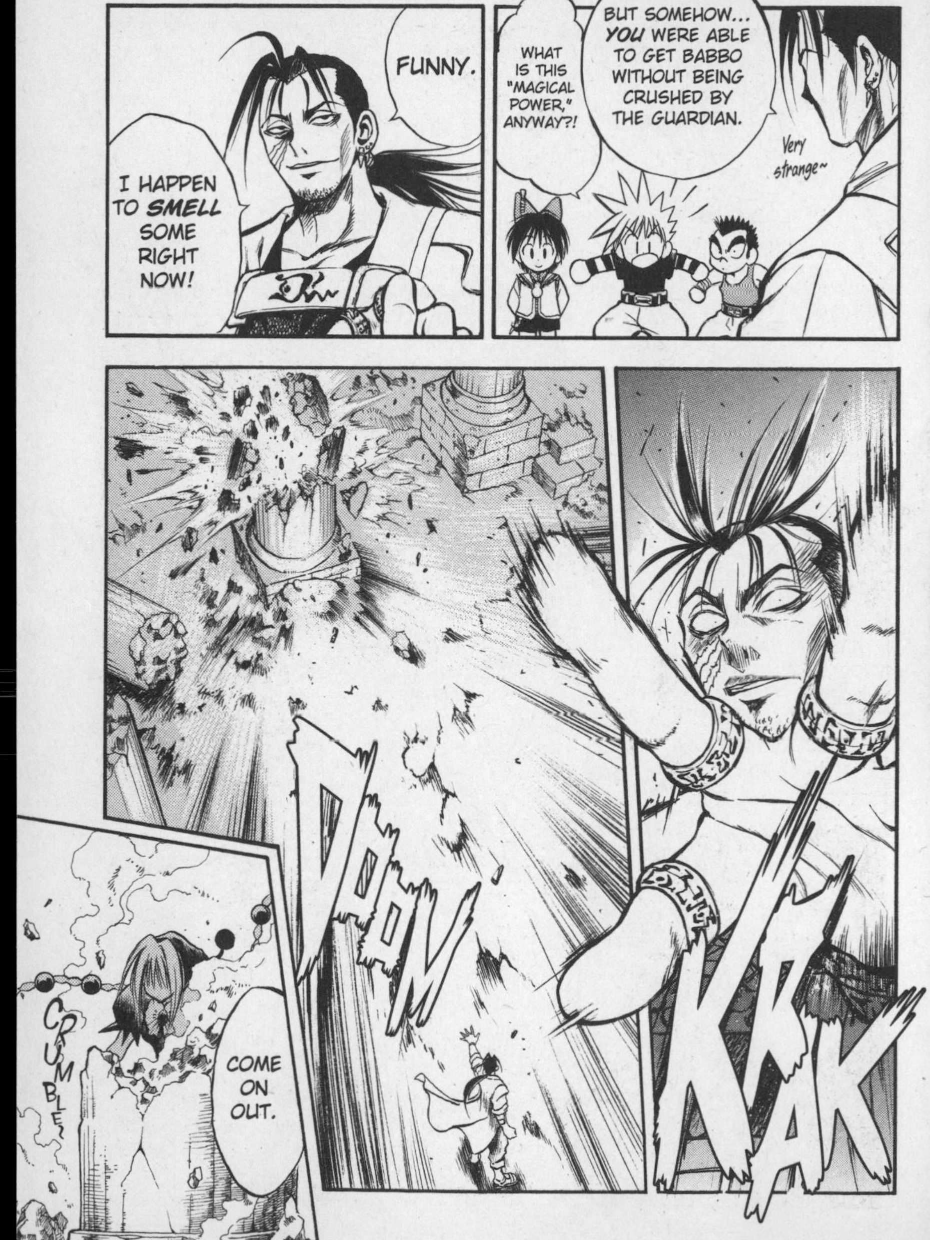
BUT SOMEHOW... YOU WERE ABLE TO GET BABBO WITHOUT BEING CRUSHED BY THE GUARDIAN.
Very strange~
WHAT IS THIS "MAGICAL POWER," ANYWAY?!
FUNNY.
I HAPPEN TO SMELL SOME RIGHT NOW!
KAK
CRUMBLE
COME ON OUT.

AKT.21/

AWAKEN THE POWER

① The Training Gate

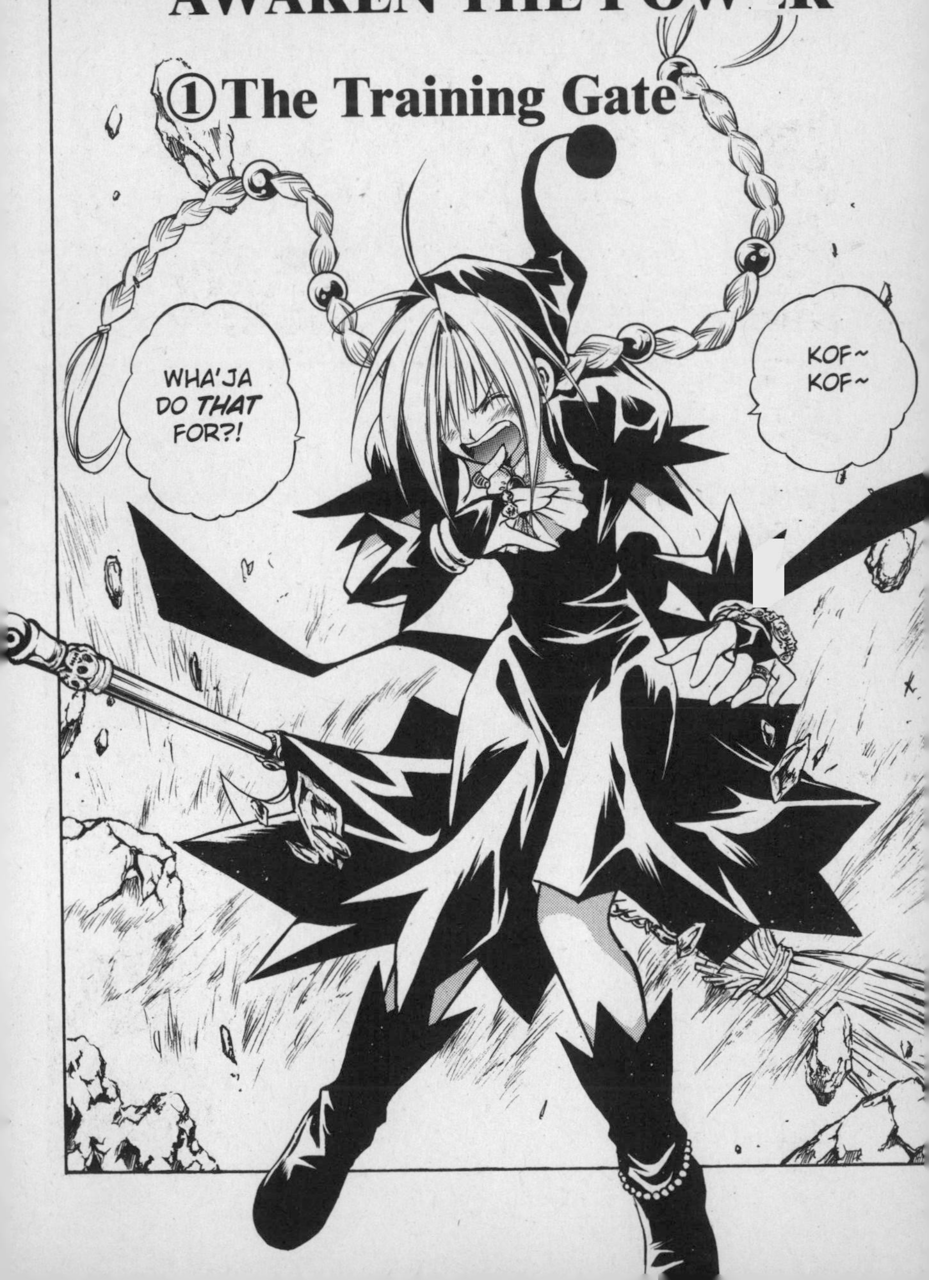
KOF~ KOF~
WHA'JA DO *THAT* FOR?!

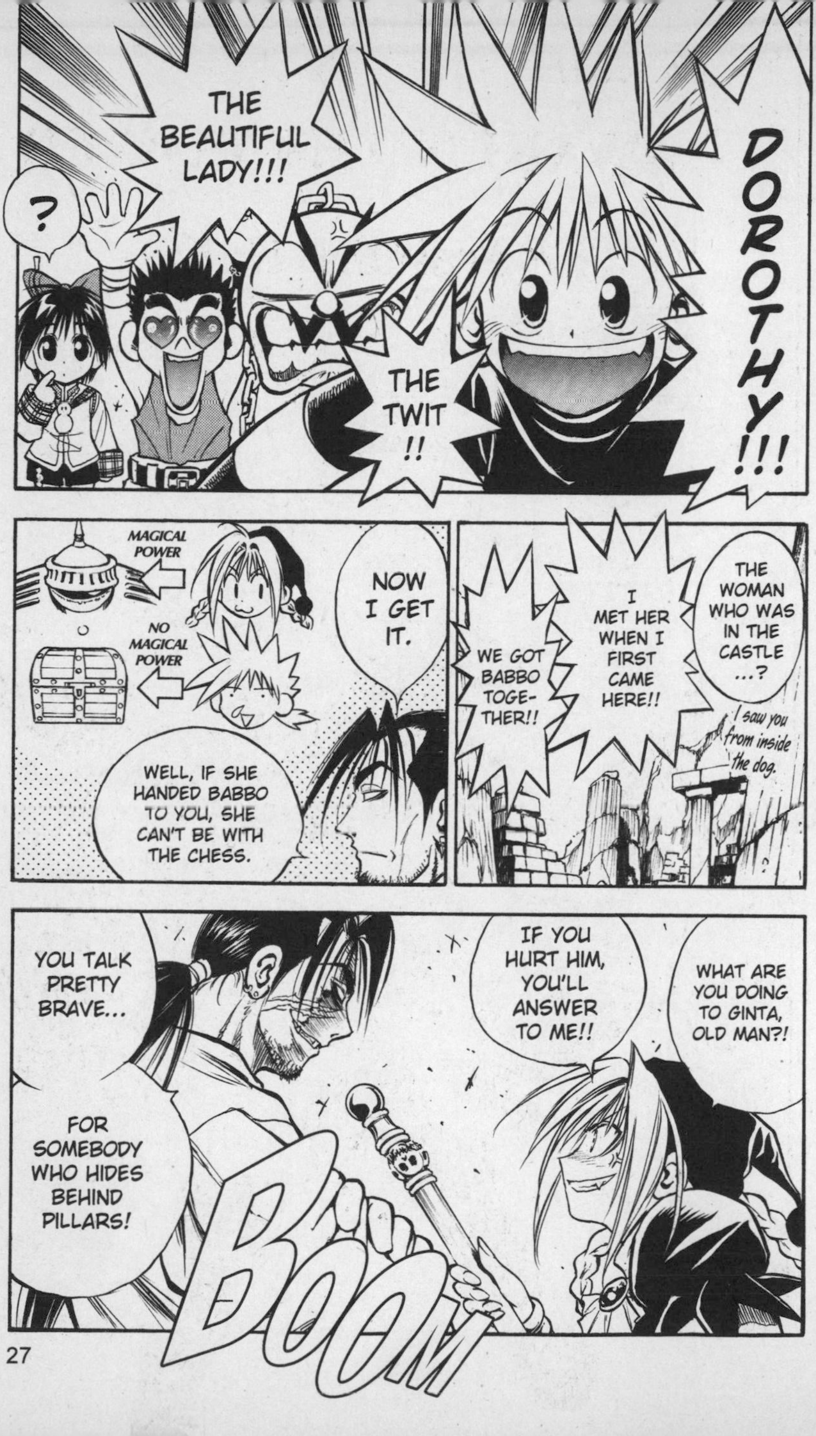
DOROTHY!!!
THE BEAUTIFUL LADY!!!
THE TWIT!!
?
THE WOMAN WHO WAS IN THE CASTLE ...?
I saw you from inside the dog.
I MET HER WHEN I FIRST CAME HERE!!
WE GOT BABBO TOGE-THER!!
NOW I GET IT.
MAGICAL POWER
NO MAGICAL POWER
WELL, IF SHE HANDED BABBO TO YOU, SHE CAN'T BE WITH THE CHESS.
WHAT ARE YOU DOING TO GINTA, OLD MAN?!
IF YOU HURT HIM, YOU'LL ANSWER TO ME!!
YOU TALK PRETTY BRAVE...
FOR SOMEBODY WHO HIDES BEHIND PILLARS!
BOOM

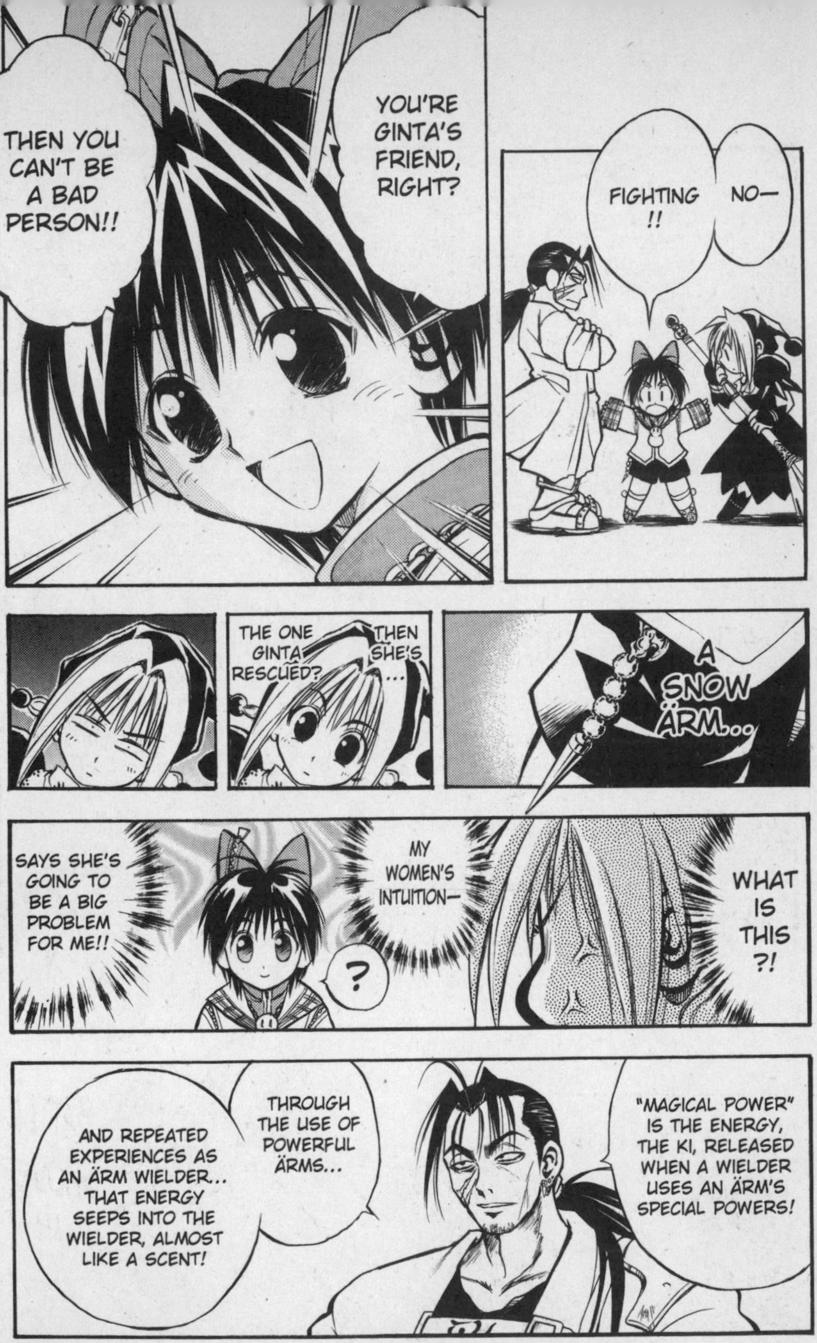
NO—
FIGHTING !!
YOU'RE GINTA'S FRIEND, RIGHT?
THEN YOU CAN'T BE A BAD PERSON!!
A SNOW ÄRM...
THEN SHE'S...
THE ONE GINTA RESCUED?
WHAT IS THIS ?!
MY WOMEN'S INTUITION—
SAYS SHE'S GOING TO BE A BIG PROBLEM FOR ME!!
?
"MAGICAL POWER" IS THE ENERGY, THE KI, RELEASED WHEN A WIELDER USES AN ÄRM'S SPECIAL POWERS!
THROUGH THE USE OF POWERFUL ÄRMS...
AND REPEATED EXPERIENCES AS AN ÄRM WIELDER... THAT ENERGY SEEPS INTO THE WIELDER, ALMOST LIKE A SCENT!

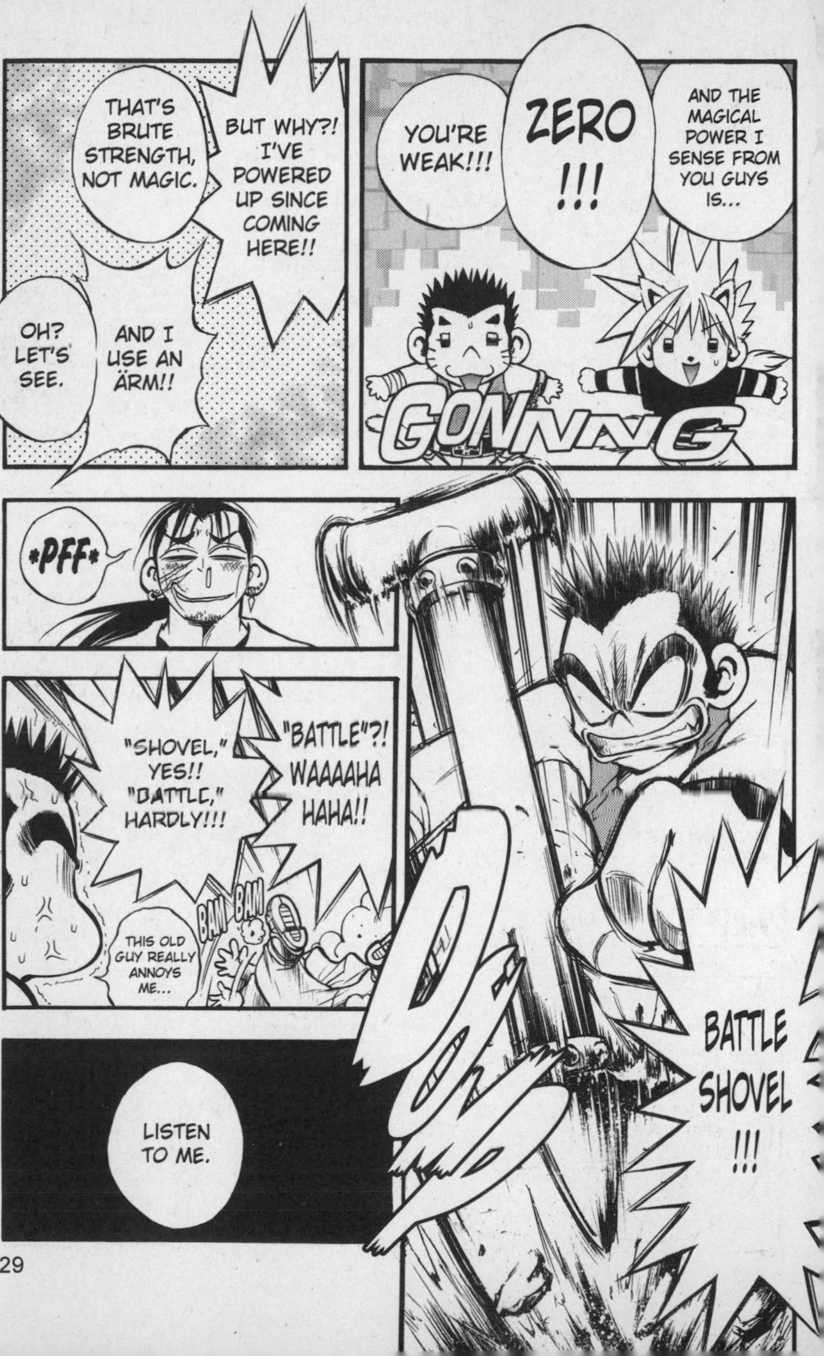
AND THE MAGICAL POWER I SENSE FROM YOU GUYS IS...
ZERO!!!
YOU'RE WEAK!!!
GONNNG
BUT WHY?! I'VE POWERED UP SINCE COMING HERE!!
THAT'S BRUTE STRENGTH, NOT MAGIC.
AND I USE AN ÄRM!!
OH? LET'S SEE.
BATTLE SHOVEL!!!
PFF
"BATTLE"?! WAAAAHA HAHA!!
"SHOVEL," YES!! "BATTLE," HARDLY!!!
BAM BAM
THIS OLD GUY REALLY ANNOYS ME...
LISTEN TO ME.

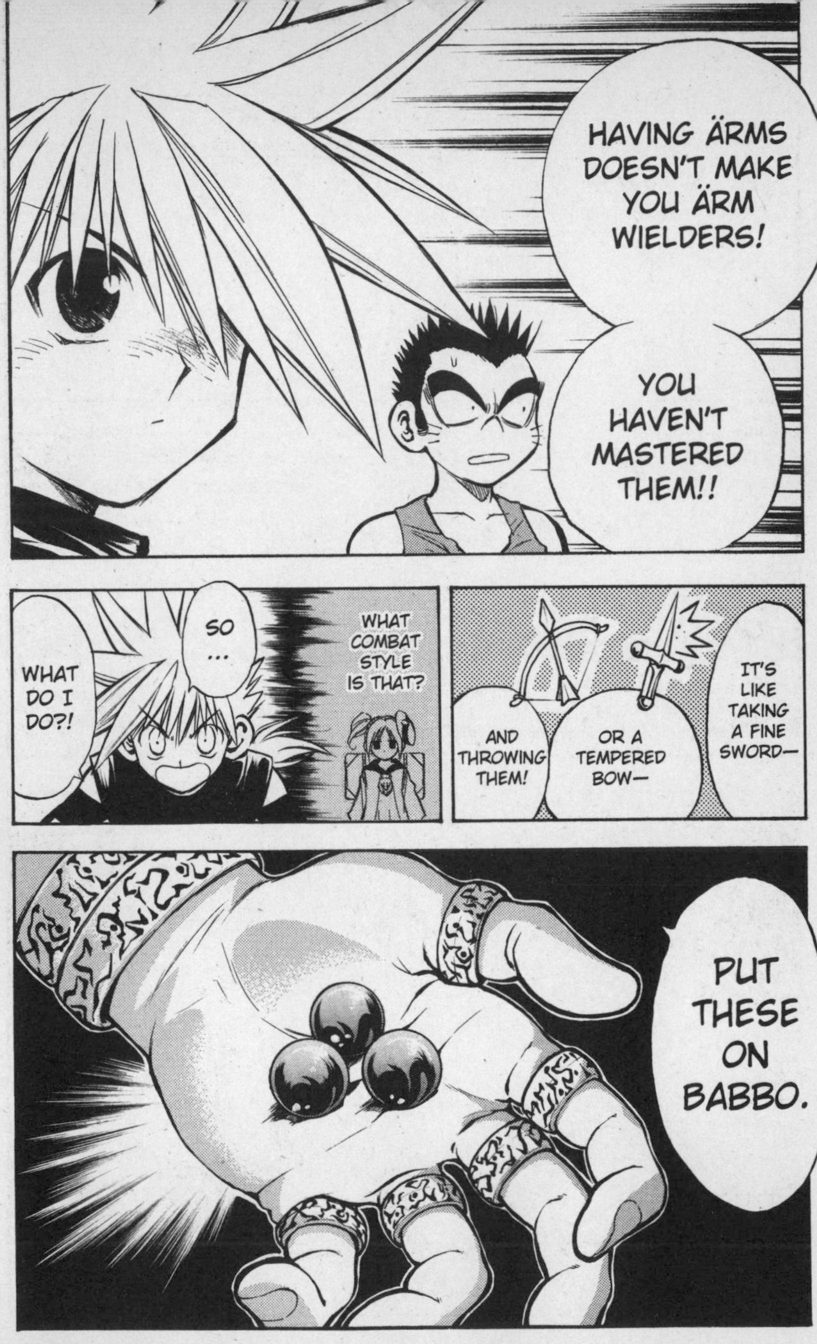
HAVING ÄRMS DOESN'T MAKE YOU ÄRM WIELDERS!
YOU HAVEN'T MASTERED THEM!!
IT'S LIKE TAKING A FINE SWORD—
OR A TEMPERED BOW—
AND THROWING THEM!
WHAT COMBAT STYLE IS THAT?
SO ...
WHAT DO I DO?!
PUT THESE ON BABBO.

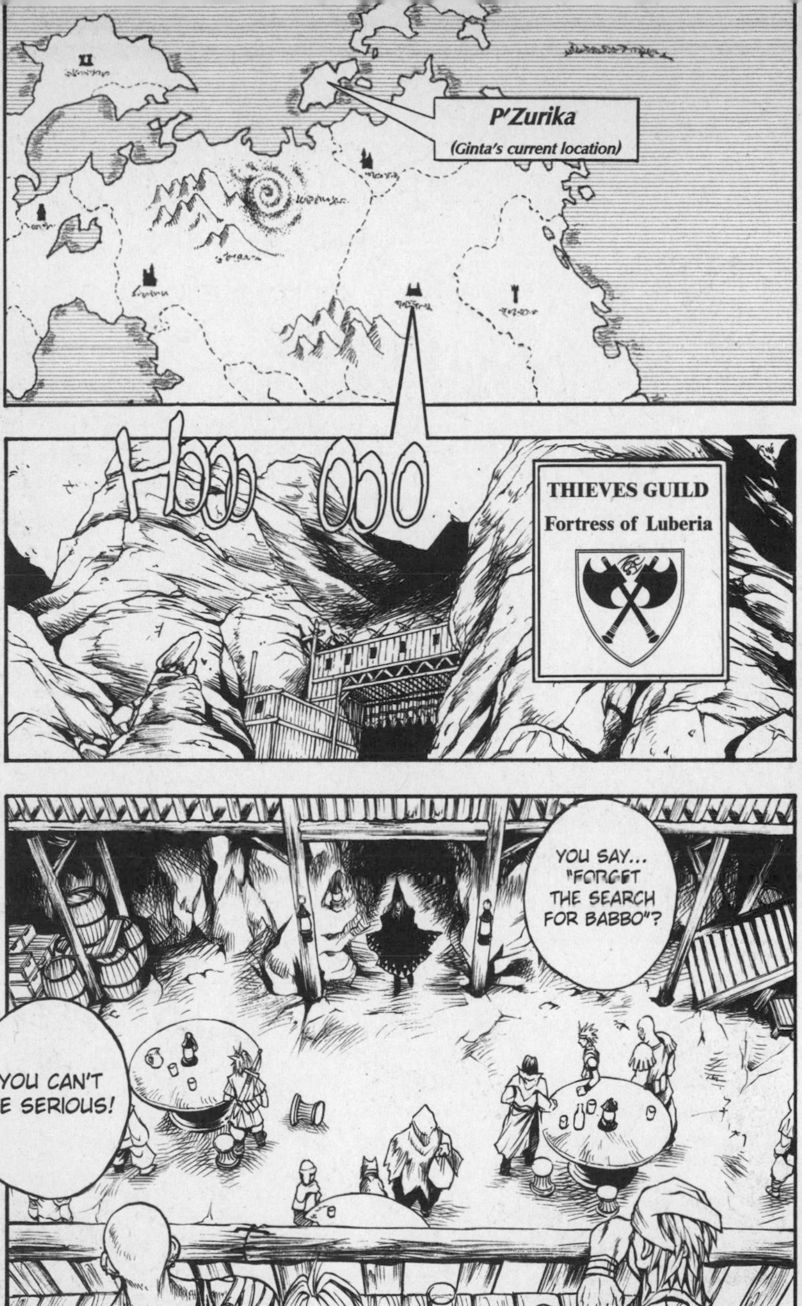
P'Zurika
(Ginta's current location)
HOOO OOO
THIEVES GUILD
Fortress of Luberia
YOU SAY... "FORGET THE SEARCH FOR BABBO"?
YOU CAN'T BE SERIOUS!

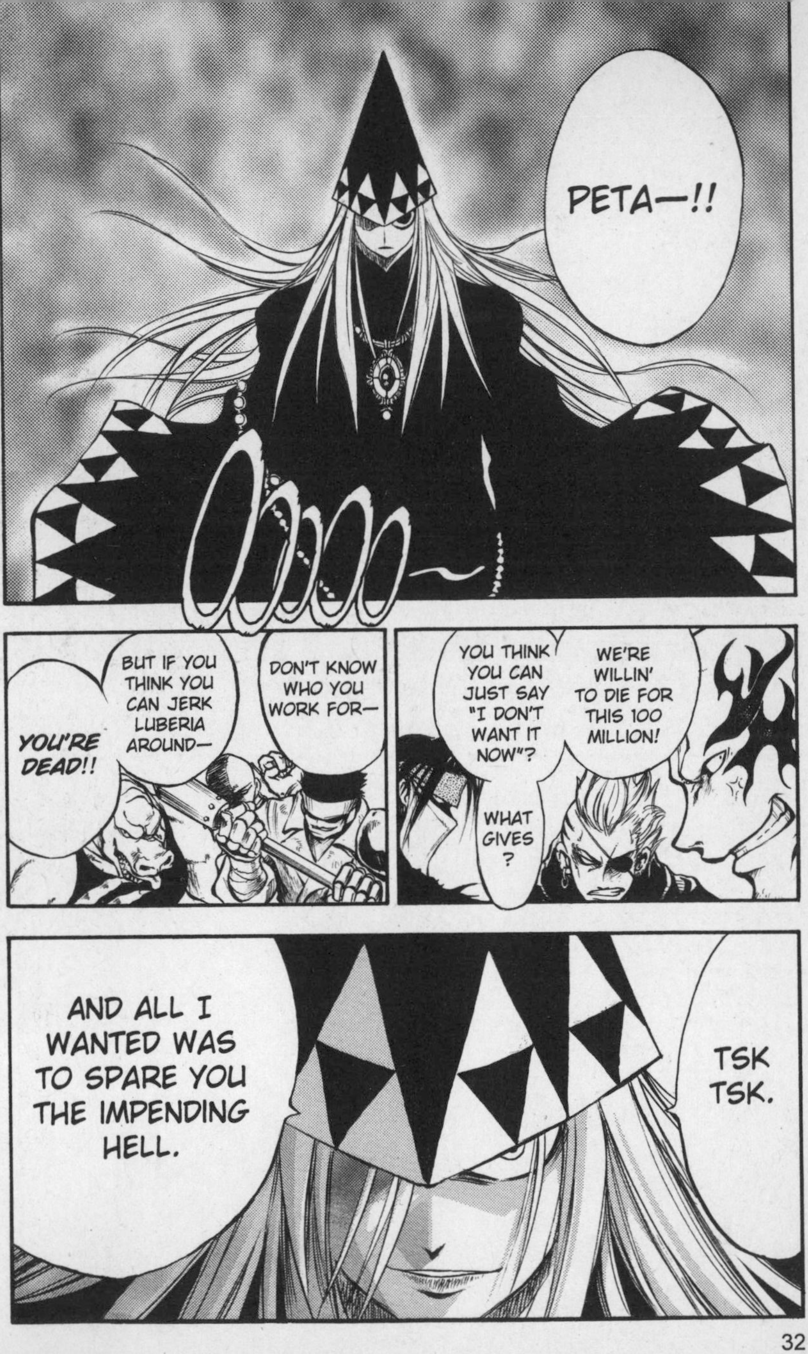
PETA—!!
WE'RE WILLIN' TO DIE FOR THIS 100 MILLION!
YOU THINK YOU CAN JUST SAY "I DON'T WANT IT NOW"?
WHAT GIVES?
DON'T KNOW WHO YOU WORK FOR—
BUT IF YOU THINK YOU CAN JERK LUBERIA AROUND—
YOU'RE DEAD!!
TSK TSK.
AND ALL I WANTED WAS TO SPARE YOU THE IMPENDING HELL.

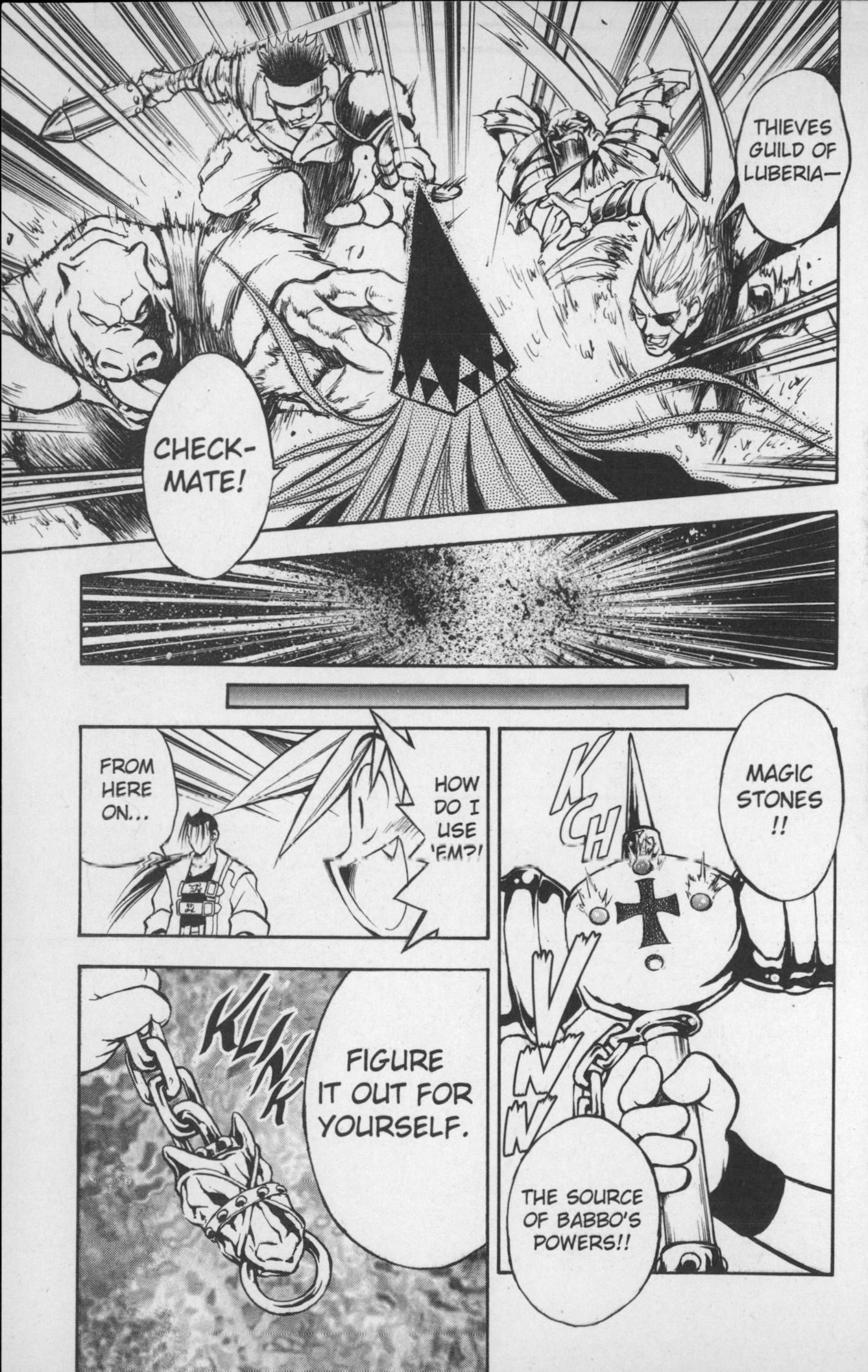
THIEVES GUILD OF LUBERIA—
CHECK-MATE!
MAGIC STONES !!
KCH
THE SOURCE OF BABBO'S POWERS!!
HOW DO I USE 'EM?!
FROM HERE ON...
KLINK
FIGURE IT OUT FOR YOURSELF.

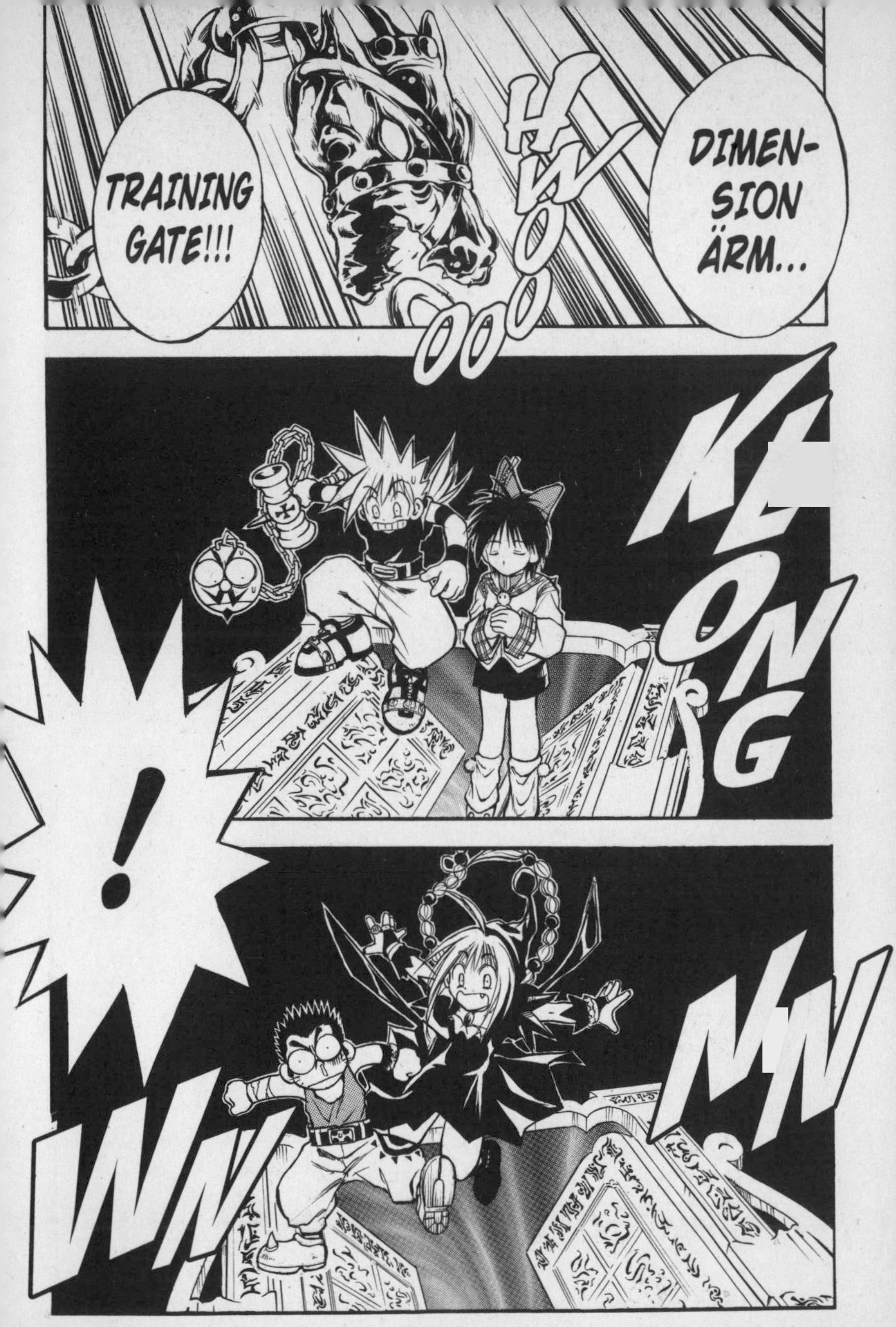
DIMEN-
SION
ÄRM...
HWOOOOO
TRAINING
GATE!!!
KLONG
!
MN
WN

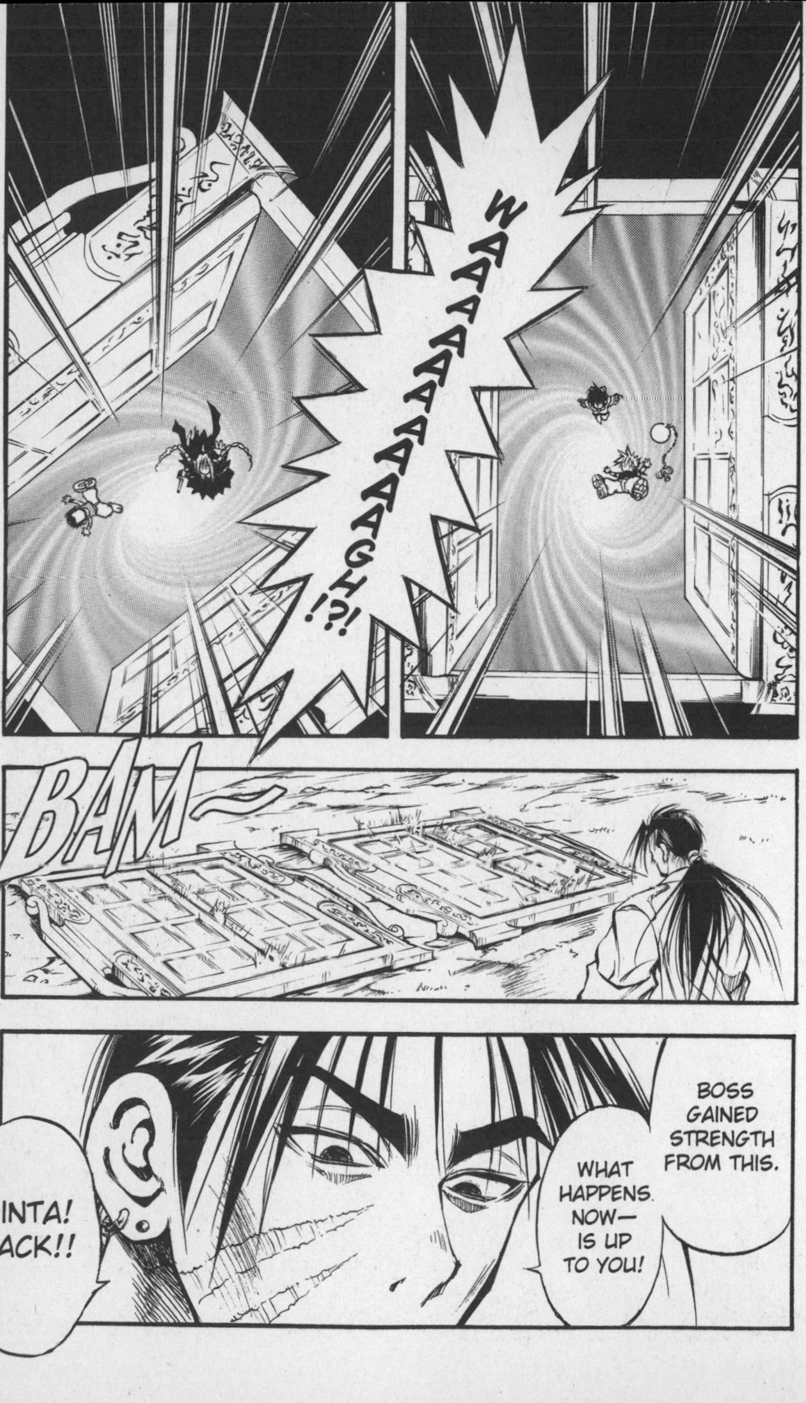
WAAAAAAAAAAGH!?!
BAM~
BOSS GAINED STRENGTH FROM THIS.
WHAT HAPPENS NOW— IS UP TO YOU!
GINTA! JACK!!

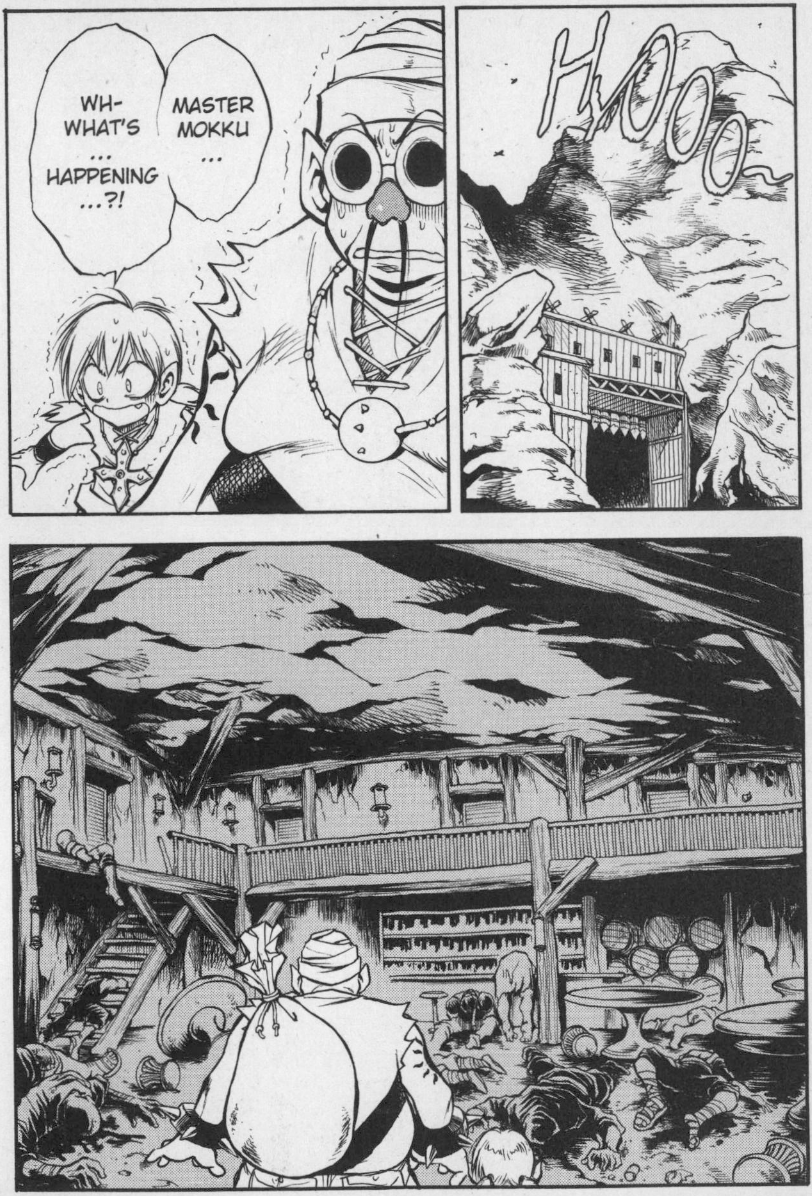
HOOO
MASTER MOKKU ...
WH- WHAT'S ... HAPPENING ...?!

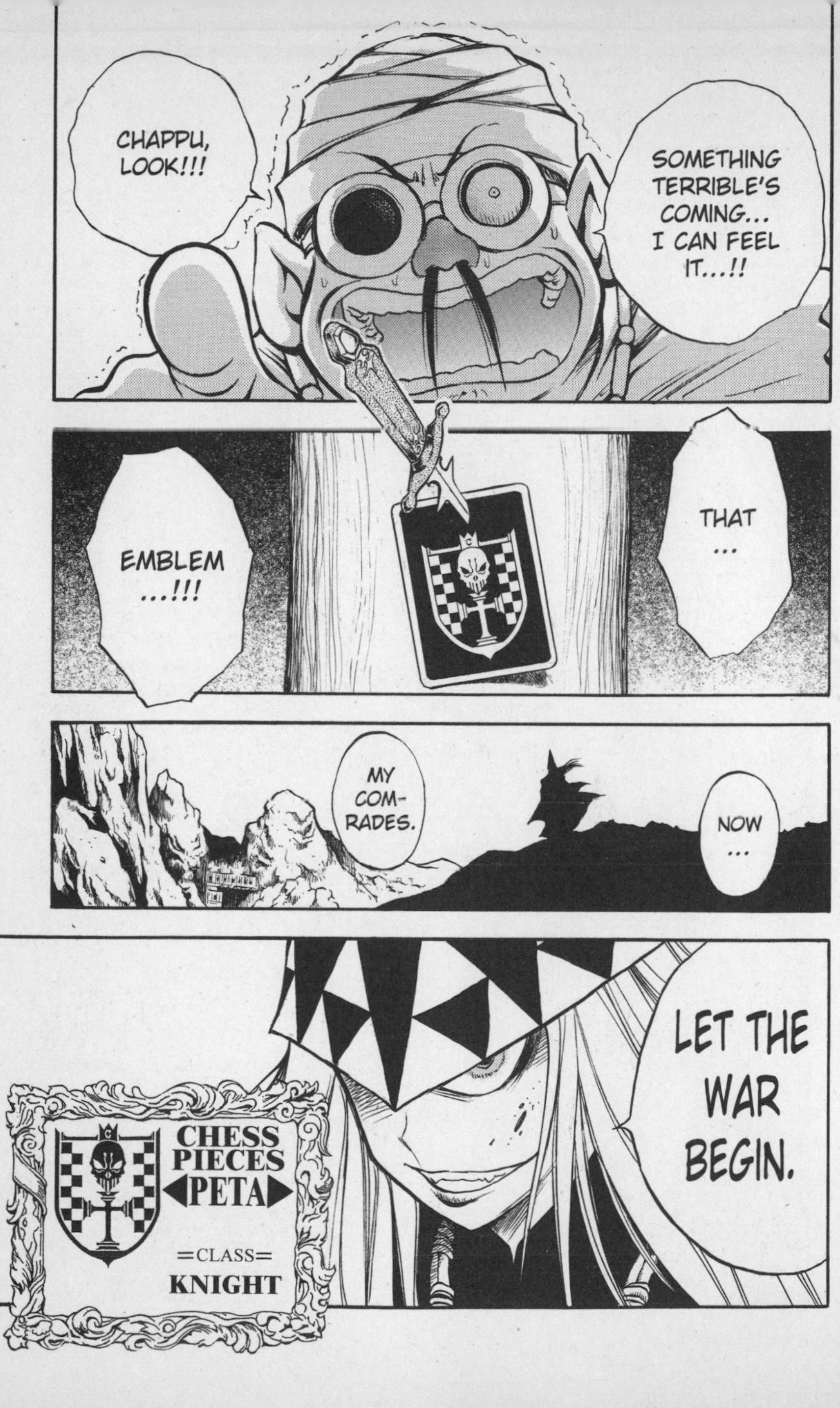
SOMETHING TERRIBLE'S COMING... I CAN FEEL IT...!!
CHAPPU, LOOK!!!
THAT ...
EMBLEM ...!!!
NOW ...
MY COM-RADES.
LET THE WAR BEGIN.
CHESS PIECES PETA
=CLASS=
KNIGHT

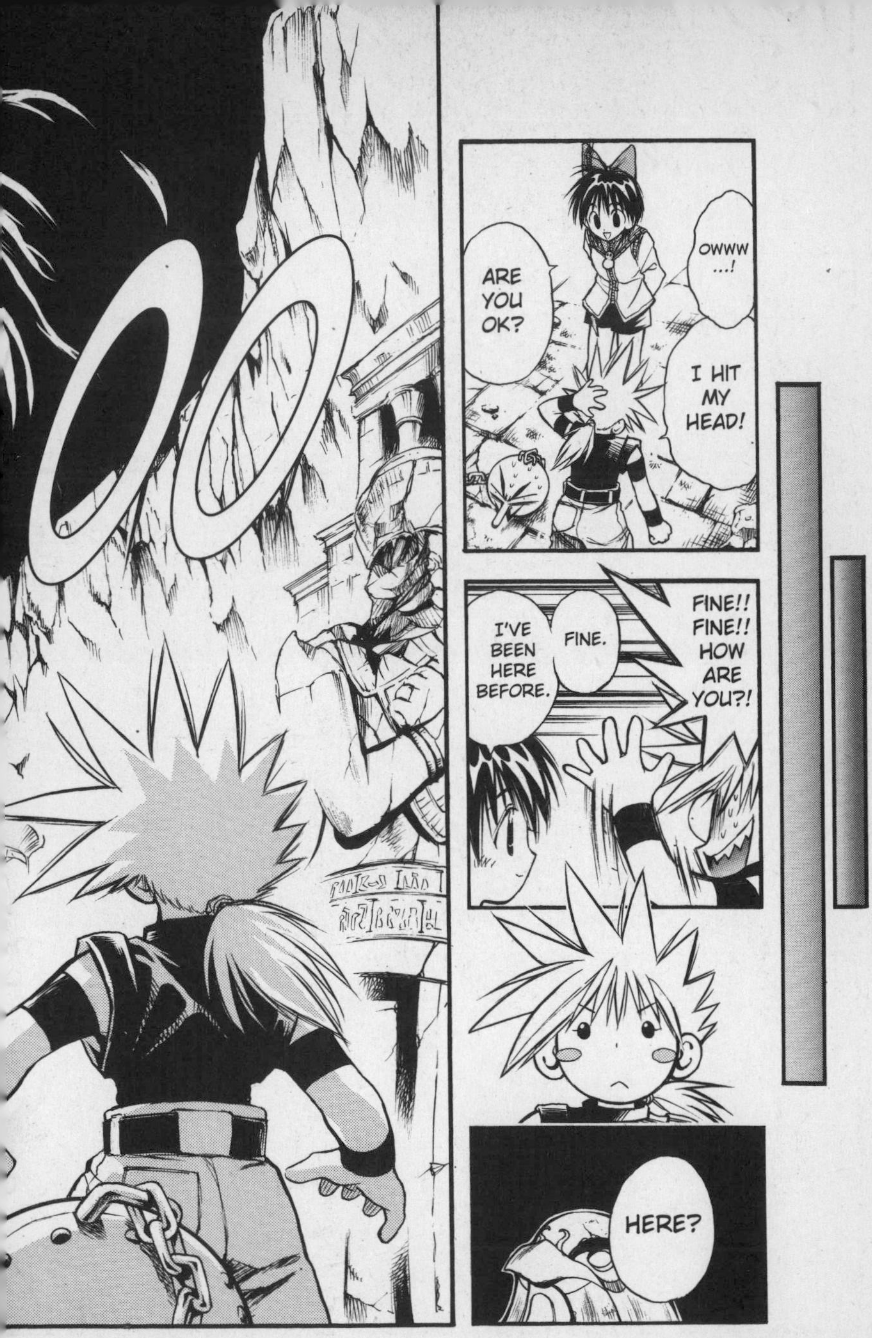
OWWW ...!
I HIT MY HEAD!
ARE YOU OK?
FINE!! FINE!! HOW ARE YOU?!
FINE.
I'VE BEEN HERE BEFORE.
HERE?

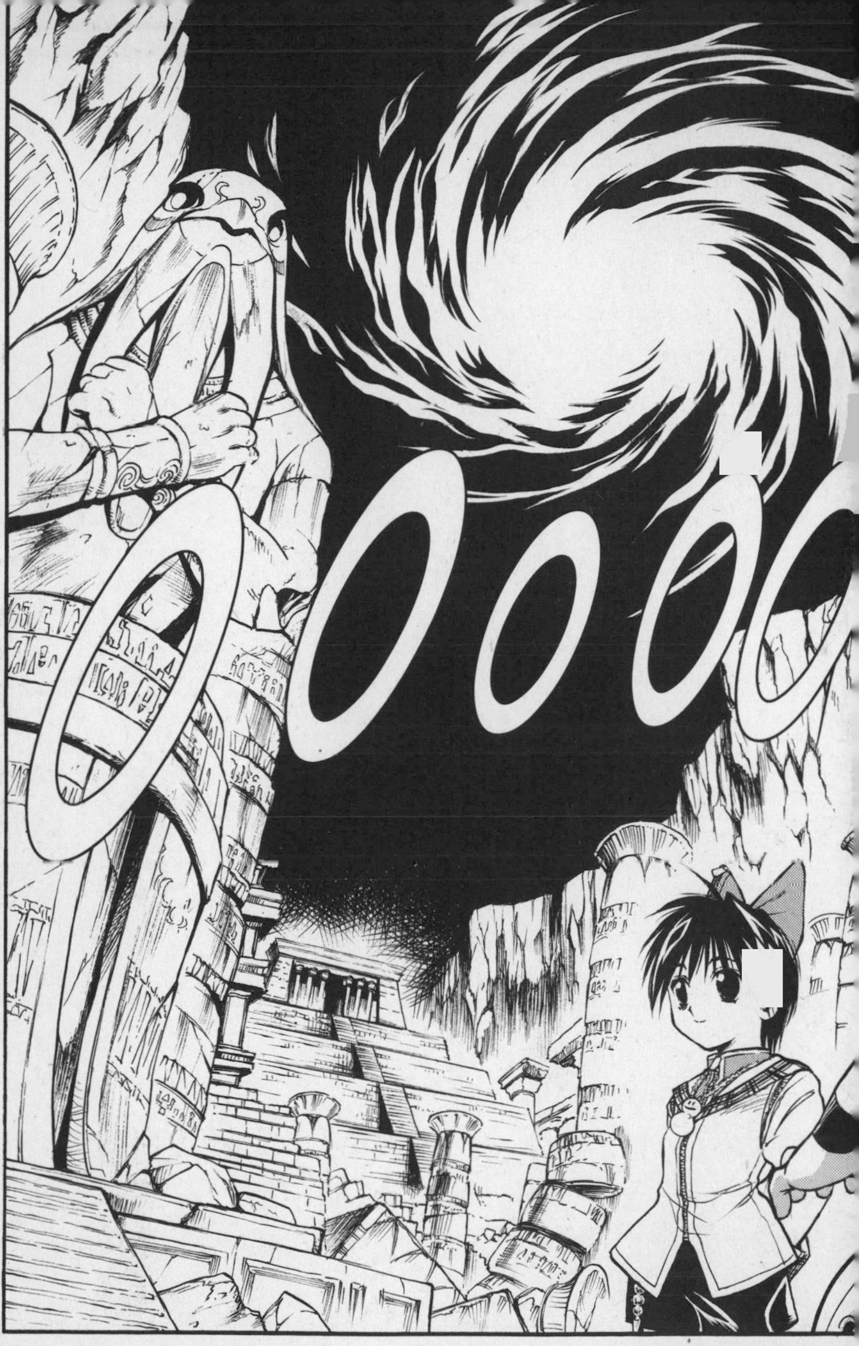

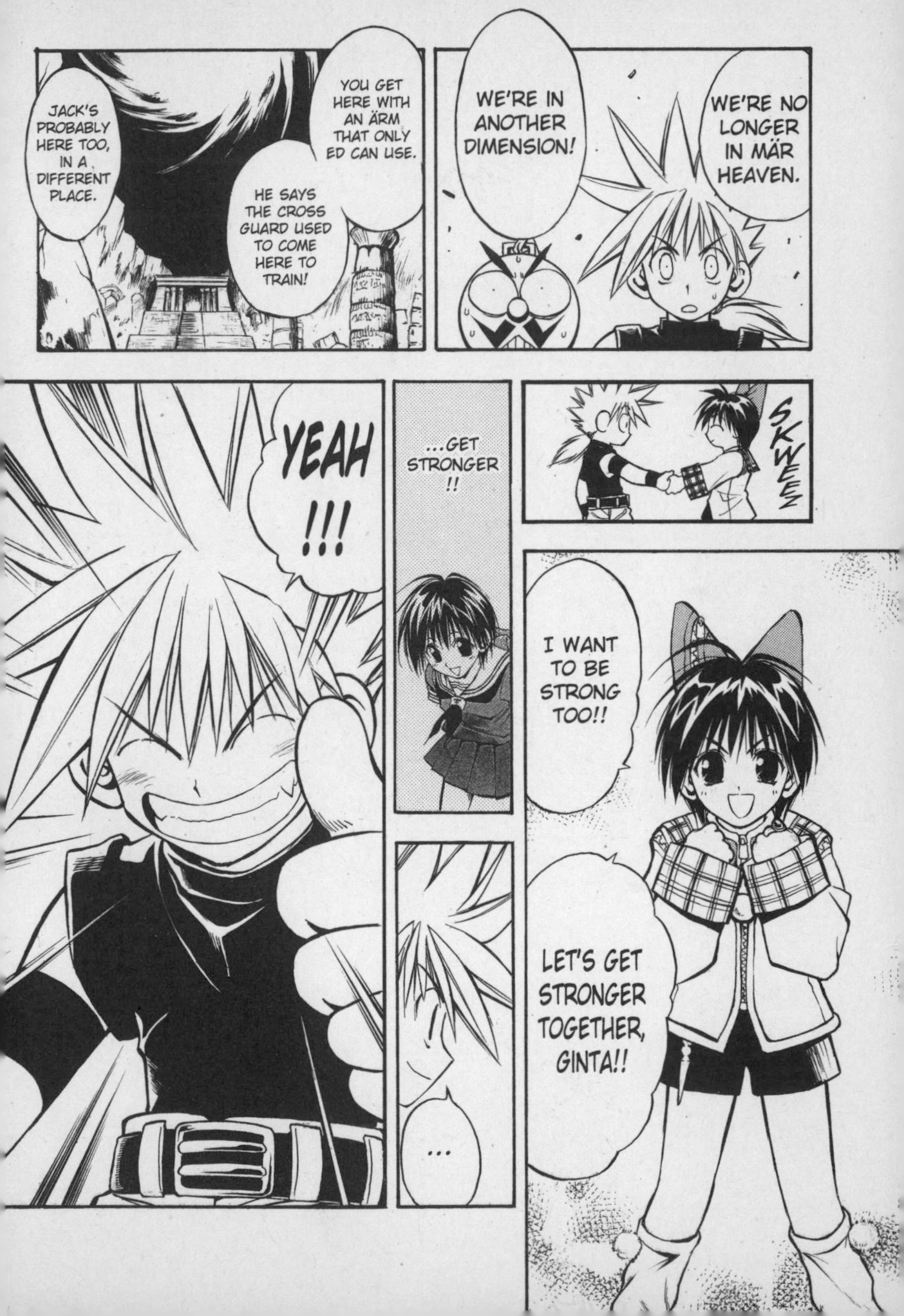
WE'RE NO LONGER IN MÄR HEAVEN.
WE'RE IN ANOTHER DIMENSION!
YOU GET HERE WITH AN ÄRM THAT ONLY ED CAN USE.
HE SAYS THE CROSS GUARD USED TO COME HERE TO TRAIN!
JACK'S PROBABLY HERE TOO, IN A DIFFERENT PLACE.
SKWEEZ
I WANT TO BE STRONG TOO!!
LET'S GET STRONGER TOGETHER, GINTA!!
...GET STRONGER !!
...
YEAH !!!

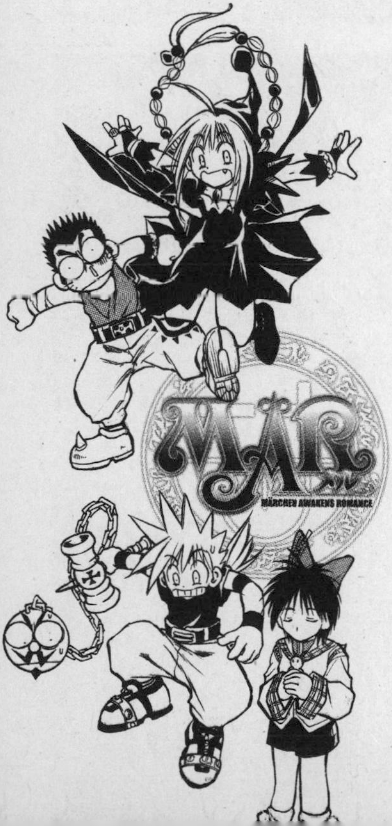
MÄR
MÄRCHEN AWAKENS ROMANCE

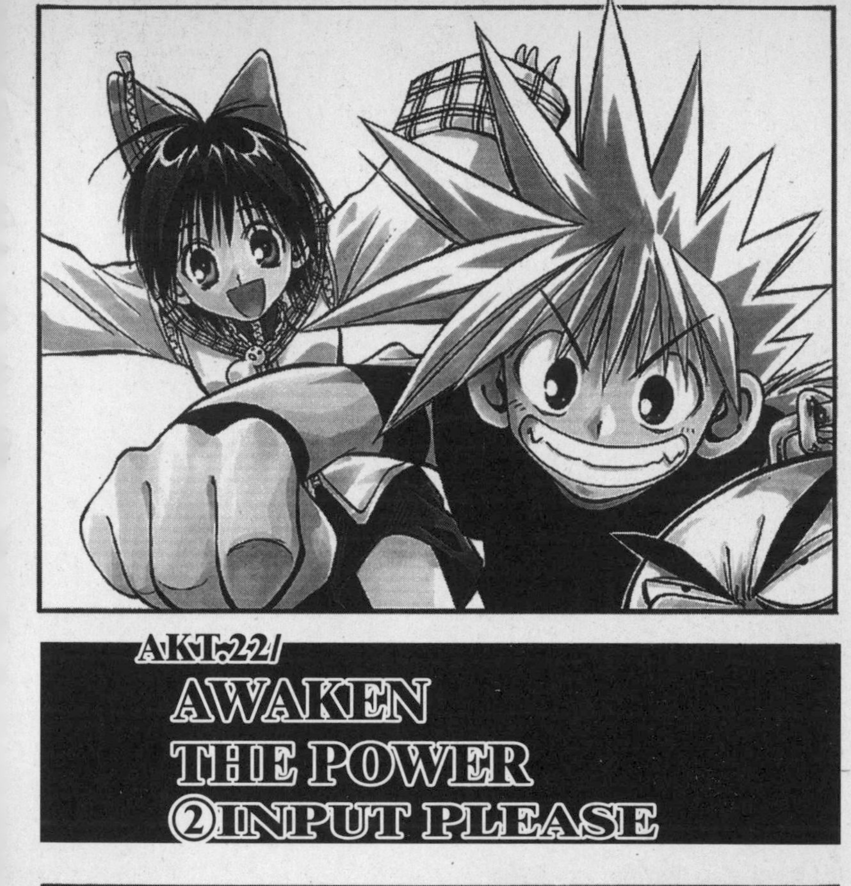

AKT.22/

AWAKEN THE POWER
② INPUT PLEASE

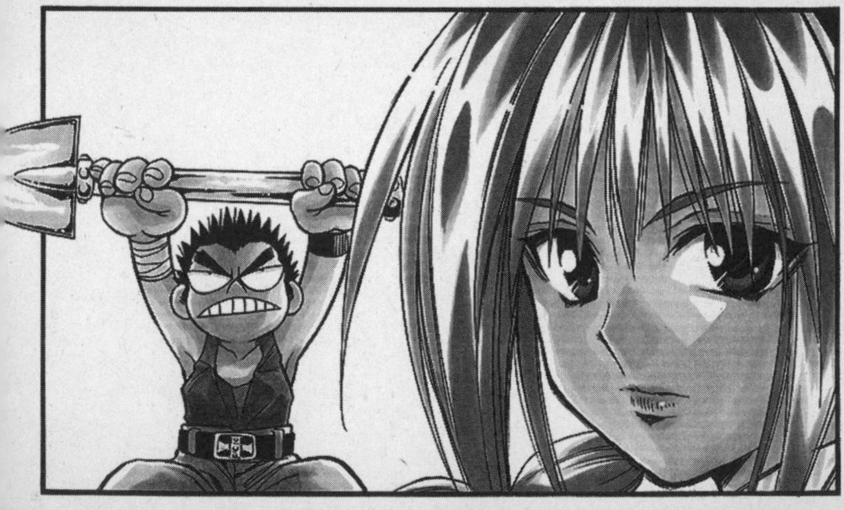

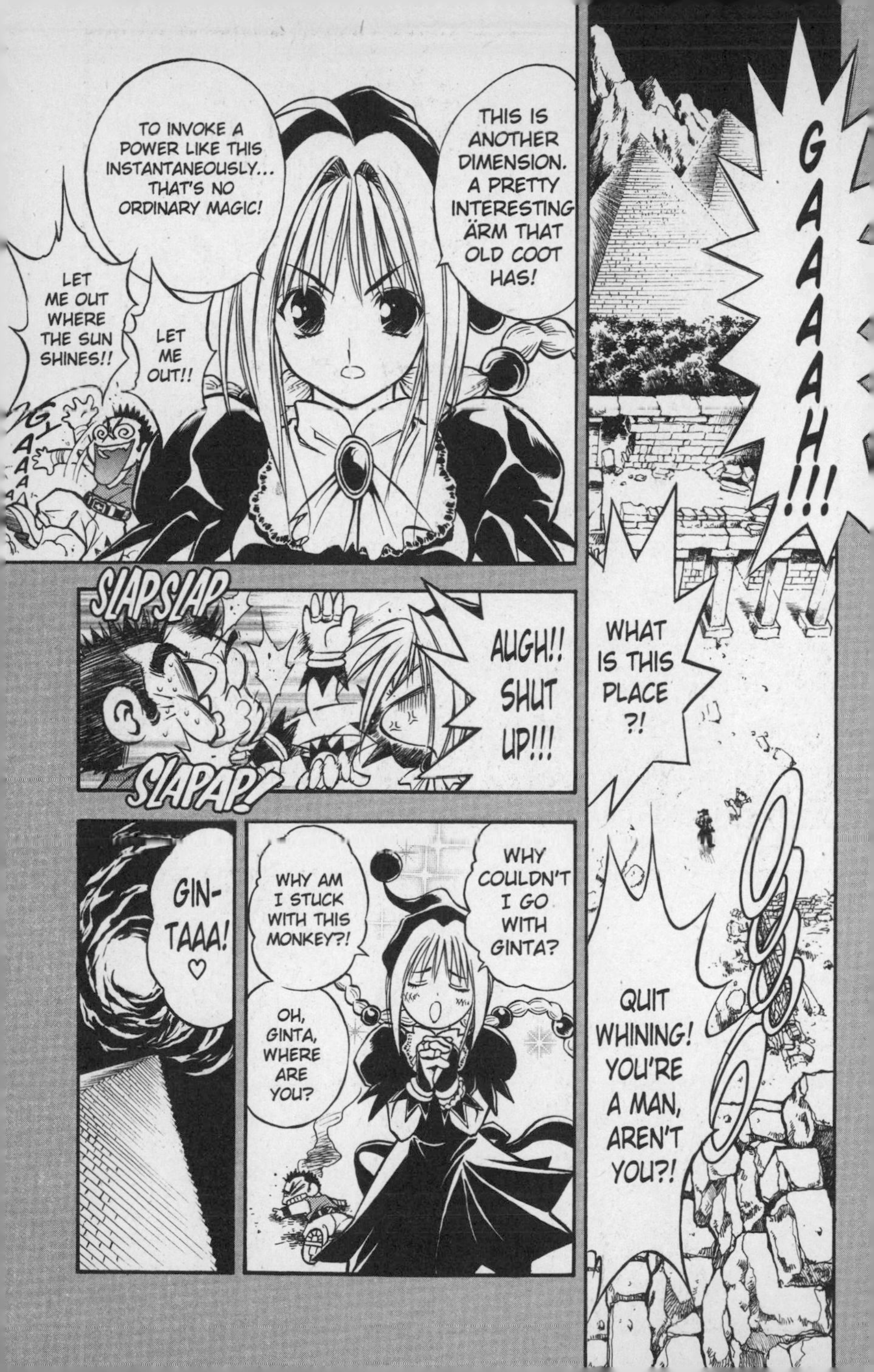
GAAAAAH!!!
WHAT IS THIS PLACE?!
QUIT WHINING! YOU'RE A MAN, AREN'T YOU?!
THIS IS ANOTHER DIMENSION. A PRETTY INTERESTING ÄRM THAT OLD COOT HAS!
TO INVOKE A POWER LIKE THIS INSTANTANEOUSLY... THAT'S NO ORDINARY MAGIC!
LET ME OUT!!
LET ME OUT WHERE THE SUN SHINES!!
AUGH!! SHUT UP!!!
SLAPSLAP
SLAPAP!
WHY COULDN'T I GO WITH GINTA?
WHY AM I STUCK WITH THIS MONKEY?!
OH, GINTA, WHERE ARE YOU?
GIN-TAAA! ♡

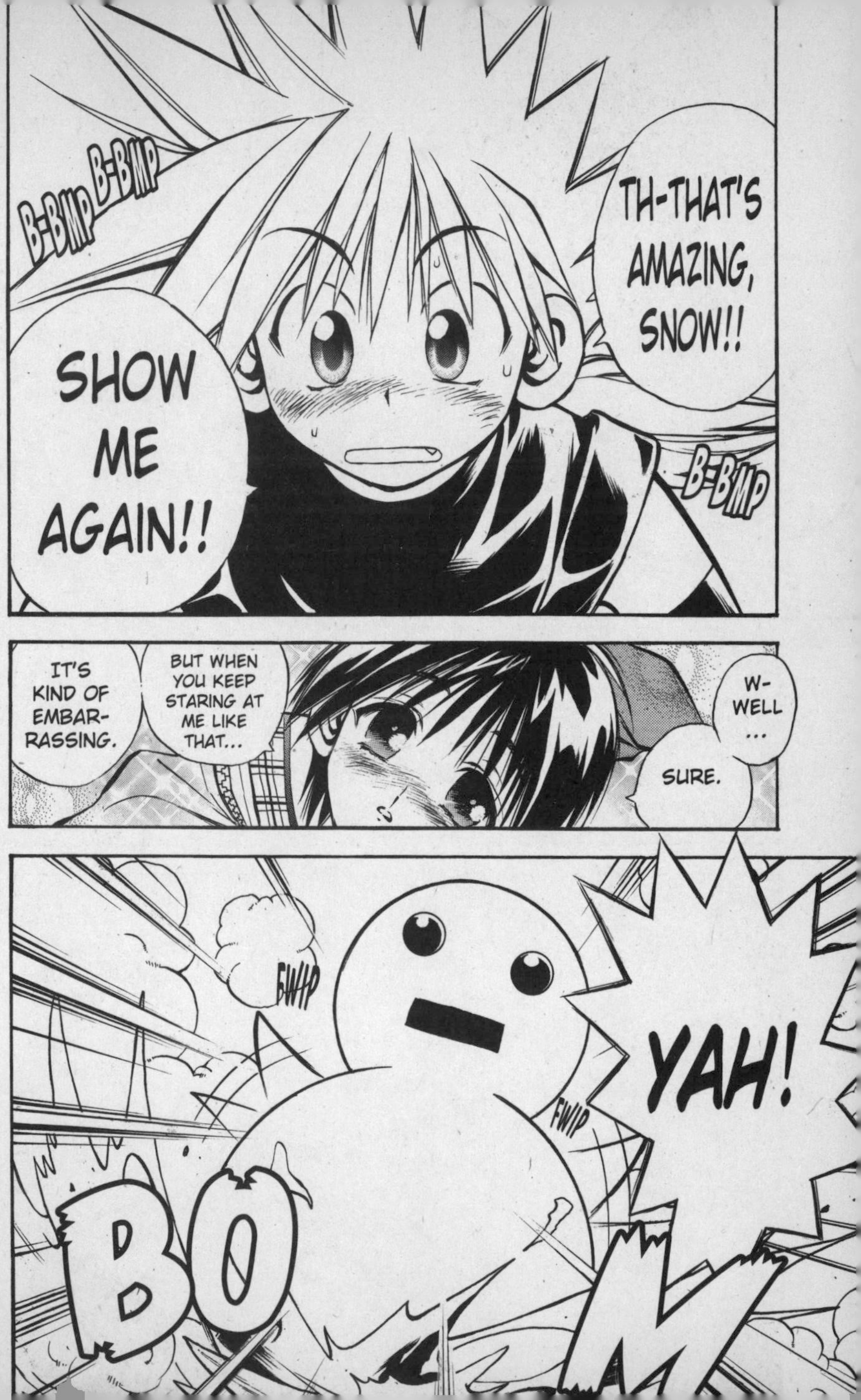
TH-THAT'S AMAZING, SNOW!!
B-B'MP B-B'MP
B-B'MP
SHOW ME AGAIN!!
W-WELL ...
SURE.
BUT WHEN YOU KEEP STARING AT ME LIKE THAT...
IT'S KIND OF EMBARRASSING.
YAH!
FWIP
FWIP
BOM

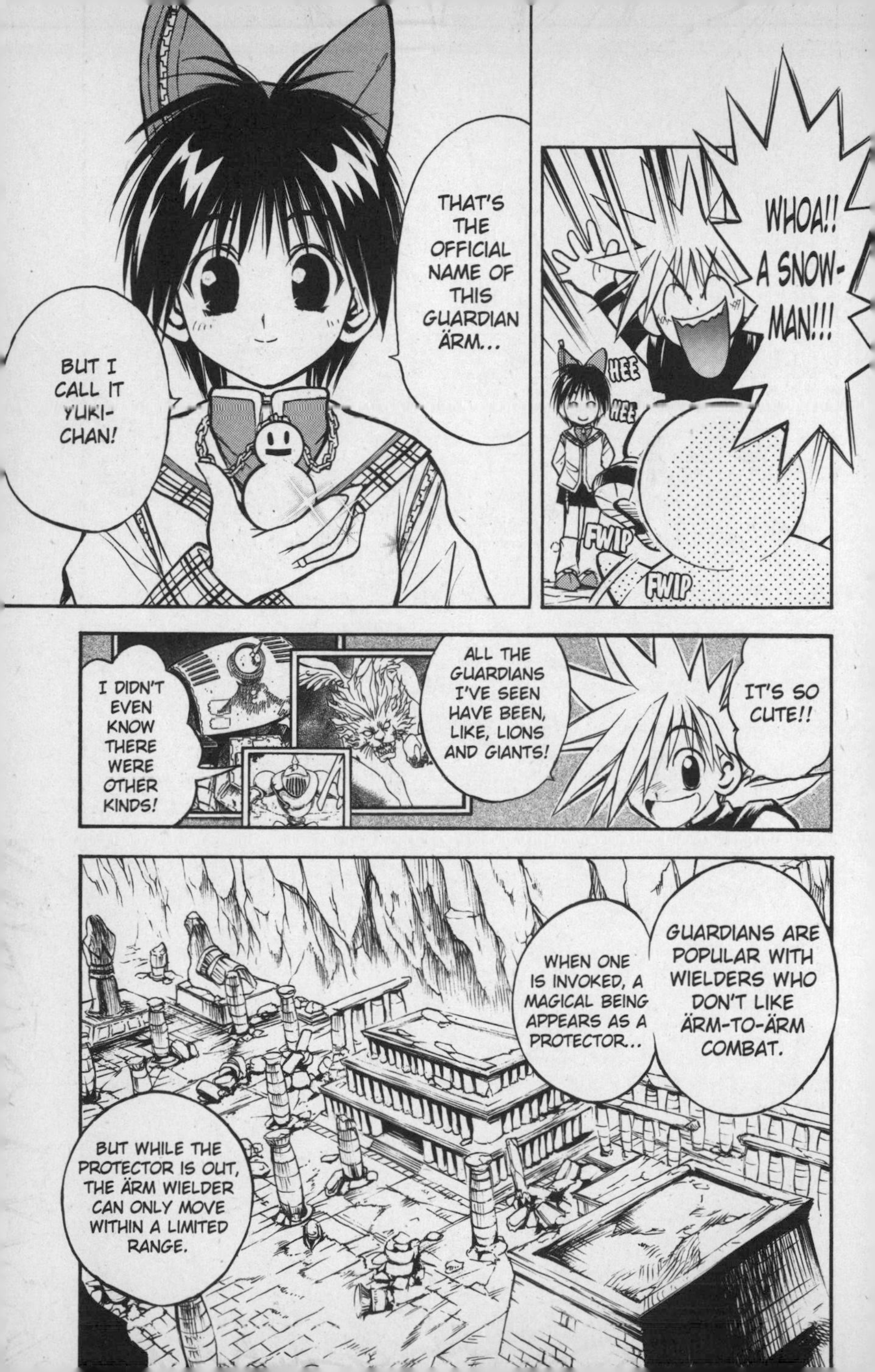
WHOA!! A SNOW-MAN!!!
HEE
HEE
FWIP
FWIP
THAT'S THE OFFICIAL NAME OF THIS GUARDIAN ÄRM...
BUT I CALL IT YUKI-CHAN!
IT'S SO CUTE!!
ALL THE GUARDIANS I'VE SEEN HAVE BEEN, LIKE, LIONS AND GIANTS!
I DIDN'T EVEN KNOW THERE WERE OTHER KINDS!
GUARDIANS ARE POPULAR WITH WIELDERS WHO DON'T LIKE ÄRM-TO-ÄRM COMBAT.
WHEN ONE IS INVOKED, A MAGICAL BEING APPEARS AS A PROTECTOR...
BUT WHILE THE PROTECTOR IS OUT, THE ÄRM WIELDER CAN ONLY MOVE WITHIN A LIMITED RANGE.

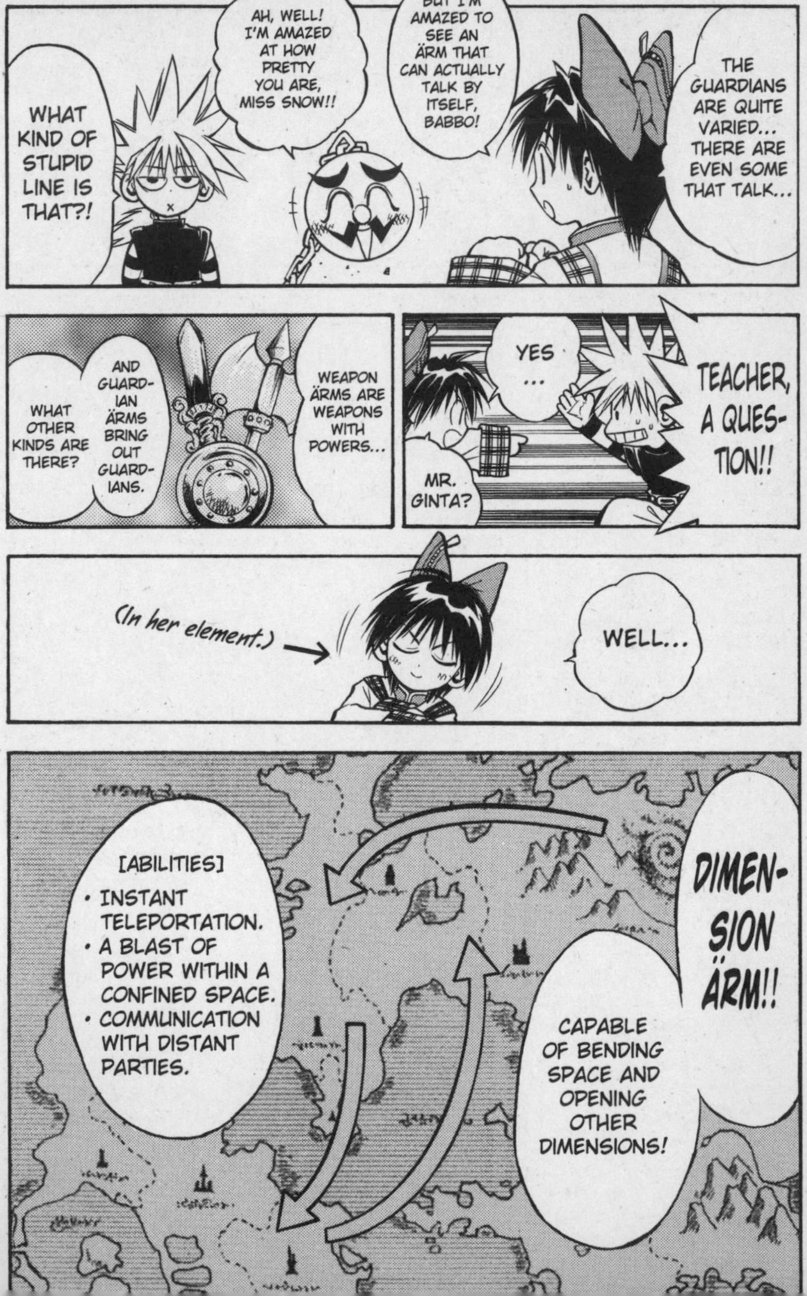
THE GUARDIANS ARE QUITE VARIED... THERE ARE EVEN SOME THAT TALK...
BUT I'M AMAZED TO SEE AN ÄRM THAT CAN ACTUALLY TALK BY ITSELF, BABBO!
AH, WELL! I'M AMAZED AT HOW PRETTY YOU ARE, MISS SNOW!!
WHAT KIND OF STUPID LINE IS THAT?!
TEACHER, A QUES-TION!!
YES...
MR. GINTA?
WEAPON ÄRMS ARE WEAPONS WITH POWERS...
AND GUARD-IAN ÄRMS BRING OUT GUARD-IANS.
WHAT OTHER KINDS ARE THERE?
WELL...
(In her element.)
DIMEN-SION ÄRM!!
CAPABLE OF BENDING SPACE AND OPENING OTHER DIMENSIONS!
[ABILITIES]
• INSTANT TELEPORTATION.
• A BLAST OF POWER WITHIN A CONFINED SPACE.
• COMMUNICATION WITH DISTANT PARTIES.

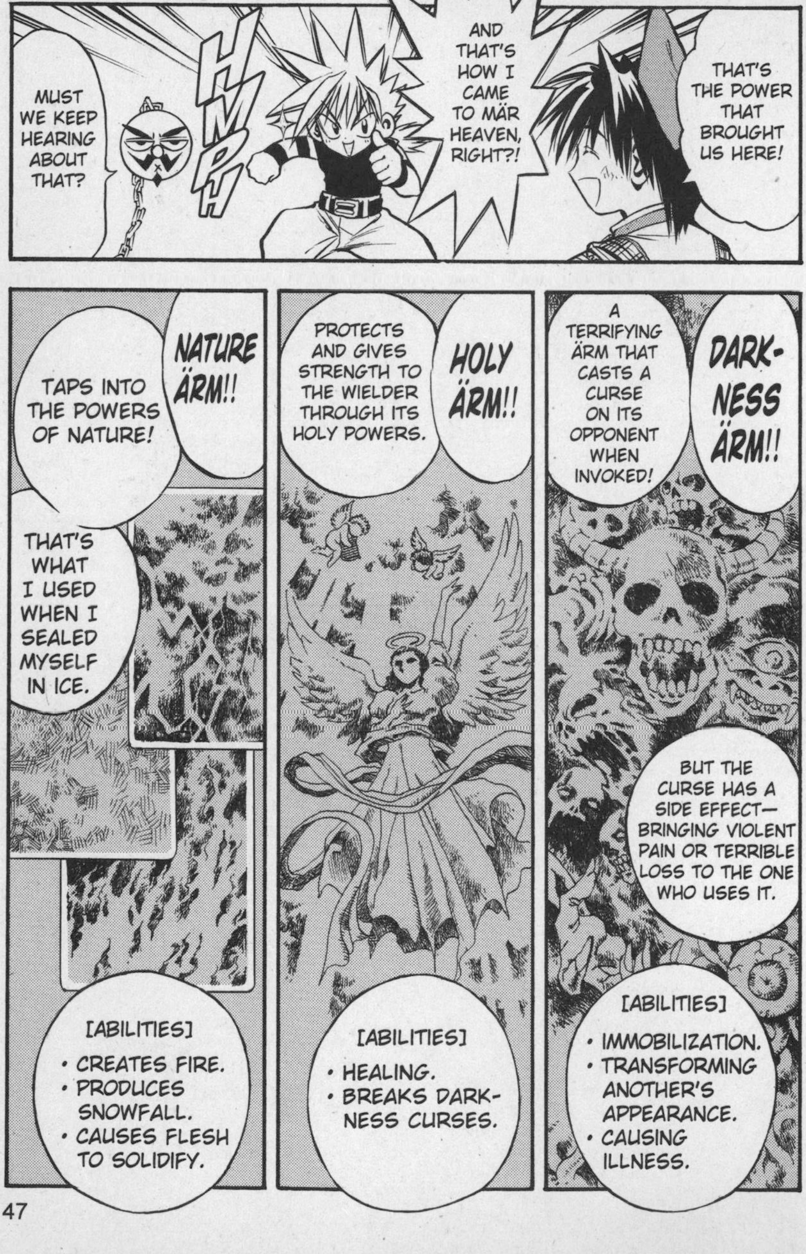
THAT'S THE POWER THAT BROUGHT US HERE!
AND THAT'S HOW I CAME TO MÄR HEAVEN, RIGHT?!
HMPH
MUST WE KEEP HEARING ABOUT THAT?
DARKNESS ÄRM!!
A TERRIFYING ÄRM THAT CASTS A CURSE ON ITS OPPONENT WHEN INVOKED!
BUT THE CURSE HAS A SIDE EFFECT—BRINGING VIOLENT PAIN OR TERRIBLE LOSS TO THE ONE WHO USES IT.
[ABILITIES]
• IMMOBILIZATION.
• TRANSFORMING ANOTHER'S APPEARANCE.
• CAUSING ILLNESS.
HOLY ÄRM!!
PROTECTS AND GIVES STRENGTH TO THE WIELDER THROUGH ITS HOLY POWERS.
[ABILITIES]
• HEALING.
• BREAKS DARKNESS CURSES.
NATURE ÄRM!!
TAPS INTO THE POWERS OF NATURE!
THAT'S WHAT I USED WHEN I SEALED MYSELF IN ICE.
[ABILITIES]
• CREATES FIRE.
• PRODUCES SNOWFALL.
• CAUSES FLESH TO SOLIDIFY.

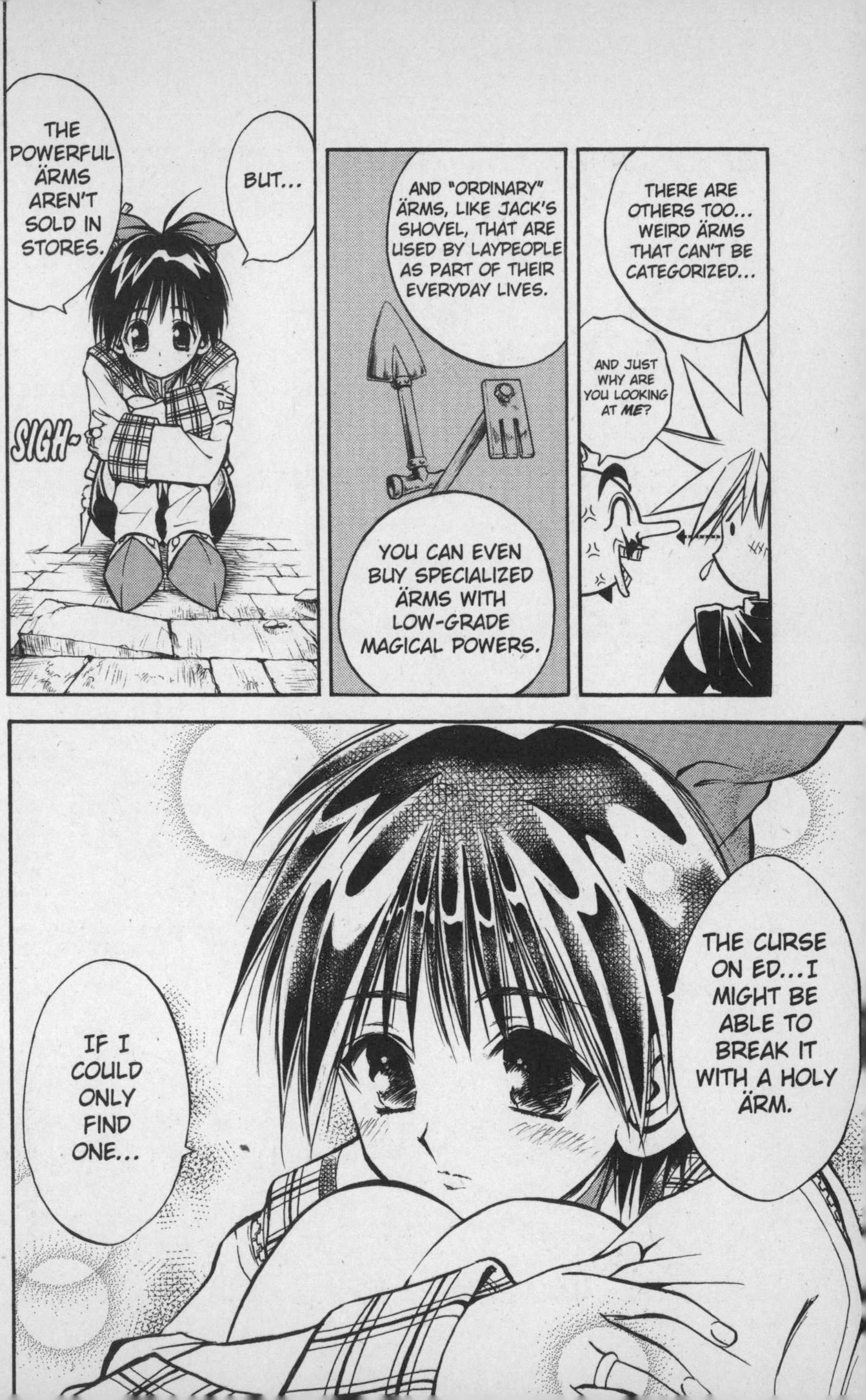
THERE ARE OTHERS TOO... WEIRD ÄRMS THAT CAN'T BE CATEGORIZED...
AND JUST WHY ARE YOU LOOKING AT *ME*?
AND "ORDINARY" ÄRMS, LIKE JACK'S SHOVEL, THAT ARE USED BY LAYPEOPLE AS PART OF THEIR EVERYDAY LIVES.
YOU CAN EVEN BUY SPECIALIZED ÄRMS WITH LOW-GRADE MAGICAL POWERS.
THE POWERFUL ÄRMS AREN'T SOLD IN STORES.
BUT...
SIGH
THE CURSE ON ED...I MIGHT BE ABLE TO BREAK IT WITH A HOLY ÄRM.
IF I COULD ONLY FIND ONE...

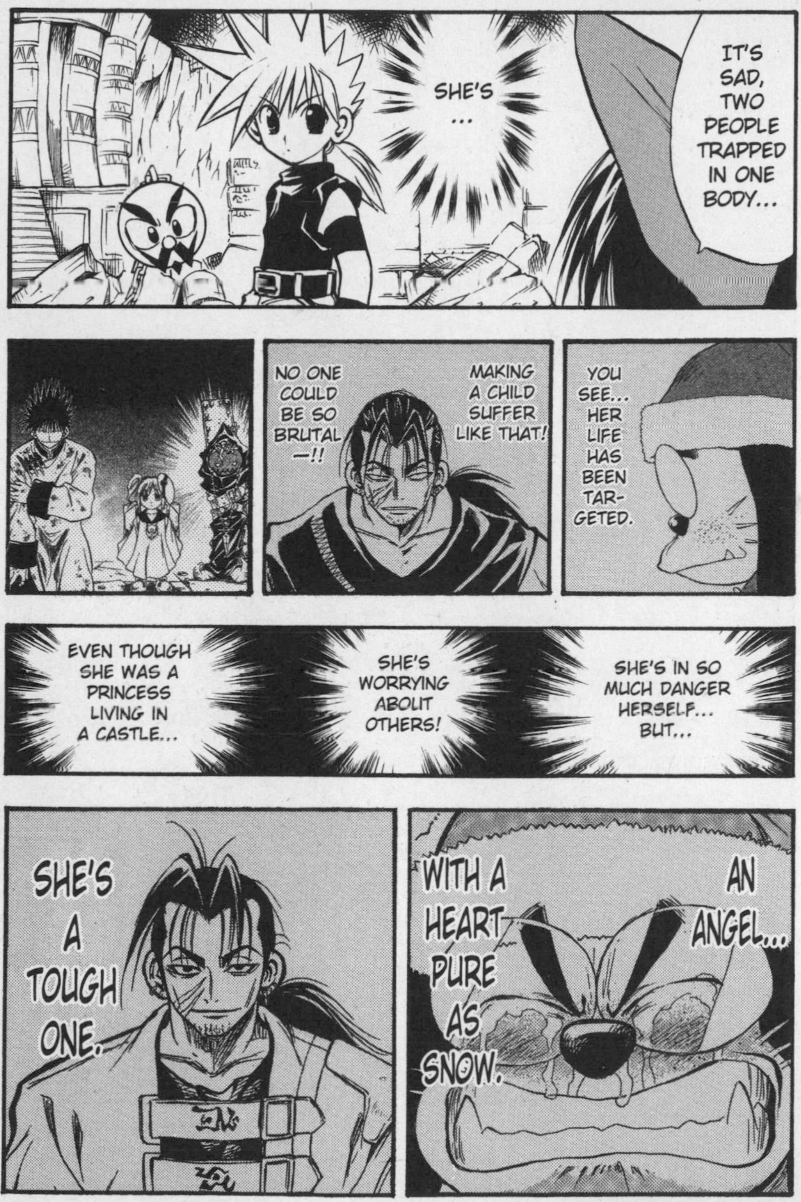
IT'S SAD, TWO PEOPLE TRAPPED IN ONE BODY...
SHE'S ...
YOU SEE... HER LIFE HAS BEEN TAR-GETED.
MAKING A CHILD SUFFER LIKE THAT!
NO ONE COULD BE SO BRUTAL—!!
SHE'S IN SO MUCH DANGER HERSELF... BUT...
SHE'S WORRYING ABOUT OTHERS!
EVEN THOUGH SHE WAS A PRINCESS LIVING IN A CASTLE...
AN ANGEL...
WITH A HEART PURE AS SNOW.
SHE'S A TOUGH ONE.

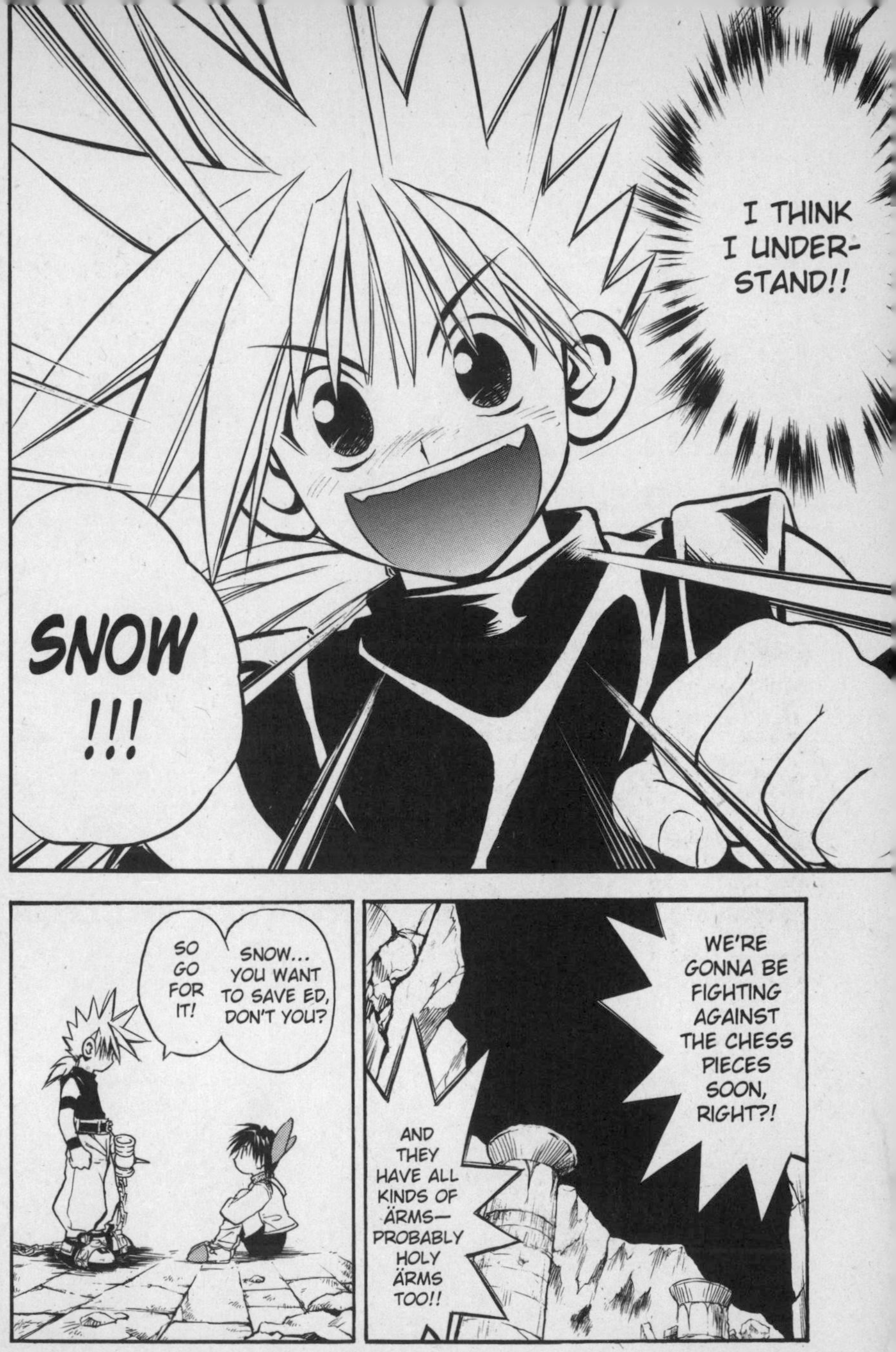
I THINK I UNDER-STAND!!
SNOW!!!
WE'RE GONNA BE FIGHTING AGAINST THE CHESS PIECES SOON, RIGHT?!
AND THEY HAVE ALL KINDS OF ÄRMS—PROBABLY HOLY ÄRMS TOO!!
SNOW... YOU WANT TO SAVE ED, DON'T YOU?
SO GO FOR IT!

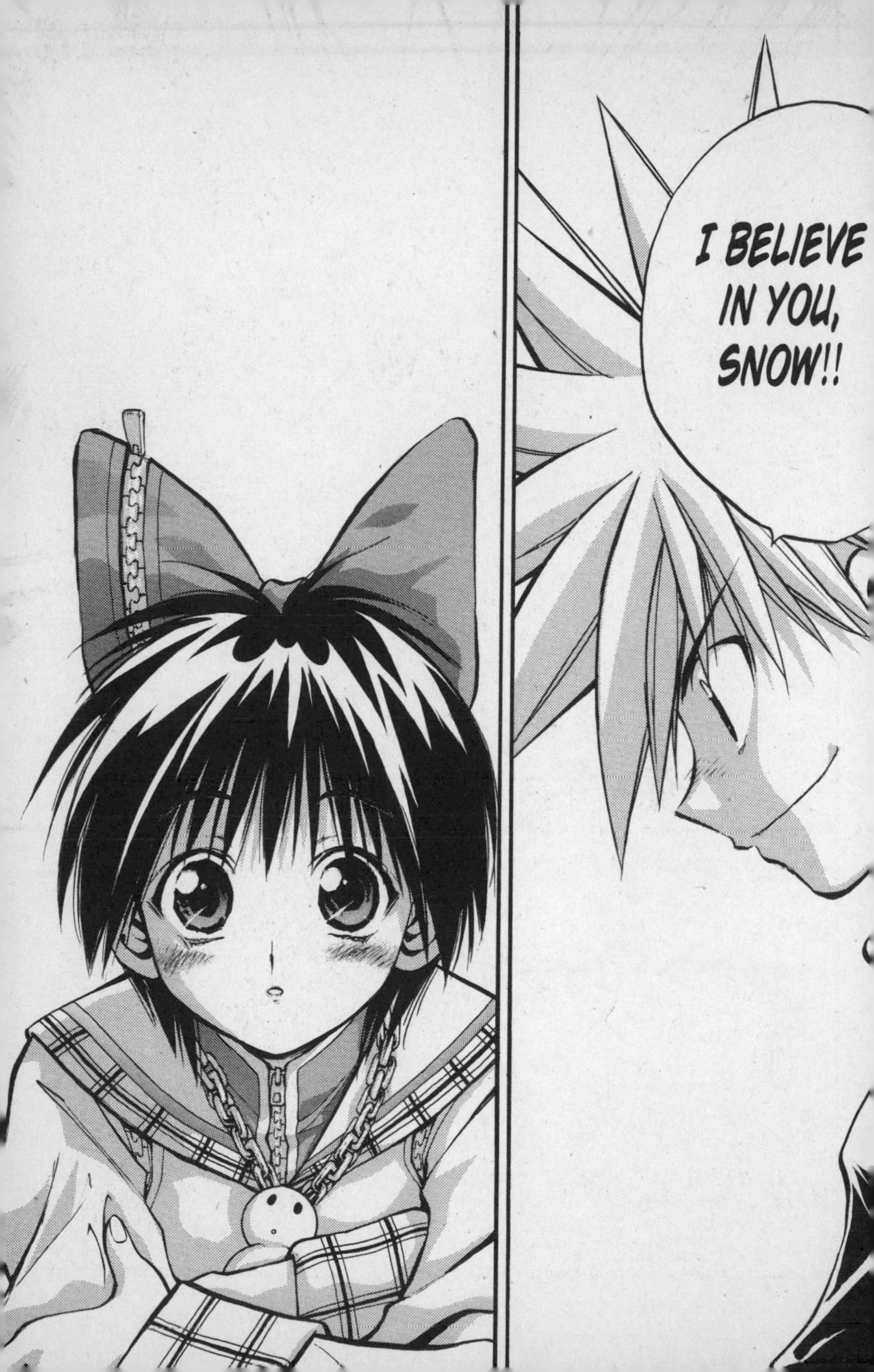
I BELIEVE IN YOU, SNOW!!

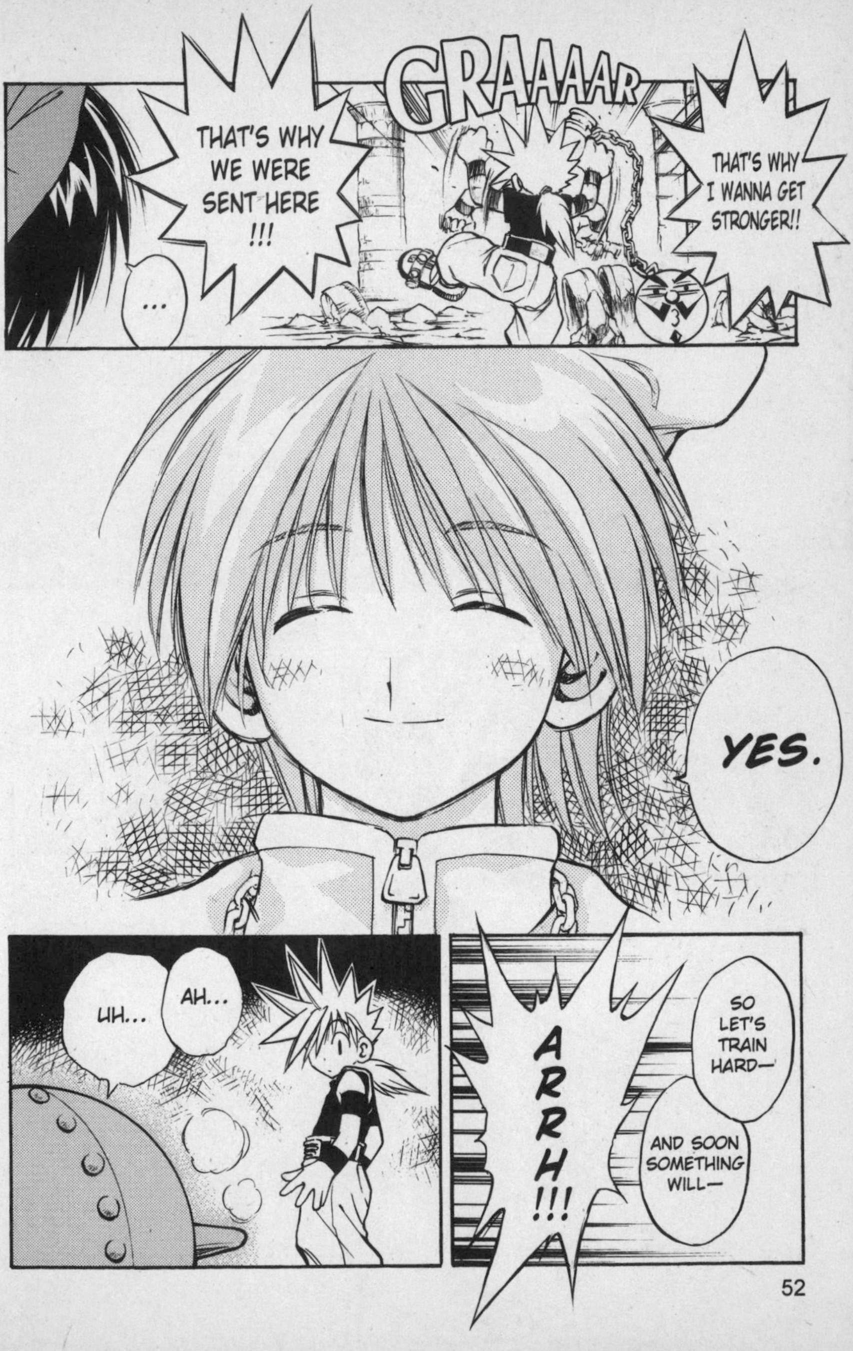
THAT'S WHY I WANNA GET STRONGER!!
GRAAAAR
THAT'S WHY WE WERE SENT HERE !!!
...
YES.
SO LET'S TRAIN HARD—
AND SOON SOMETHING WILL—
ARRH!!!
AH...
UH...

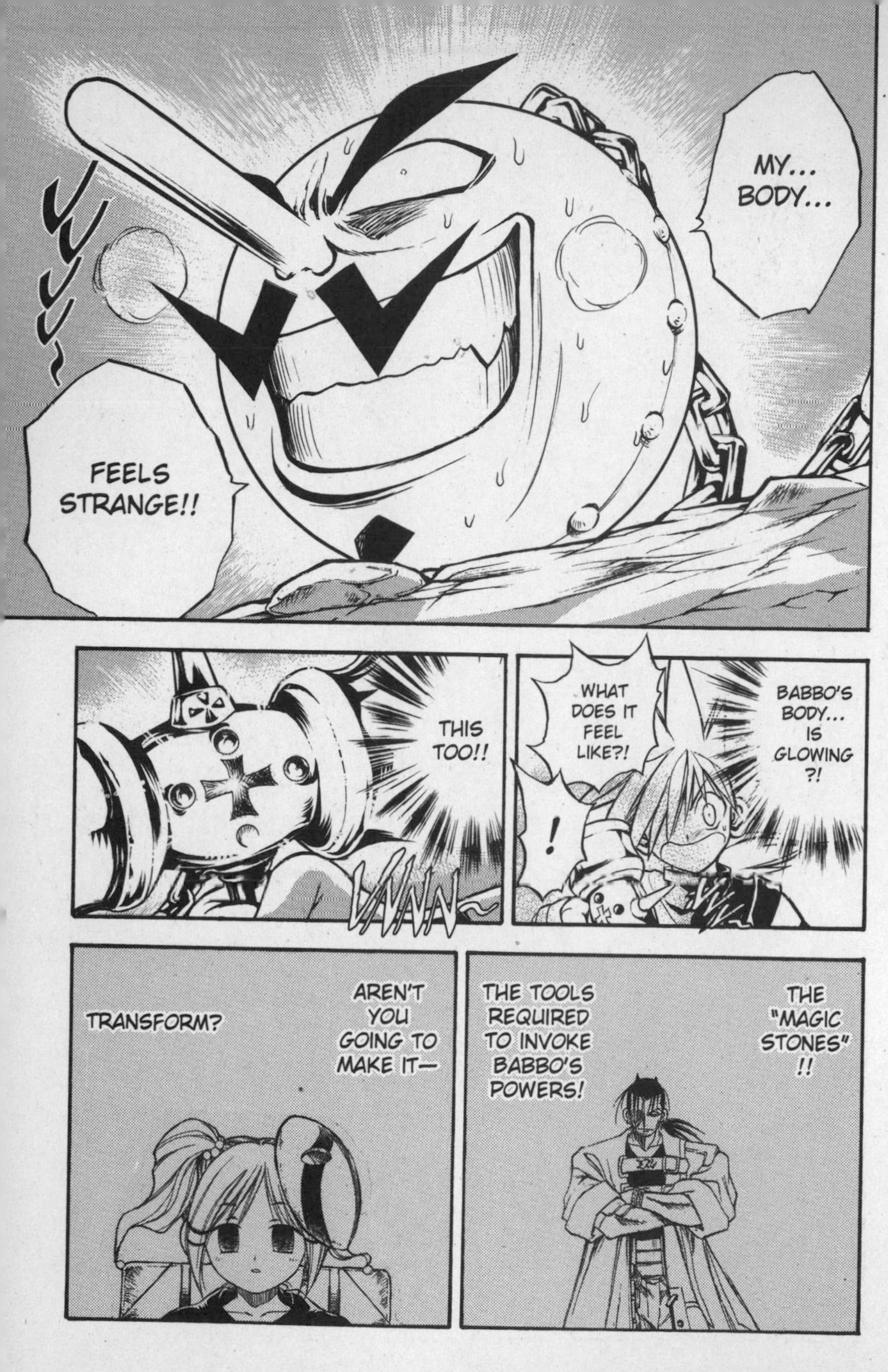
MY... BODY...
FEELS STRANGE!!
BABBO'S BODY... IS GLOWING?!
WHAT DOES IT FEEL LIKE?!
!
THIS TOO!!
THE "MAGIC STONES" !!
THE TOOLS REQUIRED TO INVOKE BABBO'S POWERS!
AREN'T YOU GOING TO MAKE IT—
TRANSFORM?

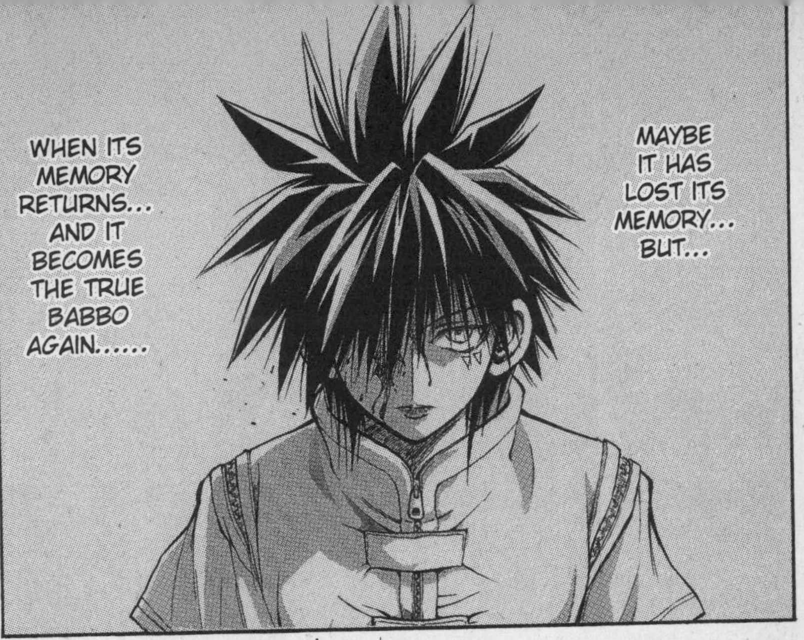
MAYBE IT HAS LOST ITS MEMORY... BUT...
WHEN ITS MEMORY RETURNS... AND IT BECOMES THE TRUE BABBO AGAIN......

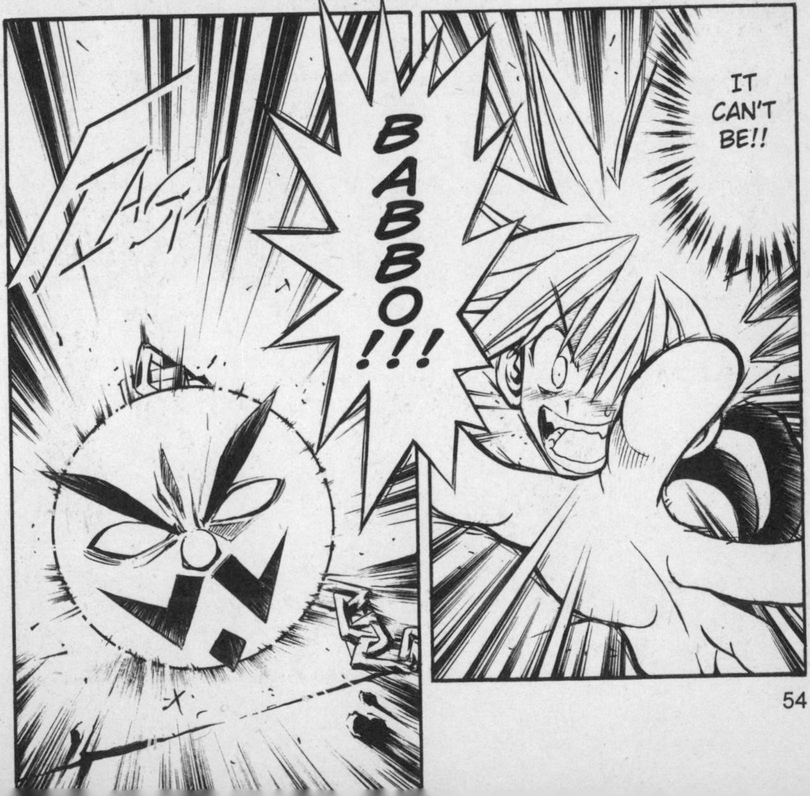
IT CAN'T BE!!
BABBO!!!

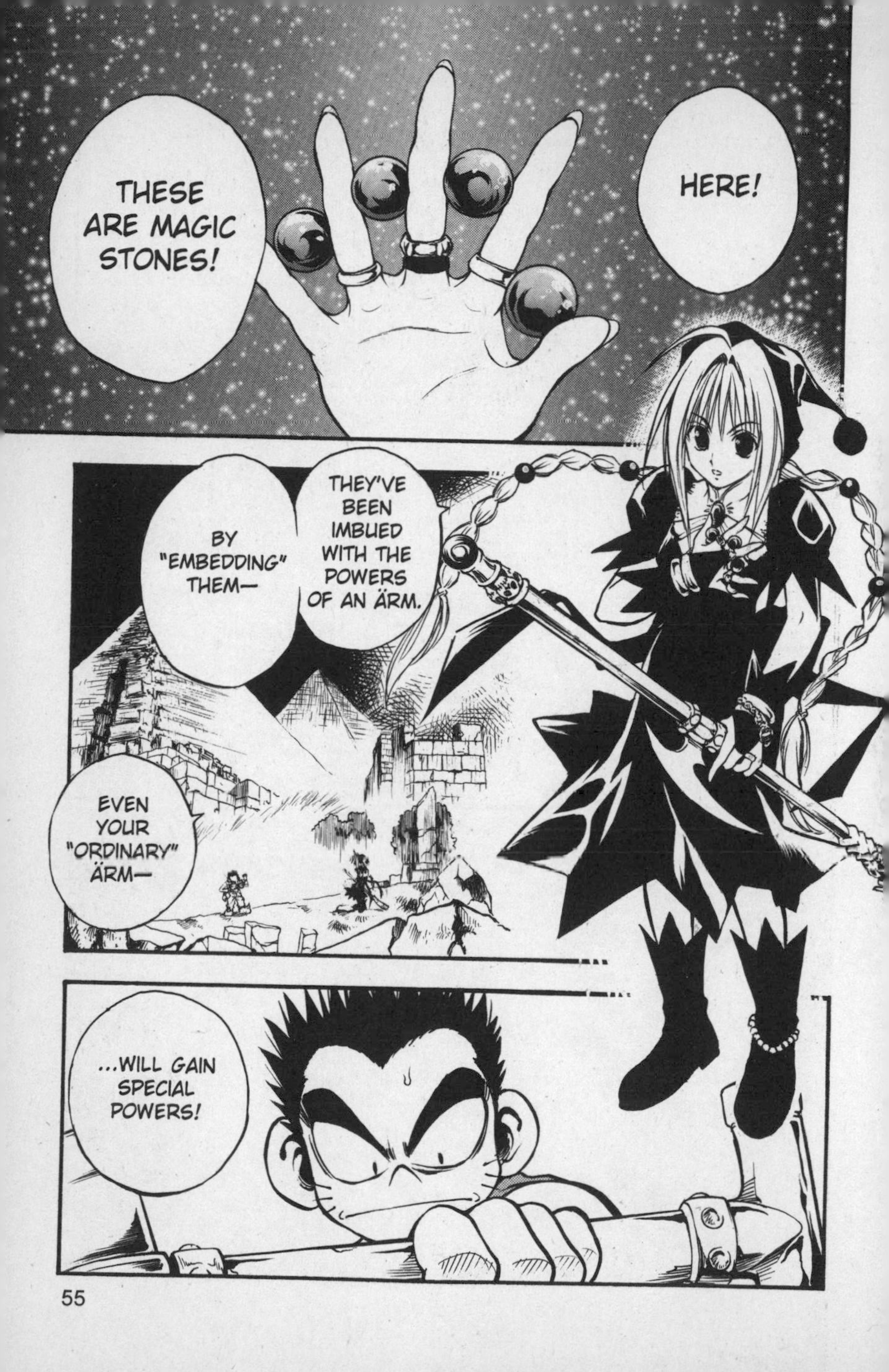
HERE!
THESE ARE MAGIC STONES!
THEY'VE BEEN IMBUED WITH THE POWERS OF AN ÄRM.
BY "EMBEDDING" THEM—
EVEN YOUR "ORDINARY" ÄRM—
...WILL GAIN SPECIAL POWERS!

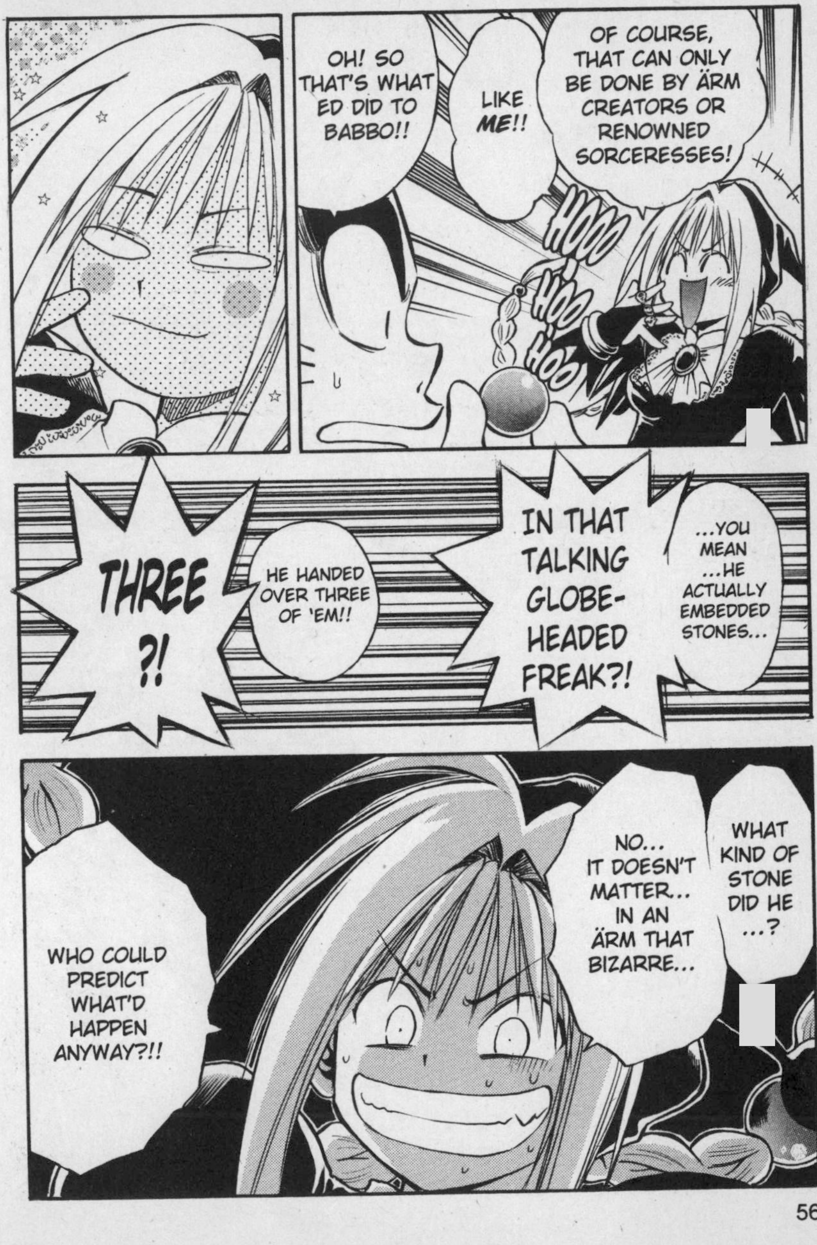
OF COURSE, THAT CAN ONLY BE DONE BY ÄRM CREATORS OR RENOWNED SORCERESSES!
LIKE ME!!
HOOO HOO HOO
OH! SO THAT'S WHAT ED DID TO BABBO!!
...YOU MEAN ...HE ACTUALLY EMBEDDED STONES...
IN THAT TALKING GLOBE-HEADED FREAK?!
HE HANDED OVER THREE OF 'EM!!
THREE ?!
WHAT KIND OF STONE DID HE ...?
NO... IT DOESN'T MATTER... IN AN ÄRM THAT BIZARRE...
WHO COULD PREDICT WHAT'D HAPPEN ANYWAY?!!

THIS ÄRM KILLED DOZENS OF MY COMRADES.

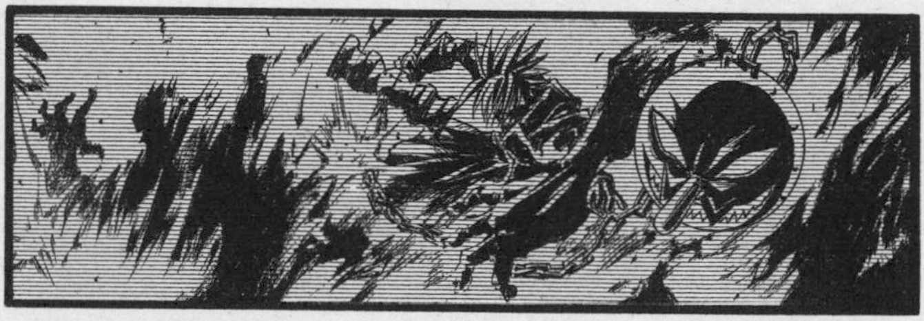

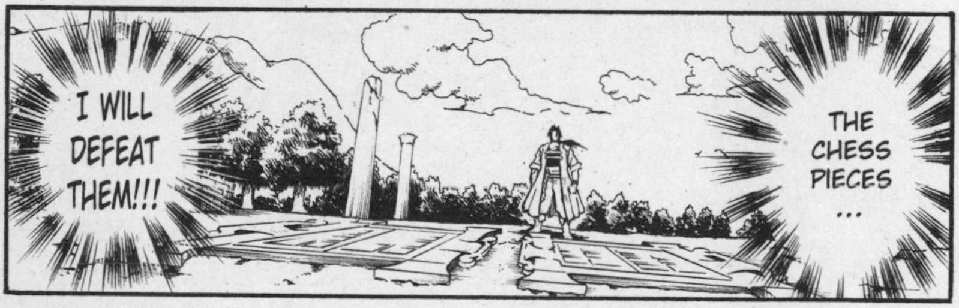
THE CHESS PIECES ...
I WILL DEFEAT THEM!!!

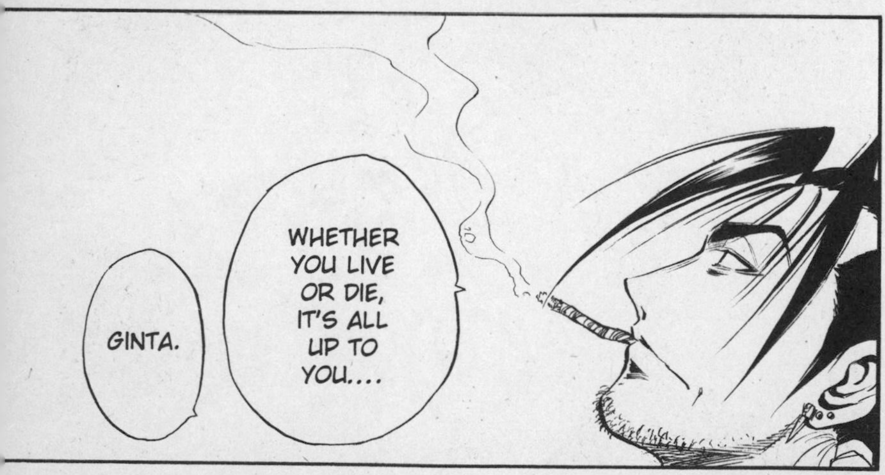
WHETHER YOU LIVE OR DIE, IT'S ALL UP TO YOU....
GINTA.

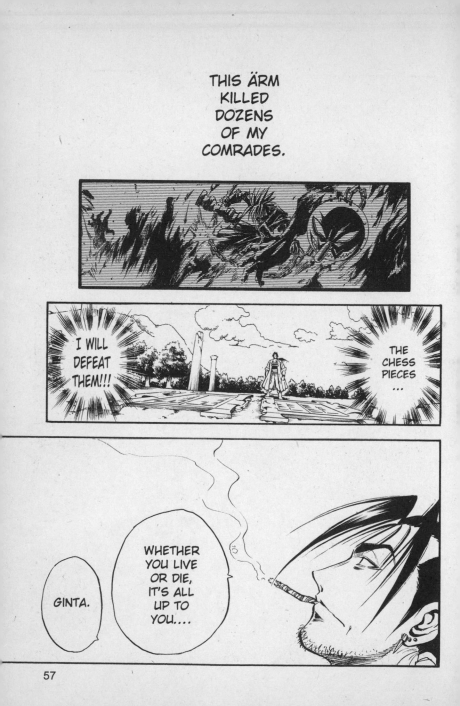

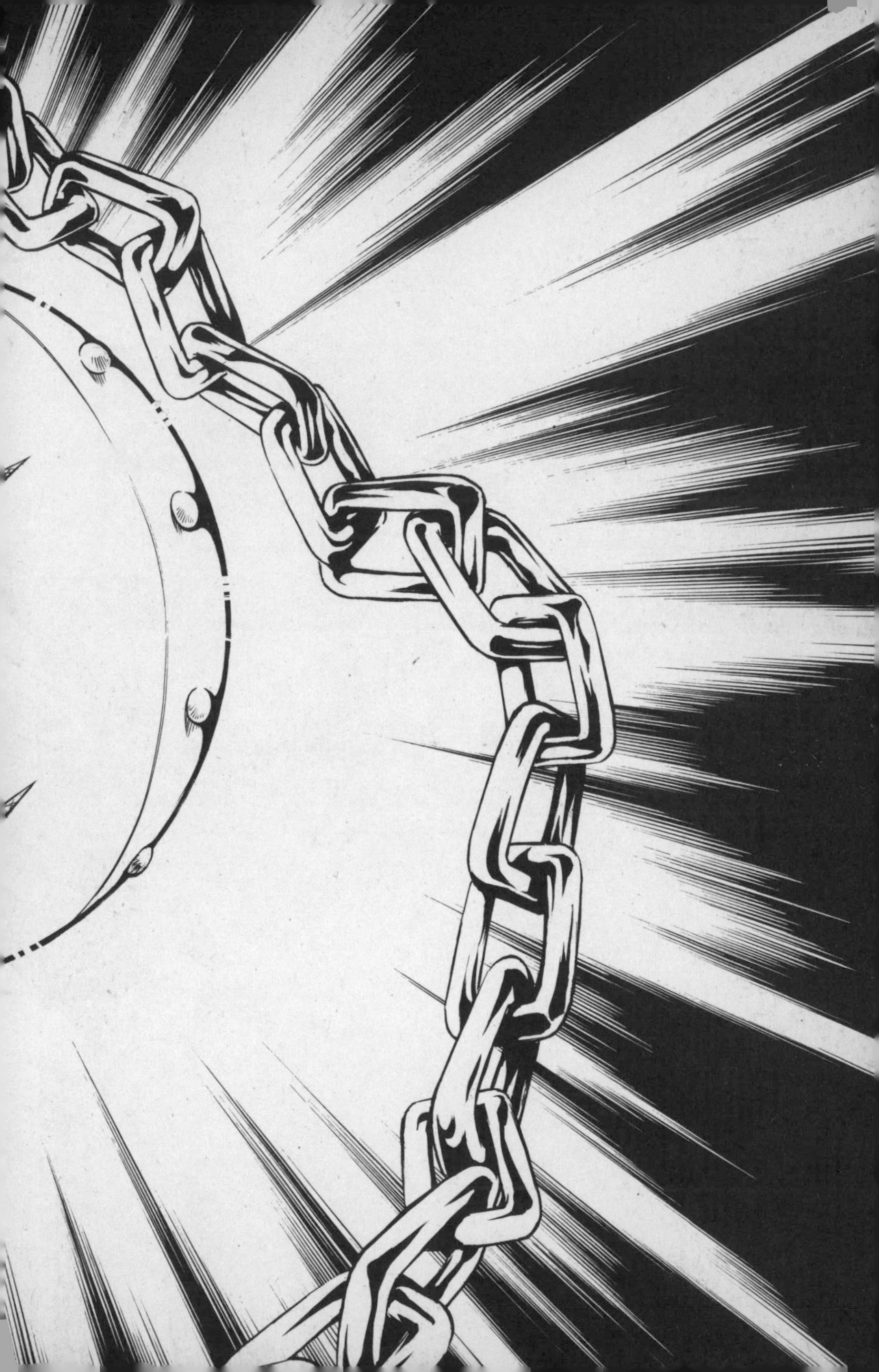

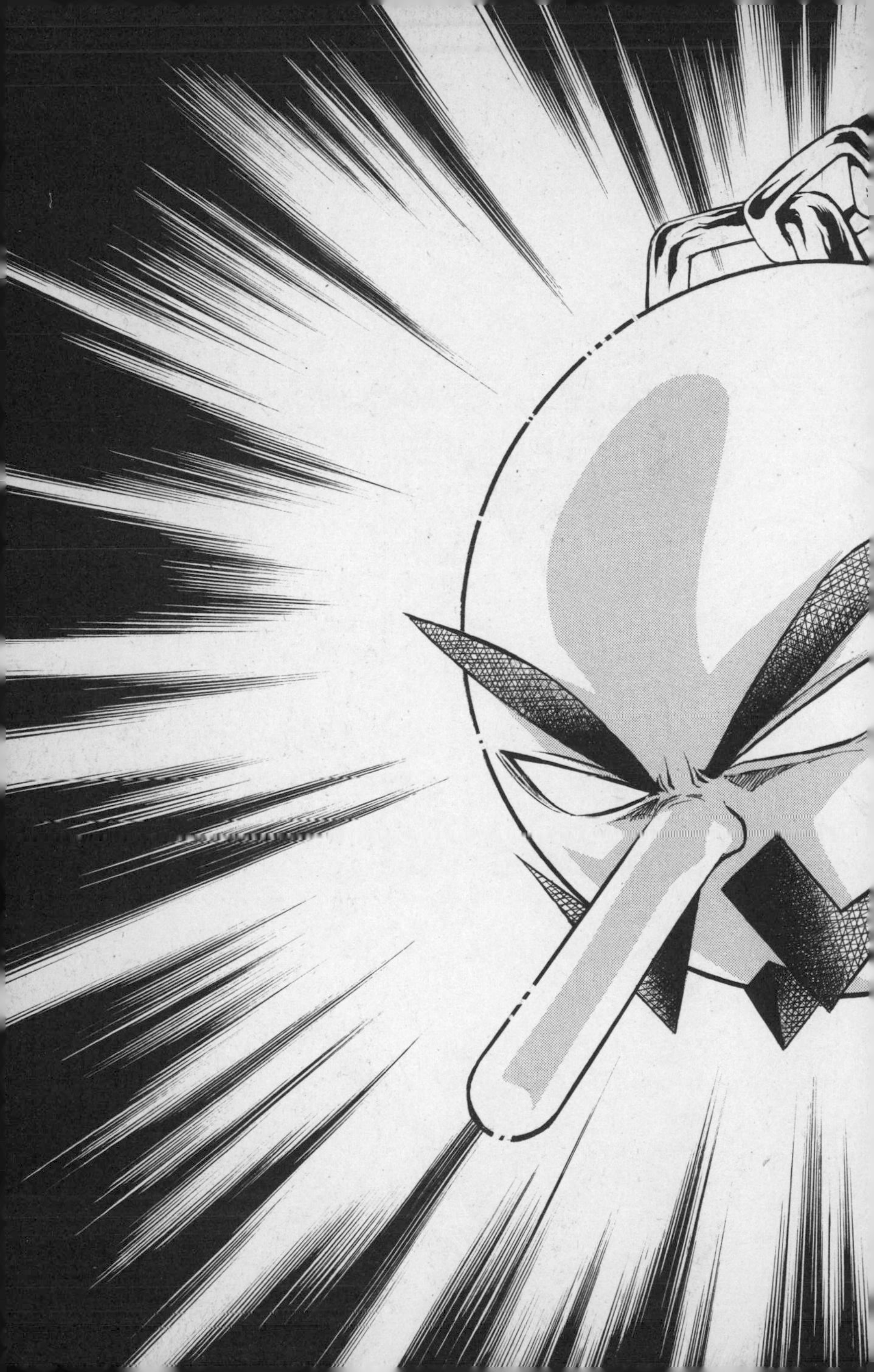

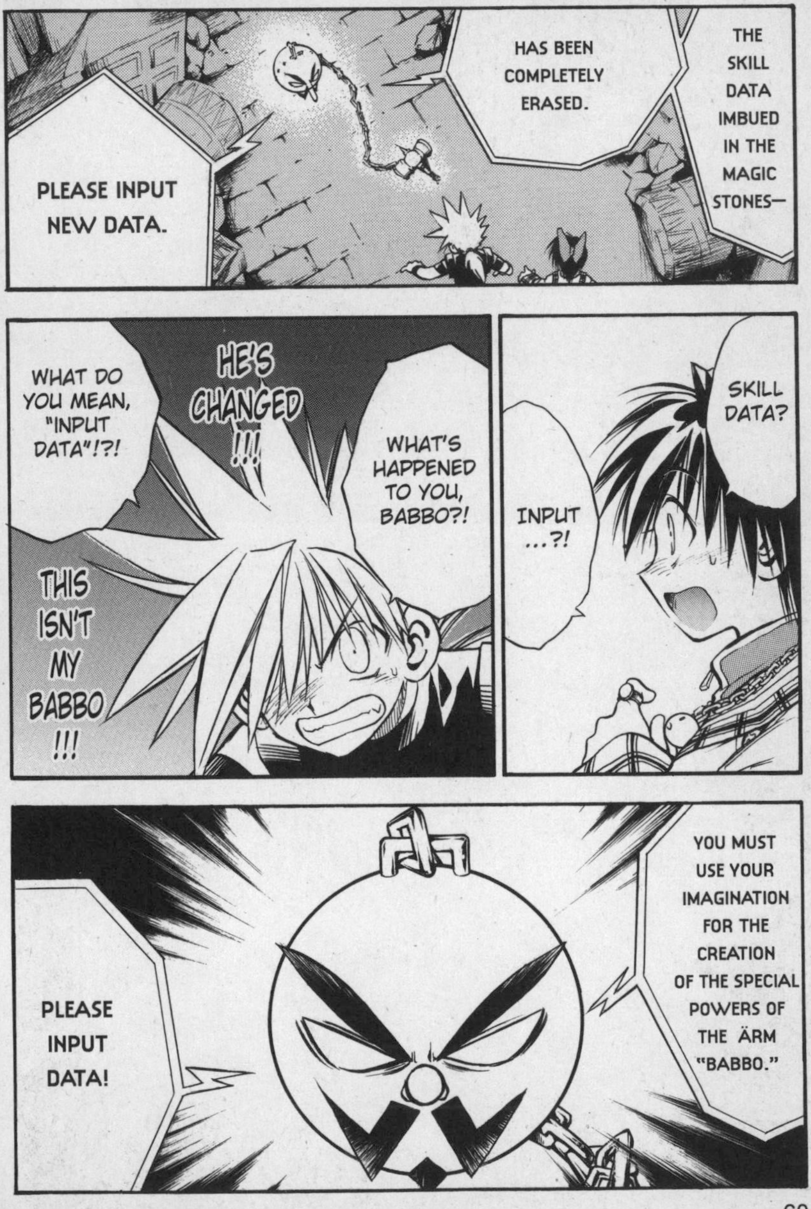
THE SKILL DATA IMBUED IN THE MAGIC STONES—
HAS BEEN COMPLETELY ERASED.
PLEASE INPUT NEW DATA.
SKILL DATA?
INPUT ...?!
HE'S CHANGED!!!
WHAT'S HAPPENED TO YOU, BABBO?!
WHAT DO YOU MEAN, "INPUT DATA"!?!
THIS ISN'T MY BABBO!!!
YOU MUST USE YOUR IMAGINATION FOR THE CREATION OF THE SPECIAL POWERS OF THE ÄRM "BABBO."
PLEASE INPUT DATA!

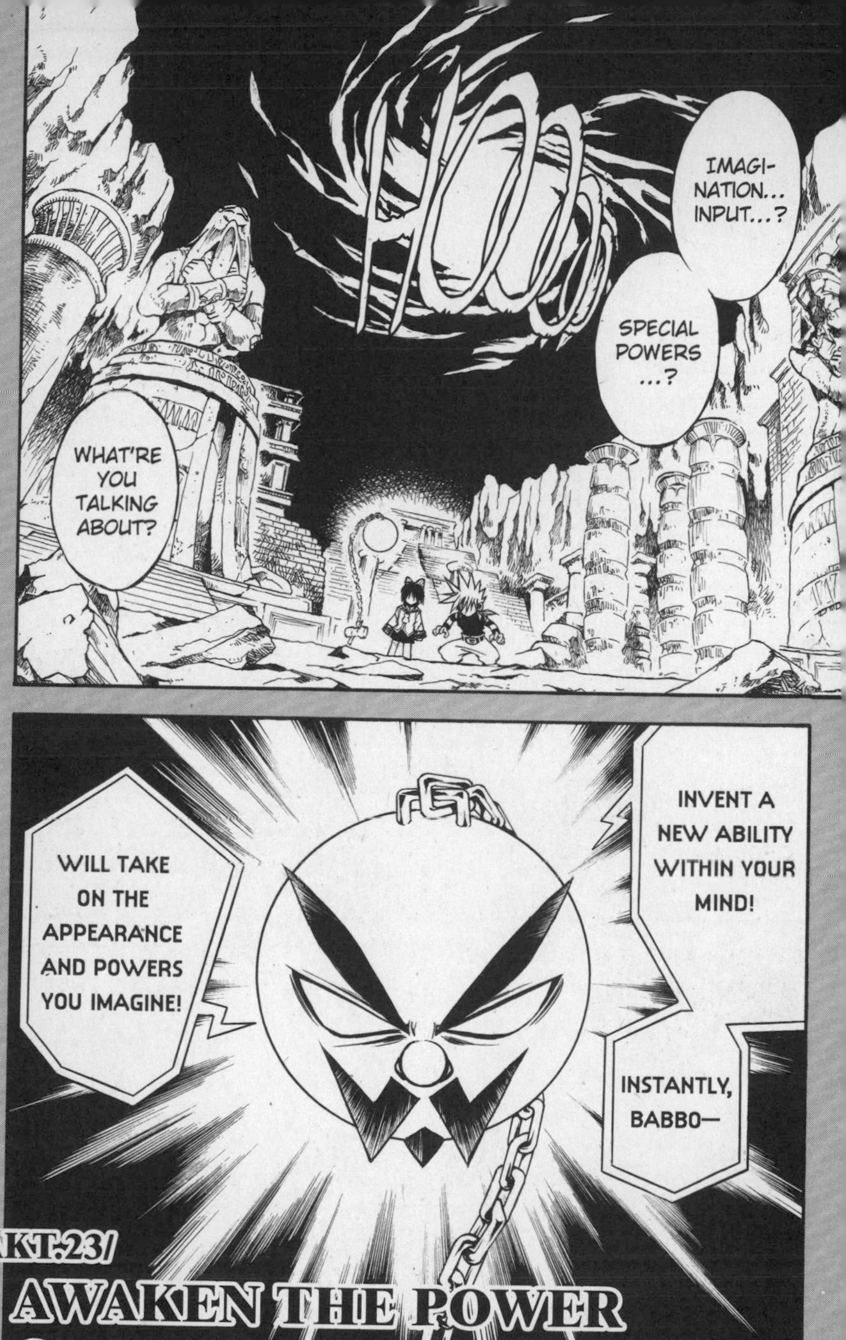
IMAGINATION... INPUT...?
SPECIAL POWERS ...?
WHAT'RE YOU TALKING ABOUT?
INVENT A NEW ABILITY WITHIN YOUR MIND!
INSTANTLY, BABBO—
WILL TAKE ON THE APPEARANCE AND POWERS YOU IMAGINE!

AKT.23/

AWAKEN THE POWER ③Babbo v1

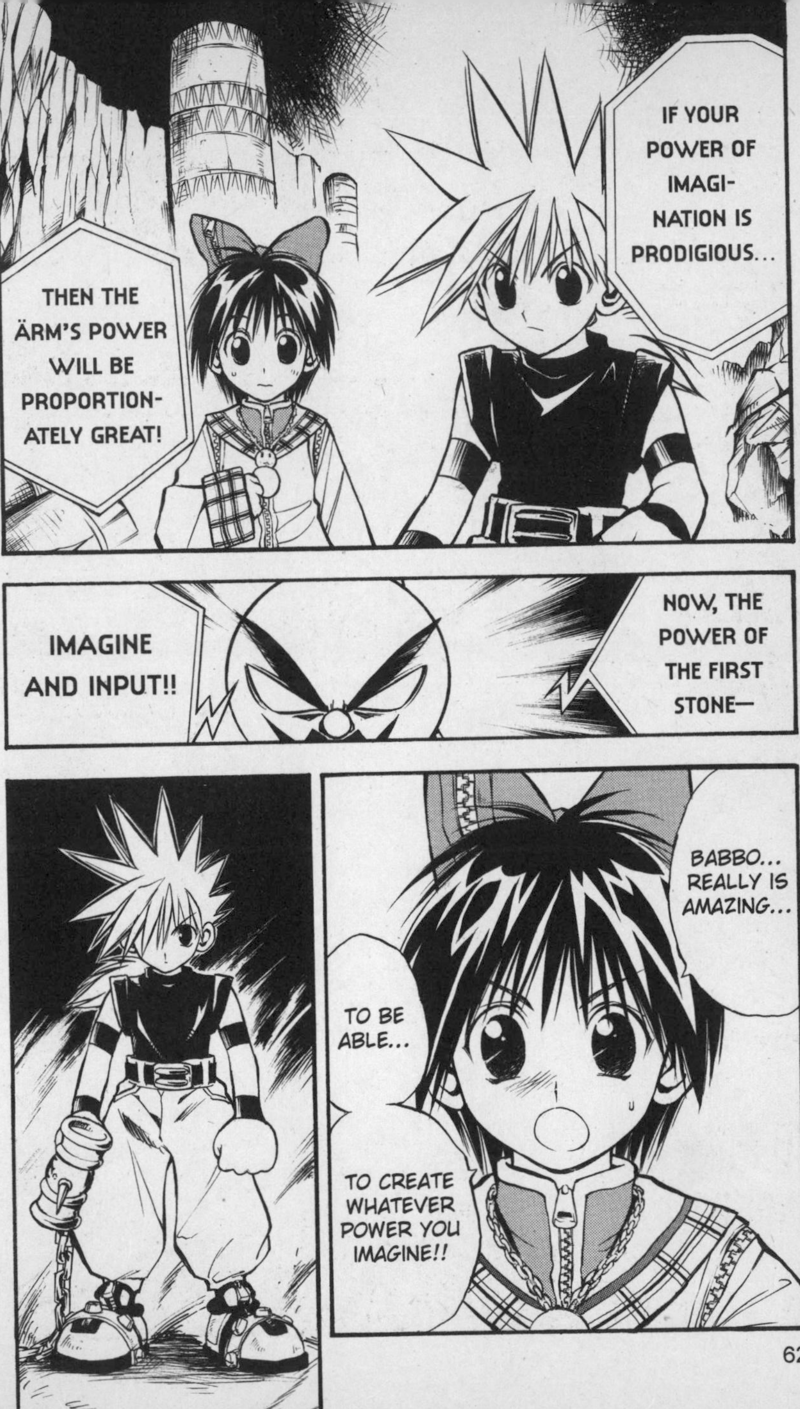
IF YOUR POWER OF IMAGI-NATION IS PRODIGIOUS...
THEN THE ÄRM'S POWER WILL BE PROPORTION-ATELY GREAT!
NOW, THE POWER OF THE FIRST STONE—
IMAGINE AND INPUT!!
BABBO... REALLY IS AMAZING...
TO BE ABLE...
TO CREATE WHATEVER POWER YOU IMAGINE!!

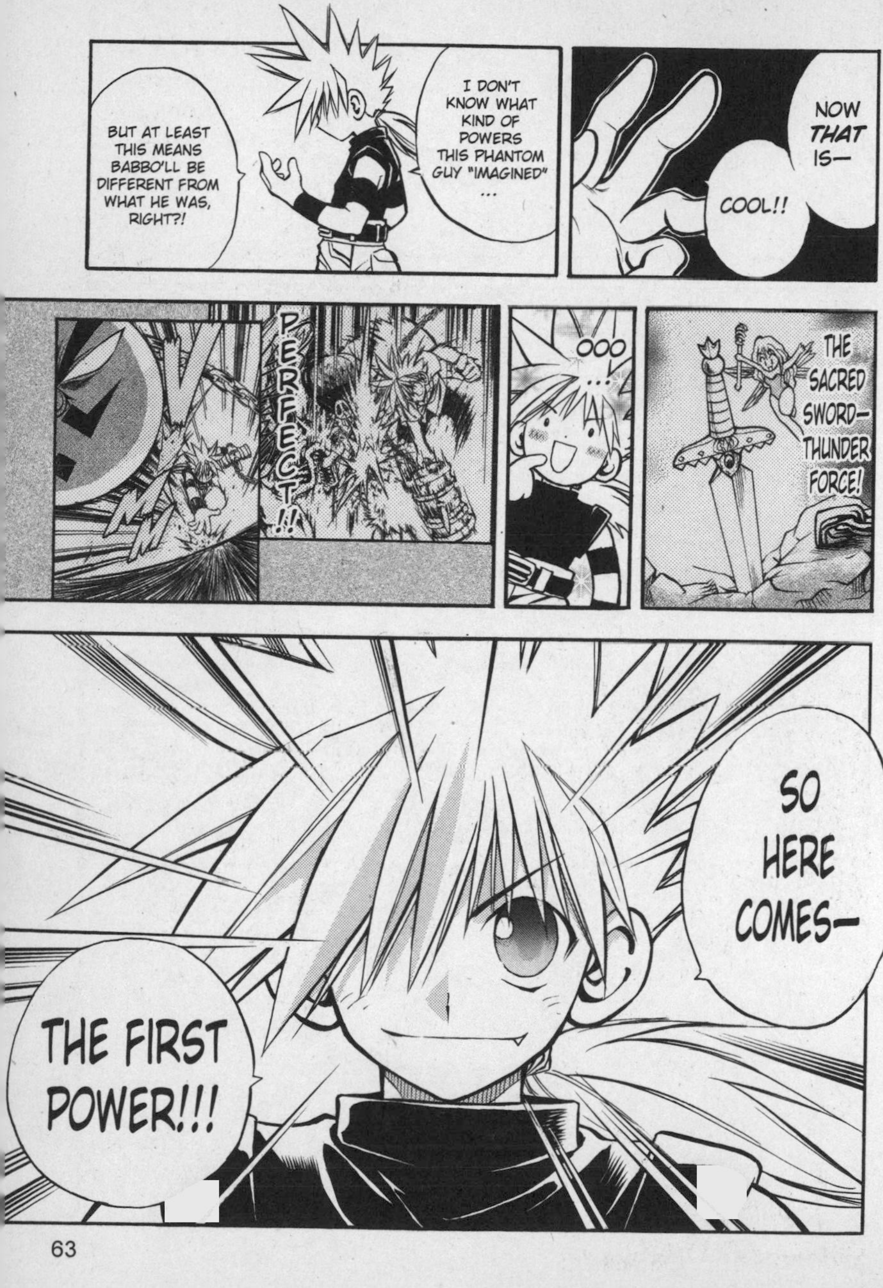
NOW *THAT* IS—
COOL!!
I DON'T KNOW WHAT KIND OF POWERS THIS PHANTOM GUY "IMAGINED" ...
BUT AT LEAST THIS MEANS BABBO'LL BE DIFFERENT FROM WHAT HE WAS, RIGHT?!
THE SACRED SWORD— THUNDER FORCE!
OOO ...
PERFECT!!
SO HERE COMES—
THE FIRST POWER!!!

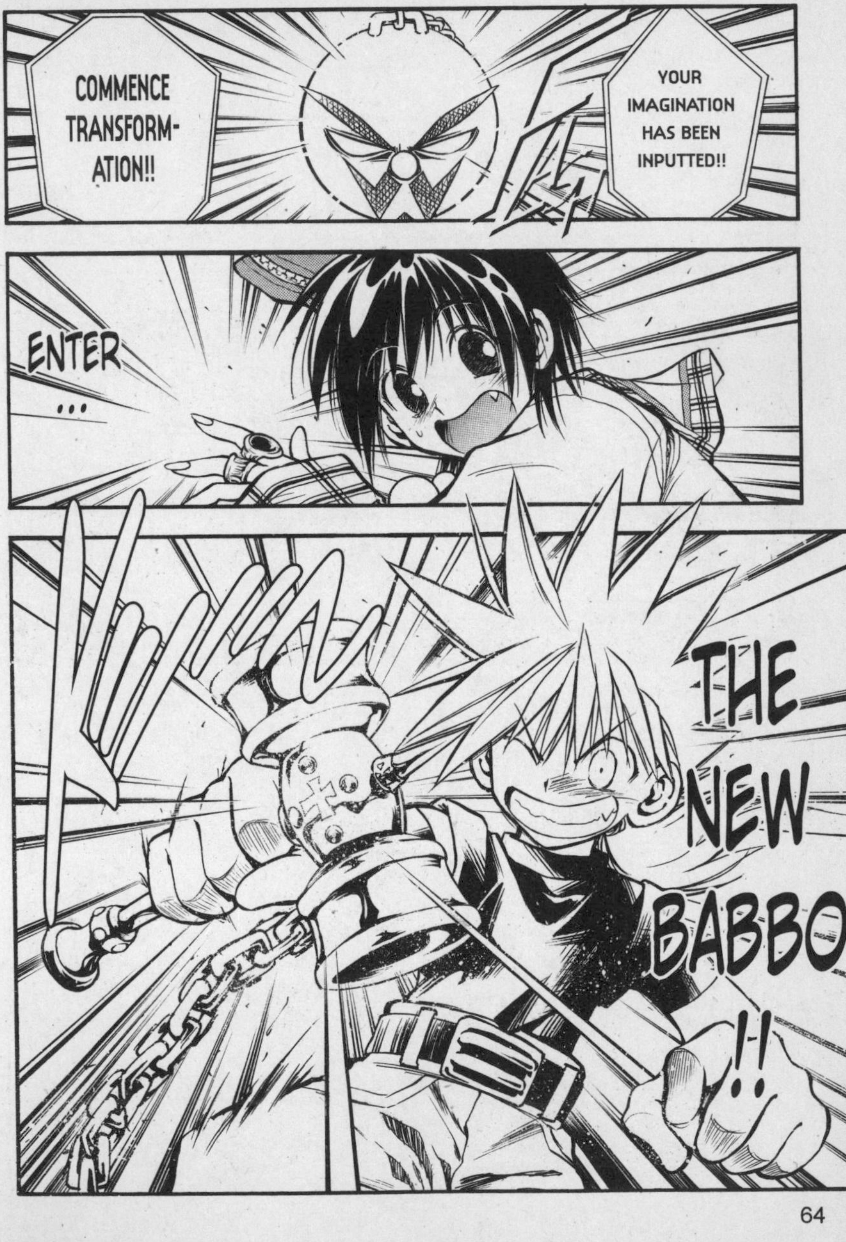
YOUR IMAGINATION HAS BEEN INPUTTED!!
COMMENCE TRANSFORM-ATION!!
ENTER ...
THE NEW BABBO!!

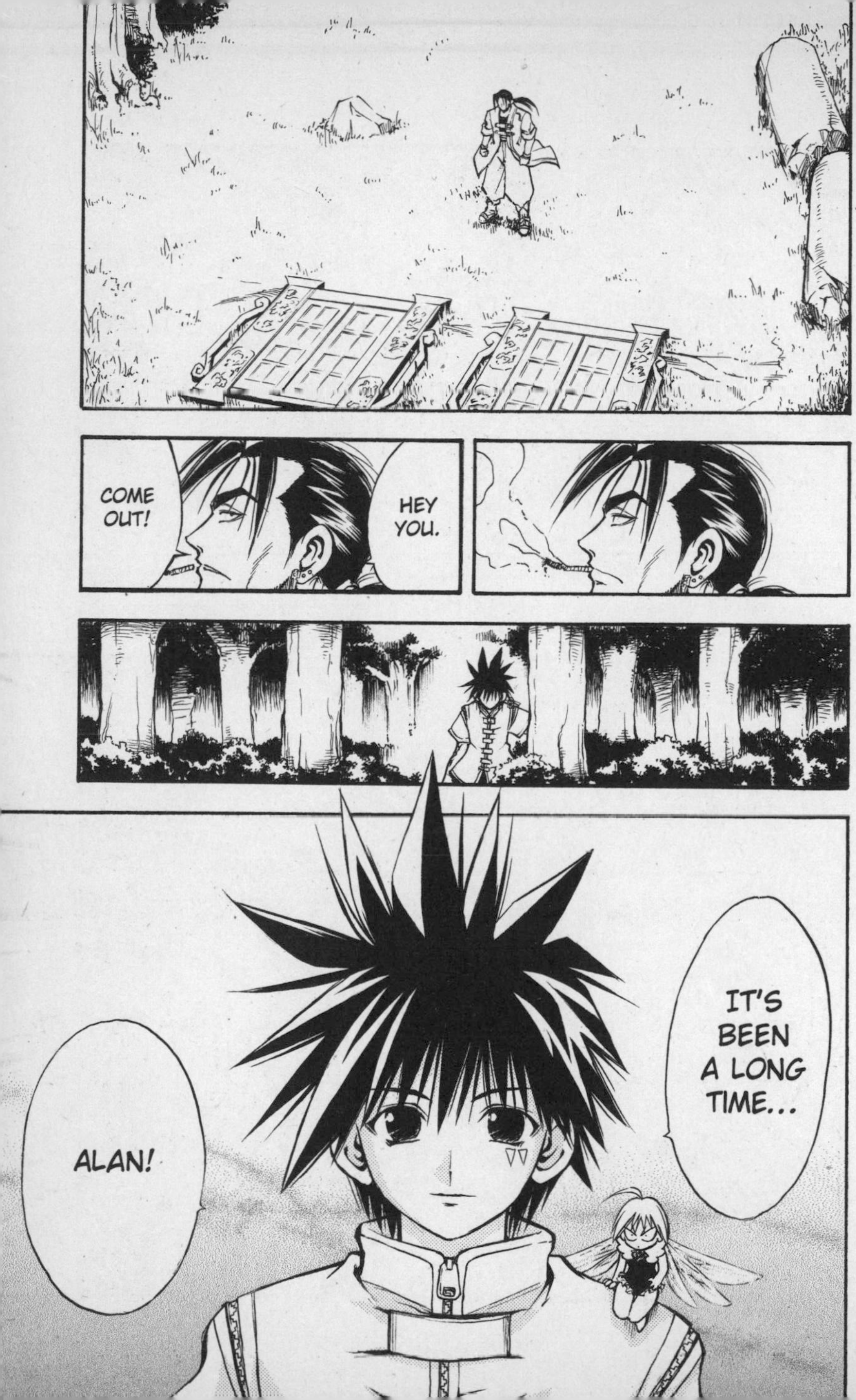
HEY YOU.
COME OUT!
IT'S BEEN A LONG TIME...
ALAN!

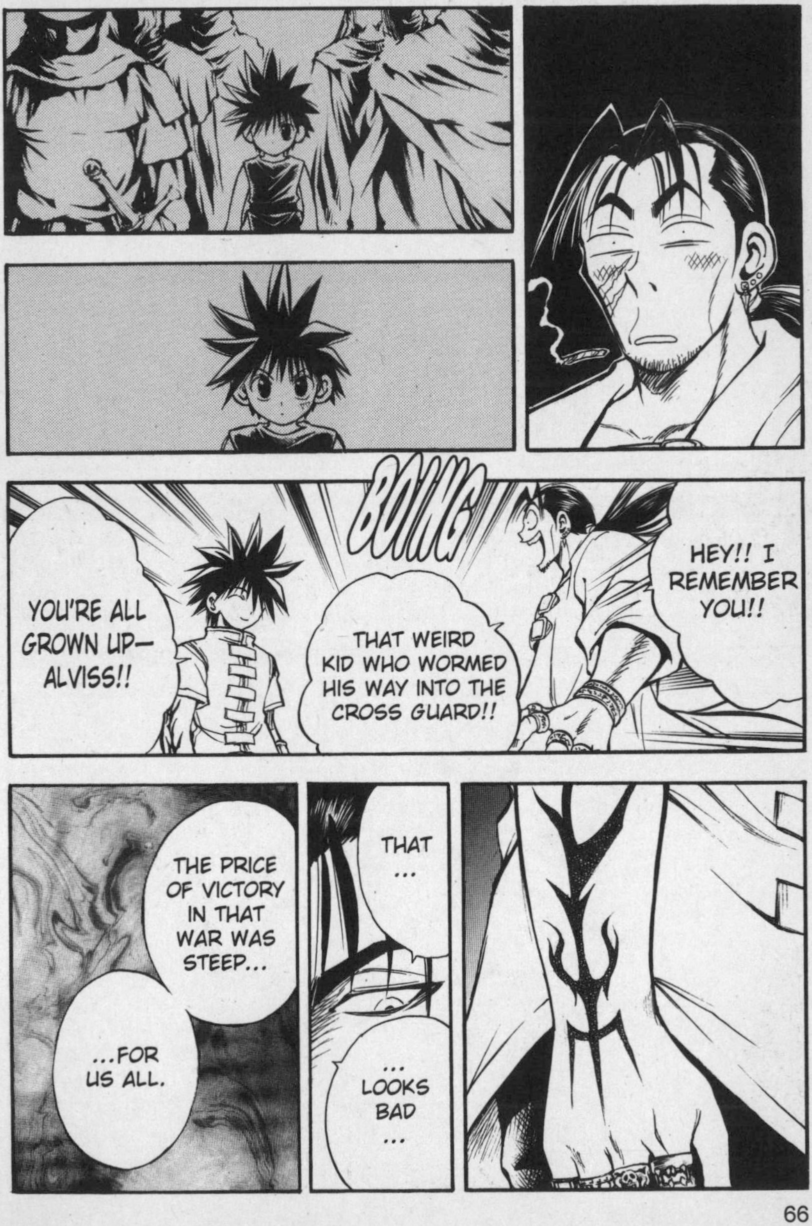
BOING
HEY!! I REMEMBER YOU!!
THAT WEIRD KID WHO WORMED HIS WAY INTO THE CROSS GUARD!!
YOU'RE ALL GROWN UP— ALVISS!!
THAT ...
... LOOKS BAD ...
THE PRICE OF VICTORY IN THAT WAR WAS STEEP...
...FOR US ALL.

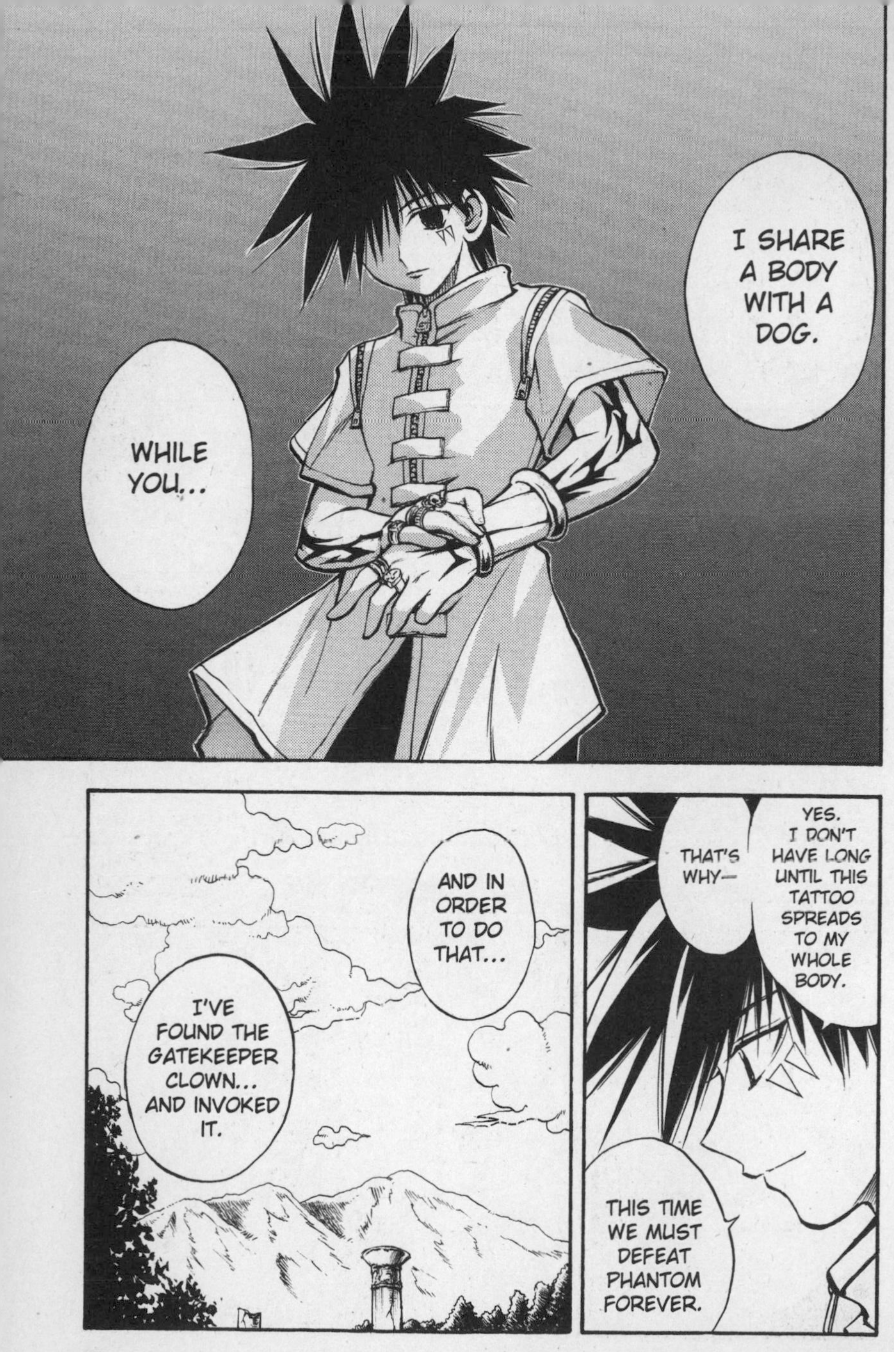
I SHARE A BODY WITH A DOG.
WHILE YOU...
YES. I DON'T HAVE LONG UNTIL THIS TATTOO SPREADS TO MY WHOLE BODY.
THAT'S WHY—
THIS TIME WE MUST DEFEAT PHANTOM FOREVER.
AND IN ORDER TO DO THAT...
I'VE FOUND THE GATEKEEPER CLOWN... AND INVOKED IT.

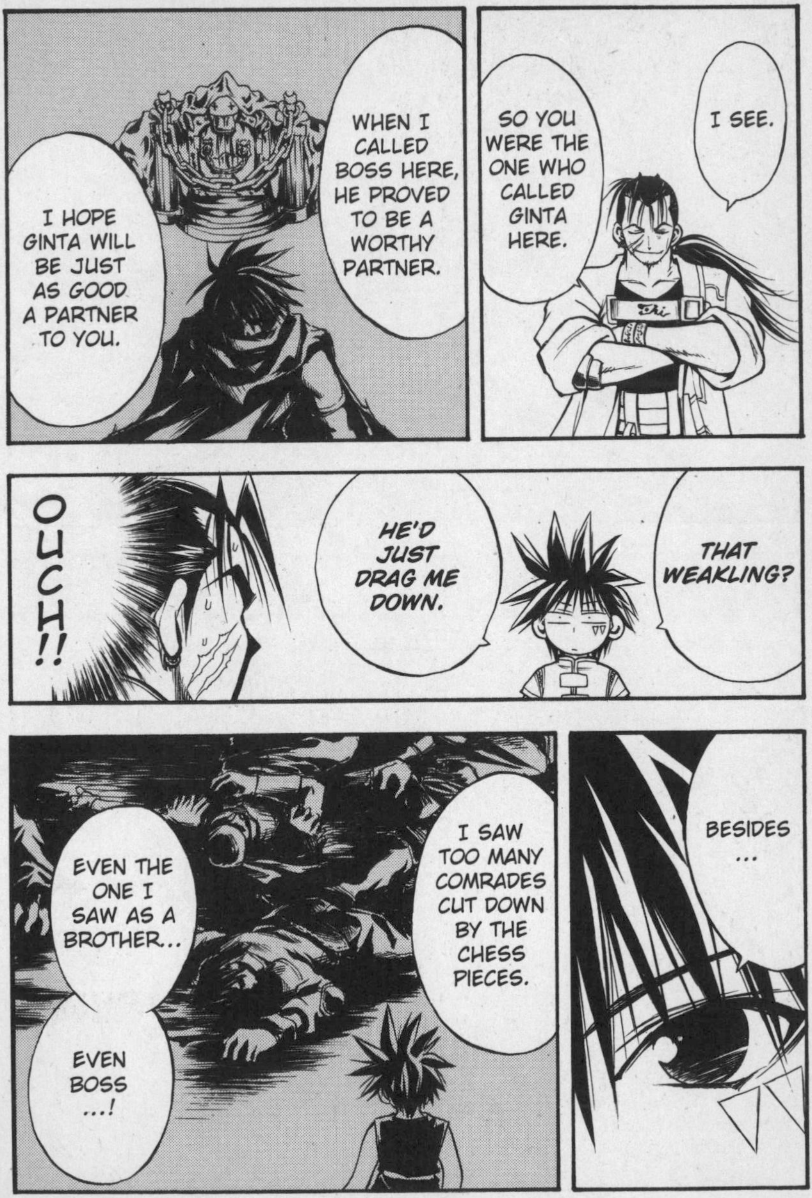
I SEE.
SO YOU WERE THE ONE WHO CALLED GINTA HERE.
WHEN I CALLED BOSS HERE, HE PROVED TO BE A WORTHY PARTNER.
I HOPE GINTA WILL BE JUST AS GOOD A PARTNER TO YOU.
THAT WEAKLING?
HE'D JUST DRAG ME DOWN.
OUCH!!
BESIDES ...
I SAW TOO MANY COMRADES CUT DOWN BY THE CHESS PIECES.
EVEN THE ONE I SAW AS A BROTHER...
EVEN BOSS ...!

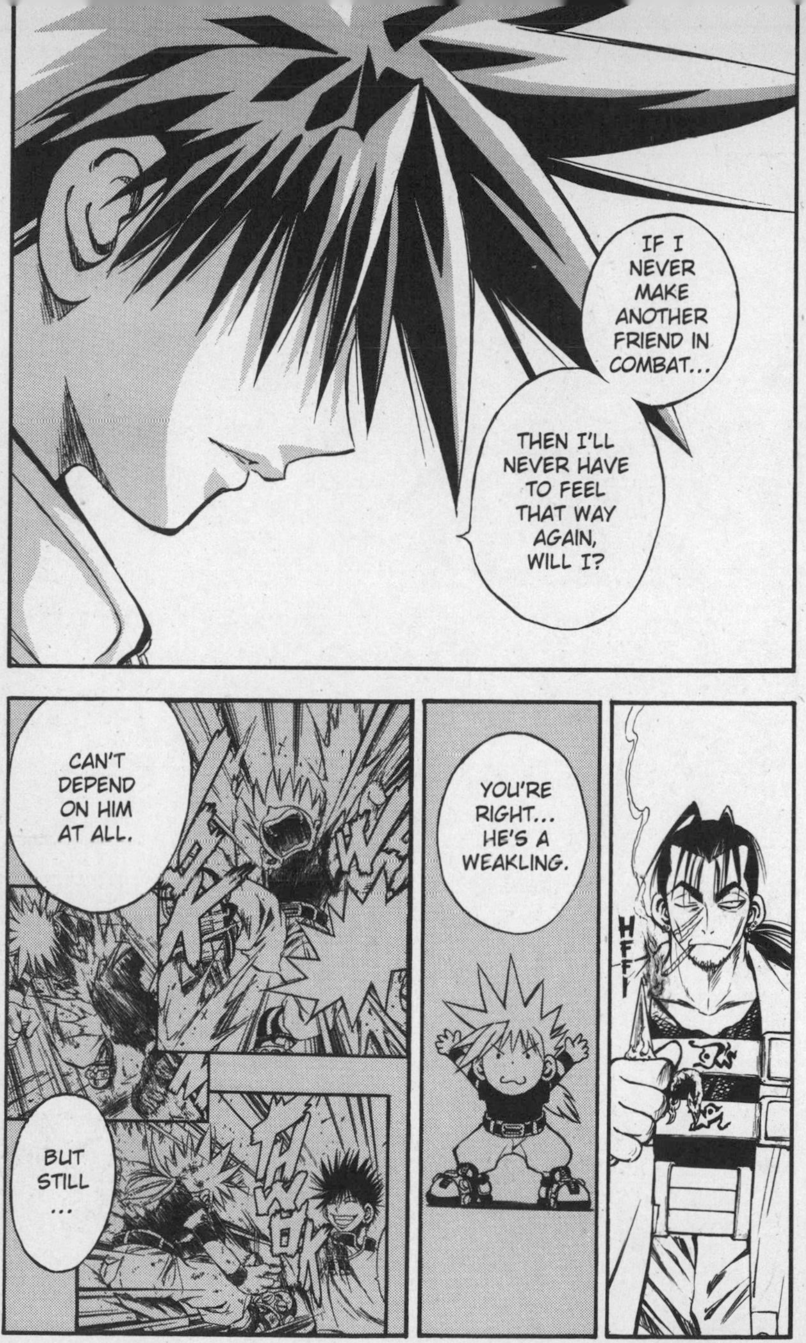
IF I NEVER MAKE ANOTHER FRIEND IN COMBAT...
THEN I'LL NEVER HAVE TO FEEL THAT WAY AGAIN, WILL I?
HFF!
YOU'RE RIGHT... HE'S A WEAKLING.
CAN'T DEPEND ON HIM AT ALL.
BUT STILL ...

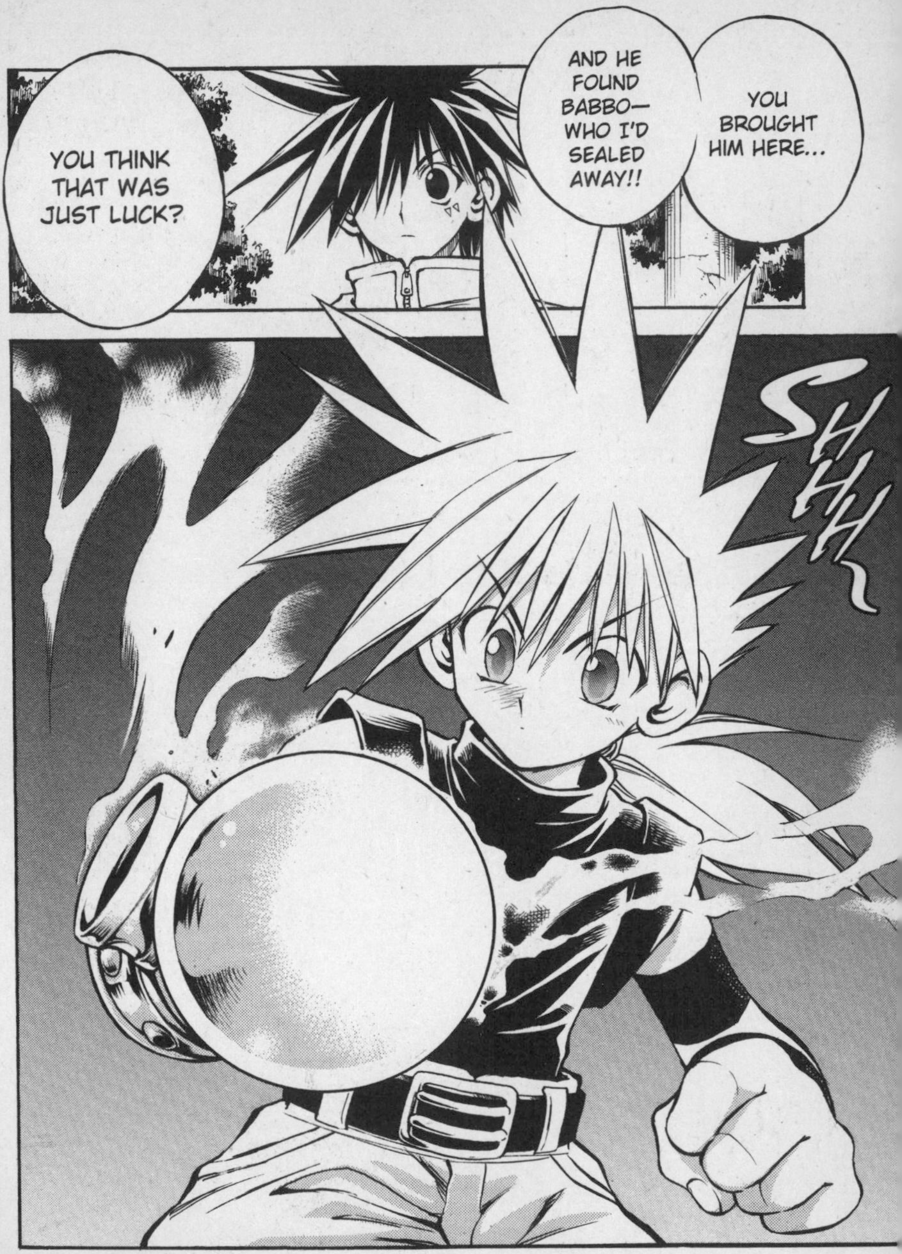
YOU BROUGHT HIM HERE...
AND HE FOUND BABBO— WHO I'D SEALED AWAY!!
YOU THINK THAT WAS JUST LUCK?
SHHH

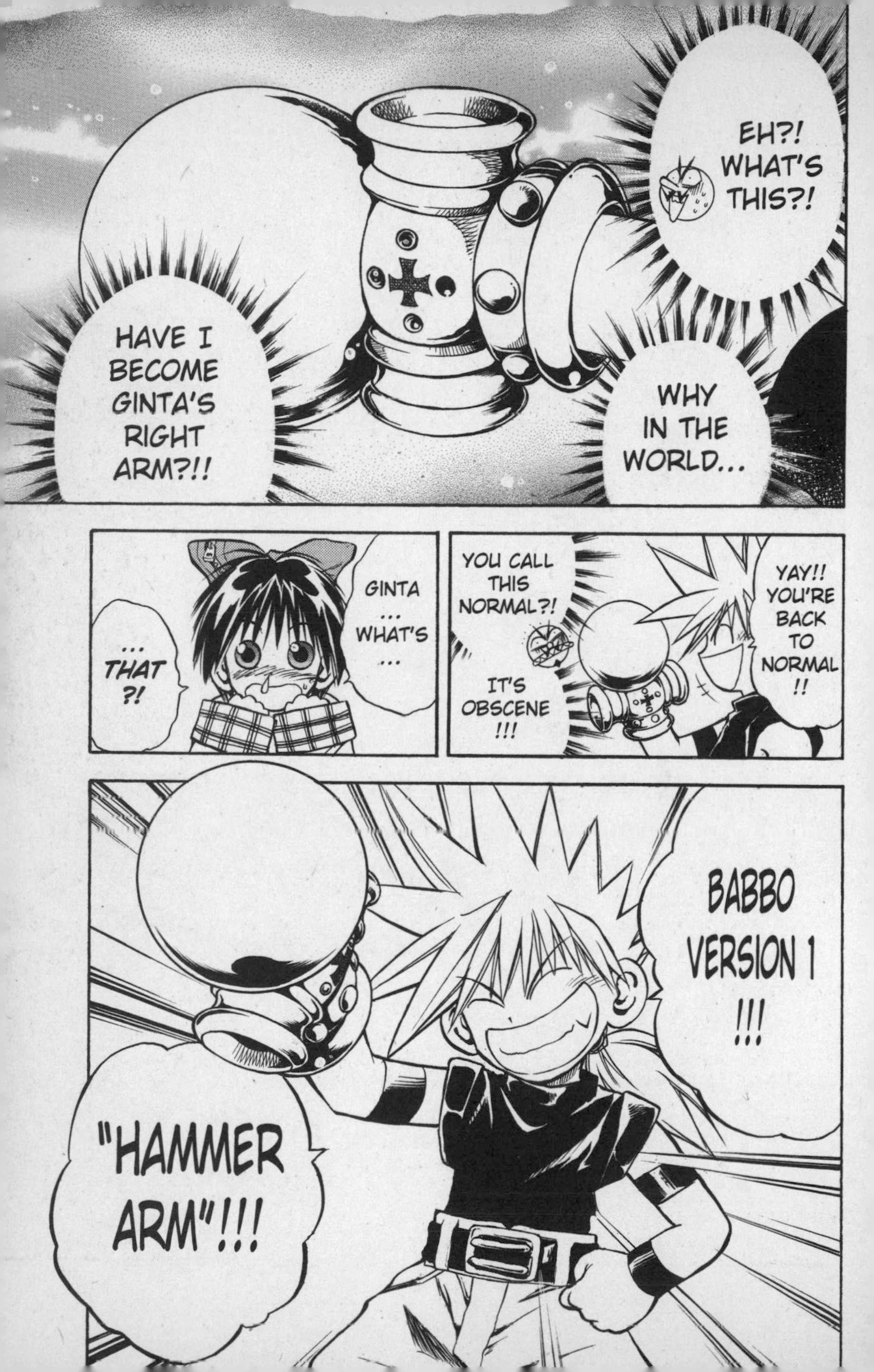
EH?! WHAT'S THIS?!
WHY IN THE WORLD...
HAVE I BECOME GINTA'S RIGHT ARM?!!
YAY!! YOU'RE BACK TO NORMAL !!
YOU CALL THIS NORMAL?!
IT'S OBSCENE !!!
GINTA ... WHAT'S ...
... THAT ?!
BABBO VERSION 1 !!!
"HAMMER ARM"!!!

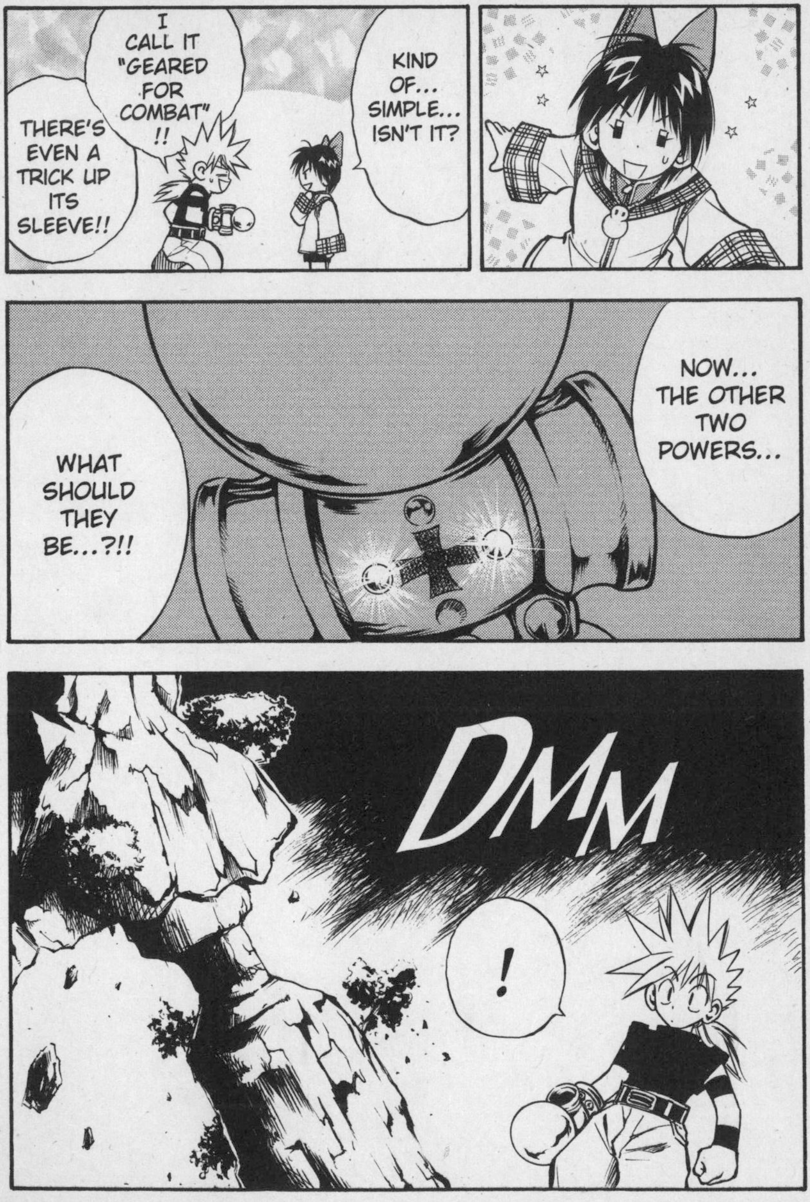
KIND OF... SIMPLE... ISN'T IT?
I CALL IT "GEARED FOR COMBAT"!!
THERE'S EVEN A TRICK UP ITS SLEEVE!!
NOW... THE OTHER TWO POWERS...
WHAT SHOULD THEY BE...?!!
DMM
!

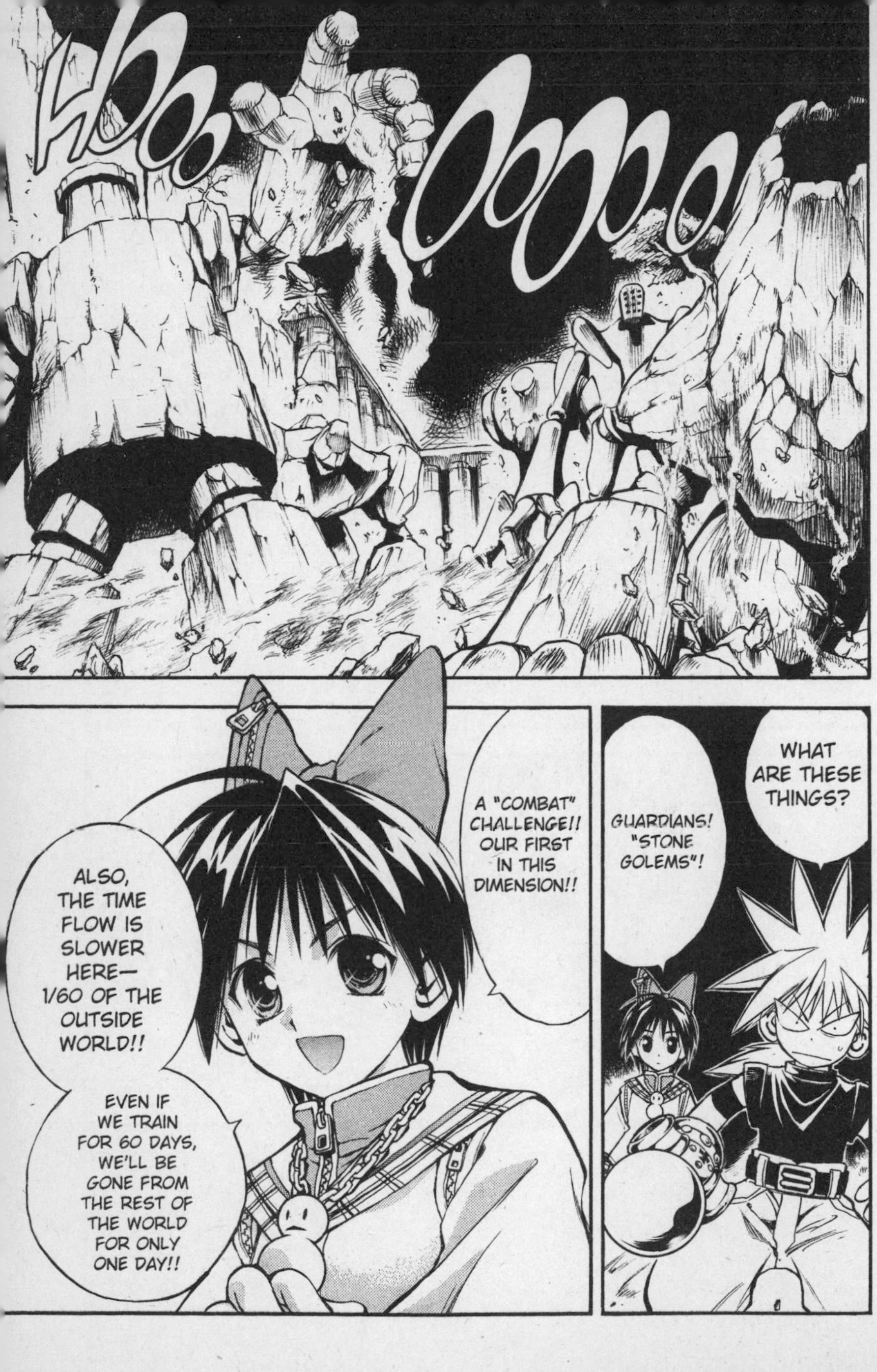
HOOOOOOOO
WHAT ARE THESE THINGS?
GUARDIANS! "STONE GOLEMS"!
A "COMBAT" CHALLENGE!! OUR FIRST IN THIS DIMENSION!!
ALSO, THE TIME FLOW IS SLOWER HERE— 1/60 OF THE OUTSIDE WORLD!!
EVEN IF WE TRAIN FOR 60 DAYS, WE'LL BE GONE FROM THE REST OF THE WORLD FOR ONLY ONE DAY!!

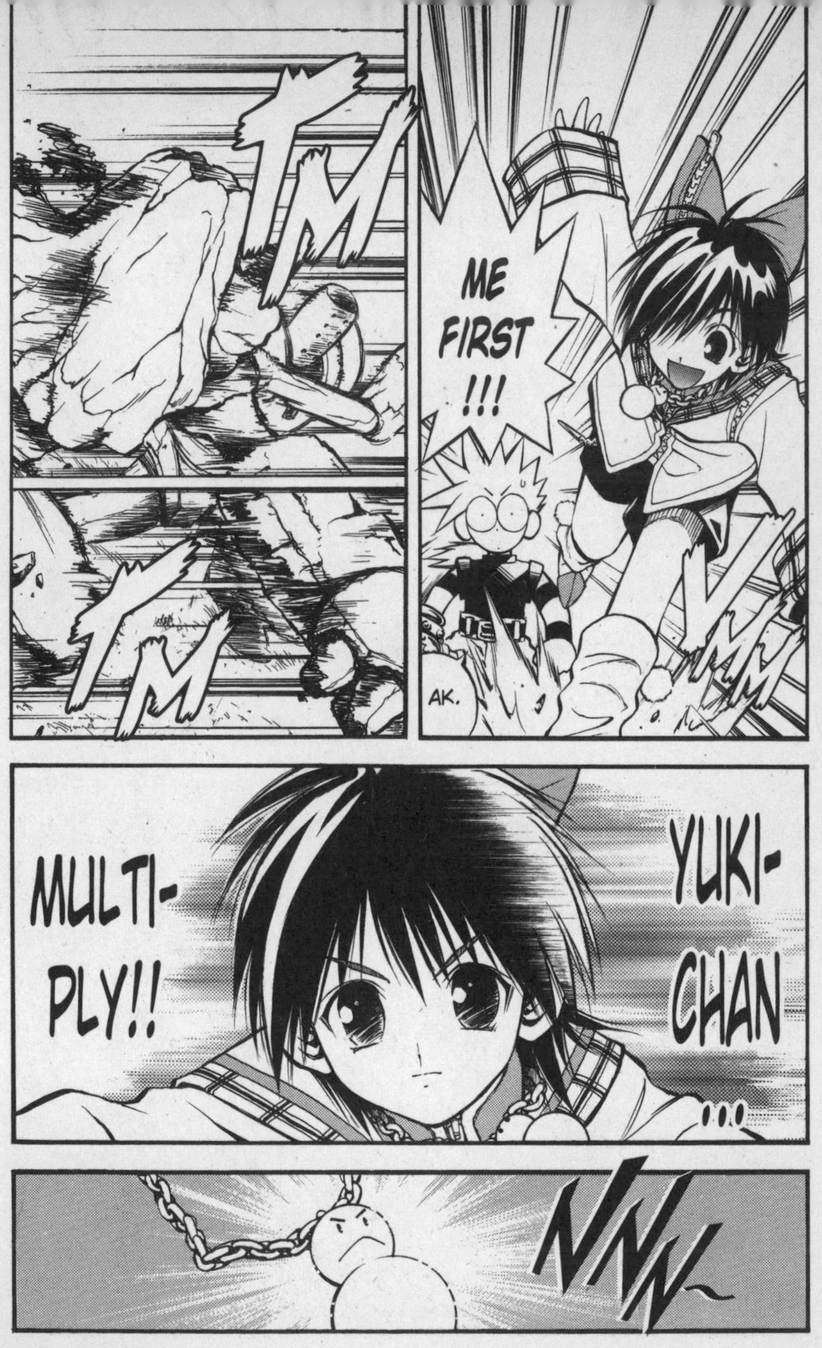
ME FIRST !!!
AK.
YUKI-CHAN...
MULTI-PLY!!
NNN~

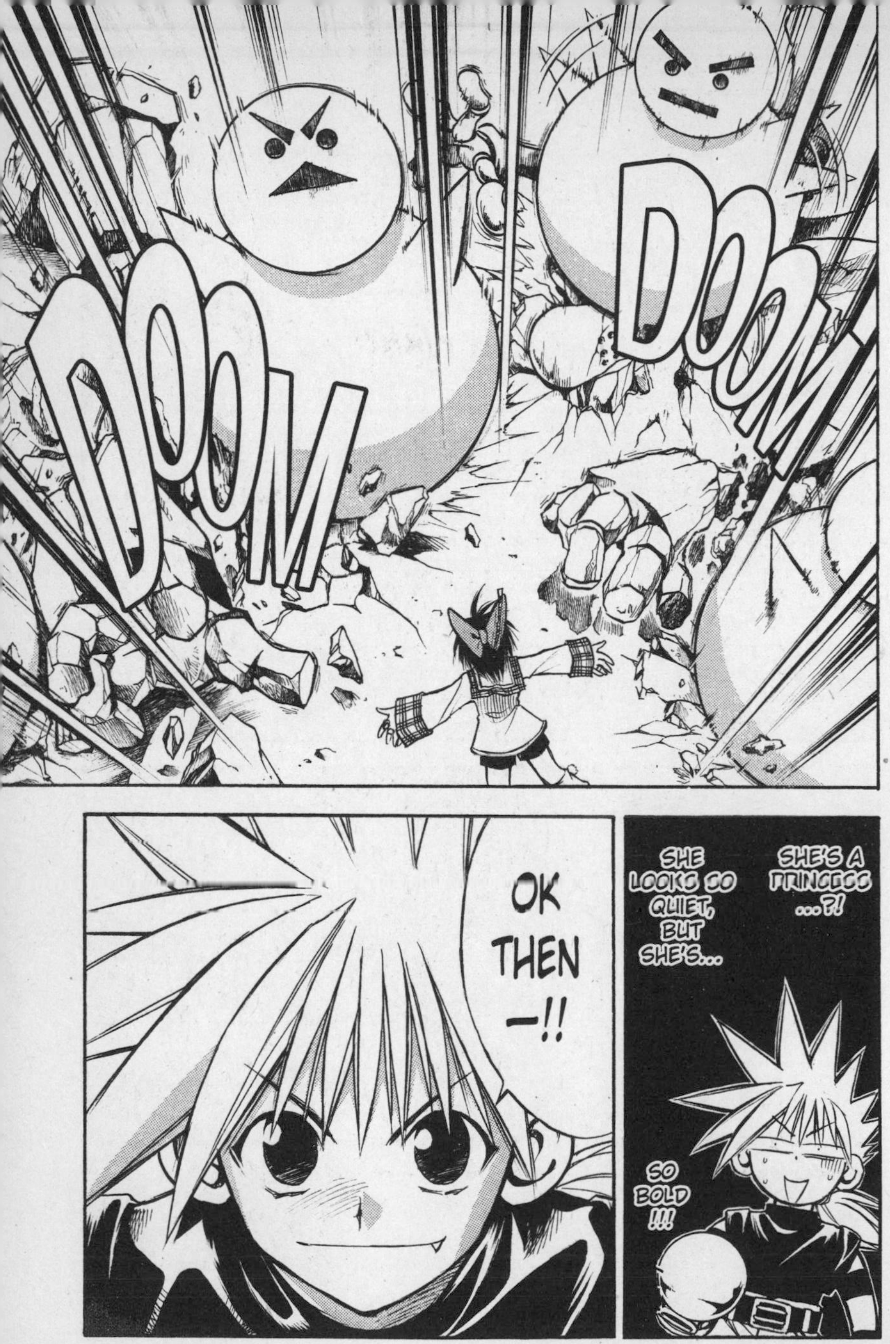
DOOM
DOOM
SHE'S A PRINCESS ...?!
SHE LOOKS SO QUIET, BUT SHE'S...
SO BOLD!!!
OK THEN—!!

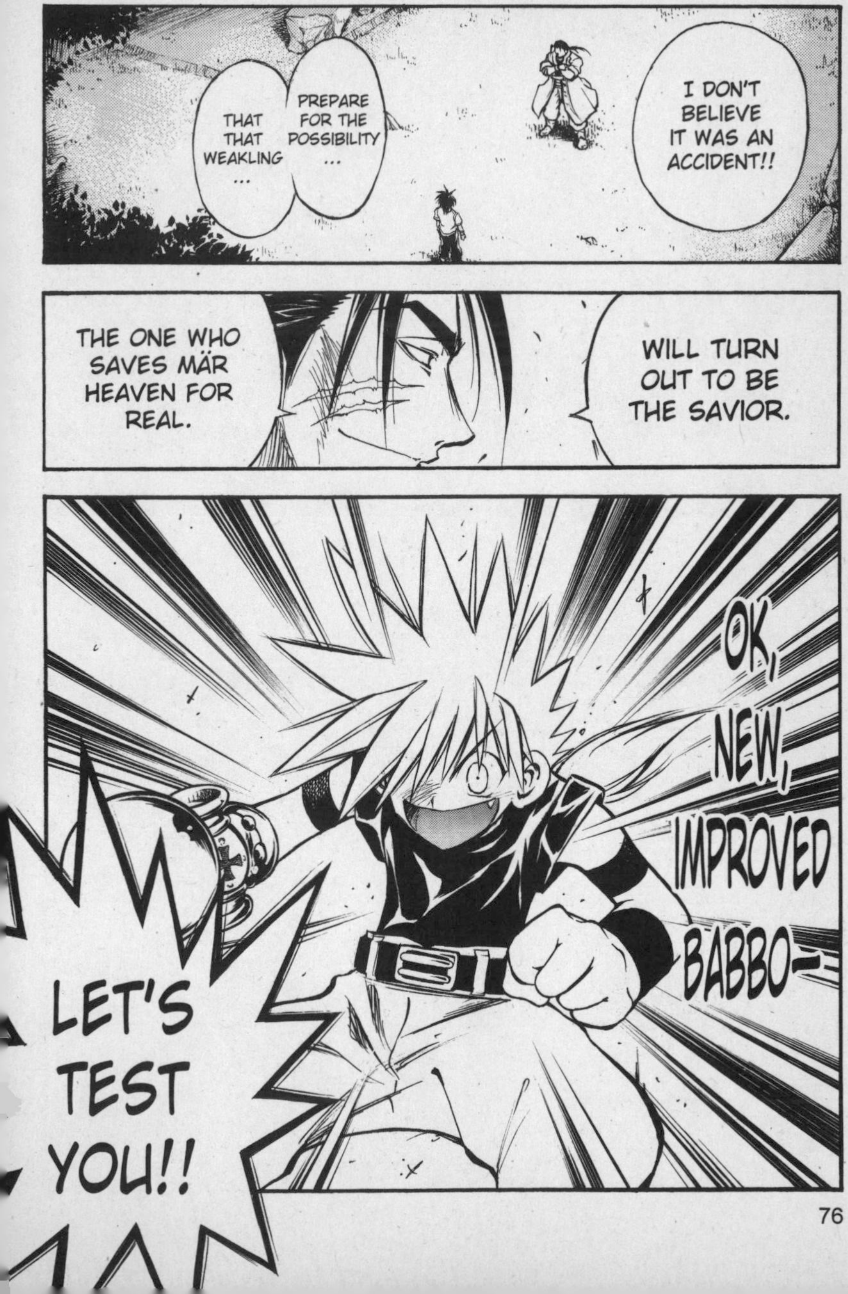
I DON'T BELIEVE IT WAS AN ACCIDENT!!
PREPARE FOR THE POSSIBILITY ...
THAT THAT WEAKLING ...
WILL TURN OUT TO BE THE SAVIOR.
THE ONE WHO SAVES MÄR HEAVEN FOR REAL.
OK, NEW, IMPROVED BABBO—
LET'S TEST YOU!!

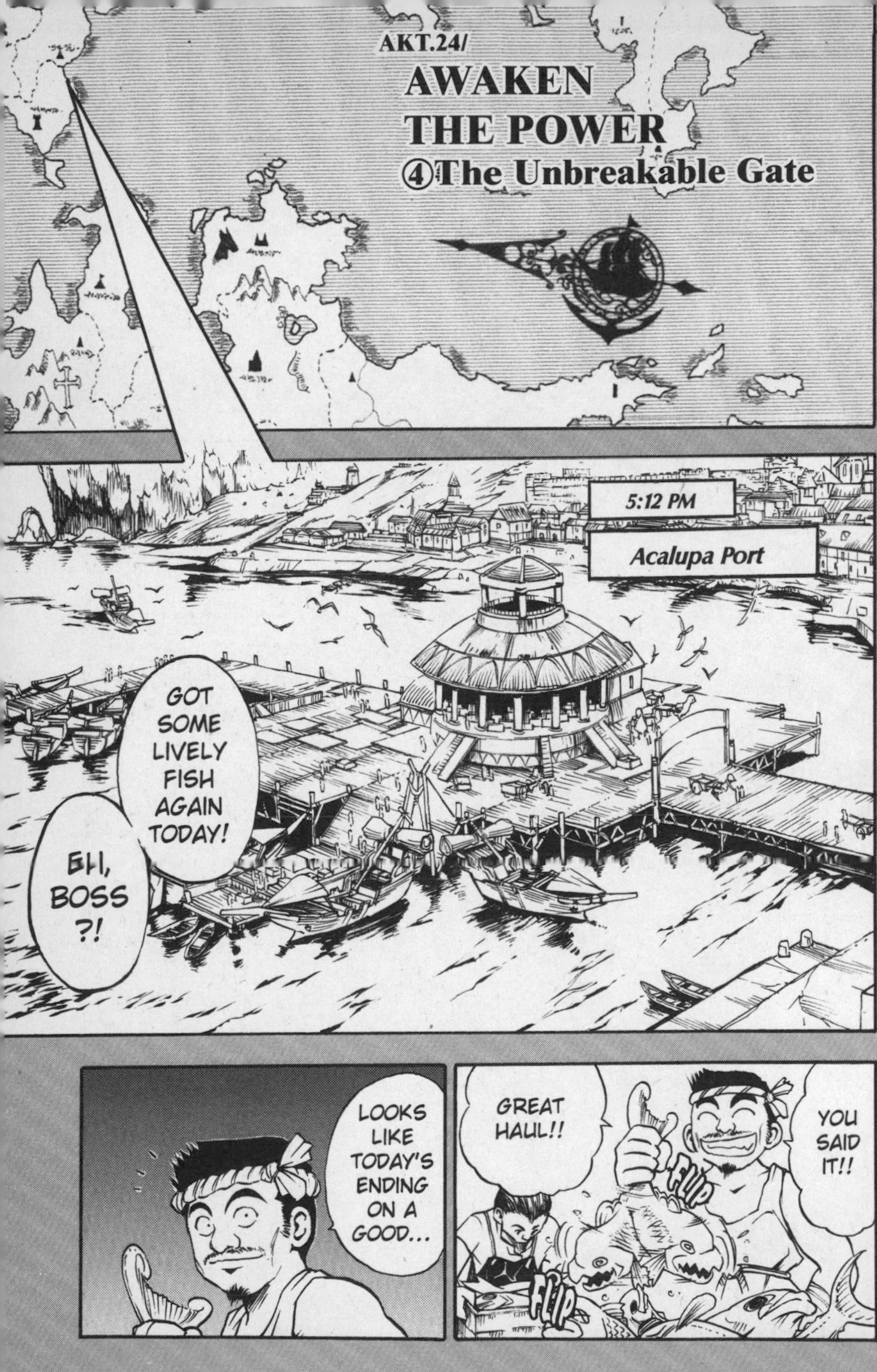
AKT.24/
AWAKEN THE POWER
④The Unbreakable Gate
5:12 PM
Acalupa Port
GOT SOME LIVELY FISH AGAIN TODAY!
EH, BOSS?!
YOU SAID IT!!
GREAT HAUL!!
FLIP
FLIP
FLIP
LOOKS LIKE TODAY'S ENDING ON A GOOD...

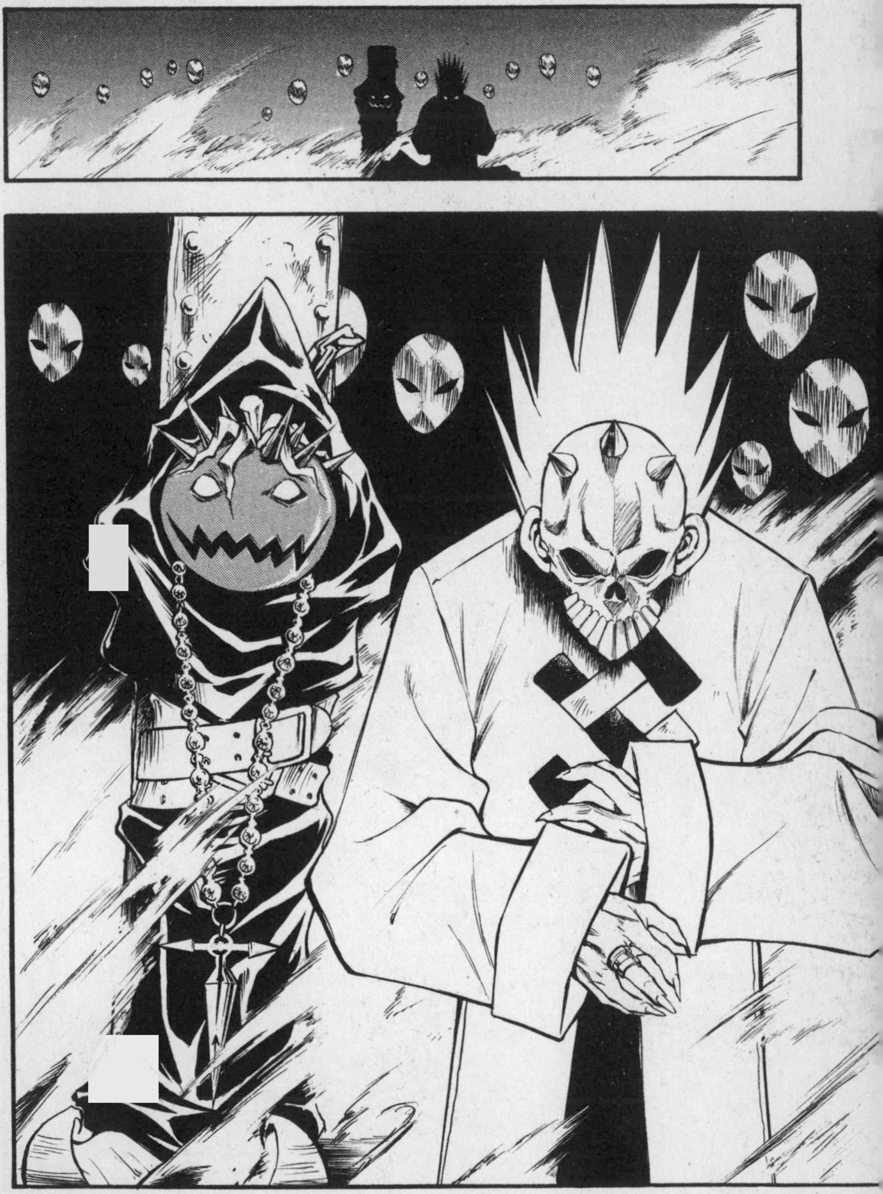

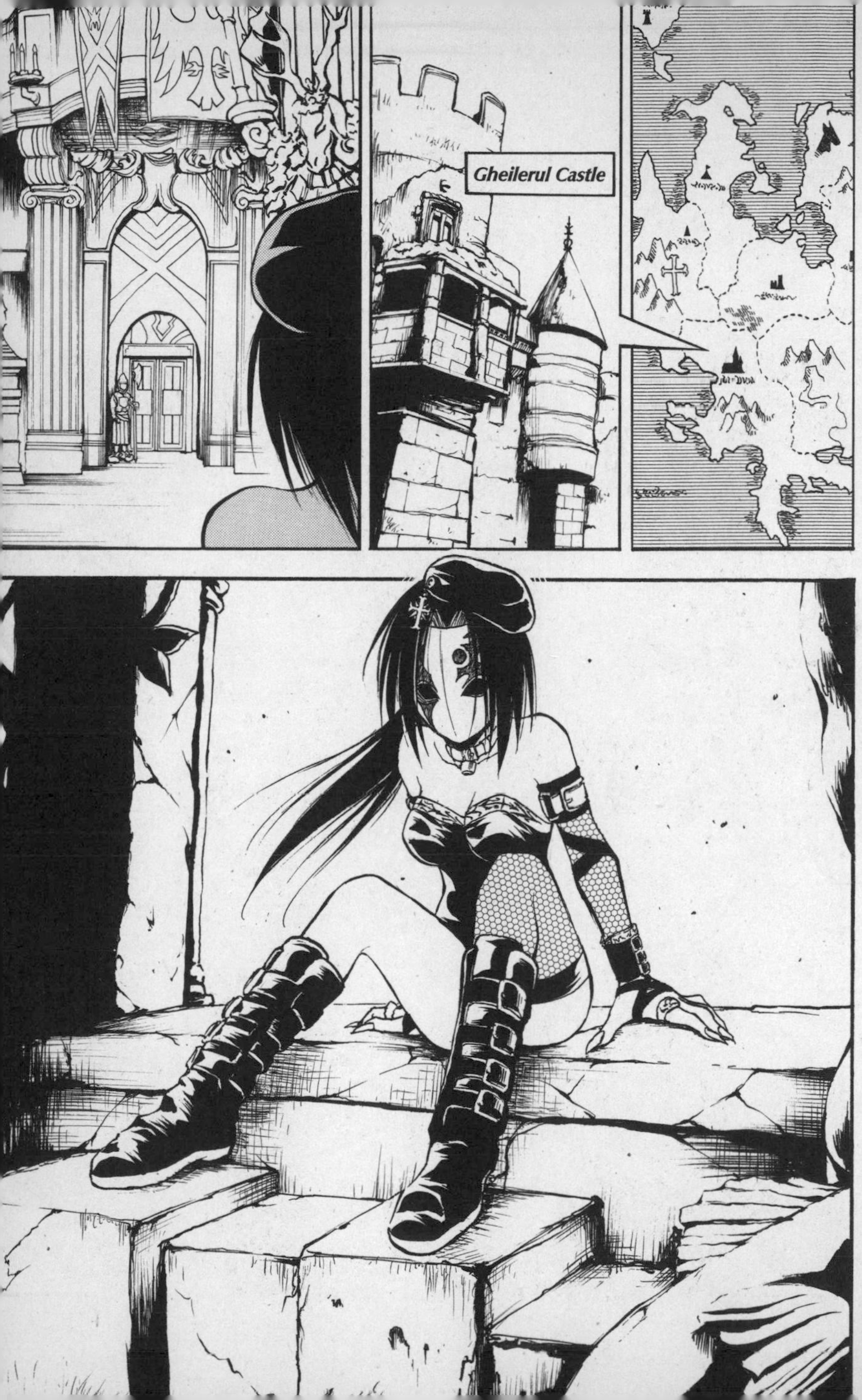
Gheilerul Castle

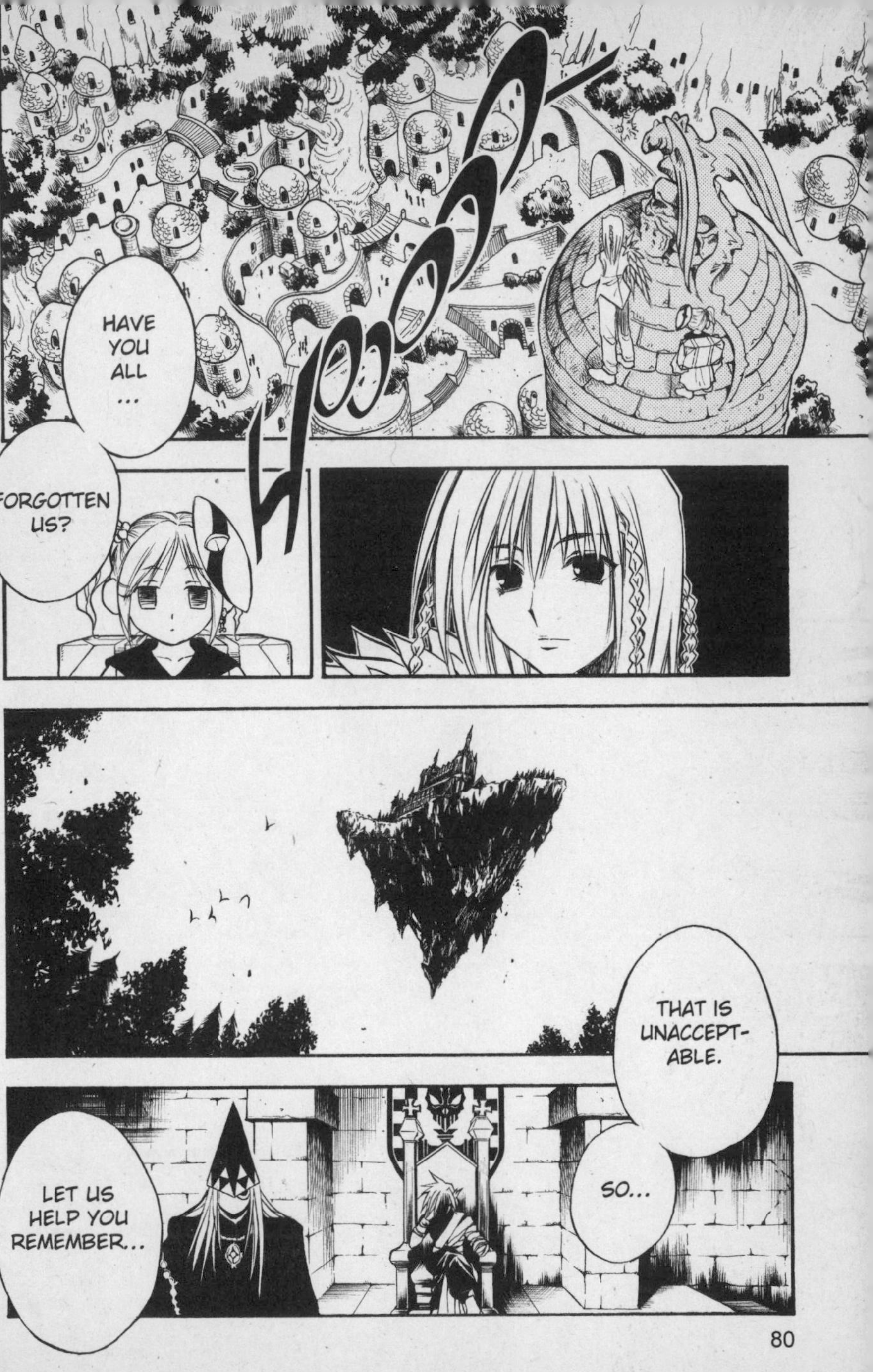
HAVE YOU ALL ...
FORGOTTEN US?
THAT IS UNACCEPT-ABLE.
SO...
LET US HELP YOU REMEMBER...

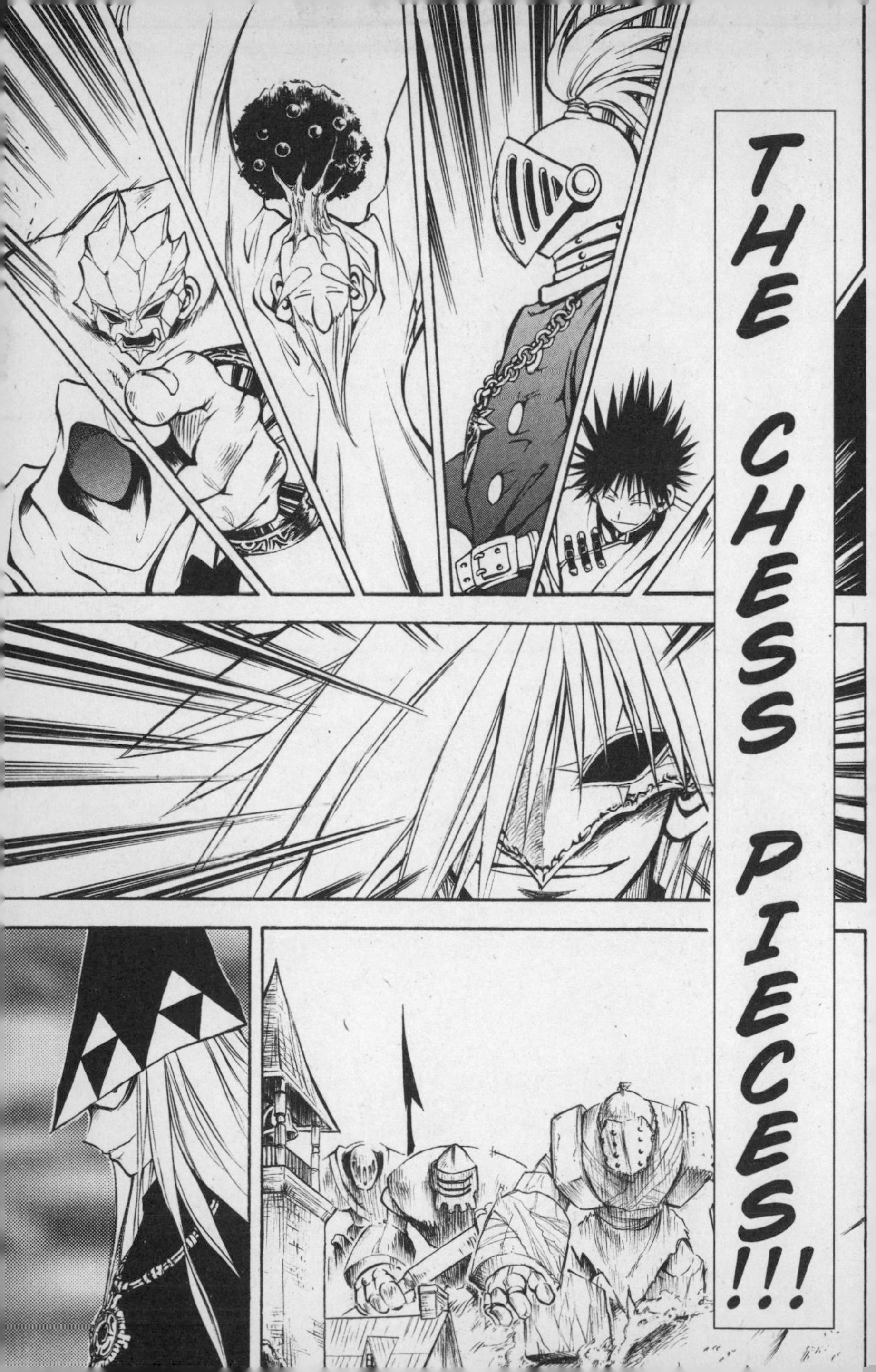
THE CHESS PIECES!!!

AKT.24/

AWAKEN THE POWER

④The Unbreakable Gate

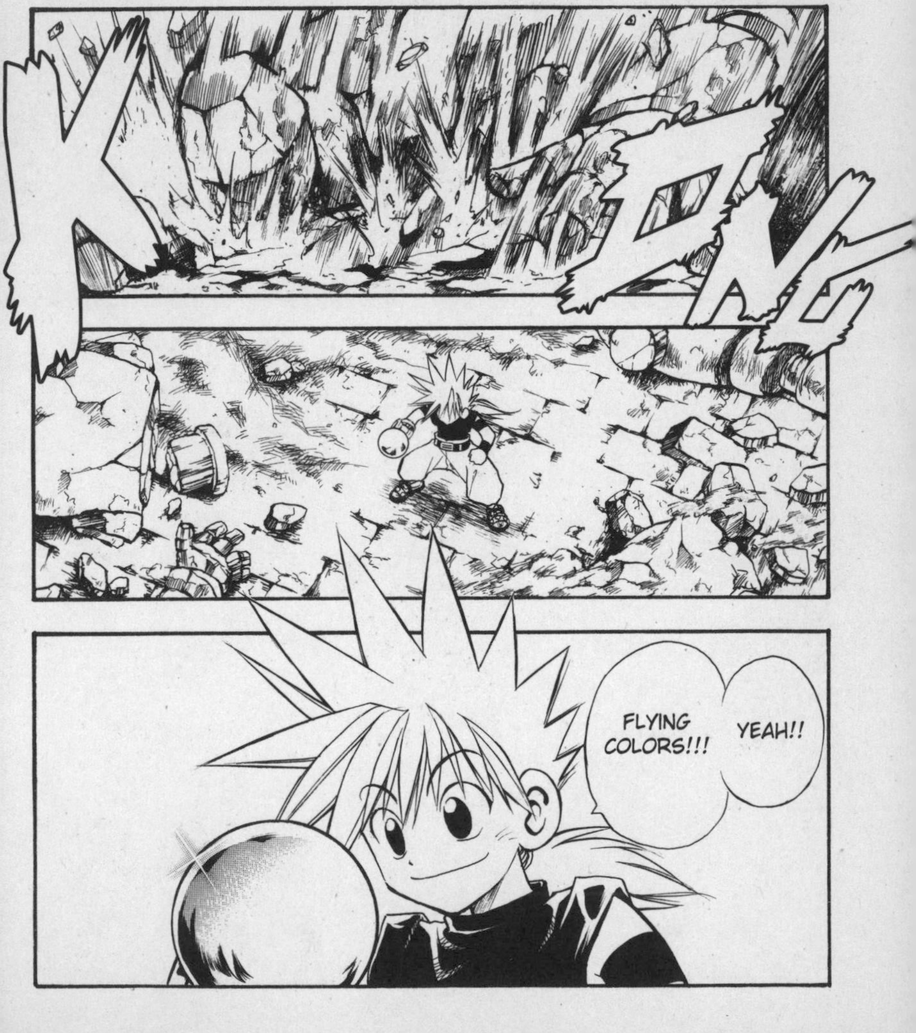
YEAH!!
FLYING COLORS!!!

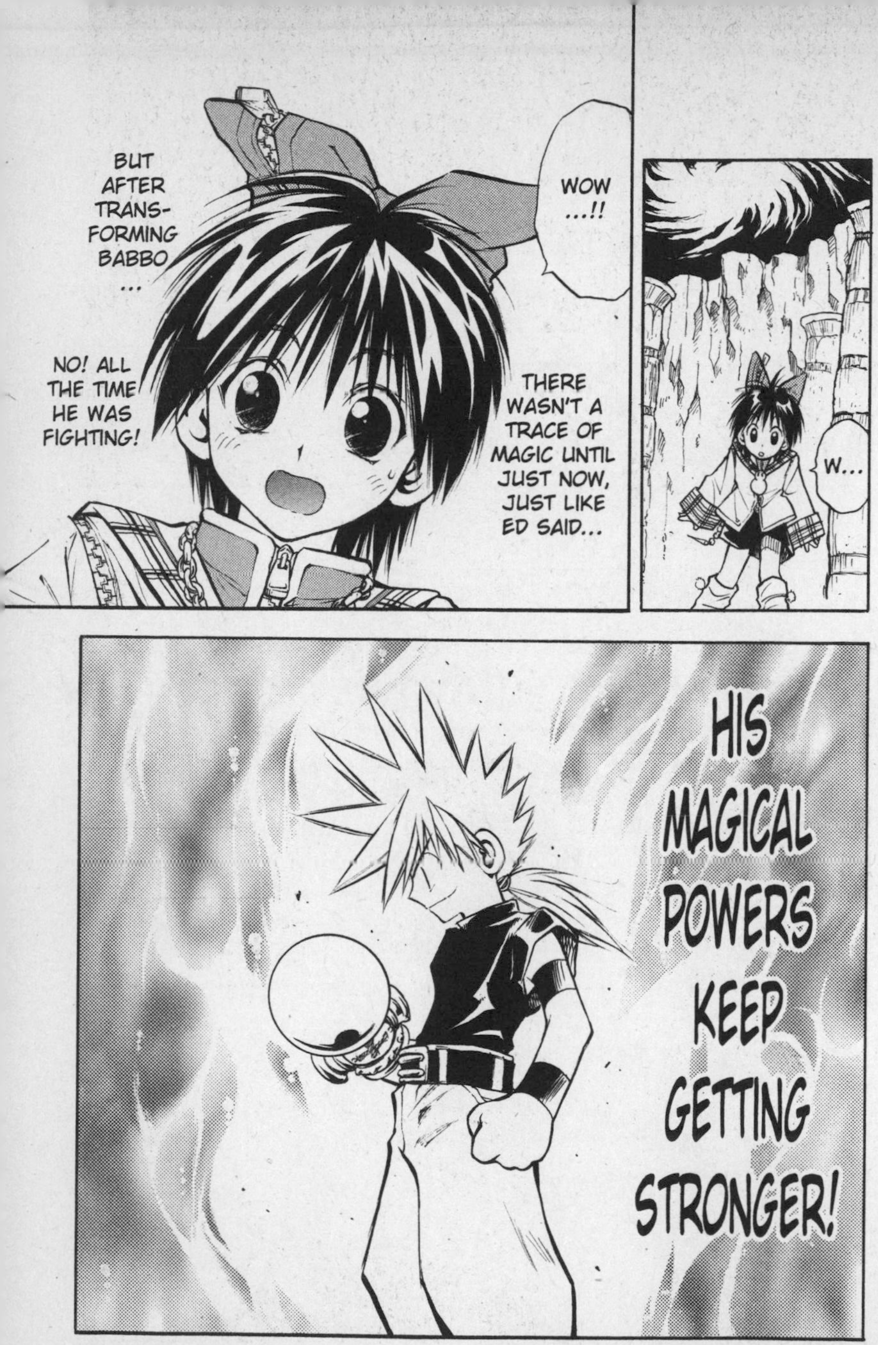
W...
WOW ...!!
THERE WASN'T A TRACE OF MAGIC UNTIL JUST NOW, JUST LIKE ED SAID...
BUT AFTER TRANS-FORMING BABBO ...
NO! ALL THE TIME HE WAS FIGHTING!
HIS MAGICAL POWERS KEEP GETTING STRONGER!

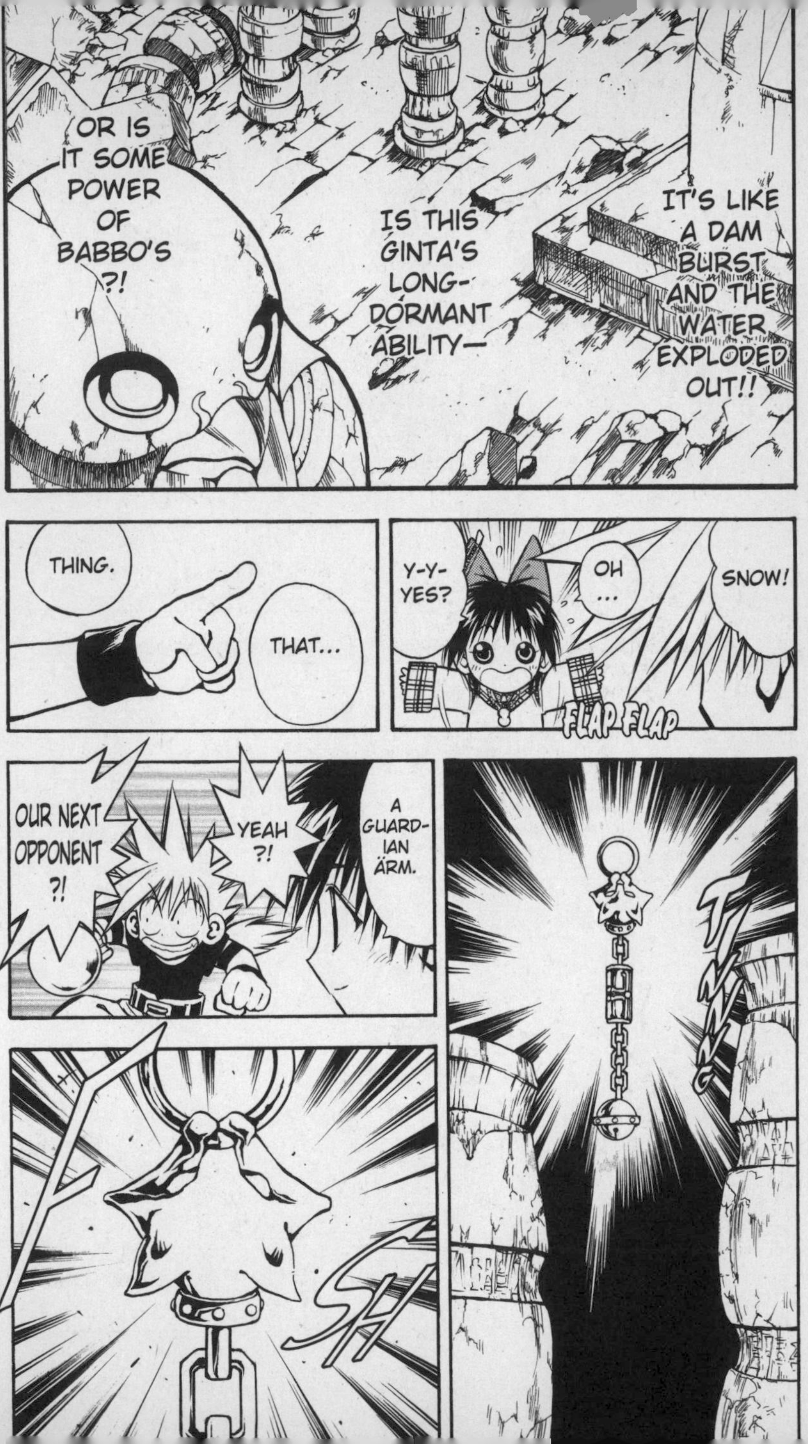
IT'S LIKE A DAM BURST AND THE WATER EXPLODED OUT!!
IS THIS GINTA'S LONG-DORMANT ABILITY—
OR IS IT SOME POWER OF BABBO'S ?!
SNOW!
OH ...
Y-Y-YES?
FLAP FLAP
THAT...
THING.
A GUARD-IAN ÄRM.
YEAH ?!
OUR NEXT OPPONENT ?!
SH

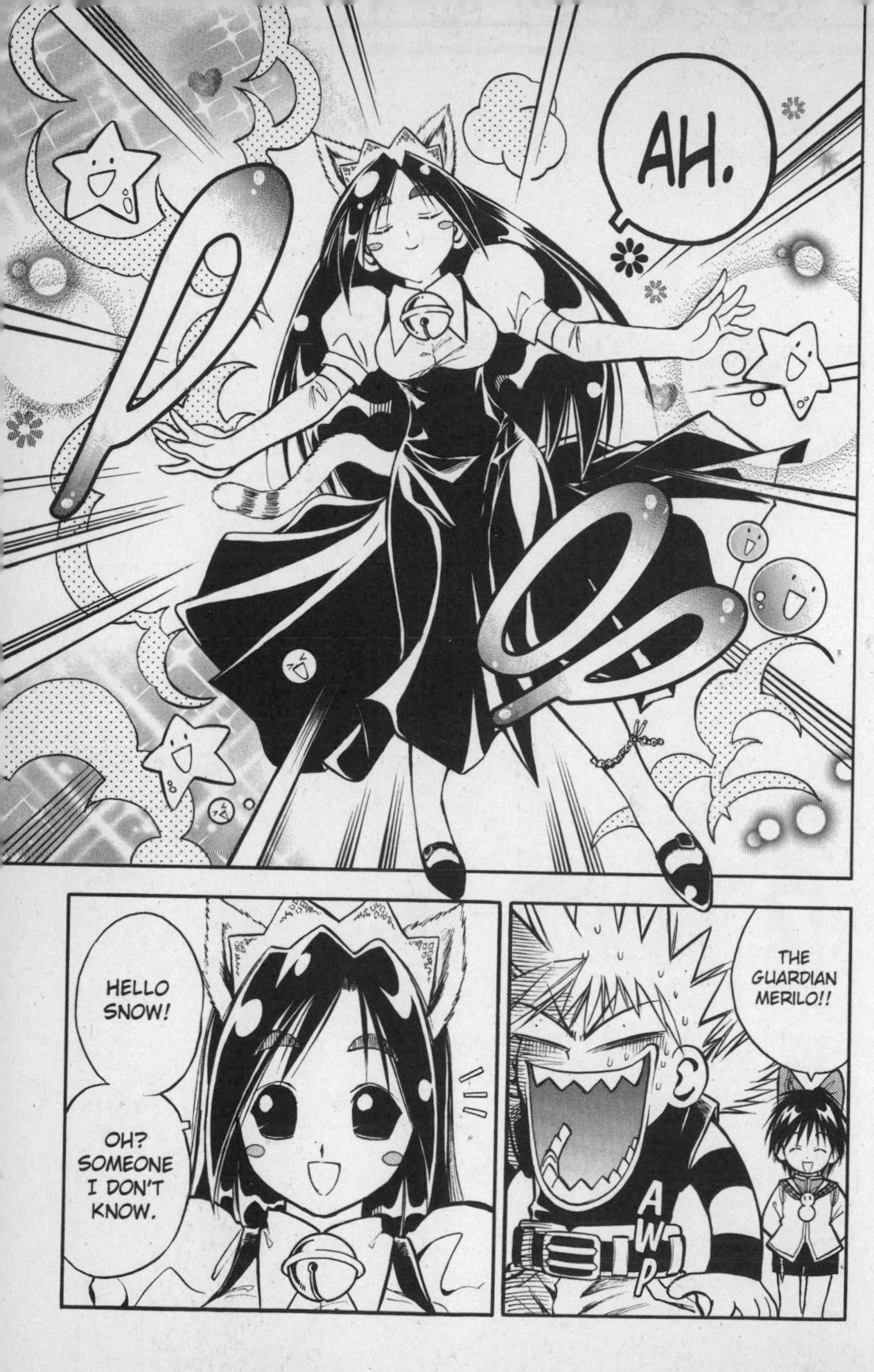
AH.
THE GUARDIAN MERILO!!
AWP
HELLO SNOW!
OH? SOMEONE I DON'T KNOW.

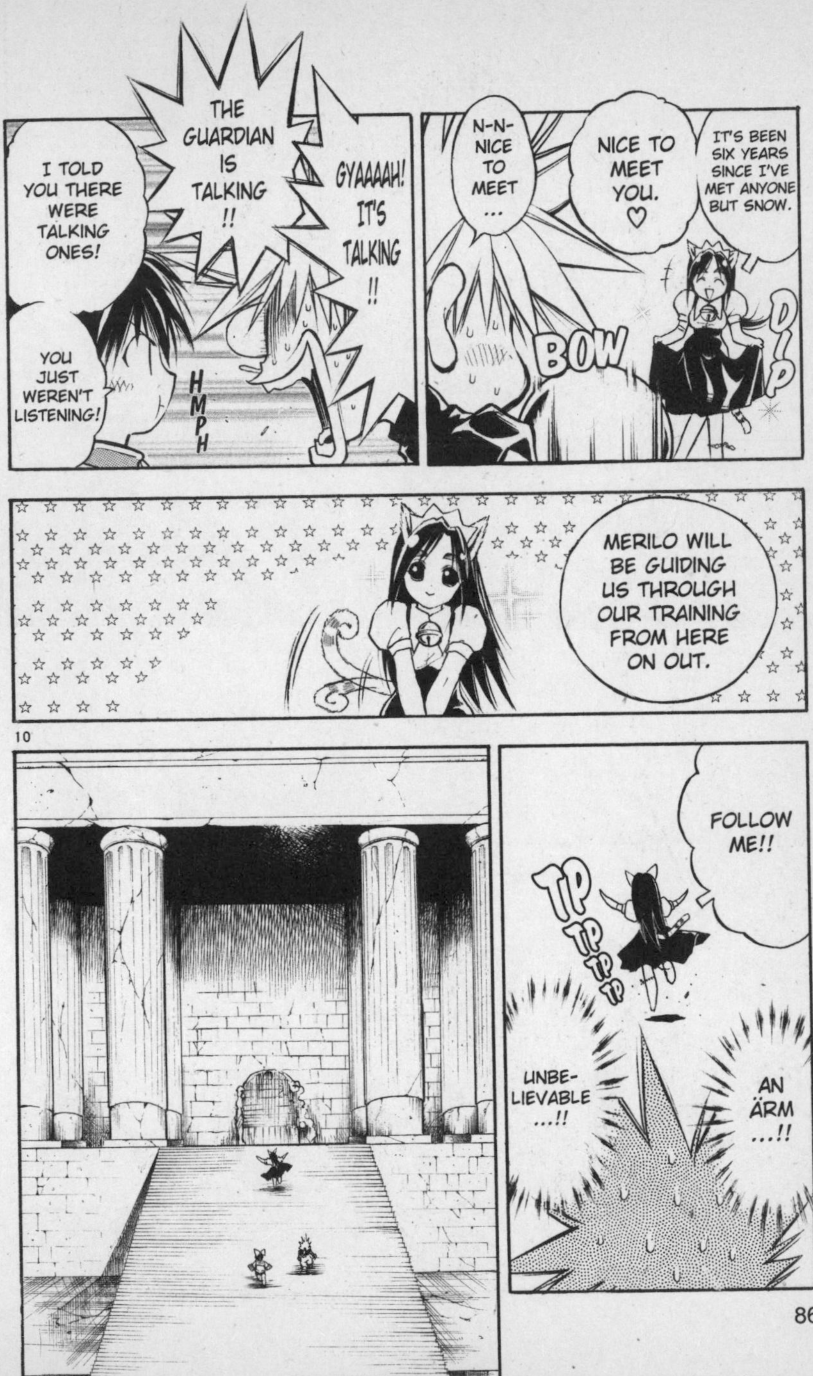
IT'S BEEN SIX YEARS SINCE I'VE MET ANYONE BUT SNOW.
NICE TO MEET YOU. ♡
N-N-NICE TO MEET ...
DIP
BOW
GYAAAAH! IT'S TALKING !!
THE GUARDIAN IS TALKING !!
I TOLD YOU THERE WERE TALKING ONES!
HMPH
YOU JUST WEREN'T LISTENING!
MERILO WILL BE GUIDING US THROUGH OUR TRAINING FROM HERE ON OUT.
10
FOLLOW ME!!
TP TP TP TP TP
AN ÄRM ...!!
UNBE-LIEVABLE ...!!

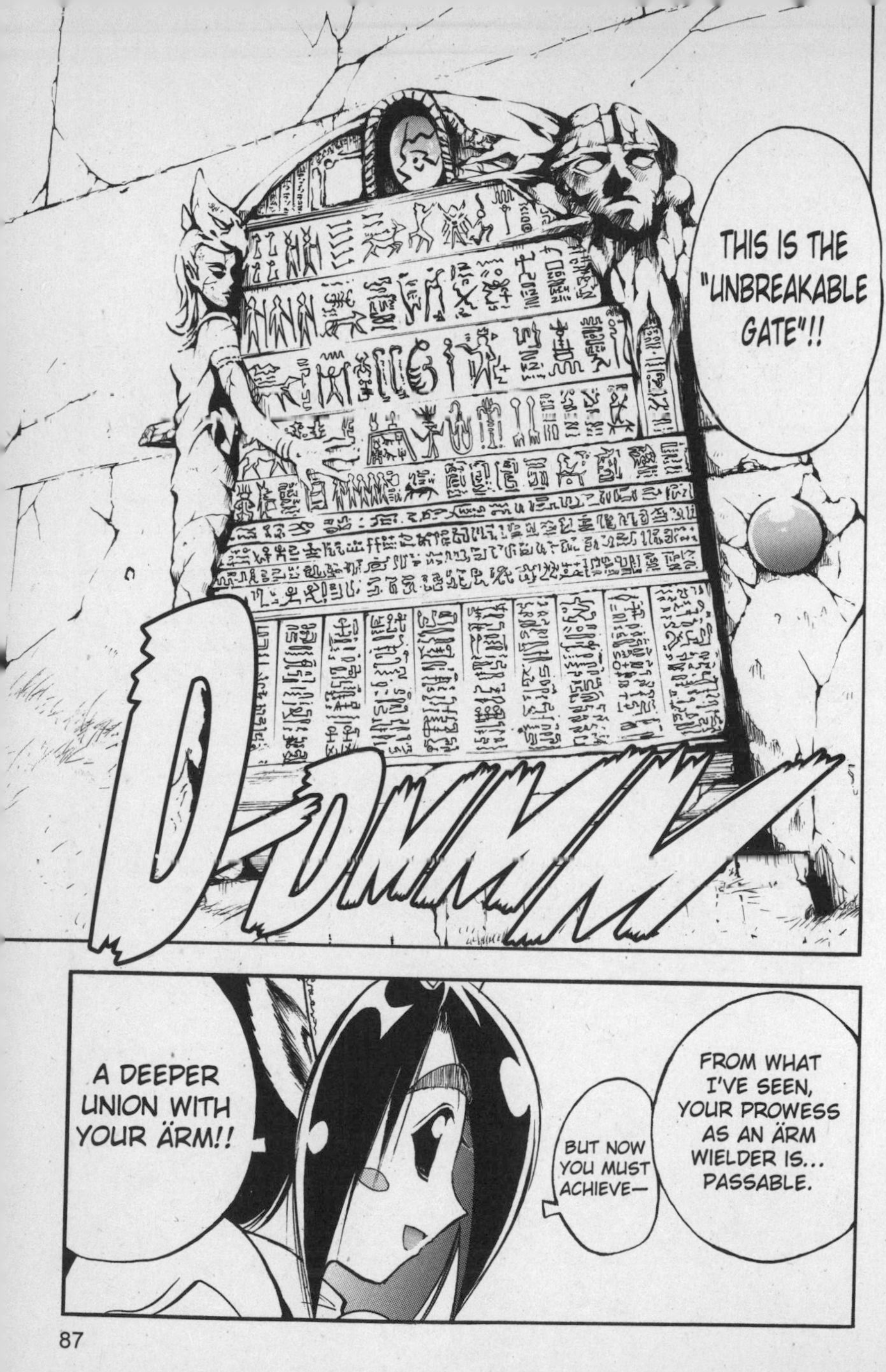
THIS IS THE "UNBREAKABLE GATE"!!
DOMMM
FROM WHAT I'VE SEEN, YOUR PROWESS AS AN ÄRM WIELDER IS... PASSABLE.
BUT NOW YOU MUST ACHIEVE—
A DEEPER UNION WITH YOUR ÄRM!!

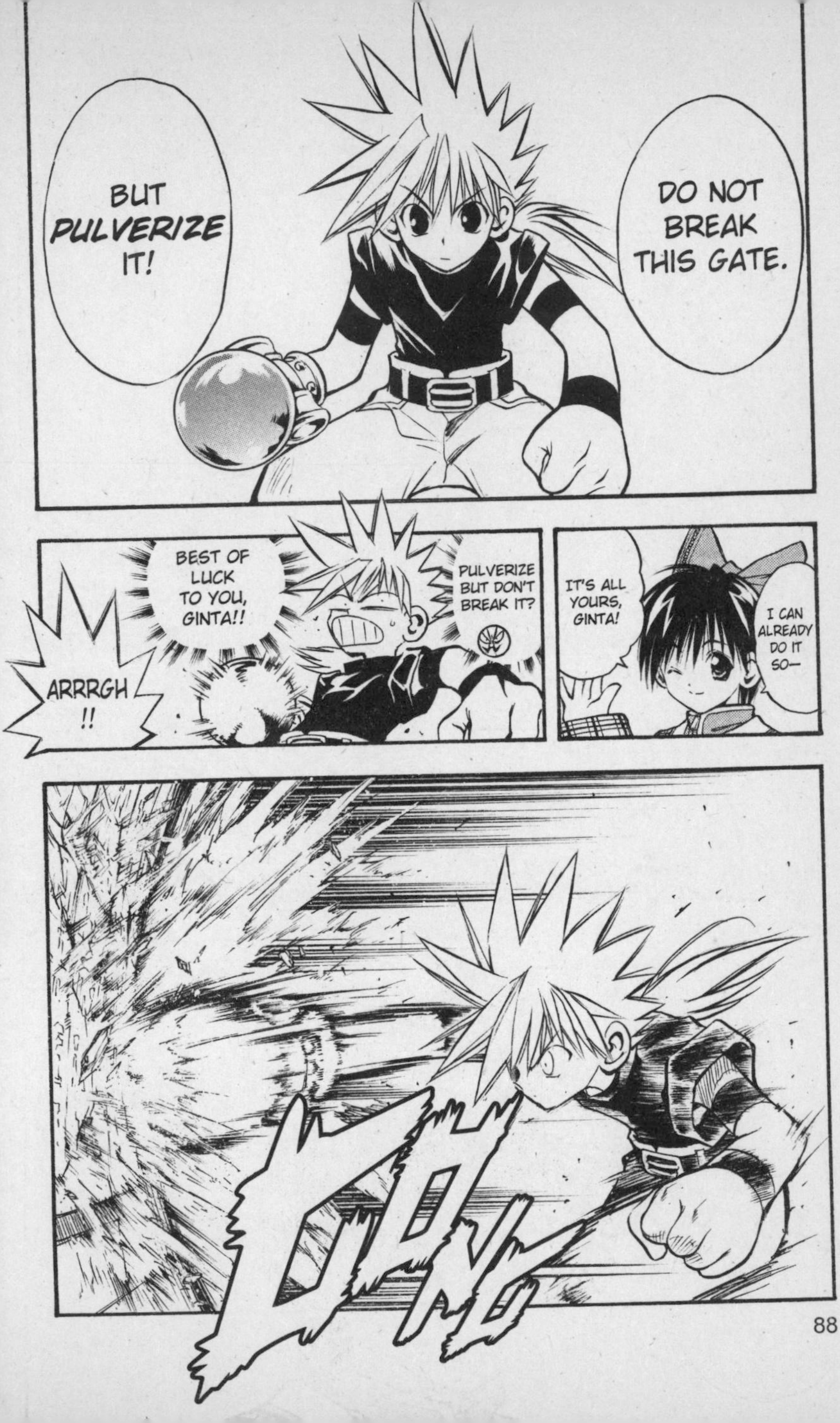
DO NOT BREAK THIS GATE.
BUT PULVERIZE IT!
I CAN ALREADY DO IT SO—
IT'S ALL YOURS, GINTA!
PULVERIZE BUT DON'T BREAK IT?
BEST OF LUCK TO YOU, GINTA!!
ARRRGH !!

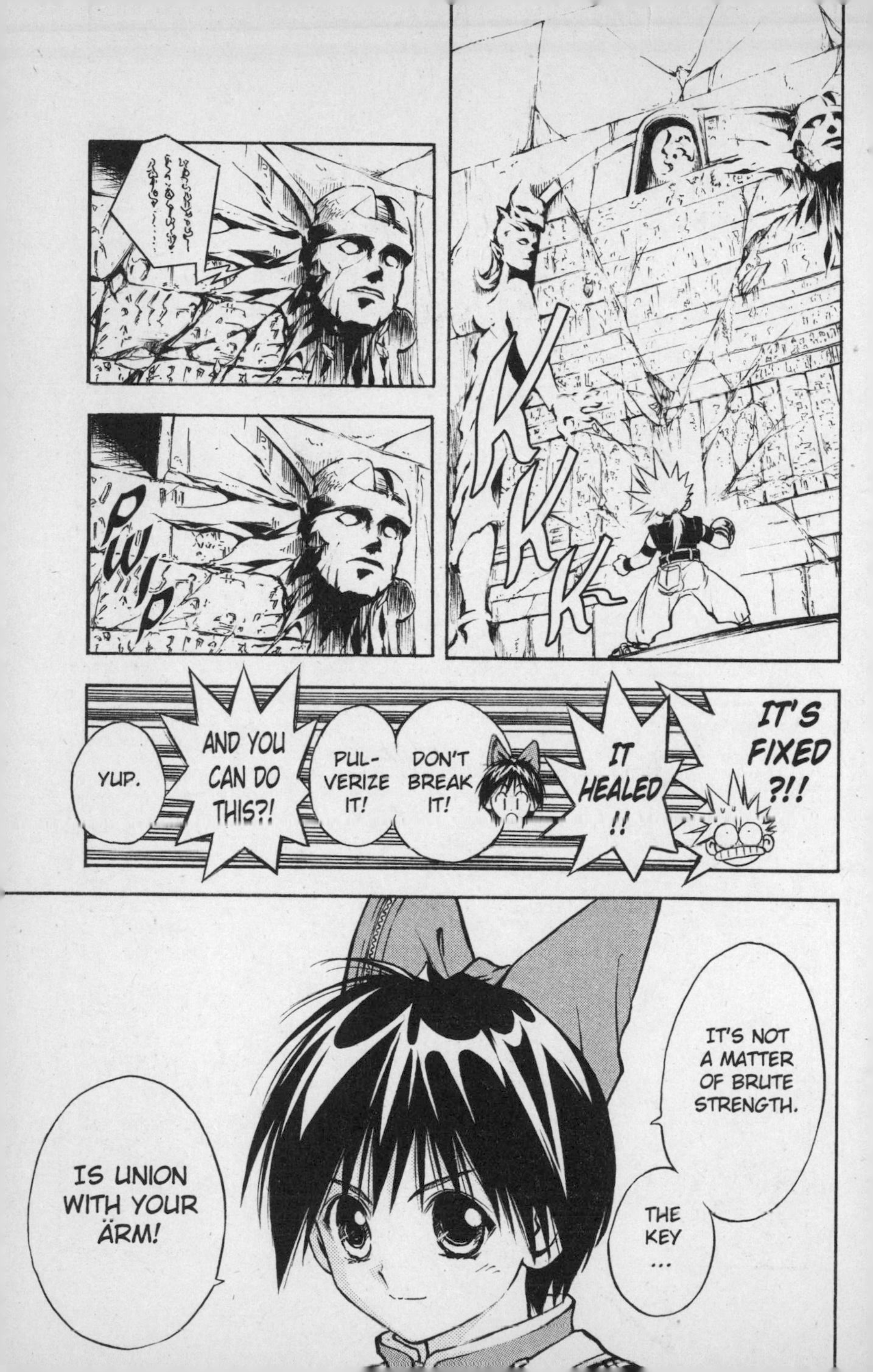
KKK
PWIP
IT'S FIXED ?!!
IT HEALED !!
DON'T BREAK IT!
PUL-VERIZE IT!
AND YOU CAN DO THIS?!
YUP.
IT'S NOT A MATTER OF BRUTE STRENGTH.
THE KEY ...
IS UNION WITH YOUR ÄRM!

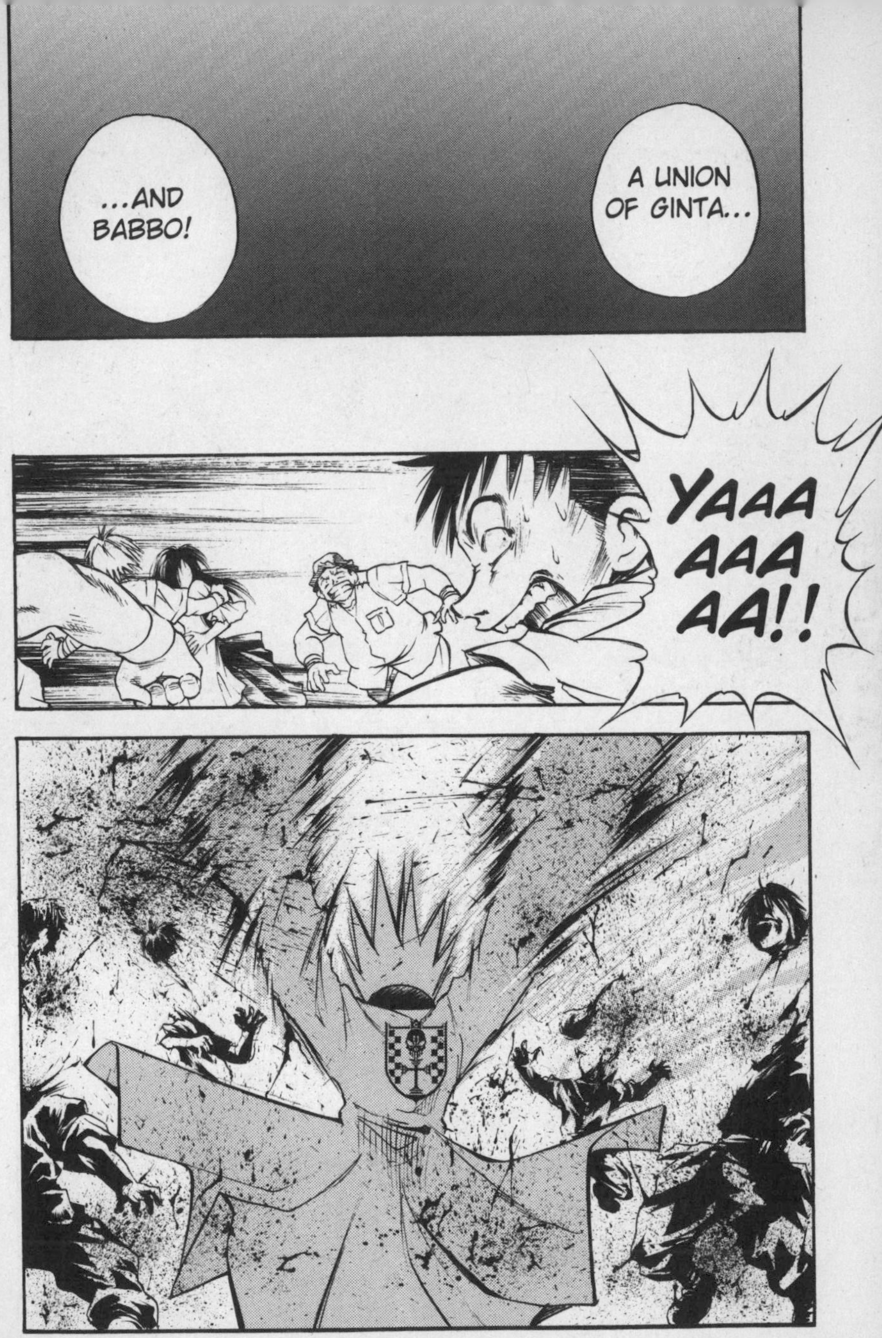
A UNION OF GINTA...
...AND BABBO!
YAAA AAA AA!!

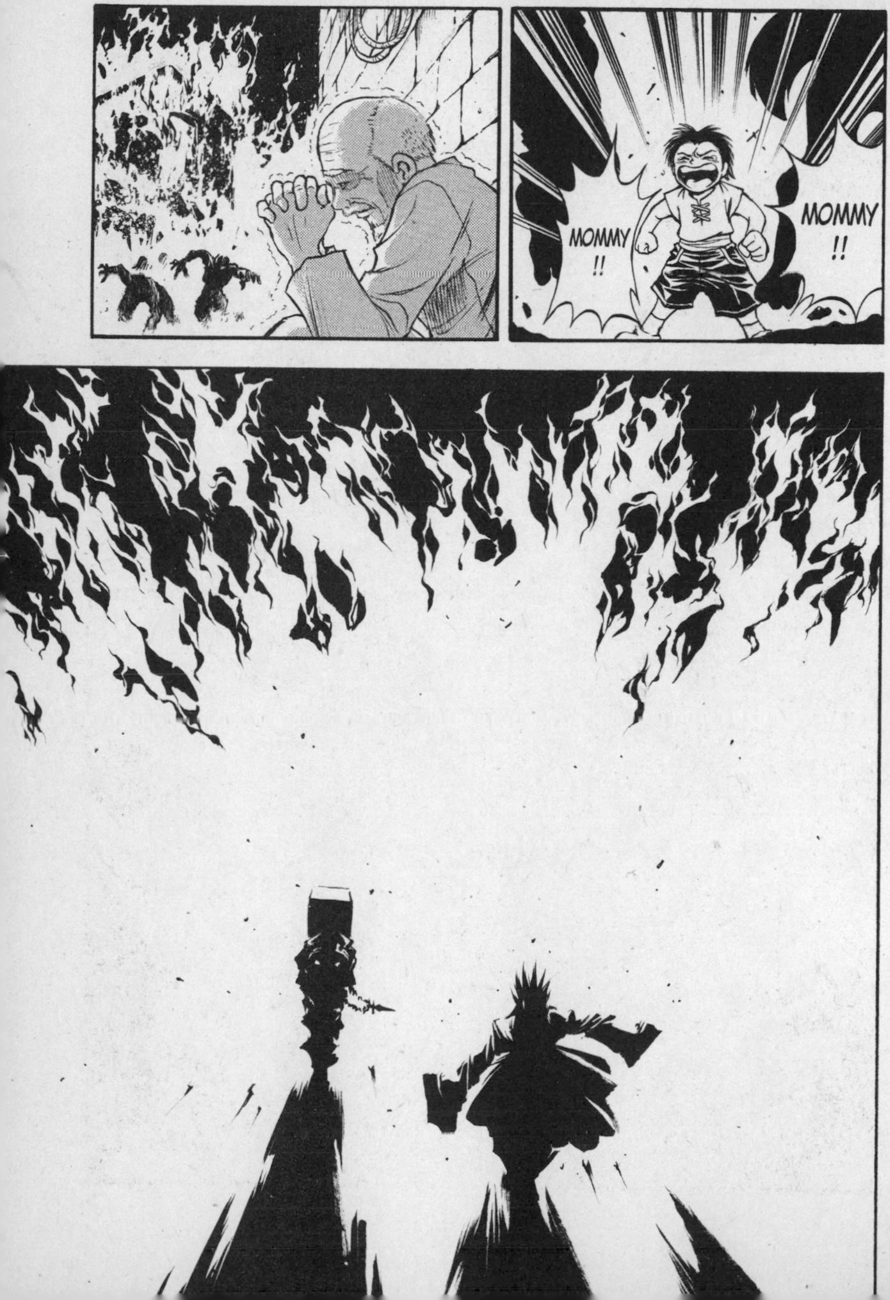
MOMMY !!
MOMMY !!

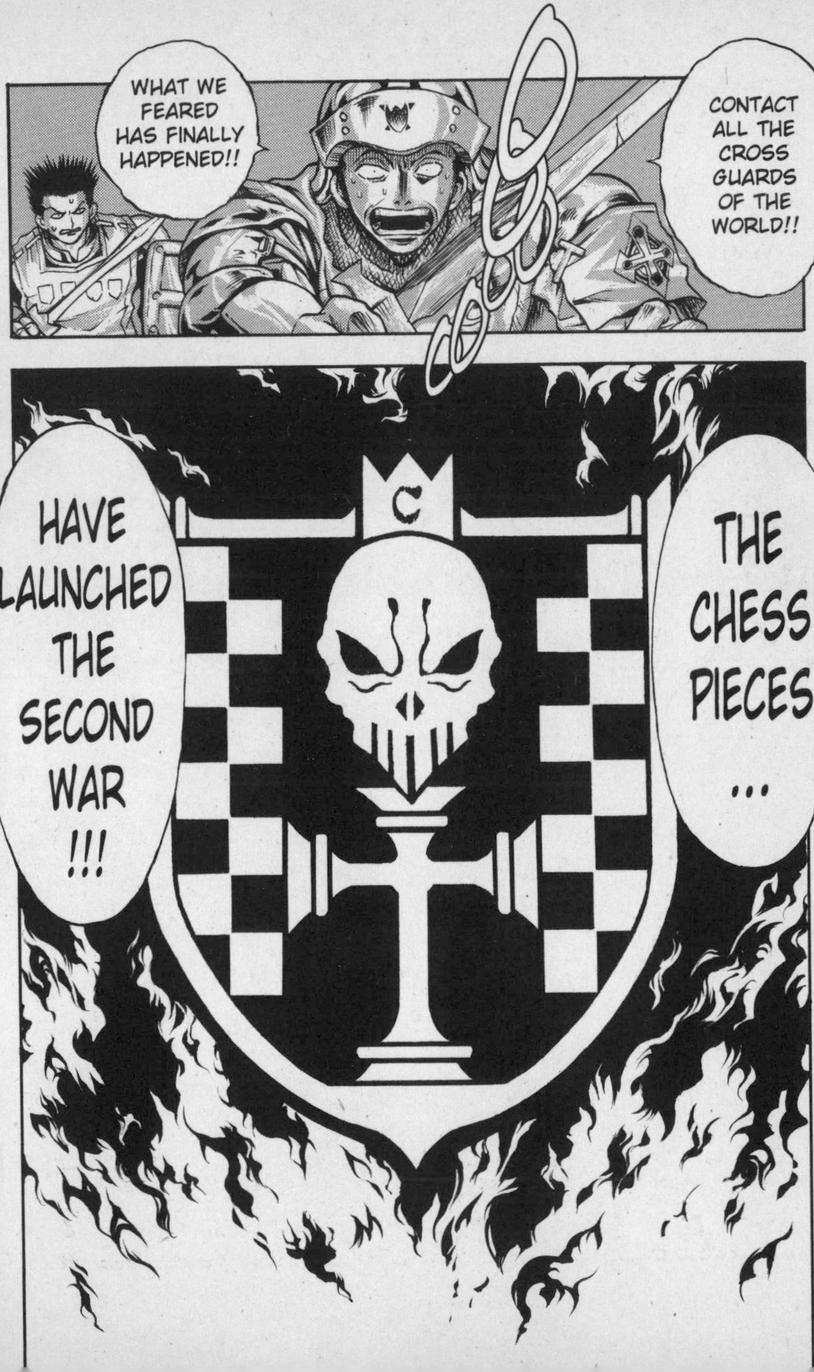
CONTACT ALL THE CROSS GUARDS OF THE WORLD!!
WHAT WE FEARED HAS FINALLY HAPPENED!!
THE CHESS PIECES ...
HAVE LAUNCHED THE SECOND WAR !!!

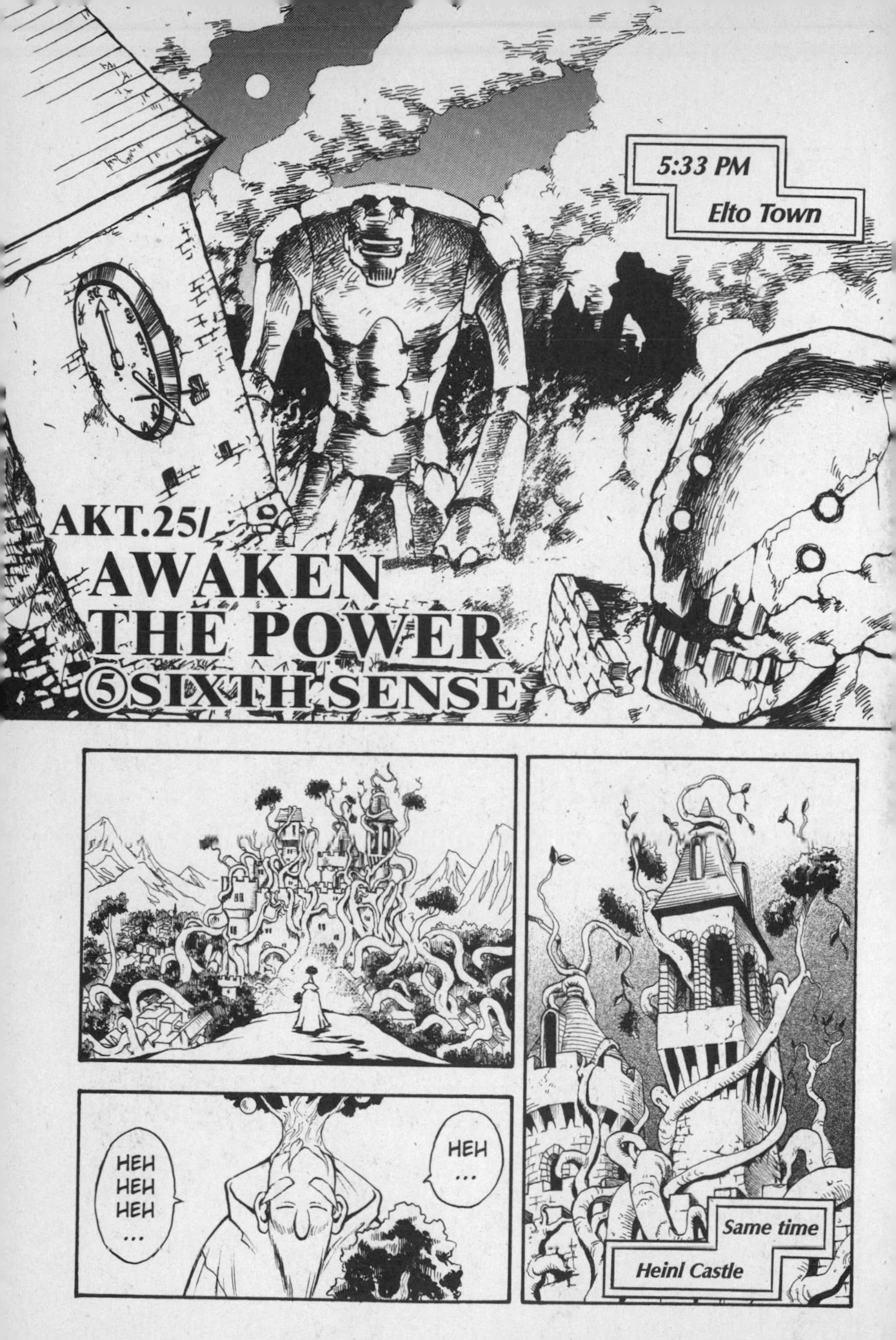
5:33 PM
Elto Town
AKT.25/
AWAKEN THE POWER
⑤SIXTH SENSE
Same time
Heinl Castle
HEH ...
HEH HEH HEH ...

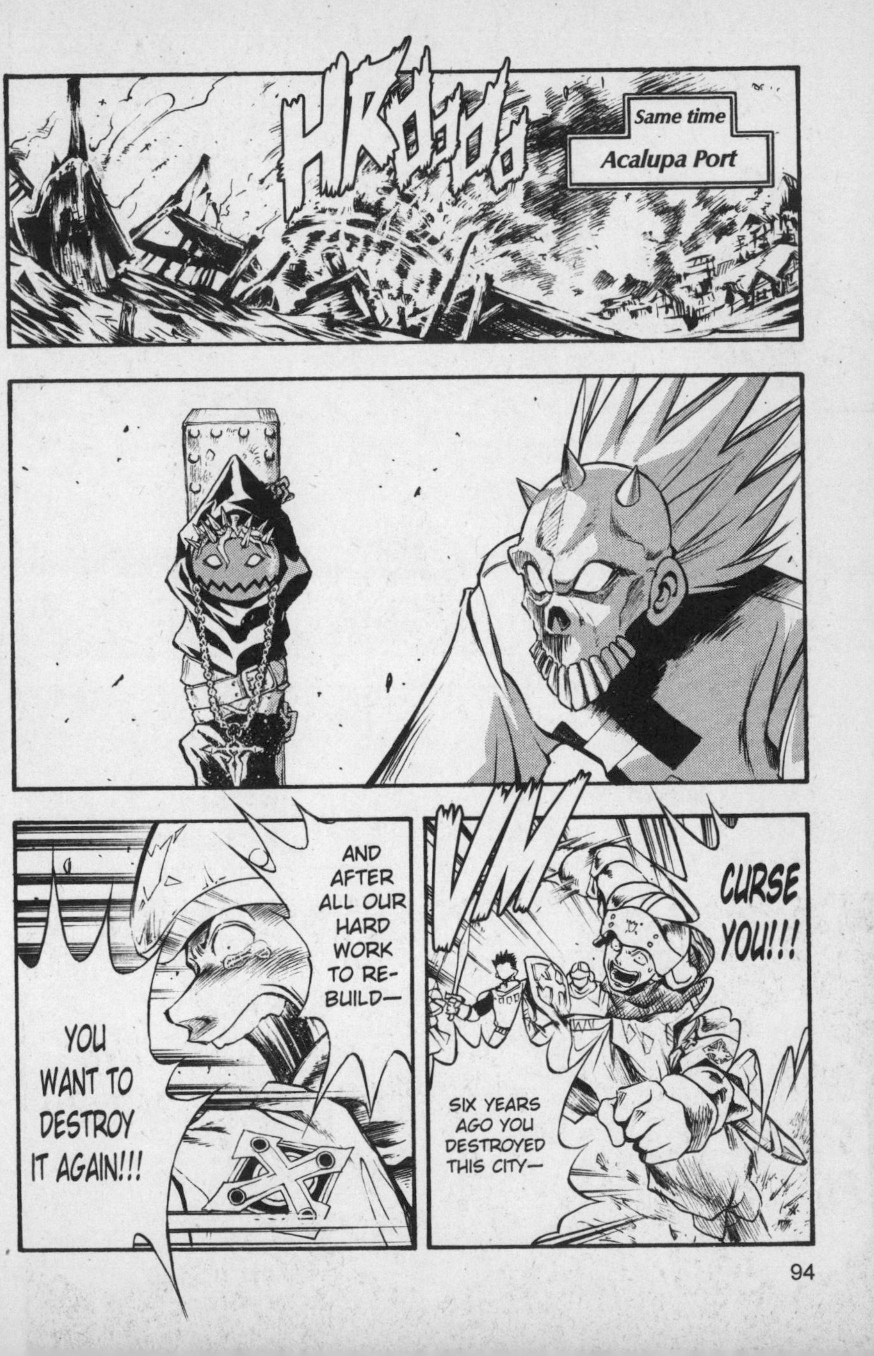
Same time
Acalupa Port
CURSE YOU!!!
SIX YEARS AGO YOU DESTROYED THIS CITY—
AND AFTER ALL OUR HARD WORK TO RE-BUILD—
YOU WANT TO DESTROY IT AGAIN!!!

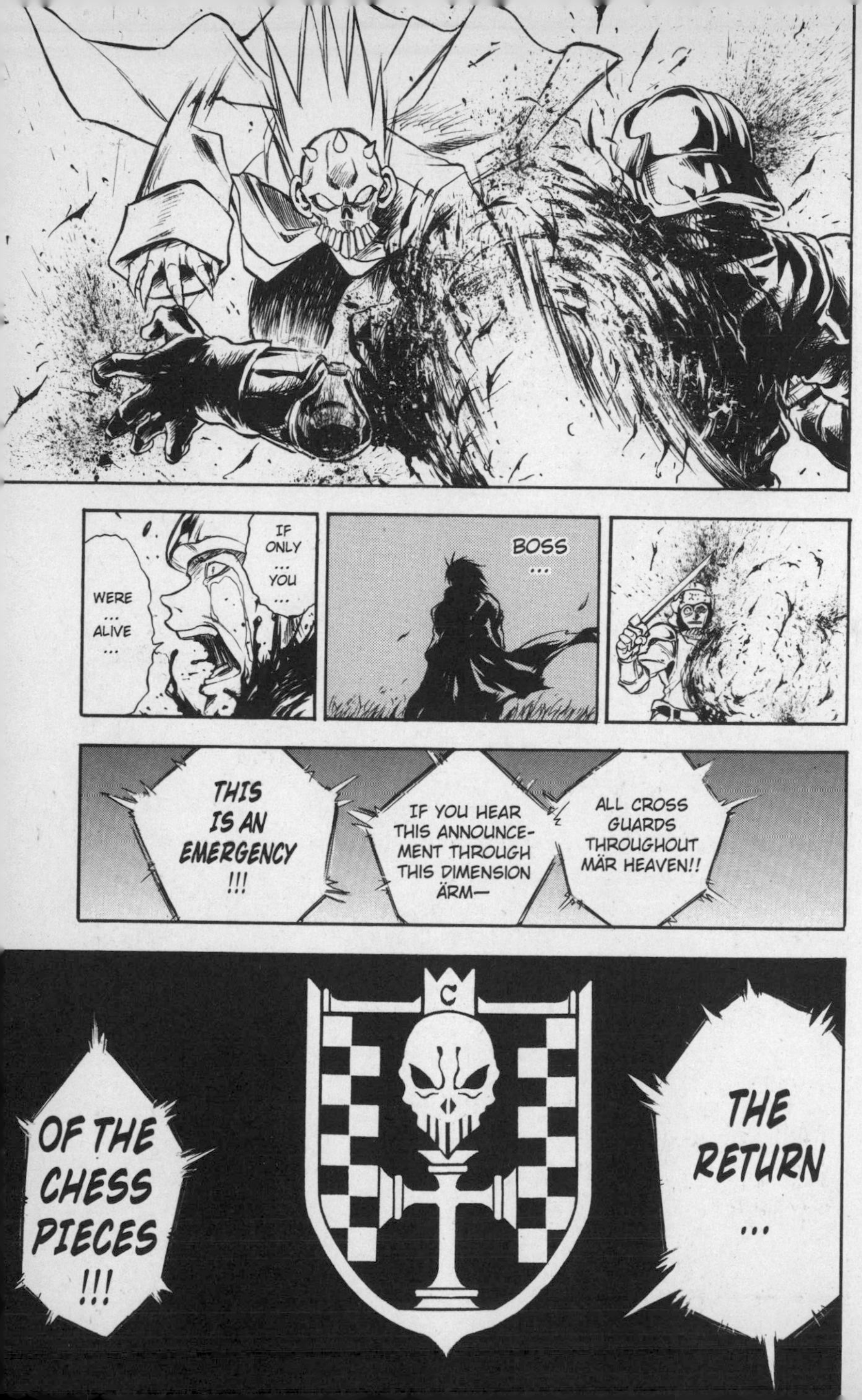
BOSS ...
IF ONLY ... YOU ...
WERE ... ALIVE ...
ALL CROSS GUARDS THROUGHOUT MÄR HEAVEN!!
IF YOU HEAR THIS ANNOUNCEMENT THROUGH THIS DIMENSION ÄRM—
THIS IS AN EMERGENCY !!!
THE RETURN ...
OF THE CHESS PIECES !!!

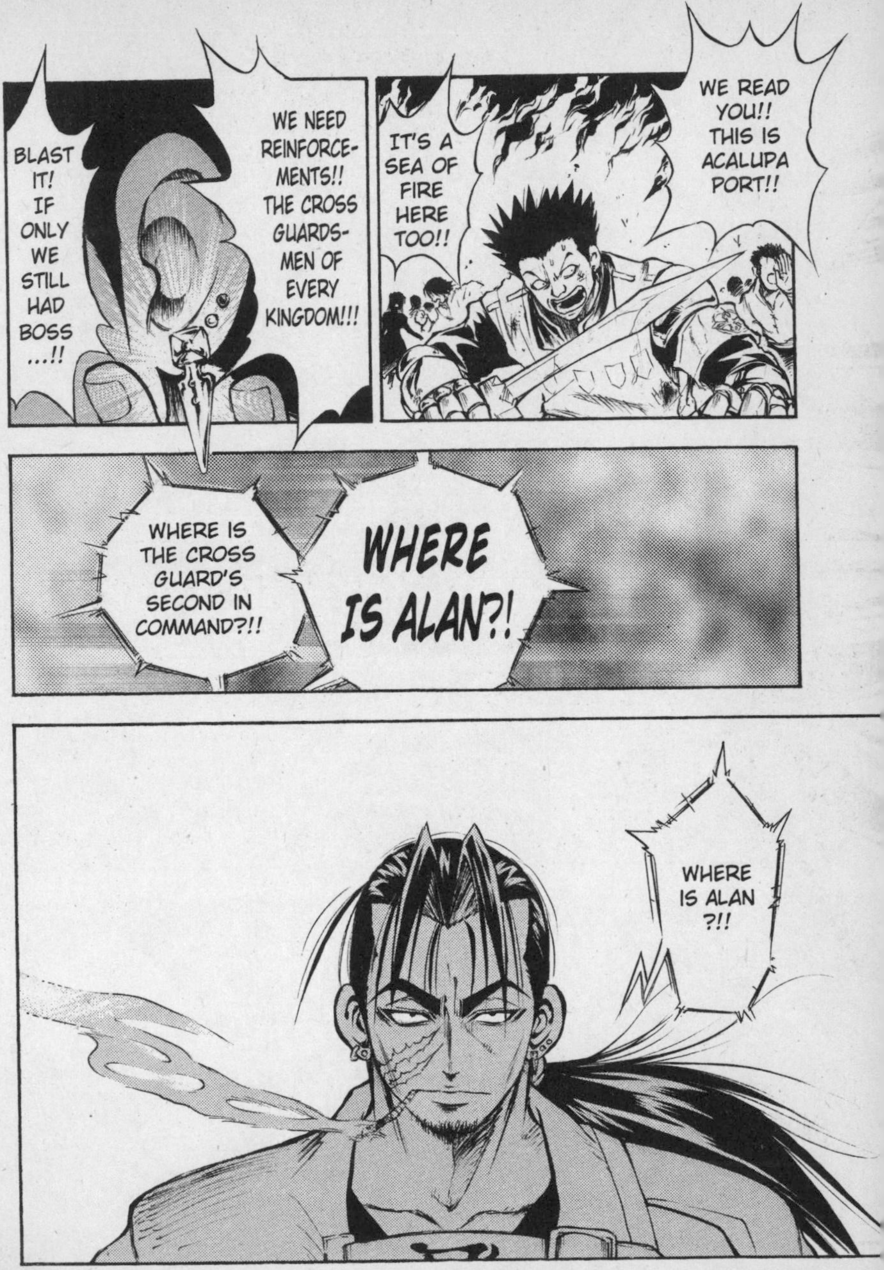
WE READ YOU!! THIS IS ACALUPA PORT!!
IT'S A SEA OF FIRE HERE TOO!!
WE NEED REINFORCEMENTS!! THE CROSS GUARDSMEN OF EVERY KINGDOM!!!
BLAST IT! IF ONLY WE STILL HAD BOSS ...!!
WHERE IS ALAN?!
WHERE IS THE CROSS GUARD'S SECOND IN COMMAND?!!
WHERE IS ALAN ?!!

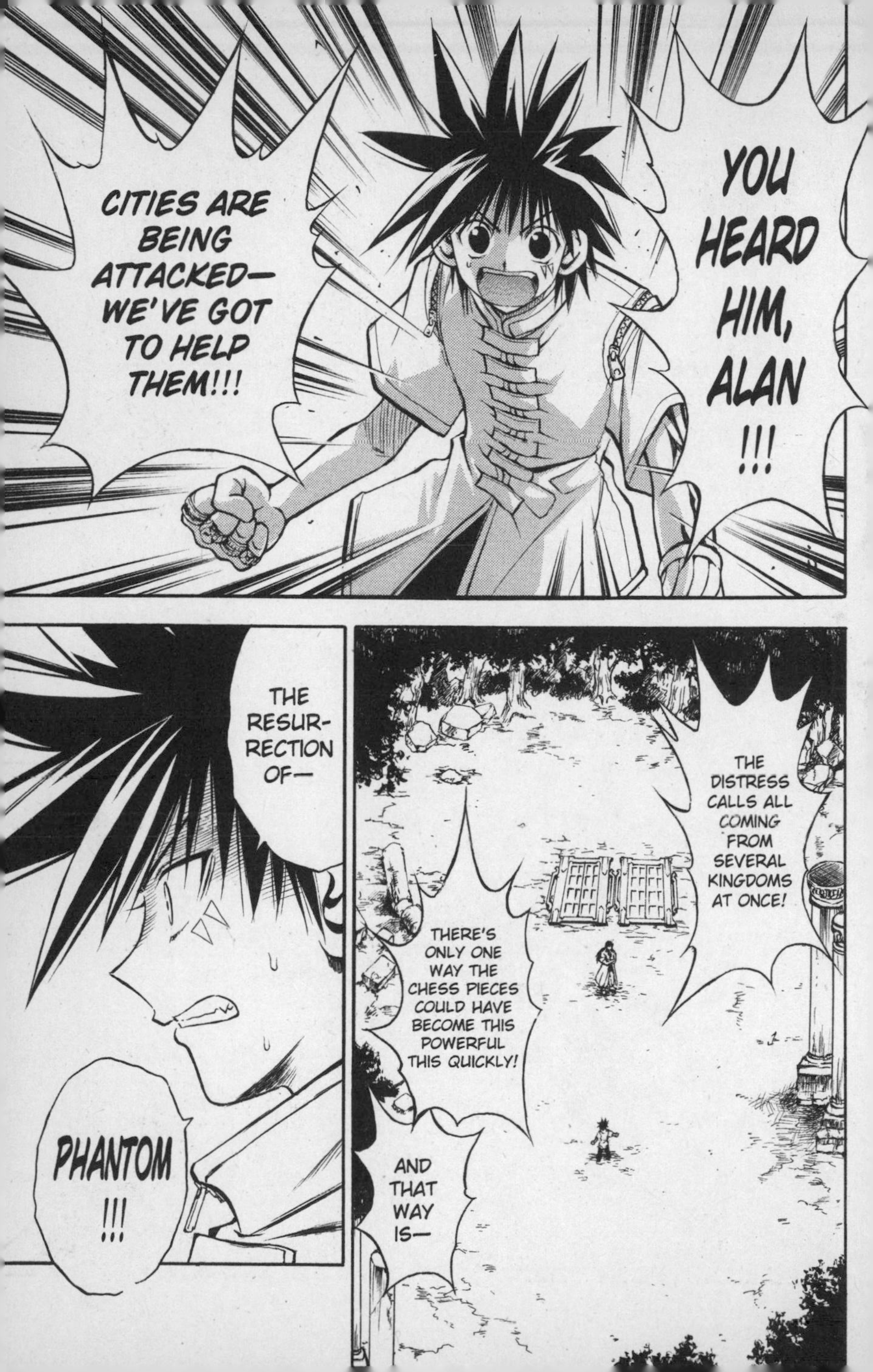
YOU HEARD HIM, ALAN!!!
CITIES ARE BEING ATTACKED—WE'VE GOT TO HELP THEM!!!
THE DISTRESS CALLS ALL COMING FROM SEVERAL KINGDOMS AT ONCE!
THERE'S ONLY ONE WAY THE CHESS PIECES COULD HAVE BECOME THIS POWERFUL THIS QUICKLY!
AND THAT WAY IS—
THE RESUR-RECTION OF—
PHANTOM!!!

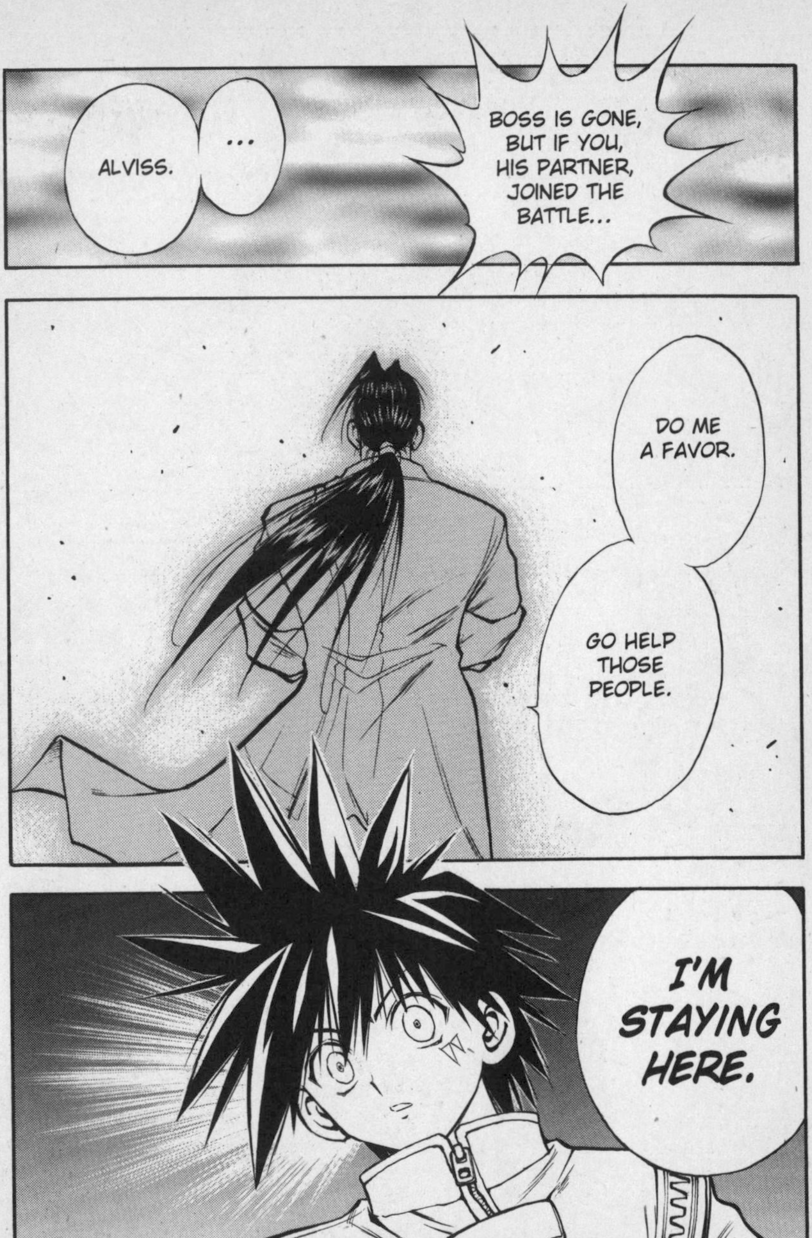
BOSS IS GONE, BUT IF YOU, HIS PARTNER, JOINED THE BATTLE...
...
ALVISS.
DO ME A FAVOR.
GO HELP THOSE PEOPLE.
I'M STAYING HERE.

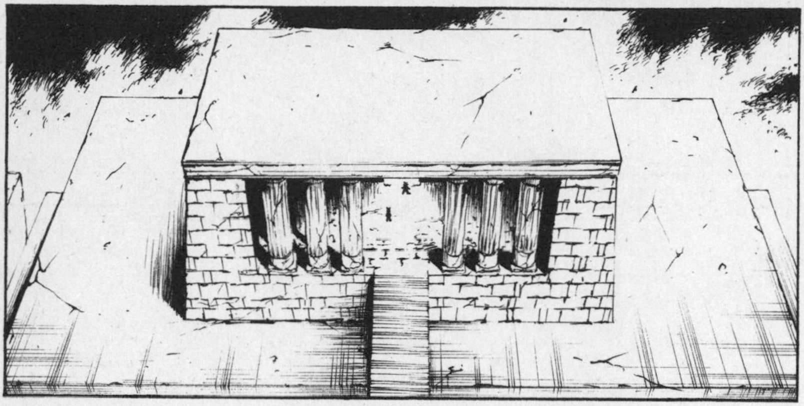

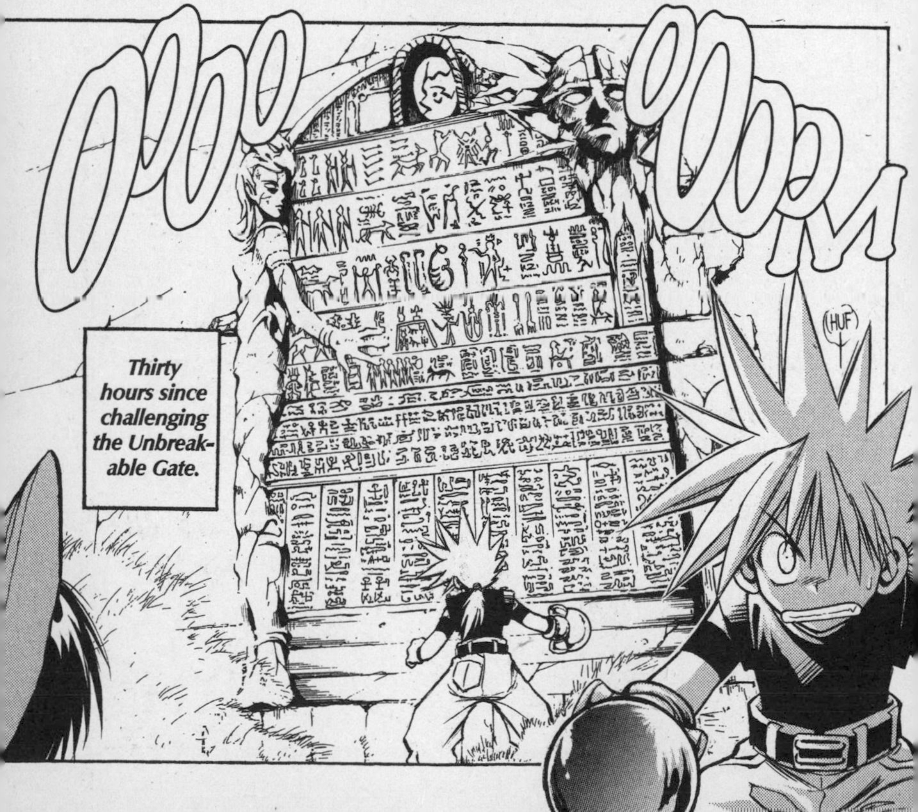
OOOOOOOM
(HUF)
Thirty hours since challenging the Unbreakable Gate.

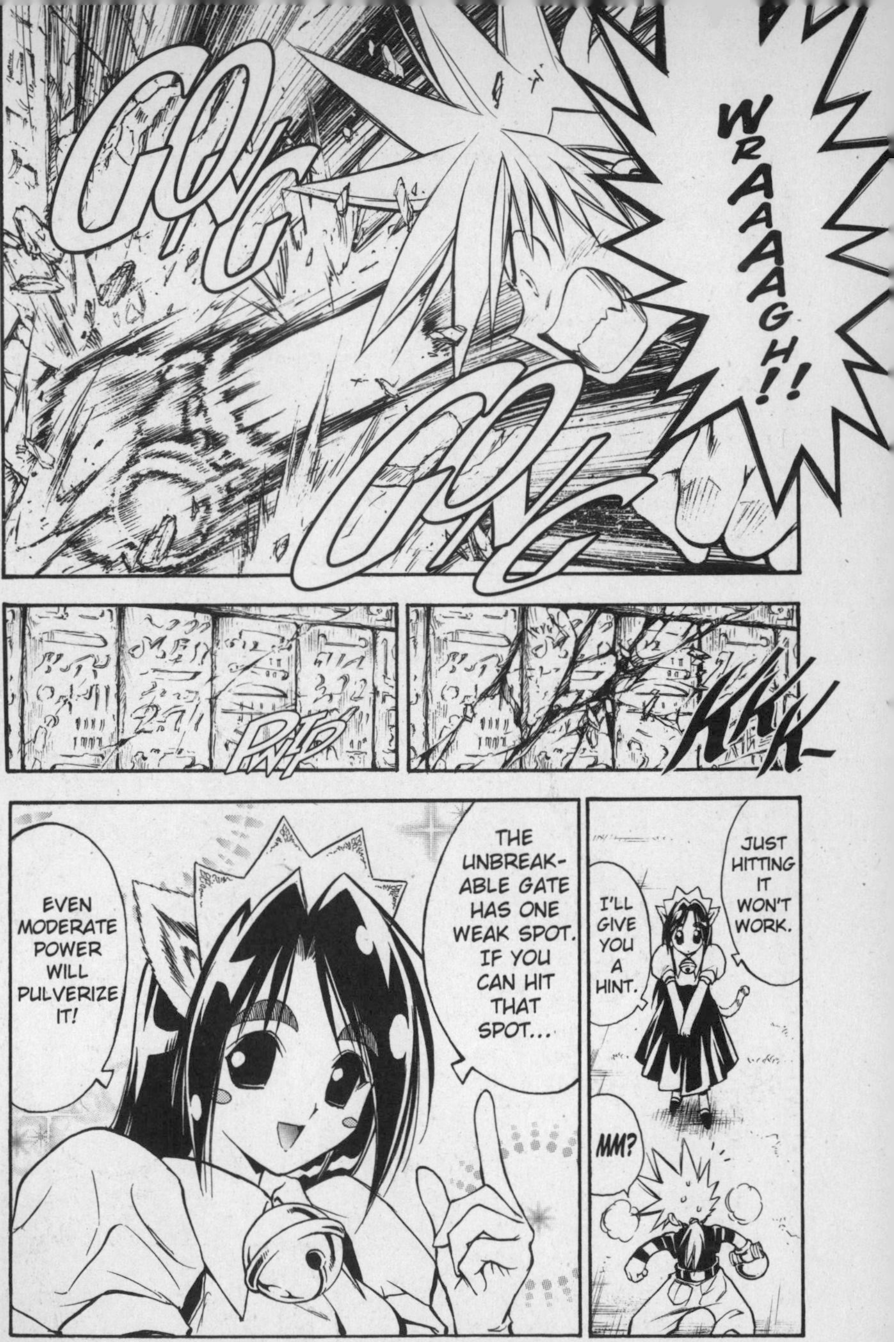
WRAAAAAGH!!
JUST HITTING IT WON'T WORK.
I'LL GIVE YOU A HINT.
MM?
THE UNBREAK-ABLE GATE HAS ONE WEAK SPOT. IF YOU CAN HIT THAT SPOT...
EVEN MODERATE POWER WILL PULVERIZE IT!

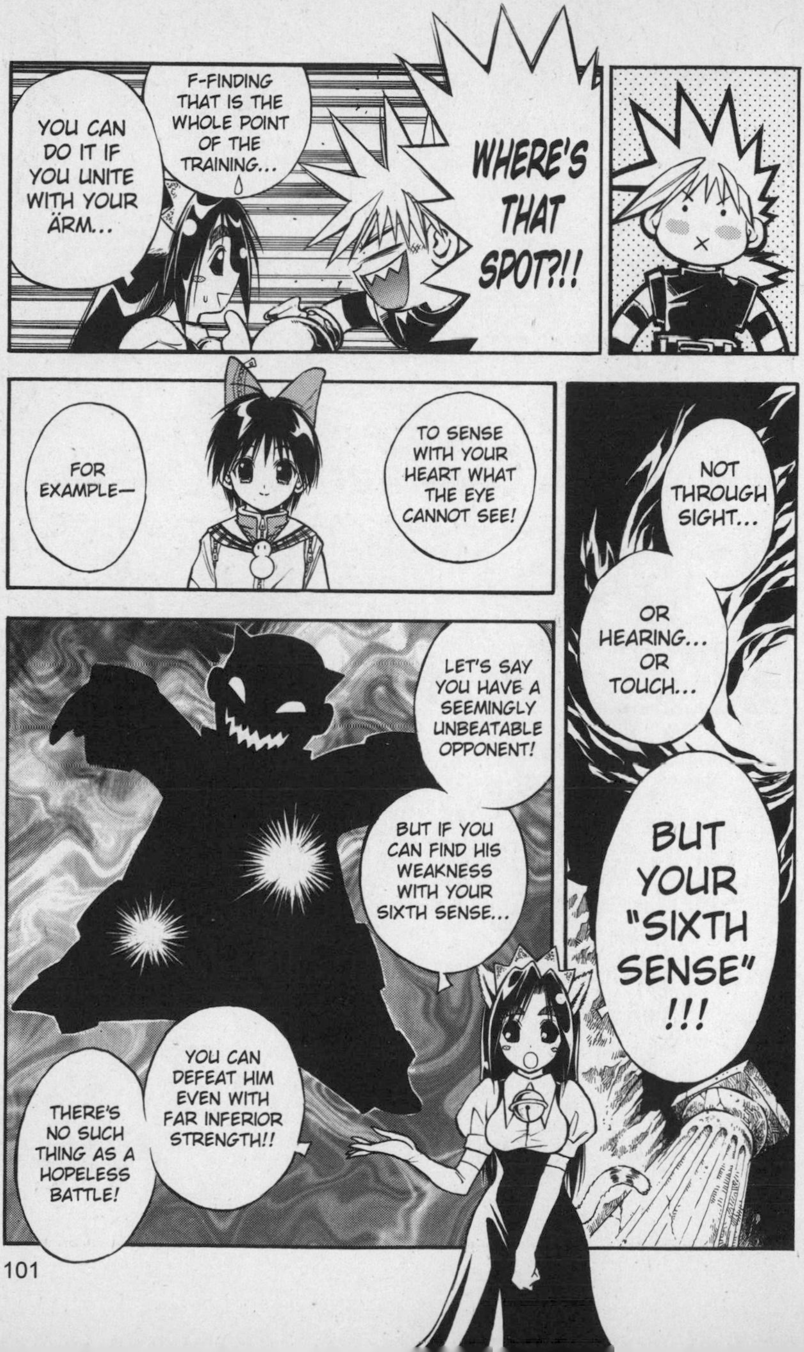
WHERE'S THAT SPOT?!!
F-FINDING THAT IS THE WHOLE POINT OF THE TRAINING...
YOU CAN DO IT IF YOU UNITE WITH YOUR ÄRM...
NOT THROUGH SIGHT...
OR HEARING... OR TOUCH...
BUT YOUR "SIXTH SENSE" !!!
TO SENSE WITH YOUR HEART WHAT THE EYE CANNOT SEE!
FOR EXAMPLE—
LET'S SAY YOU HAVE A SEEMINGLY UNBEATABLE OPPONENT!
BUT IF YOU CAN FIND HIS WEAKNESS WITH YOUR SIXTH SENSE...
YOU CAN DEFEAT HIM EVEN WITH FAR INFERIOR STRENGTH!!
THERE'S NO SUCH THING AS A HOPELESS BATTLE!

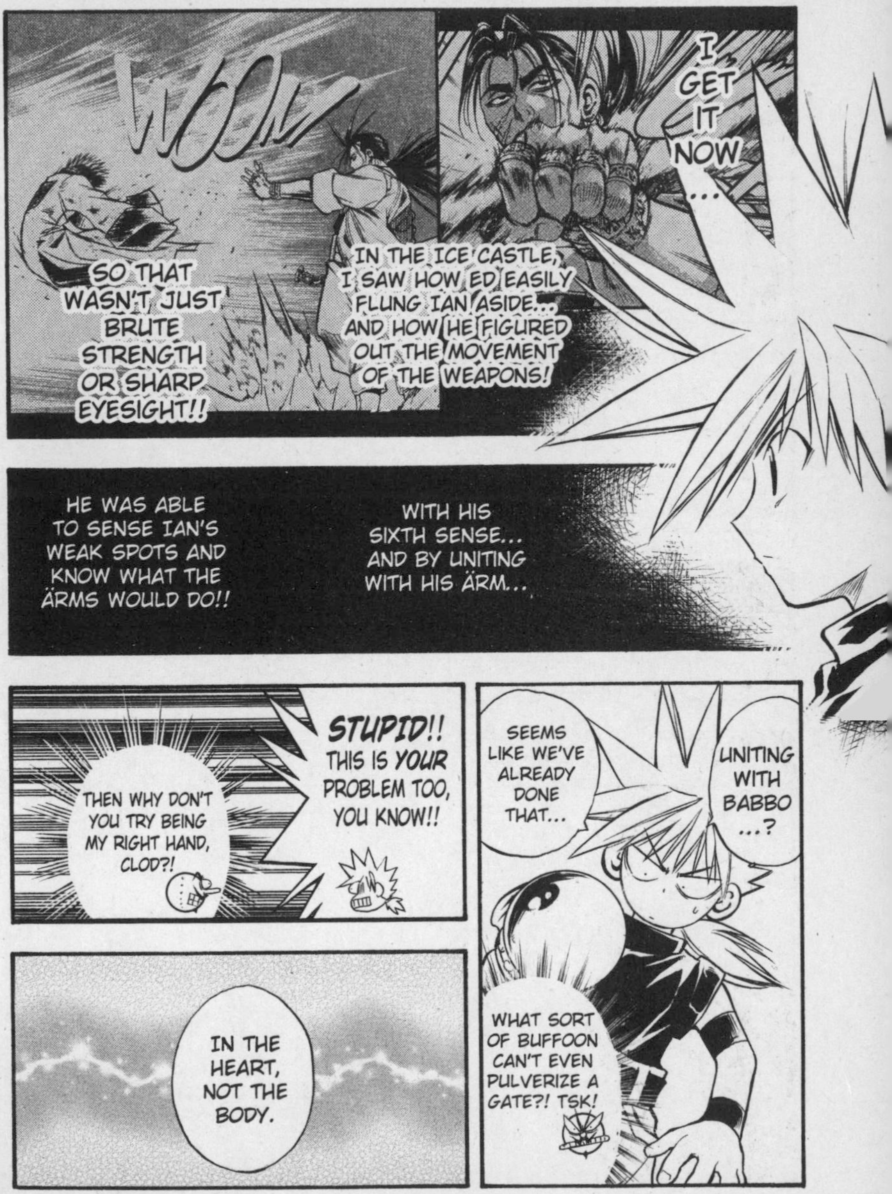
I GET IT NOW...
IN THE ICE CASTLE, I SAW HOW ED EASILY FLUNG IAN ASIDE... AND HOW HE FIGURED OUT THE MOVEMENT OF THE WEAPONS!
WOOM
SO THAT WASN'T JUST BRUTE STRENGTH OR SHARP EYESIGHT!!
WITH HIS SIXTH SENSE... AND BY UNITING WITH HIS ÄRM...
HE WAS ABLE TO SENSE IAN'S WEAK SPOTS AND KNOW WHAT THE ÄRMS WOULD DO!!
UNITING WITH BABBO ...?
SEEMS LIKE WE'VE ALREADY DONE THAT...
WHAT SORT OF BUFFOON CAN'T EVEN PULVERIZE A GATE?! TSK!
STUPID!! THIS IS YOUR PROBLEM TOO, YOU KNOW!!
THEN WHY DON'T YOU TRY BEING MY RIGHT HAND, CLOD?!
IN THE HEART, NOT THE BODY.

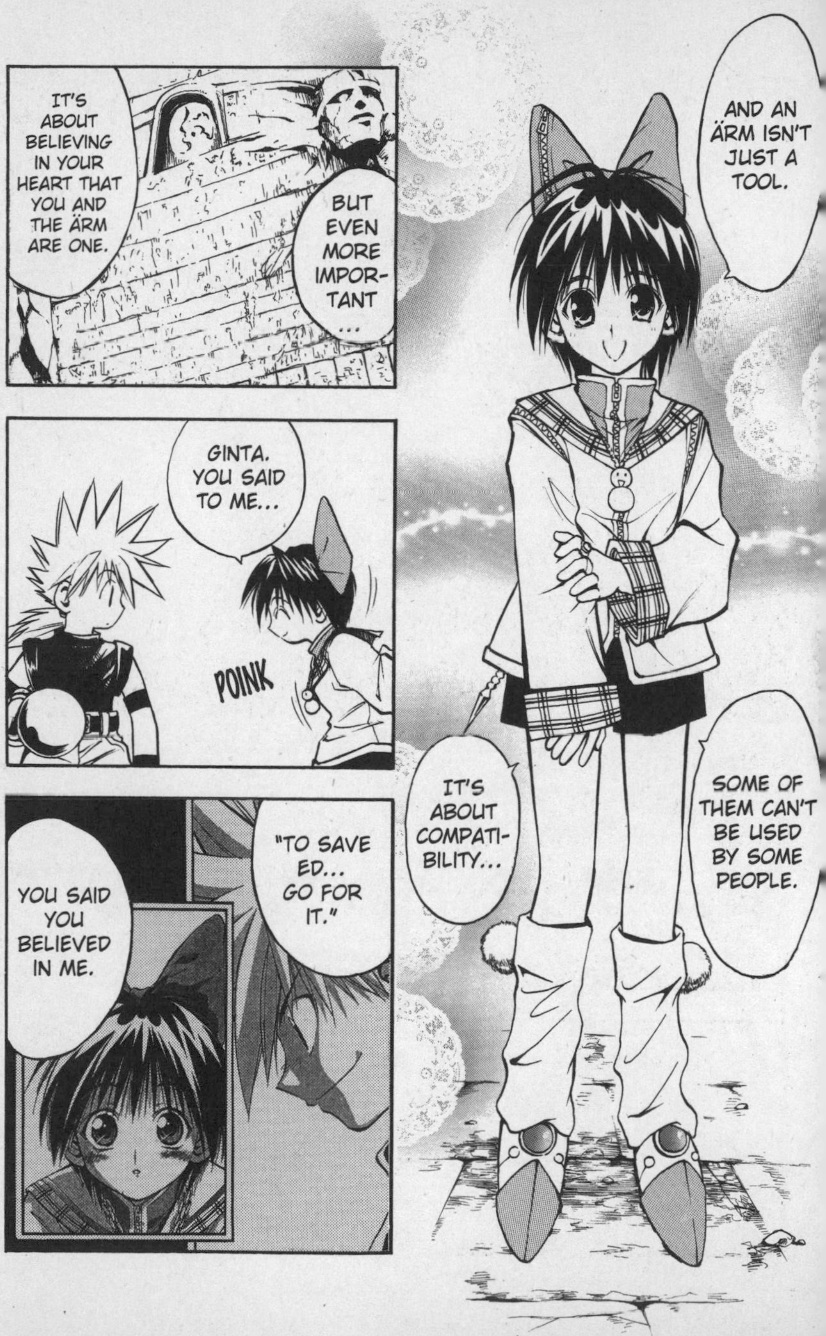
AND AN ÄRM ISN'T JUST A TOOL.
SOME OF THEM CAN'T BE USED BY SOME PEOPLE.
IT'S ABOUT COMPATIBILITY...
IT'S ABOUT BELIEVING IN YOUR HEART THAT YOU AND THE ÄRM ARE ONE.
BUT EVEN MORE IMPORTANT...
GINTA. YOU SAID TO ME...
POINK
"TO SAVE ED... GO FOR IT."
YOU SAID YOU BELIEVED IN ME.

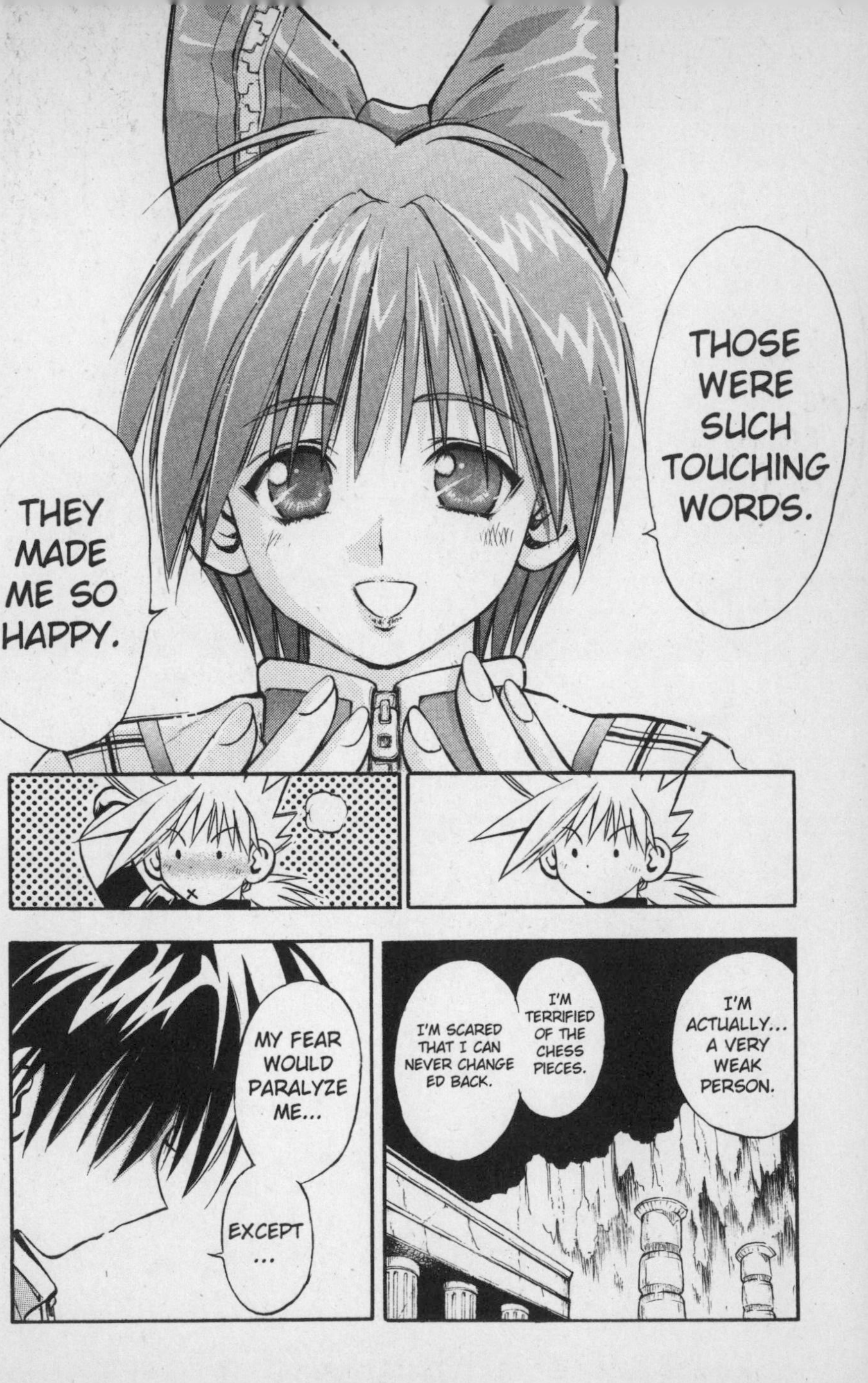
THOSE WERE SUCH TOUCHING WORDS.
THEY MADE ME SO HAPPY.
I'M ACTUALLY... A VERY WEAK PERSON.
I'M TERRIFIED OF THE CHESS PIECES.
I'M SCARED THAT I CAN NEVER CHANGE ED BACK.
MY FEAR WOULD PARALYZE ME...
EXCEPT ...

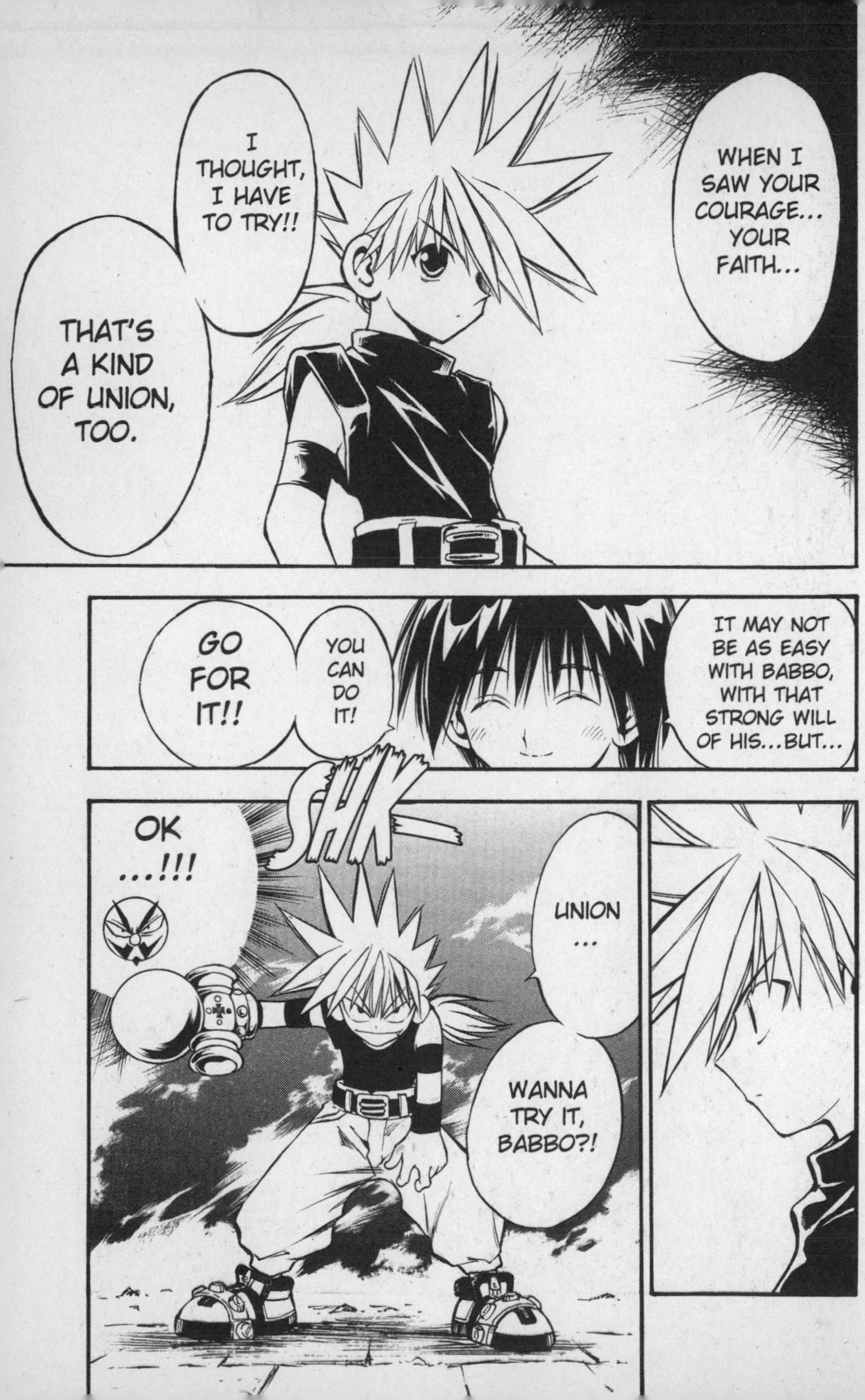
WHEN I SAW YOUR COURAGE... YOUR FAITH...
I THOUGHT, I HAVE TO TRY!!
THAT'S A KIND OF UNION, TOO.
IT MAY NOT BE AS EASY WITH BABBO, WITH THAT STRONG WILL OF HIS...BUT...
YOU CAN DO IT!
GO FOR IT!!
SHK
UNION ...
WANNA TRY IT, BABBO?!
OK ...!!!

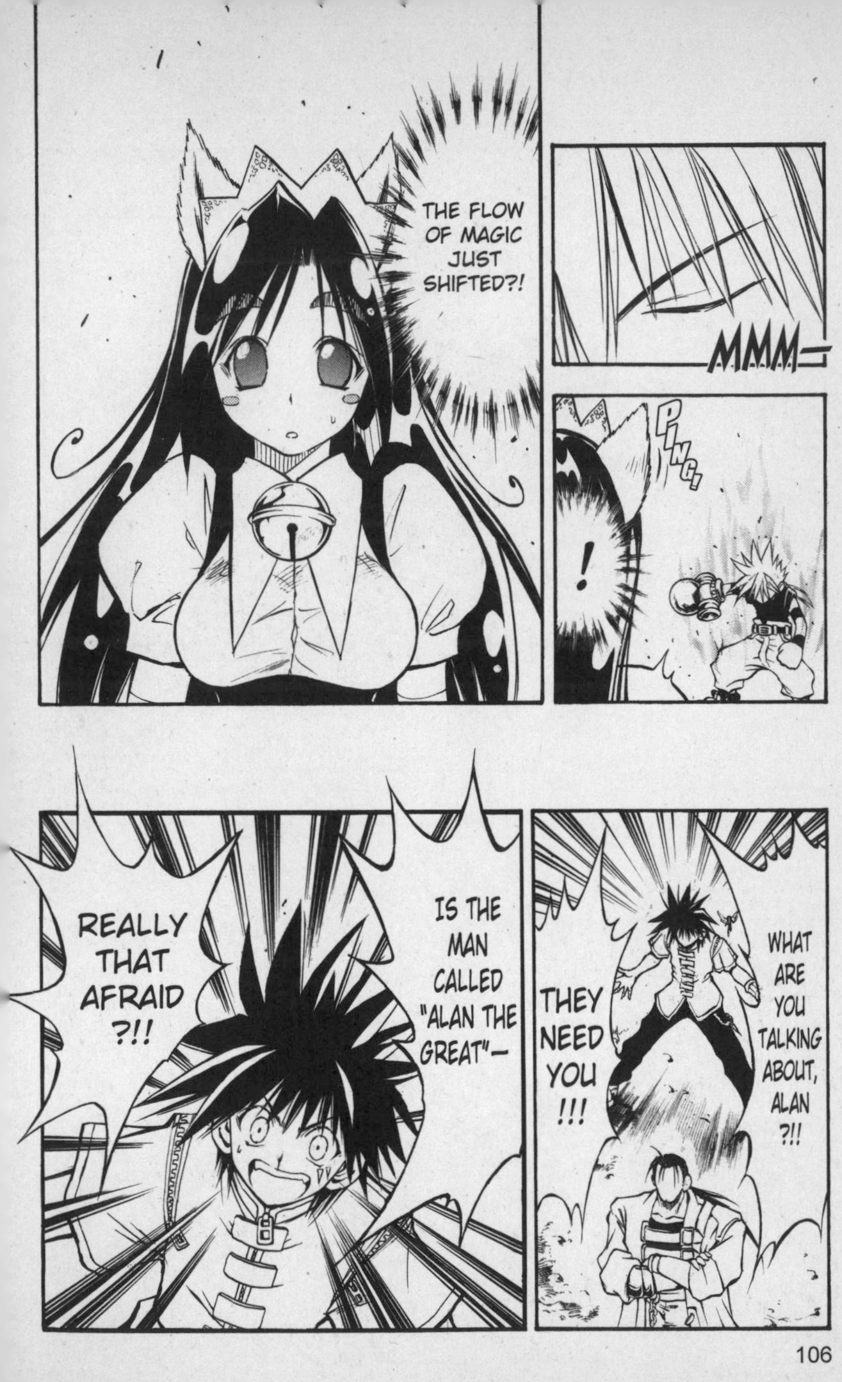
MMM—
PING!
!
THE FLOW OF MAGIC JUST SHIFTED?!
WHAT ARE YOU TALKING ABOUT, ALAN?!!
THEY NEED YOU!!!
IS THE MAN CALLED "ALAN THE GREAT"—
REALLY THAT AFRAID?!!

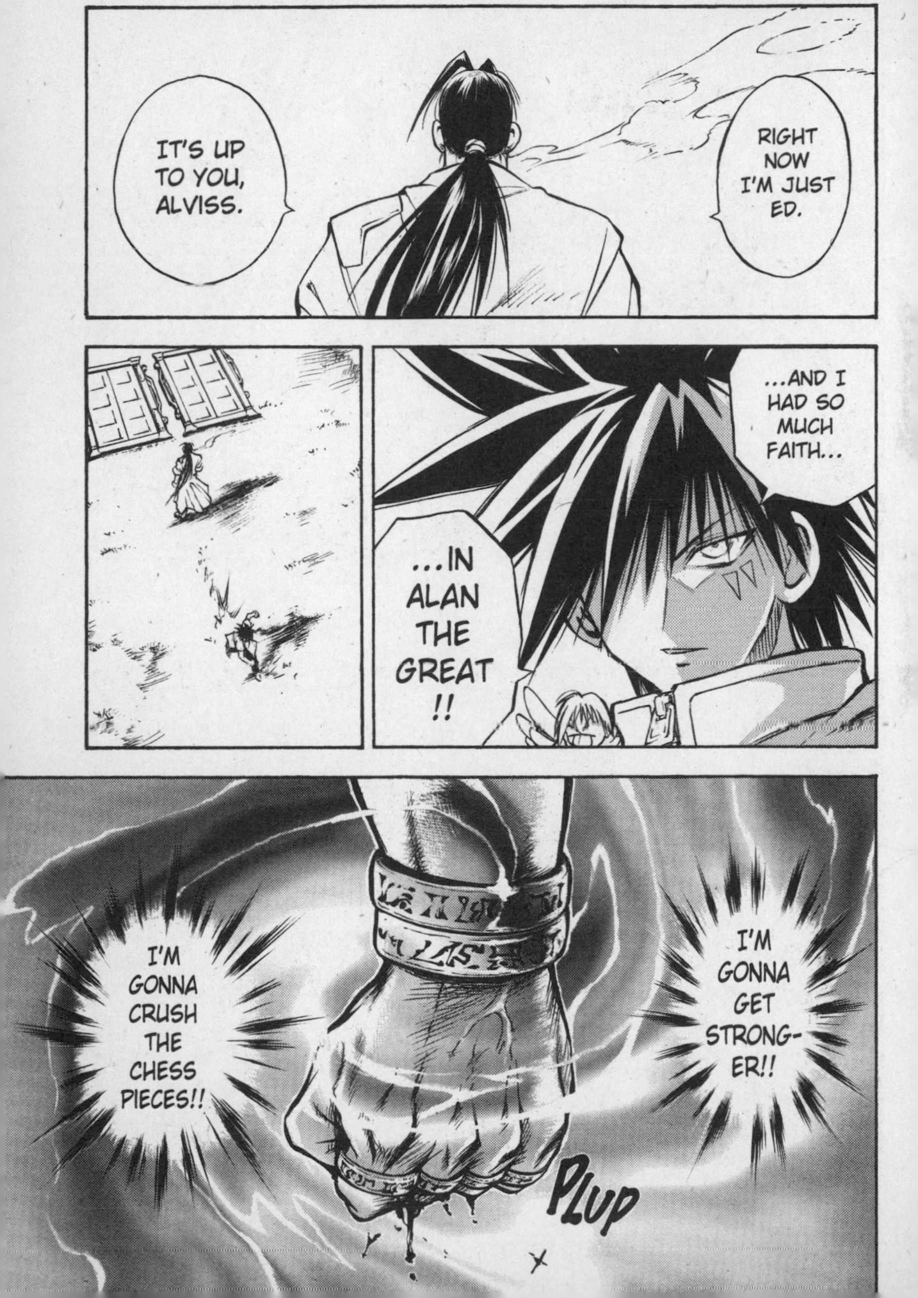
RIGHT NOW I'M JUST ED.
IT'S UP TO YOU, ALVISS.
...AND I HAD SO MUCH FAITH...
...IN ALAN THE GREAT!!
I'M GONNA GET STRONG-ER!!
I'M GONNA CRUSH THE CHESS PIECES!!
PLUP

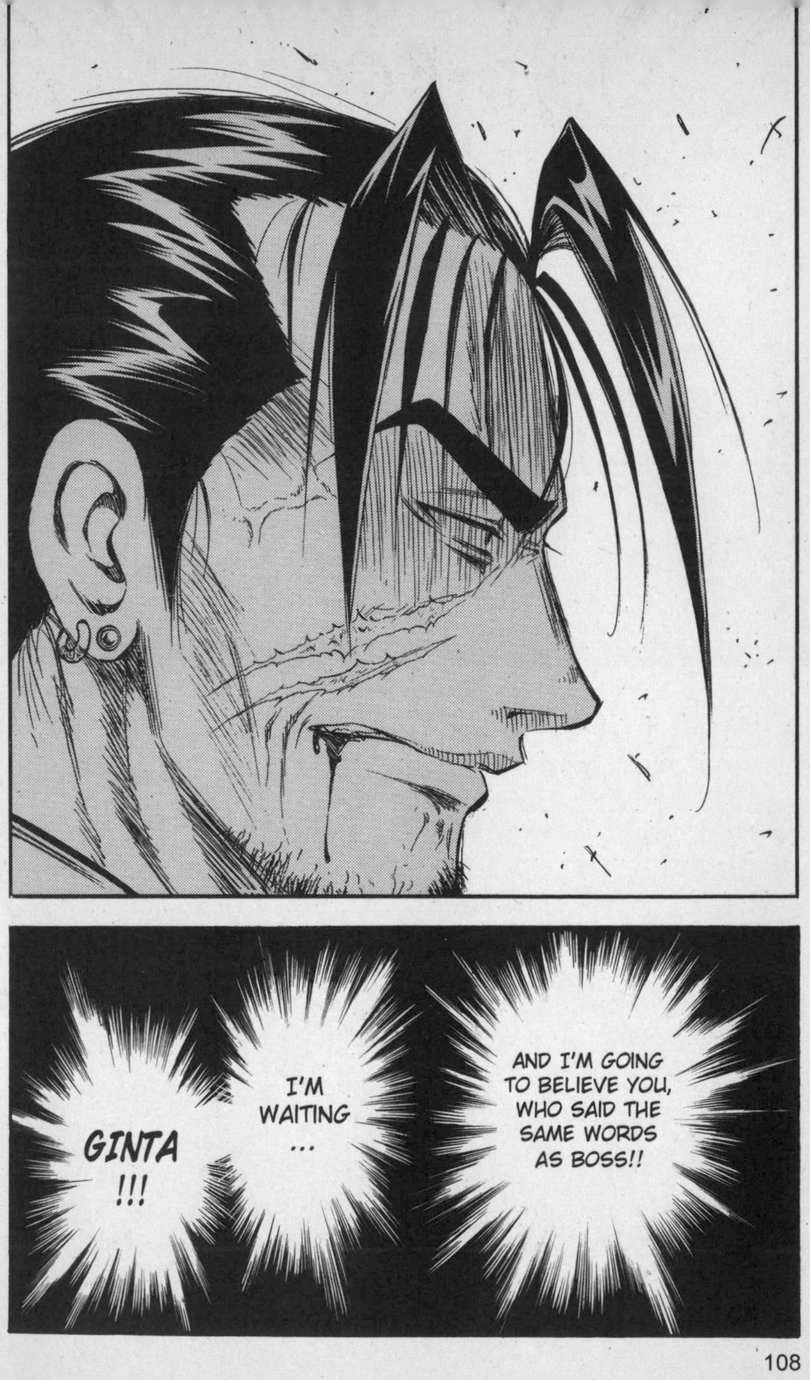
AND I'M GOING TO BELIEVE YOU, WHO SAID THE SAME WORDS AS BOSS!!
I'M WAITING ...
GINTA !!!

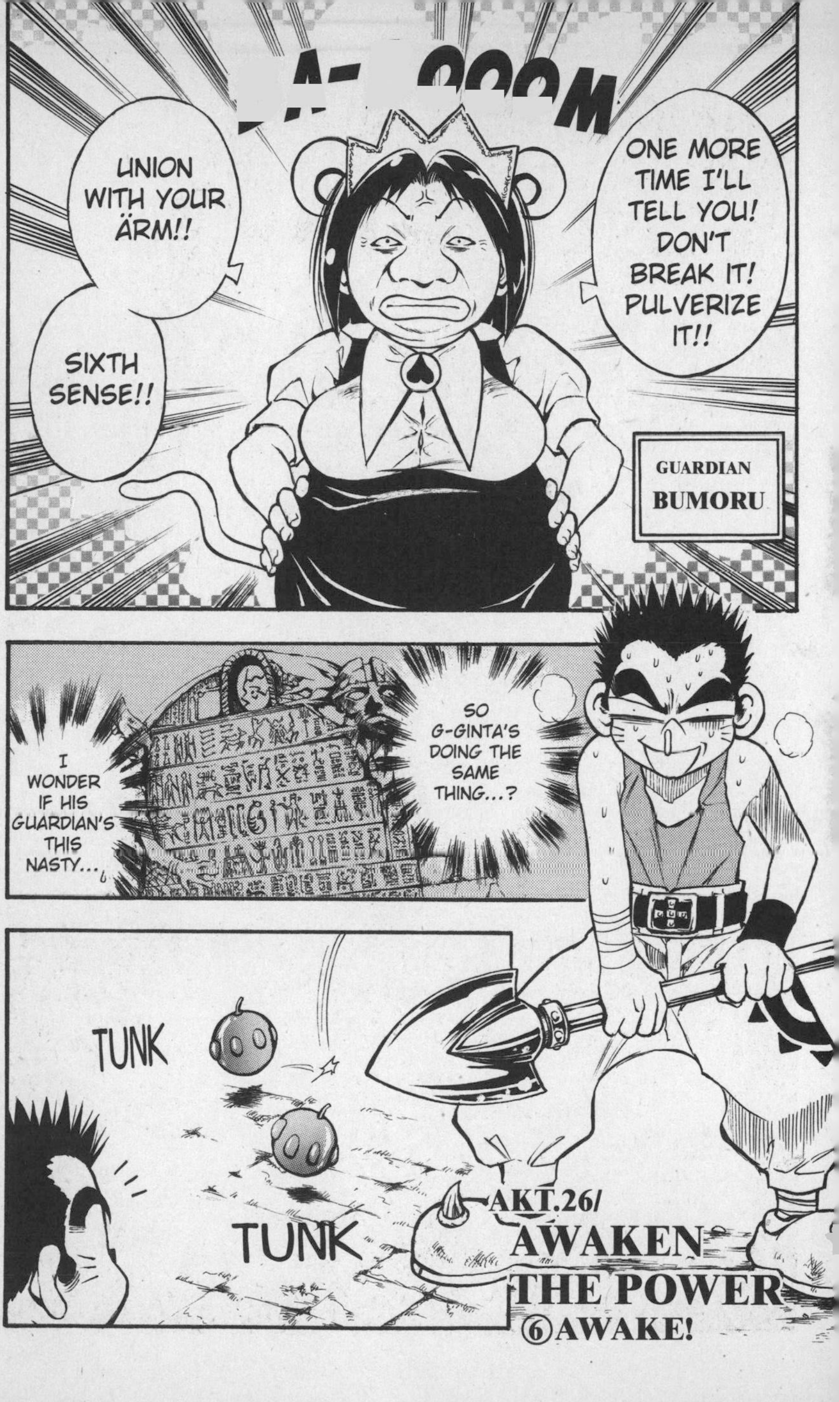
ONE MORE TIME I'LL TELL YOU! DON'T BREAK IT! PULVERIZE IT!!
UNION WITH YOUR ÄRM!!
SIXTH SENSE!!
GUARDIAN BUMORU
SO G-GINTA'S DOING THE SAME THING...?
I WONDER IF HIS GUARDIAN'S THIS NASTY...
TUNK
TUNK
AKT.26/ AWAKEN THE POWER ⑥AWAKE!

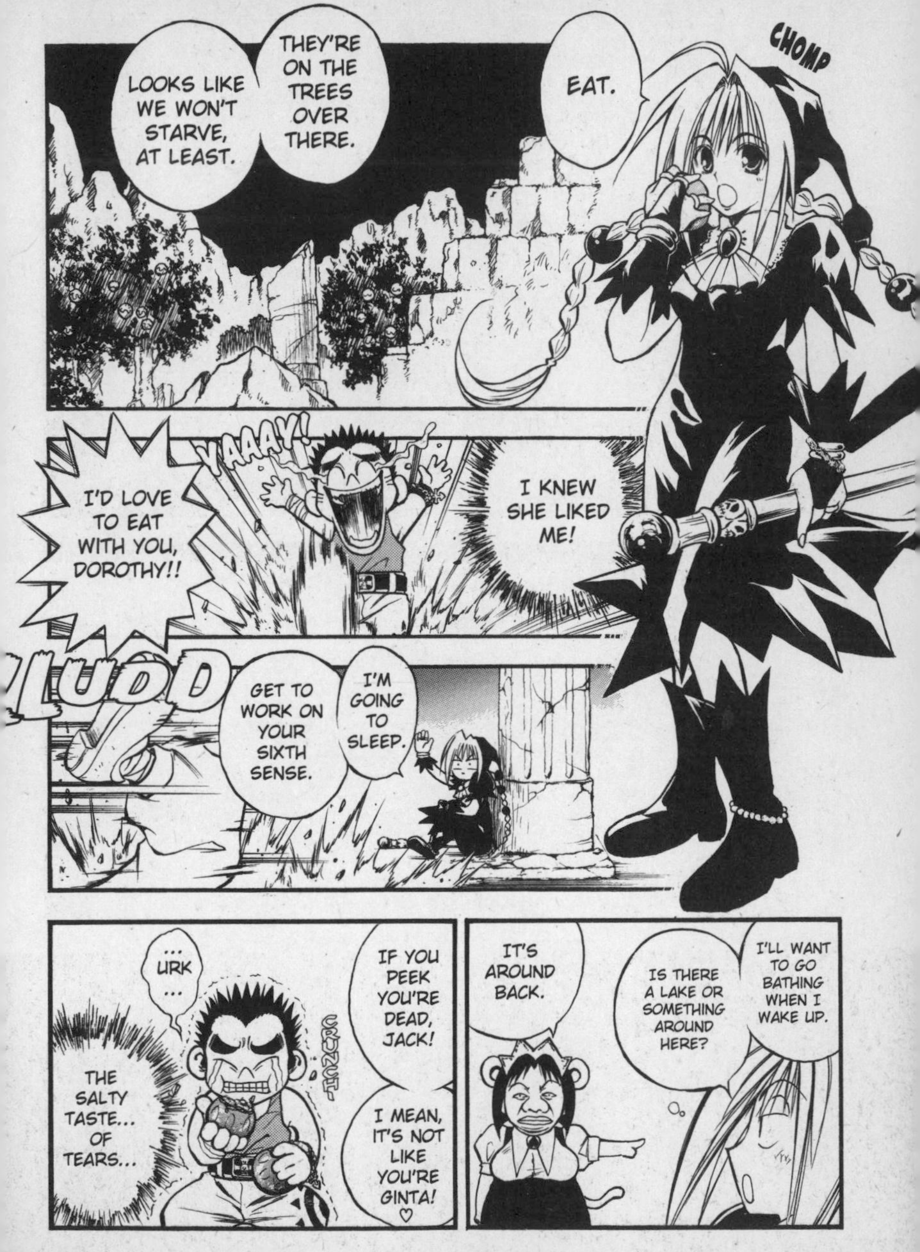
CHOMP
EAT.
THEY'RE ON THE TREES OVER THERE.
LOOKS LIKE WE WON'T STARVE, AT LEAST.
YAAAY!
I KNEW SHE LIKED ME!
I'D LOVE TO EAT WITH YOU, DOROTHY!!
I'M GOING TO SLEEP.
GET TO WORK ON YOUR SIXTH SENSE.
LUDD
I'LL WANT TO GO BATHING WHEN I WAKE UP.
IS THERE A LAKE OR SOMETHING AROUND HERE?
IT'S AROUND BACK.
IF YOU PEEK YOU'RE DEAD, JACK!
I MEAN, IT'S NOT LIKE YOU'RE GINTA! ♡
CRUNCH
... URK ...
THE SALTY TASTE... OF TEARS...

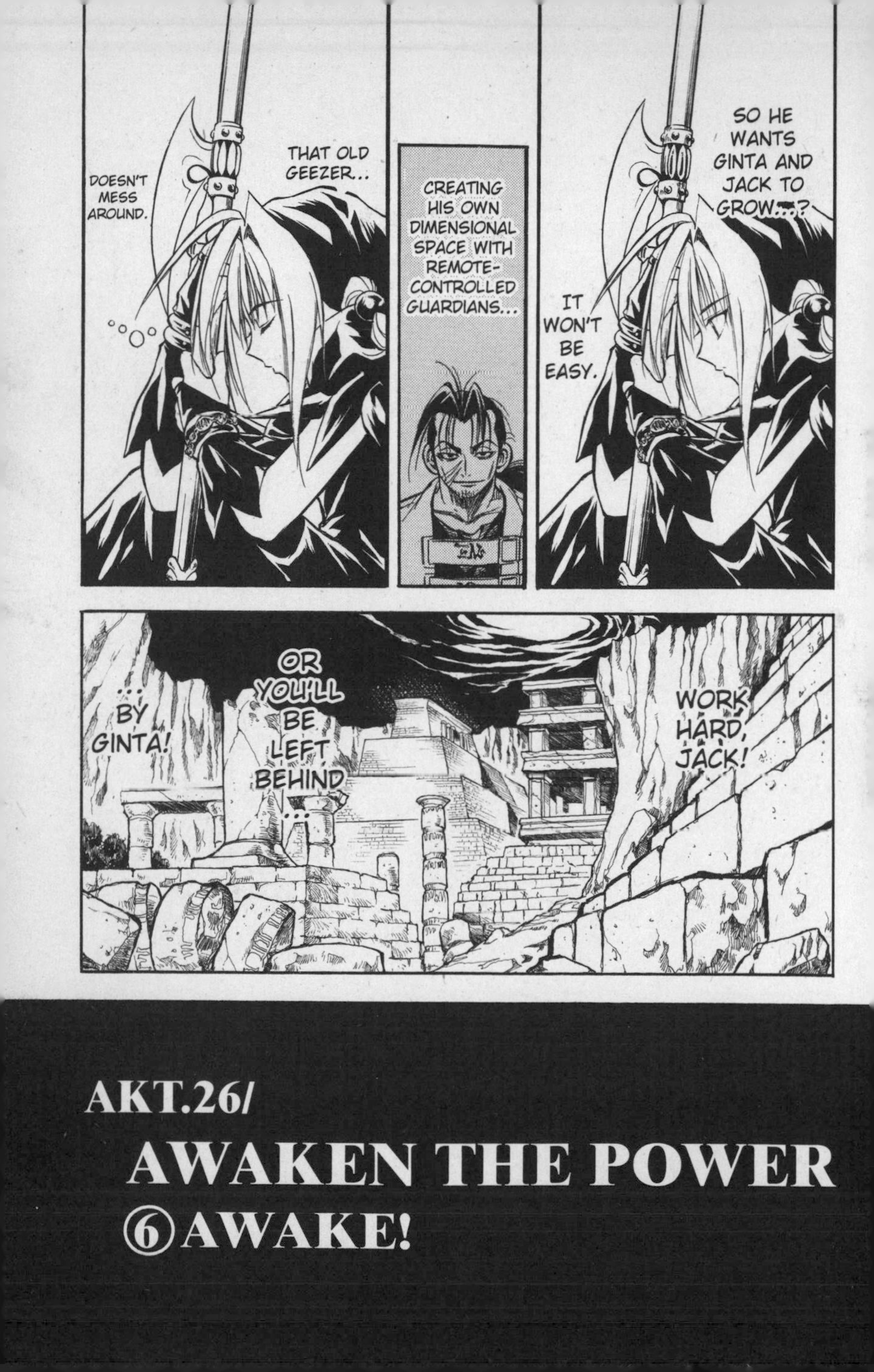
SO HE WANTS GINTA AND JACK TO GROW...?
IT WON'T BE EASY.
CREATING HIS OWN DIMENSIONAL SPACE WITH REMOTE-CONTROLLED GUARDIANS...
THAT OLD GEEZER...
DOESN'T MESS AROUND.
WORK HARD, JACK!
OR YOU'LL BE LEFT BEHIND...
...BY GINTA!

AKT.26/ AWAKEN THE POWER ⑥ AWAKE!

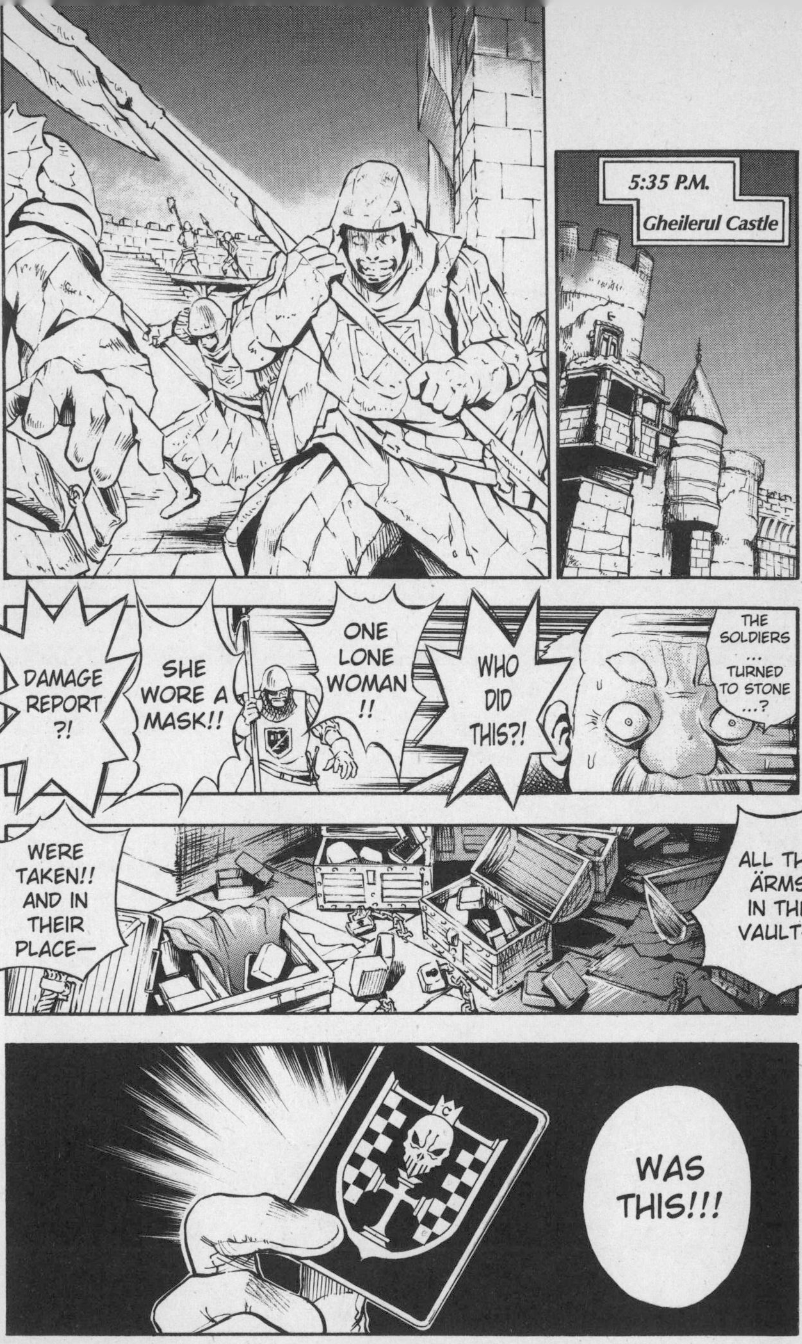
5:35 P.M.
Gheilerul Castle
THE SOLDIERS ... TURNED TO STONE ...?
WHO DID THIS?!
ONE LONE WOMAN !!
SHE WORE A MASK!!
DAMAGE REPORT ?!
ALL THE ÄRMS IN THE VAULT—
WERE TAKEN!! AND IN THEIR PLACE—
WAS THIS!!!

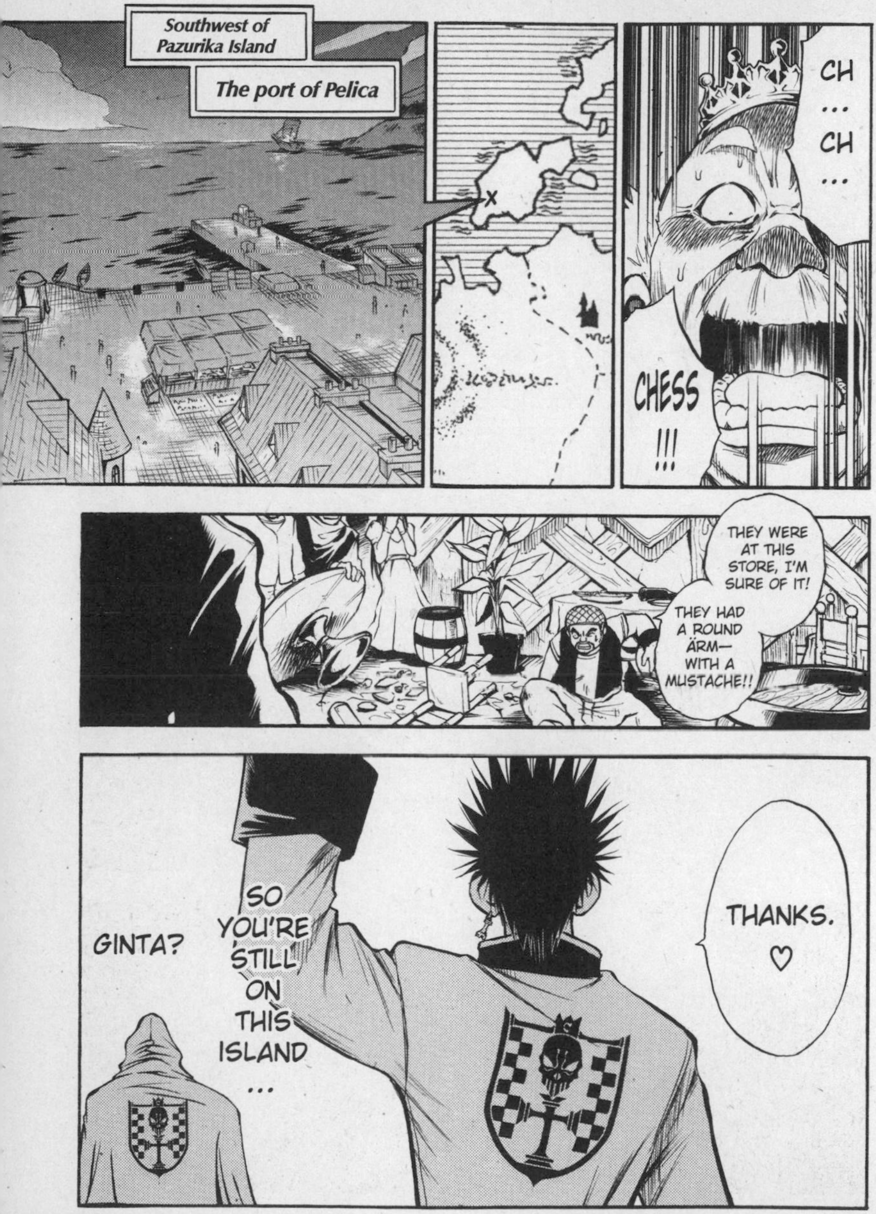
CH... CH...
CHESS!!!
Southwest of Pazurika Island
The port of Pelica
THEY WERE AT THIS STORE, I'M SURE OF IT!
THEY HAD A ROUND ÄRM— WITH A MUSTACHE!!
THANKS. ♡
SO YOU'RE STILL ON THIS ISLAND...
GINTA?

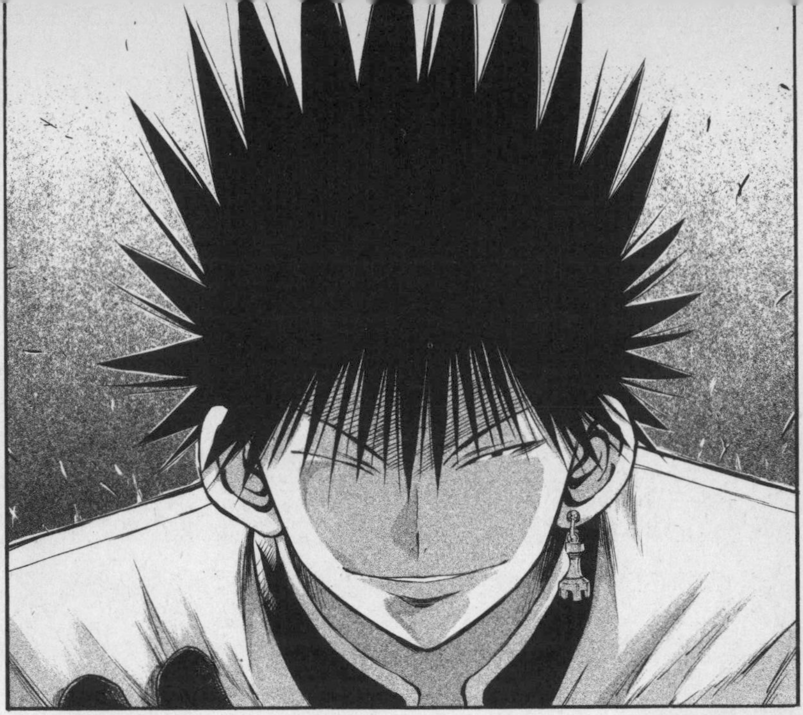

THIS TIME...

YOU WILL DIE.

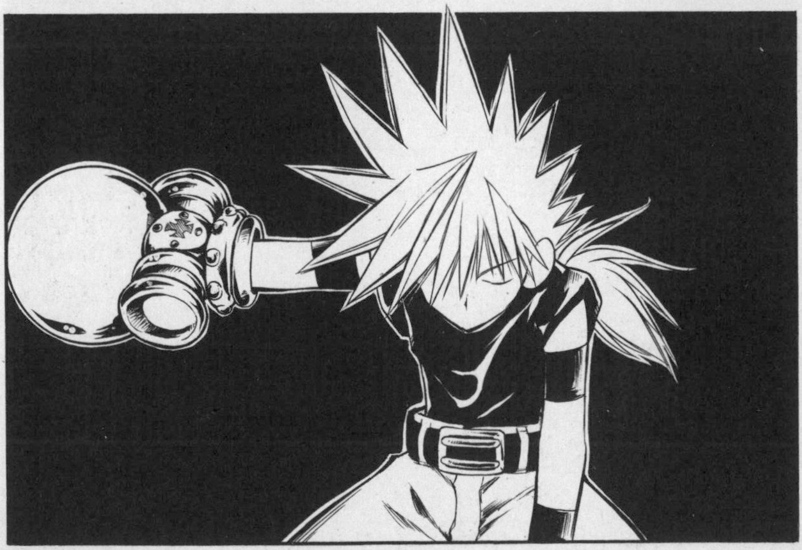

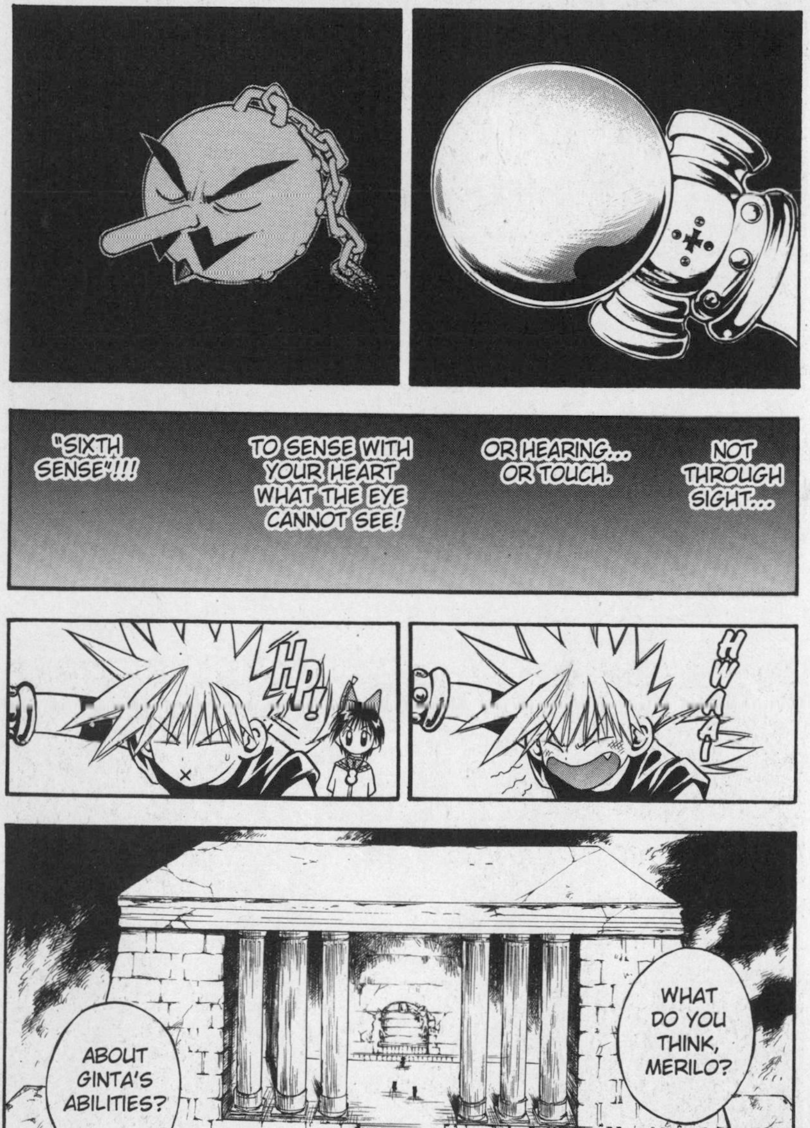
NOT THROUGH SIGHT...
OR HEARING... OR TOUCH.
TO SENSE WITH YOUR HEART WHAT THE EYE CANNOT SEE!
"SIXTH SENSE"!!!
HWAA!
HP!
WHAT DO YOU THINK, MERILO?
ABOUT GINTA'S ABILITIES?

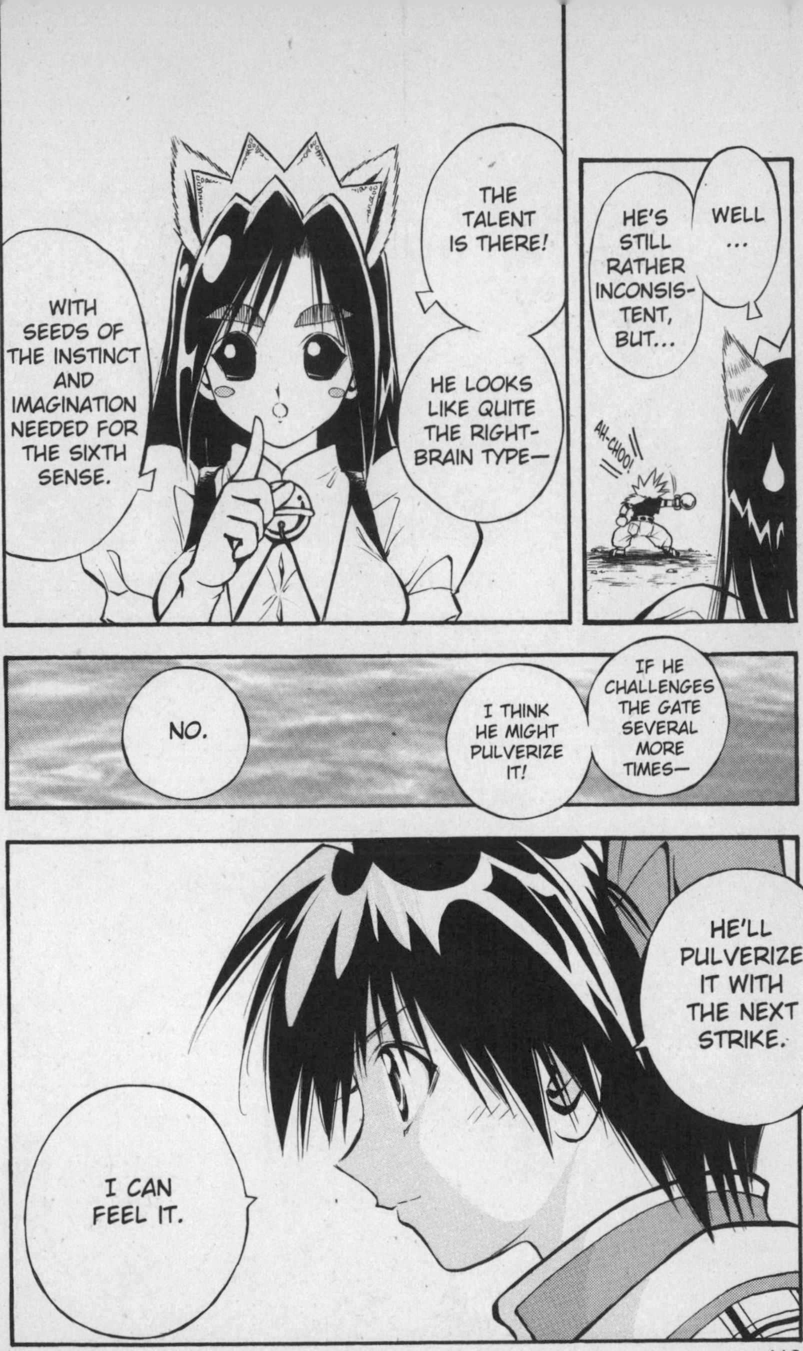
WELL...
HE'S STILL RATHER INCONSIS-TENT, BUT...
AH-CHOO!
THE TALENT IS THERE!
HE LOOKS LIKE QUITE THE RIGHT-BRAIN TYPE—
WITH SEEDS OF THE INSTINCT AND IMAGINATION NEEDED FOR THE SIXTH SENSE.
IF HE CHALLENGES THE GATE SEVERAL MORE TIMES—
I THINK HE MIGHT PULVERIZE IT!
NO.
HE'LL PULVERIZE IT WITH THE NEXT STRIKE.
I CAN FEEL IT.

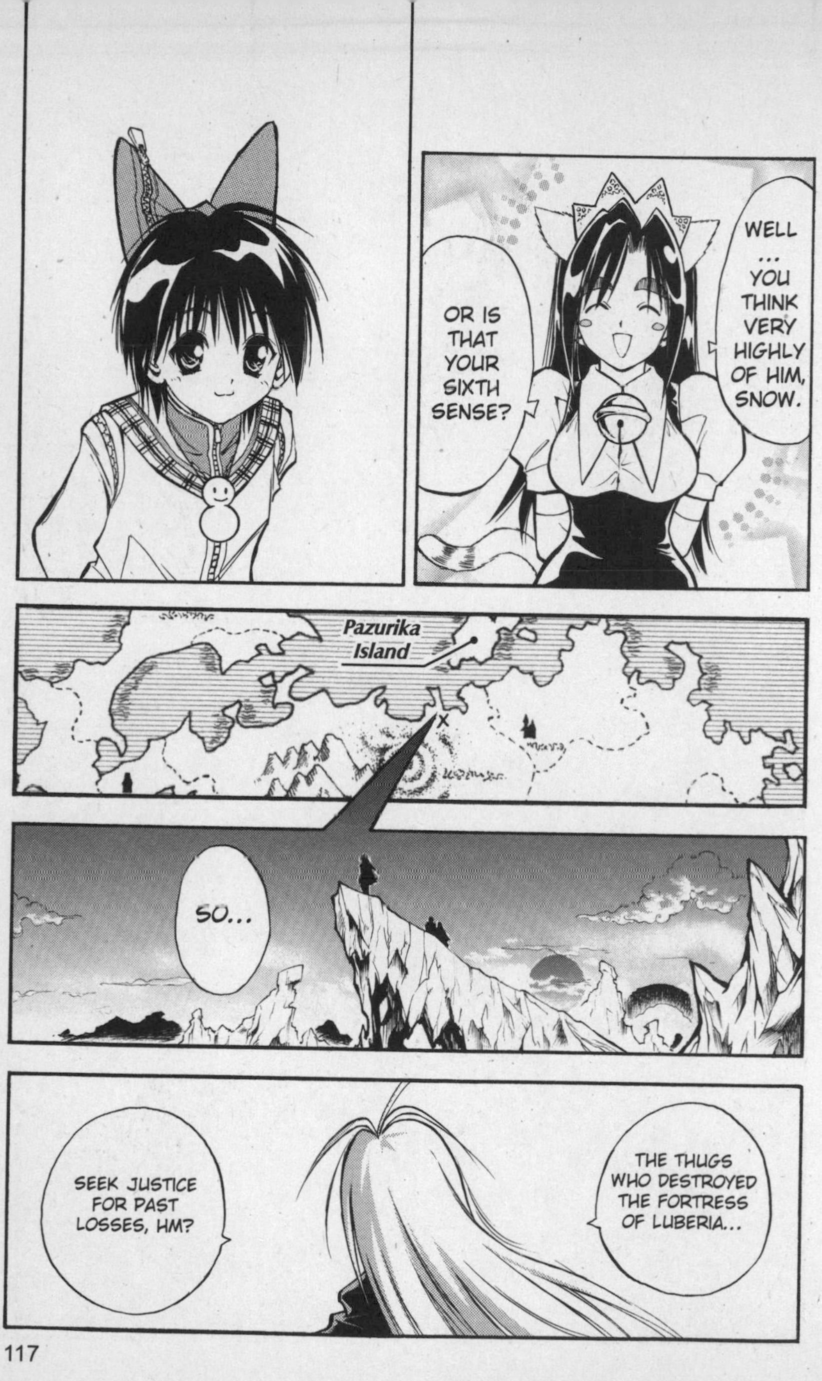
WELL ... YOU THINK VERY HIGHLY OF HIM, SNOW.
OR IS THAT YOUR SIXTH SENSE?
Pazurika Island
X
SO...
THE THUGS WHO DESTROYED THE FORTRESS OF LUBERIA...
SEEK JUSTICE FOR PAST LOSSES, HM?

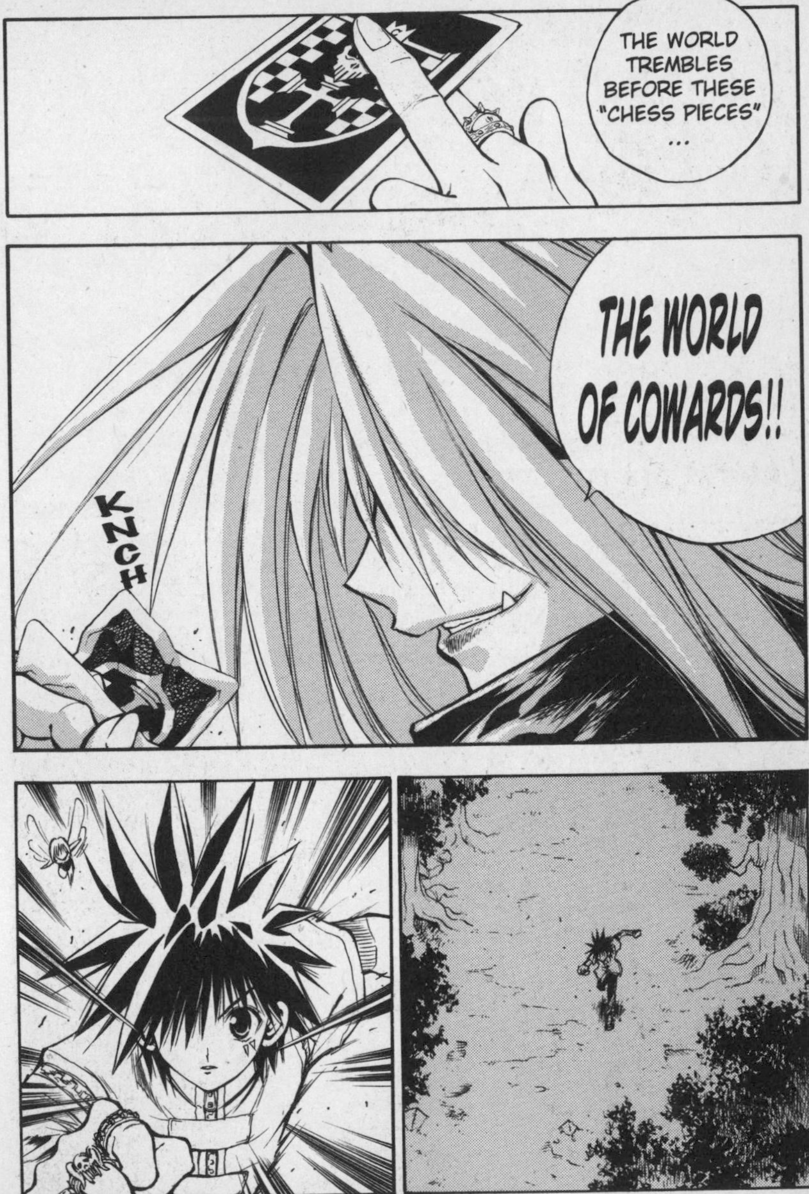
THE WORLD TREMBLES BEFORE THESE "CHESS PIECES" ...
THE WORLD OF COWARDS!!
KNCH

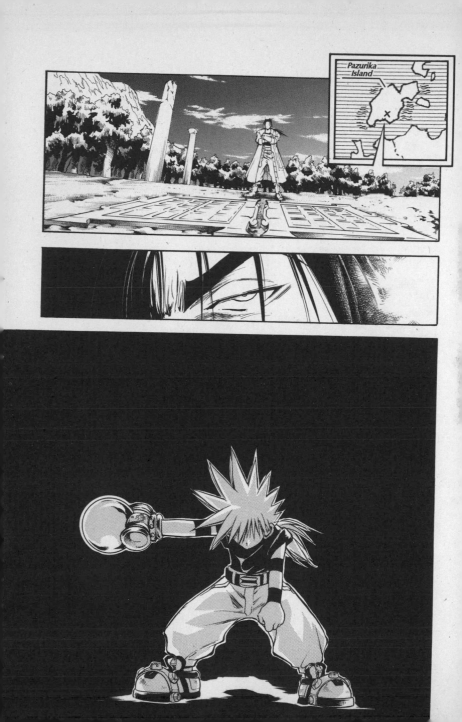

Pazurika
Island

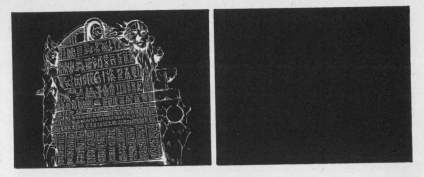

BUT EVEN MORE IMPORTANT...

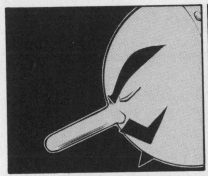

IT'S ABOUT BELIEVING IN YOUR HEART
THAT YOU AND THE ÄRM ARE ONE.

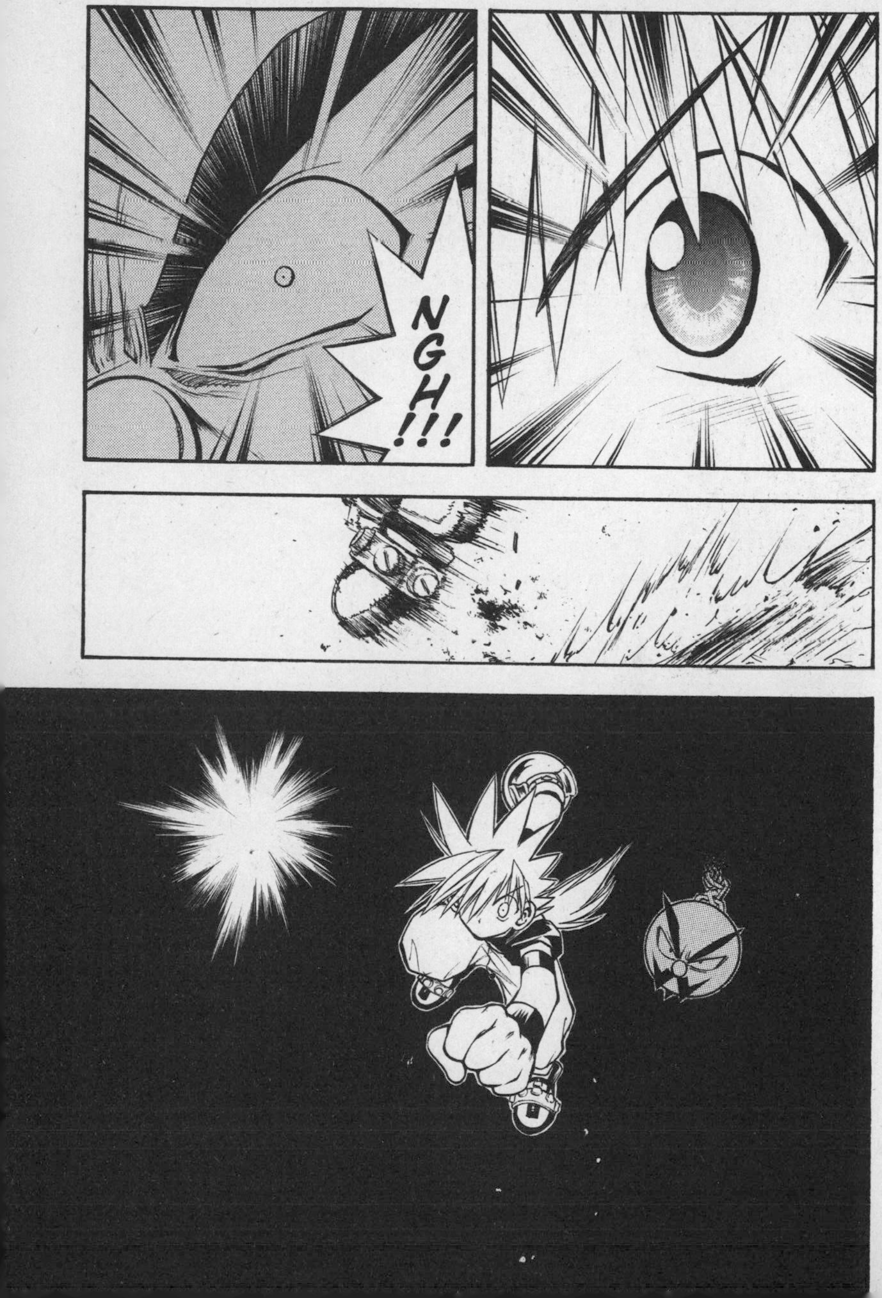
NGH!!!

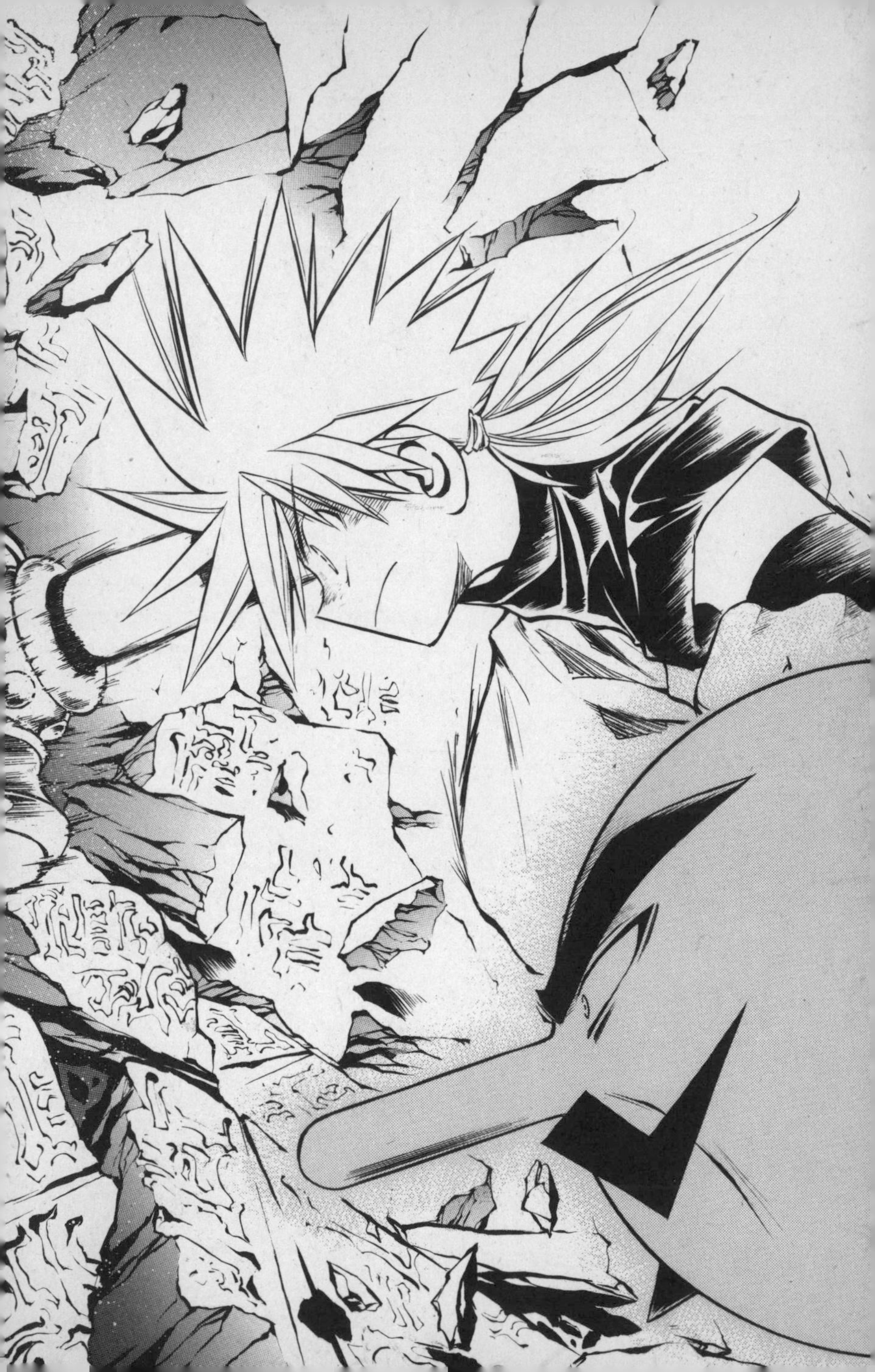

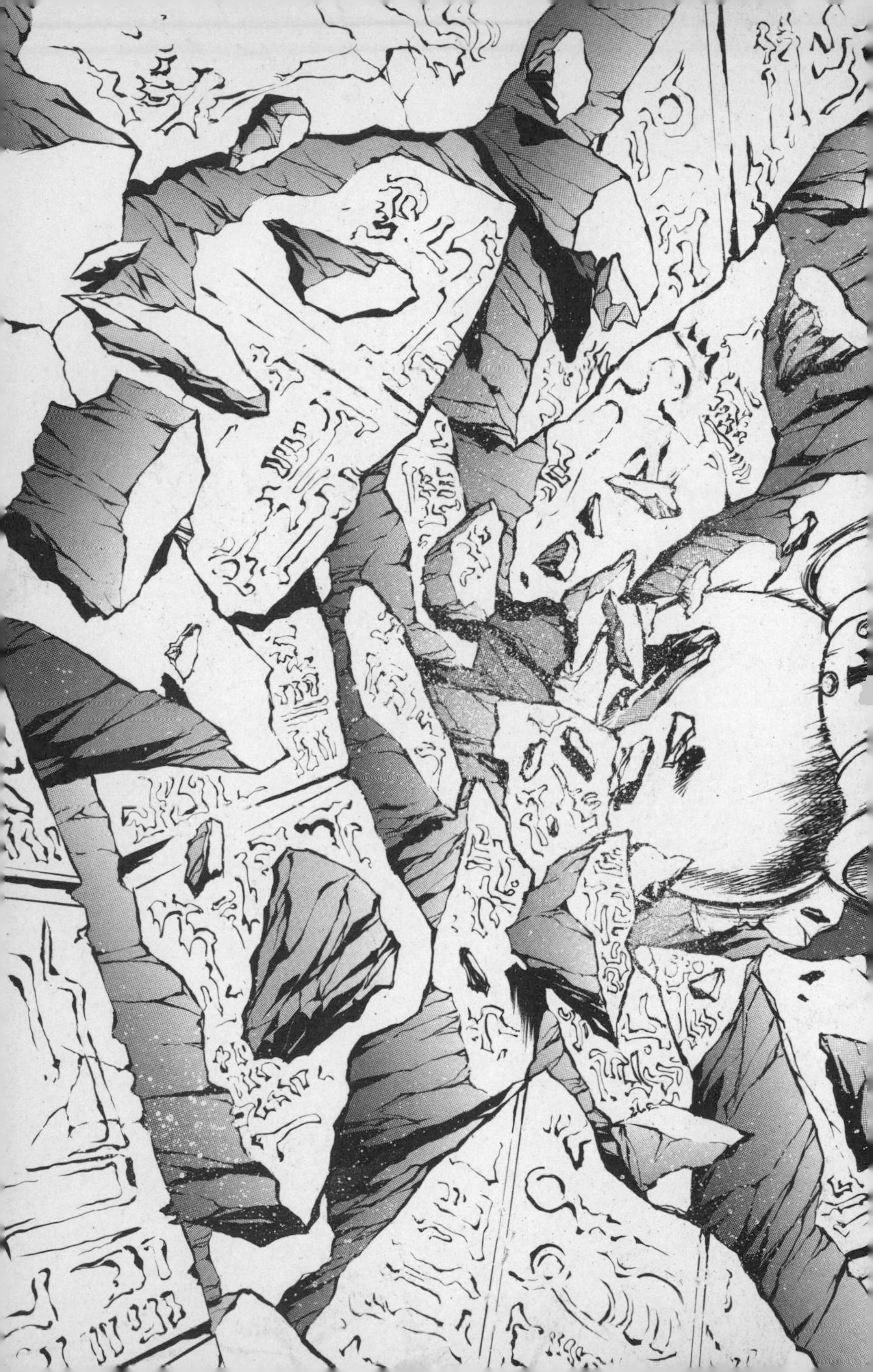

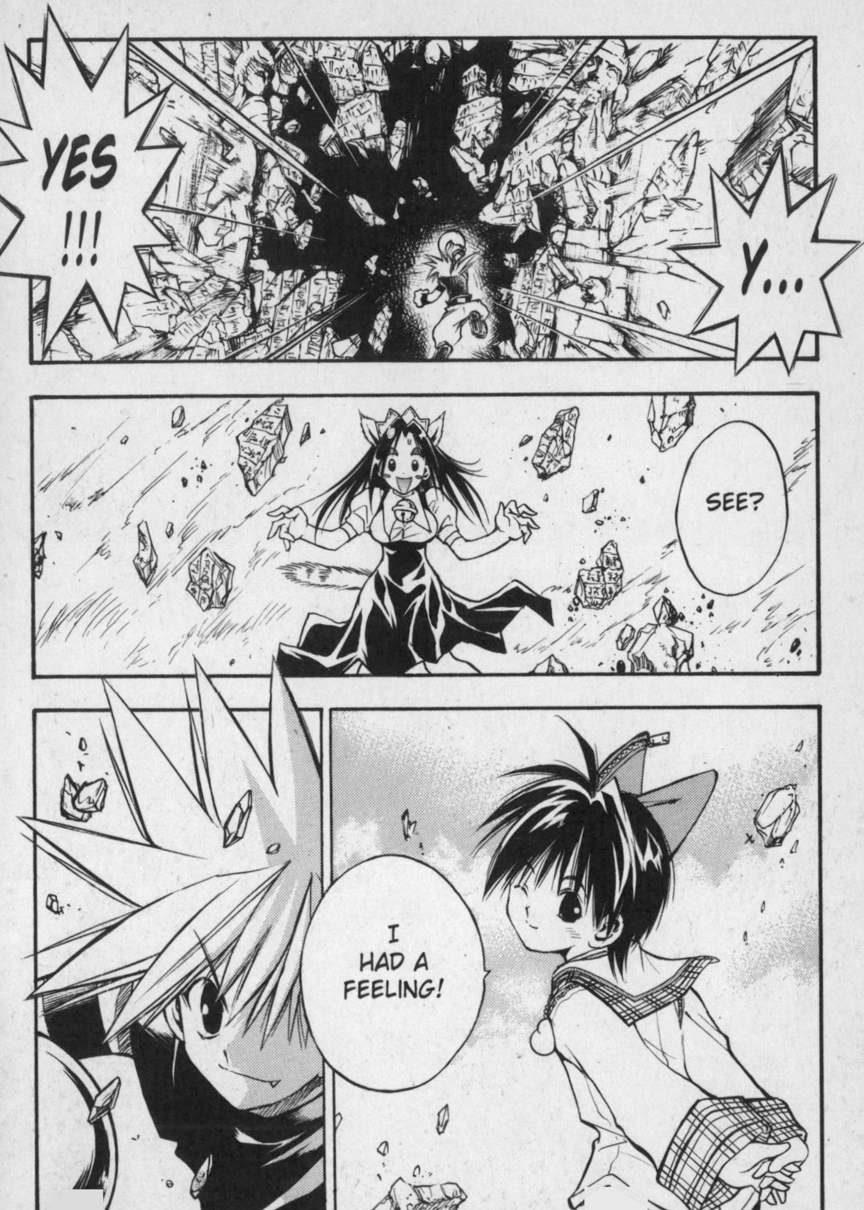
Y...
YES !!!
SEE?
I HAD A FEELING!

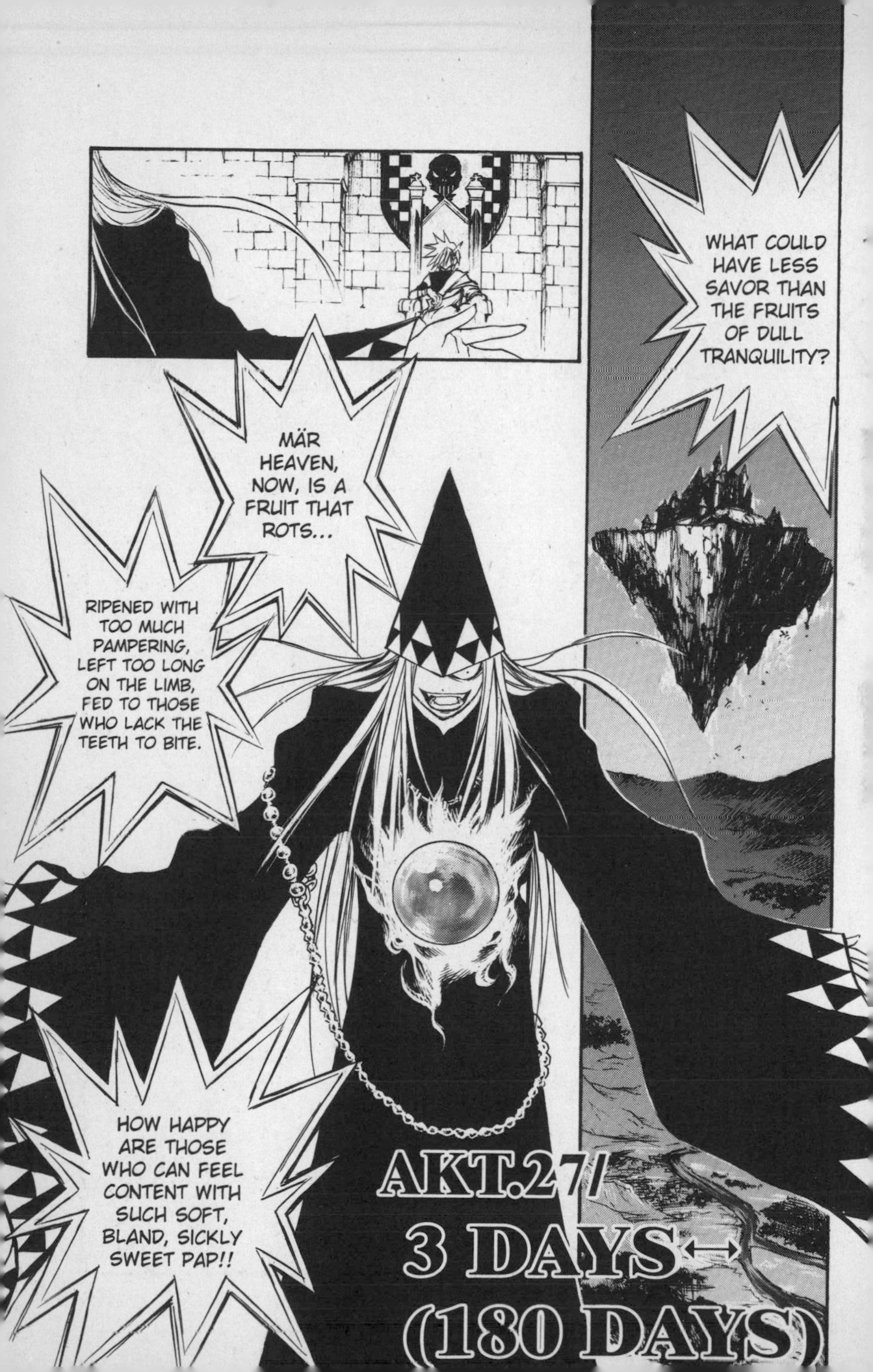
WHAT COULD HAVE LESS SAVOR THAN THE FRUITS OF DULL TRANQUILITY?
MÄR HEAVEN, NOW, IS A FRUIT THAT ROTS...
RIPENED WITH TOO MUCH PAMPERING, LEFT TOO LONG ON THE LIMB, FED TO THOSE WHO LACK THE TEETH TO BITE.
HOW HAPPY ARE THOSE WHO CAN FEEL CONTENT WITH SUCH SOFT, BLAND, SICKLY SWEET PAP!!
AKT.27/
3 DAYS↔
(180 DAYS)

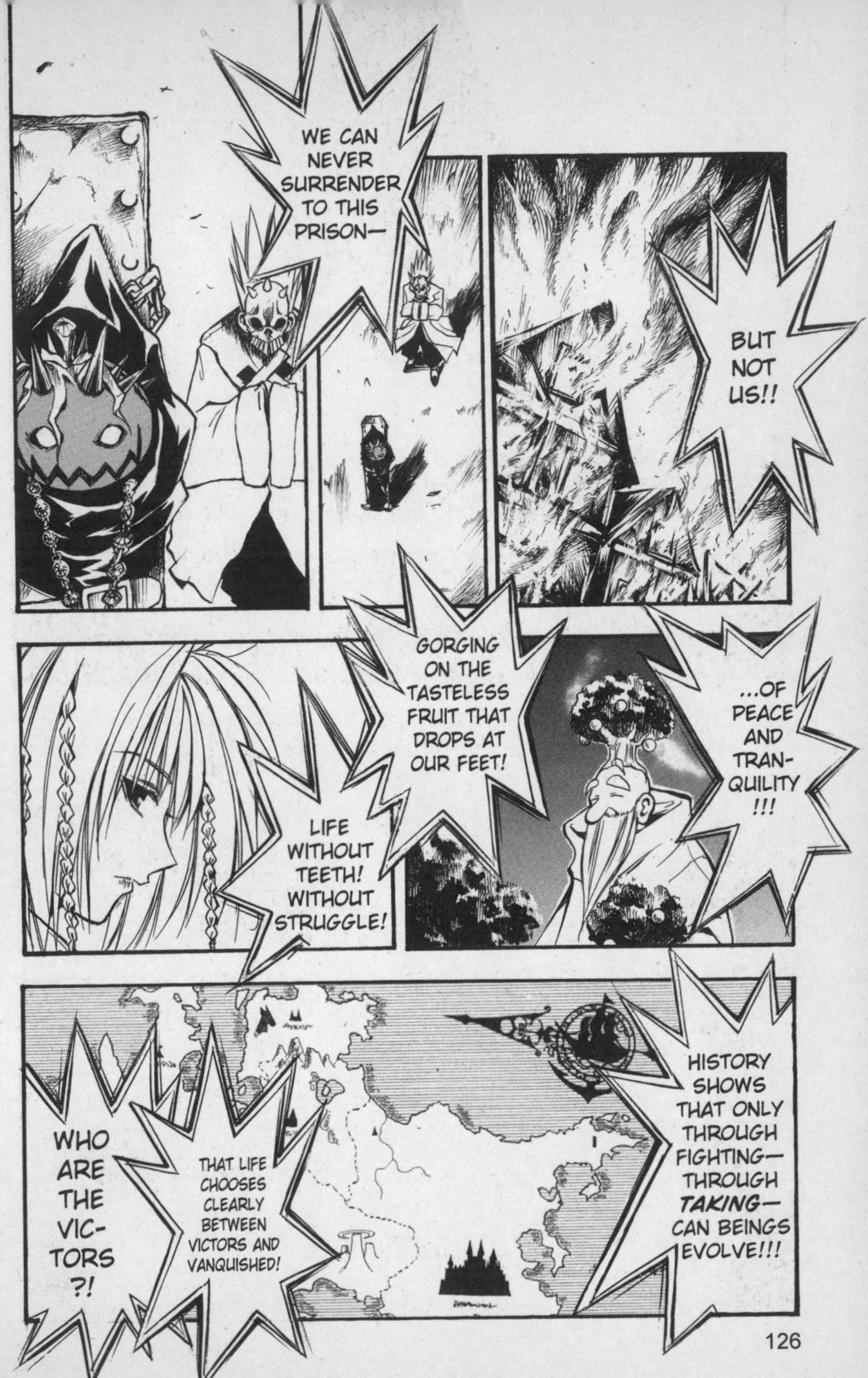
BUT NOT US!!
WE CAN NEVER SURRENDER TO THIS PRISON—
...OF PEACE AND TRAN-QUILITY!!!
GORGING ON THE TASTELESS FRUIT THAT DROPS AT OUR FEET!
LIFE WITHOUT TEETH! WITHOUT STRUGGLE!
HISTORY SHOWS THAT ONLY THROUGH FIGHTING— THROUGH *TAKING*— CAN BEINGS EVOLVE!!!
THAT LIFE CHOOSES CLEARLY BETWEEN VICTORS AND VANQUISHED!
WHO ARE THE VIC-TORS?!

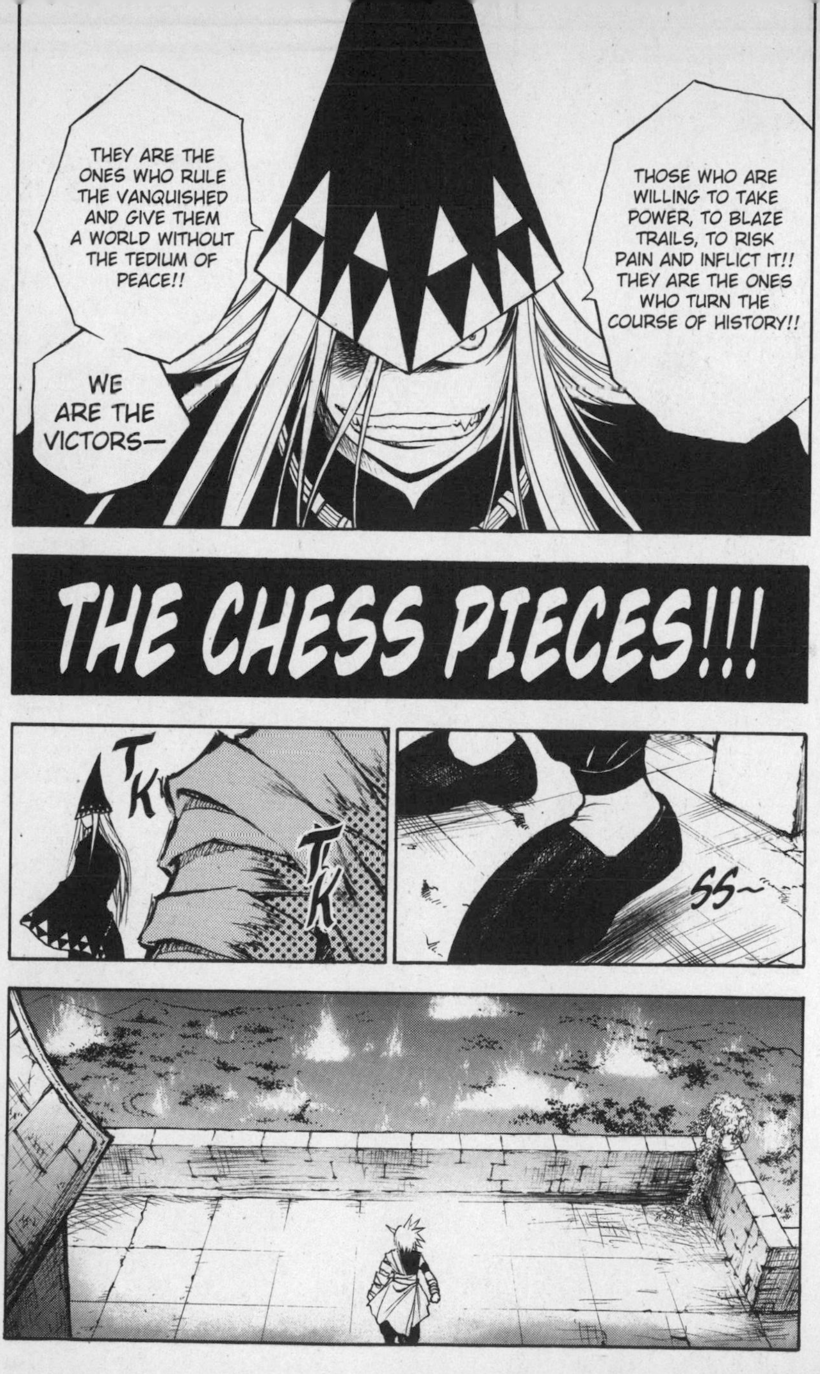
THOSE WHO ARE WILLING TO TAKE POWER, TO BLAZE TRAILS, TO RISK PAIN AND INFLICT IT!! THEY ARE THE ONES WHO TURN THE COURSE OF HISTORY!!
THEY ARE THE ONES WHO RULE THE VANQUISHED AND GIVE THEM A WORLD WITHOUT THE TEDIUM OF PEACE!!
WE ARE THE VICTORS—
THE CHESS PIECES!!!
SS~
TK
TK

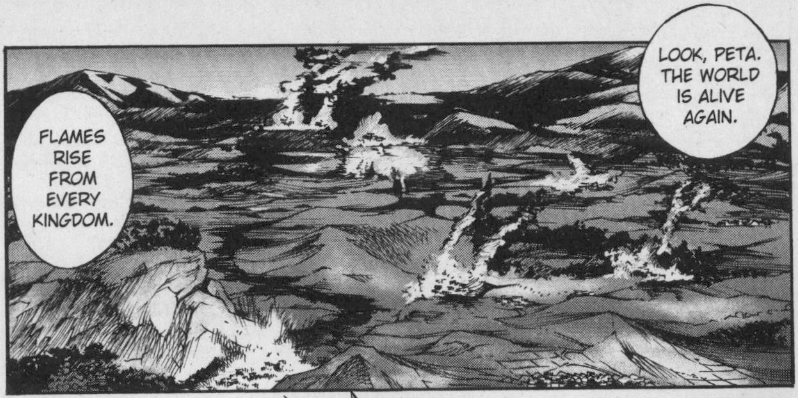
LOOK, PETA. THE WORLD IS ALIVE AGAIN.
FLAMES RISE FROM EVERY KINGDOM.

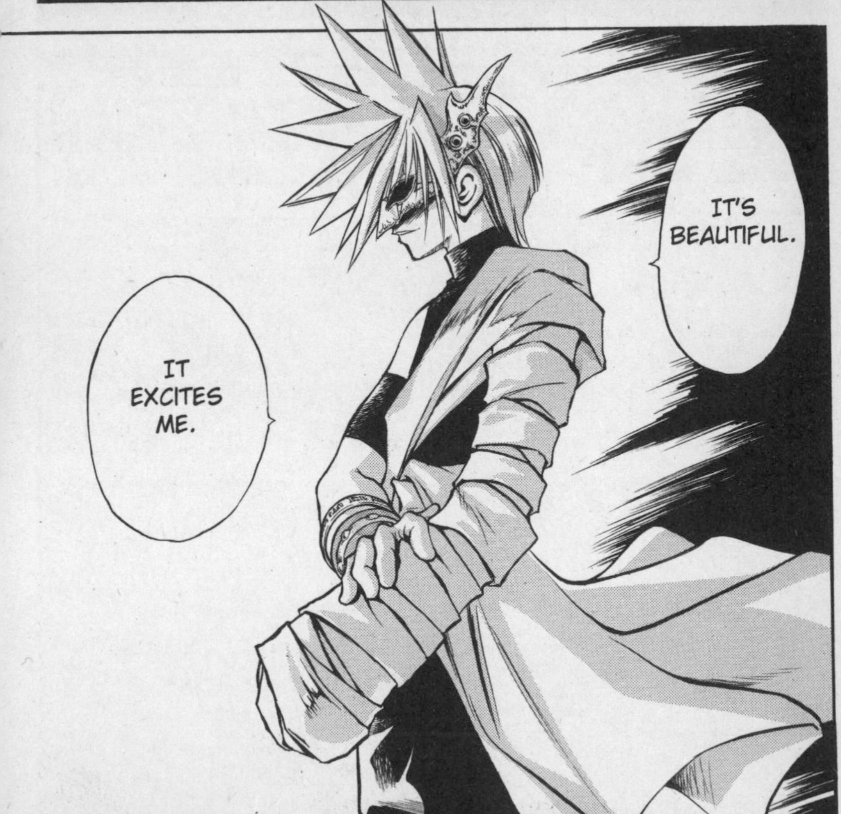
IT'S BEAUTIFUL.
IT EXCITES ME.

BUT WOULDN'T IT BE EVEN MORE FUN...
IF A FOE EMERGED TO BARE ITS FANGS AGAINST US, AS IN THE TIME OF THE LAST WAR?
SIX YEARS AGO I LOST TO A MAN NAMED BOSS... BUT I ENJOYED THE FIGHT.
THIS BOSS DIED AT MY HAND, I HEAR.
WILL THE CROSS GUARD CHALLENGE ME TO ANOTHER BATTLE SUCH AS THAT...?
ANOTHER OUTLANDER WILL MAKE THINGS INTERESTING.
I HOPE THEY FIND ONE WORTHY OF US...

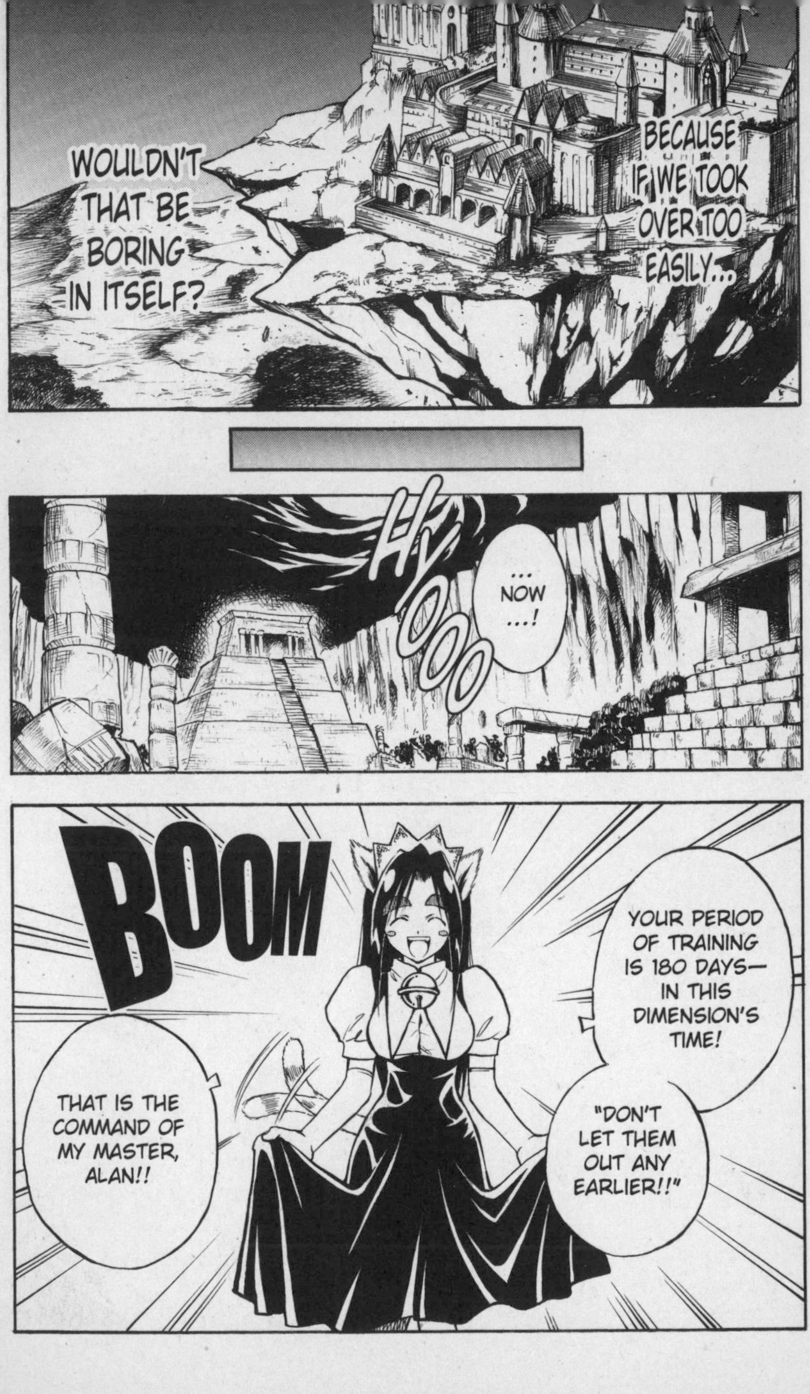
BECAUSE IF WE TOOK OVER TOO EASILY...
WOULDN'T THAT BE BORING IN ITSELF?
... NOW ...!
HYOOO
YOUR PERIOD OF TRAINING IS 180 DAYS— IN THIS DIMENSION'S TIME!
"DON'T LET THEM OUT ANY EARLIER!!"
BOOM
THAT IS THE COMMAND OF MY MASTER, ALAN!!

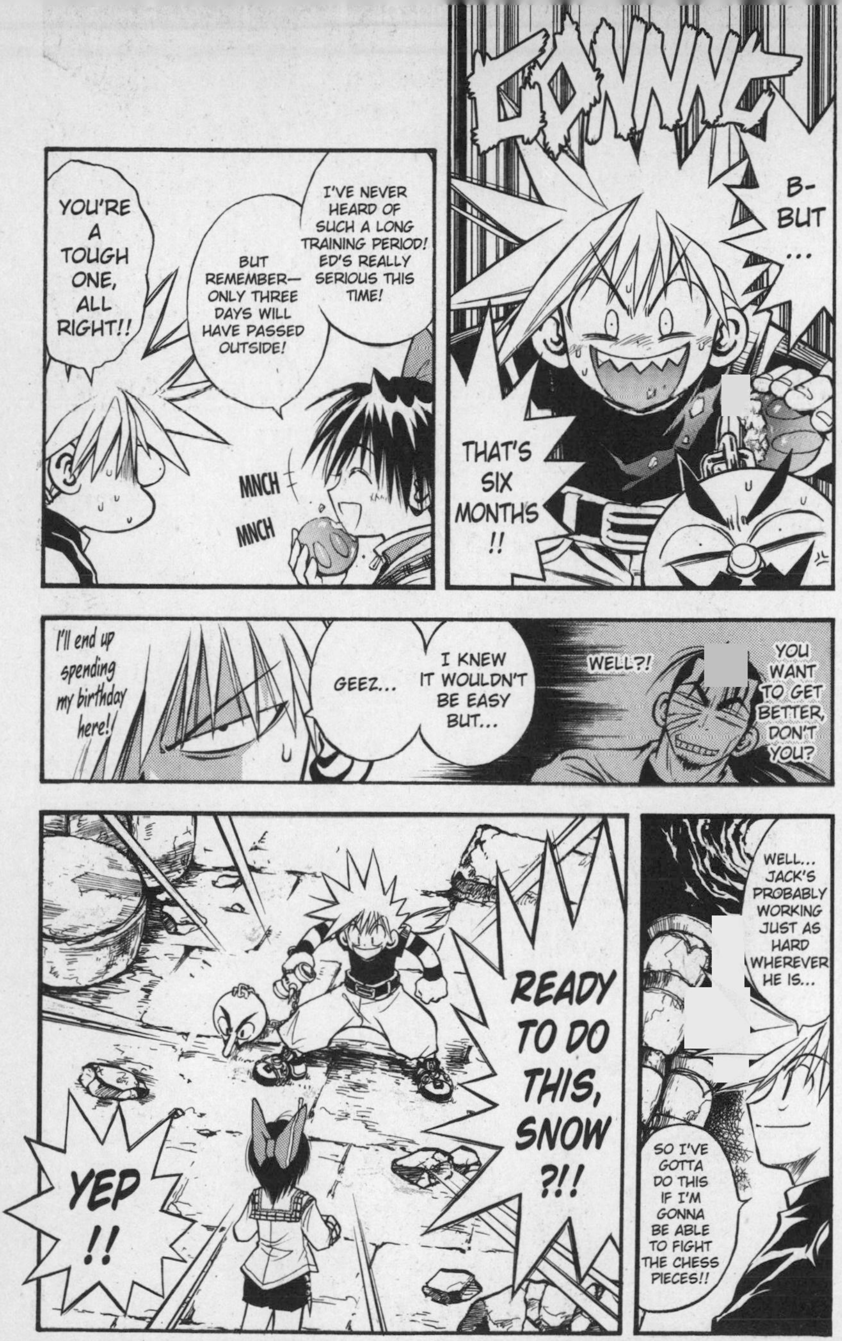
GONNNG
B-BUT...
THAT'S SIX MONTHS!!
I'VE NEVER HEARD OF SUCH A LONG TRAINING PERIOD! ED'S REALLY SERIOUS THIS TIME!
BUT REMEMBER—ONLY THREE DAYS WILL HAVE PASSED OUTSIDE!
YOU'RE A TOUGH ONE, ALL RIGHT!!
MNCH
MNCH
YOU WANT TO GET BETTER, DON'T YOU?
WELL?!
I KNEW IT WOULDN'T BE EASY BUT...
GEEZ...
I'll end up spending my birthday here!
WELL... JACK'S PROBABLY WORKING JUST AS HARD WHEREVER HE IS...
SO I'VE GOTTA DO THIS IF I'M GONNA BE ABLE TO FIGHT THE CHESS PIECES!!
READY TO DO THIS, SNOW?!!
YEP!!

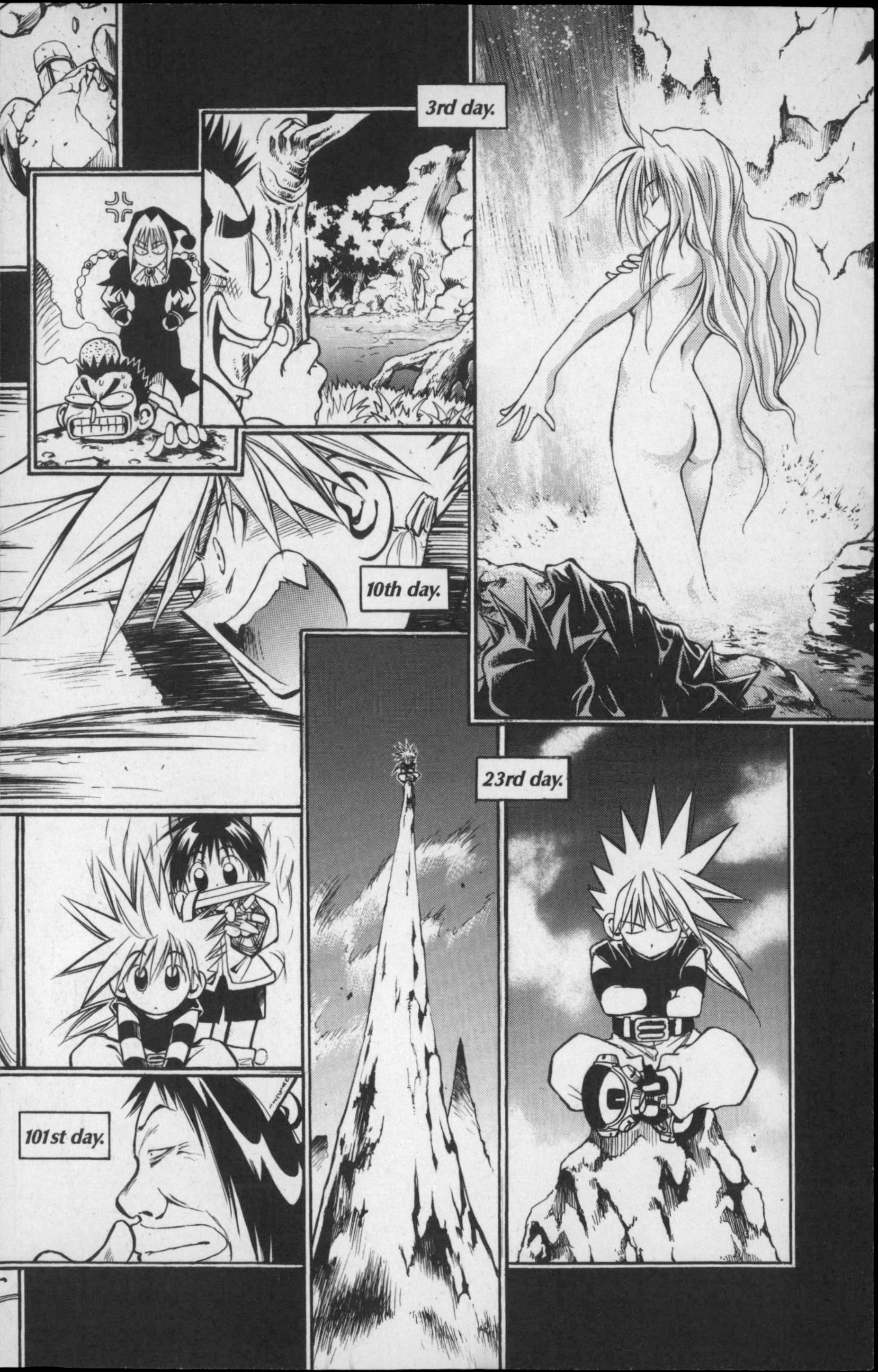
3rd day.
10th day.
23rd day.
101st day.

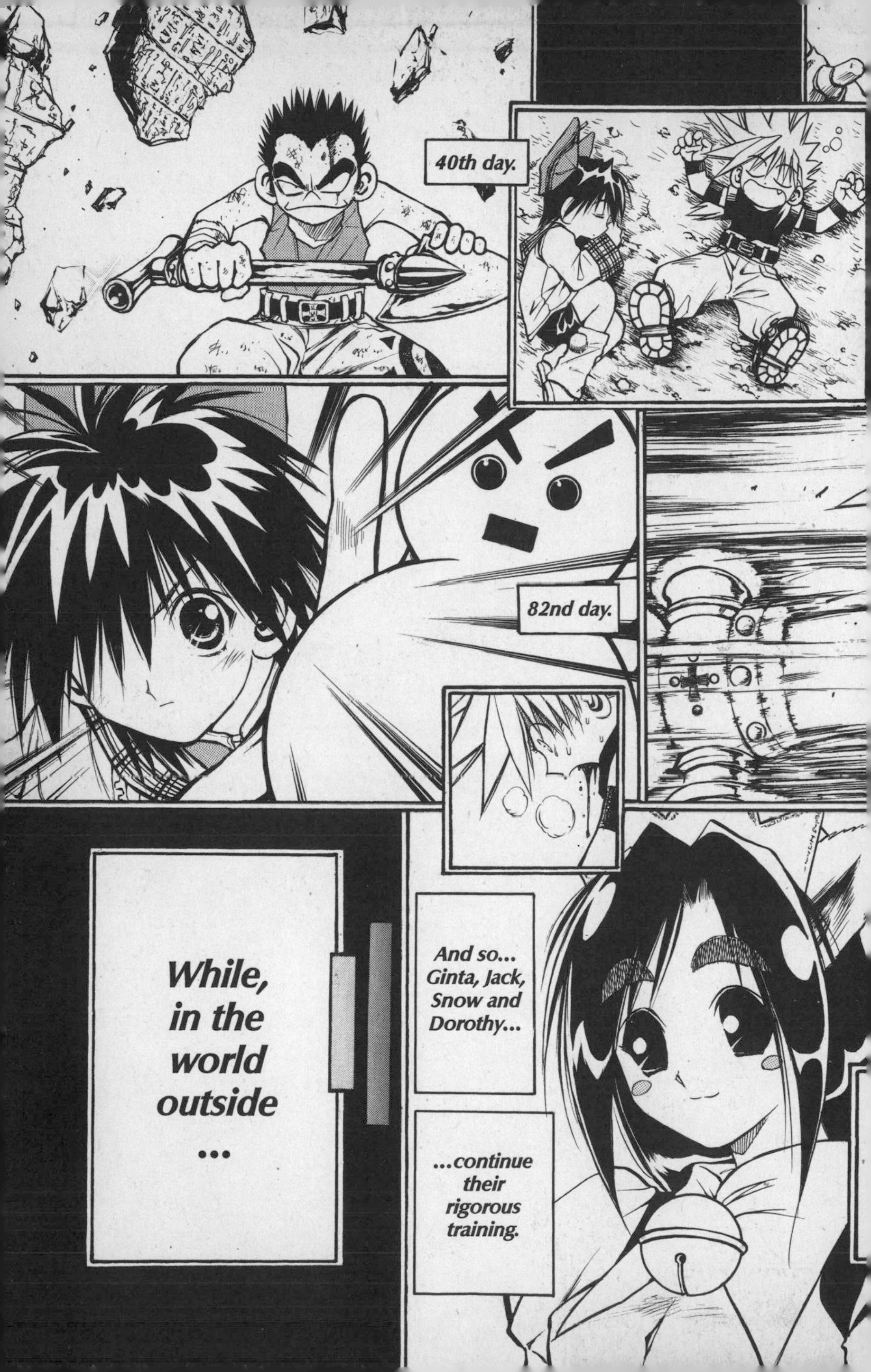
40th day.
82nd day.
And so... Ginta, Jack, Snow and Dorothy...
...continue their rigorous training.
While, in the world outside ...

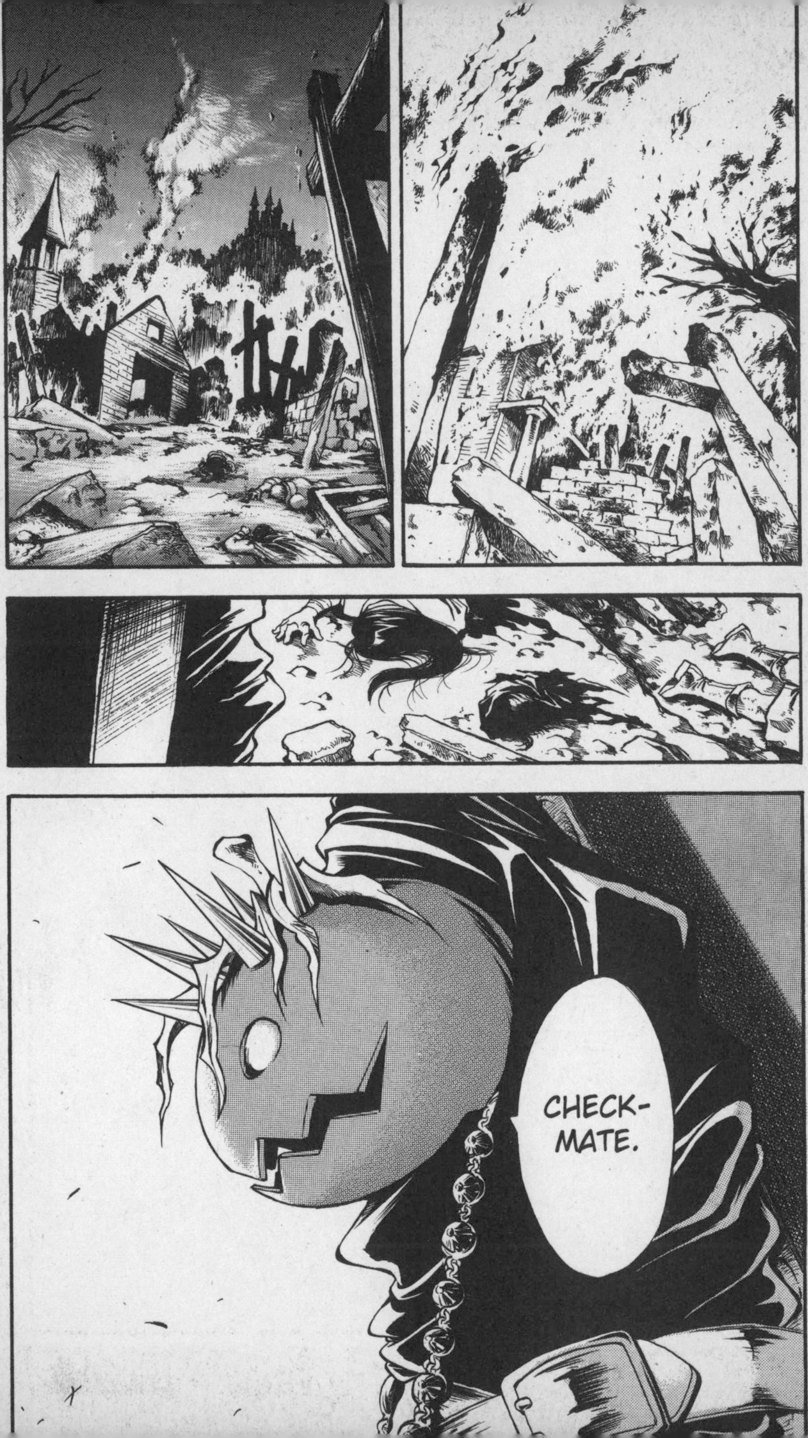
CHECK-
MATE.

...four-
tenths
of all the
land in
Mär
Heaven
falls
to the
conqueror
!!!

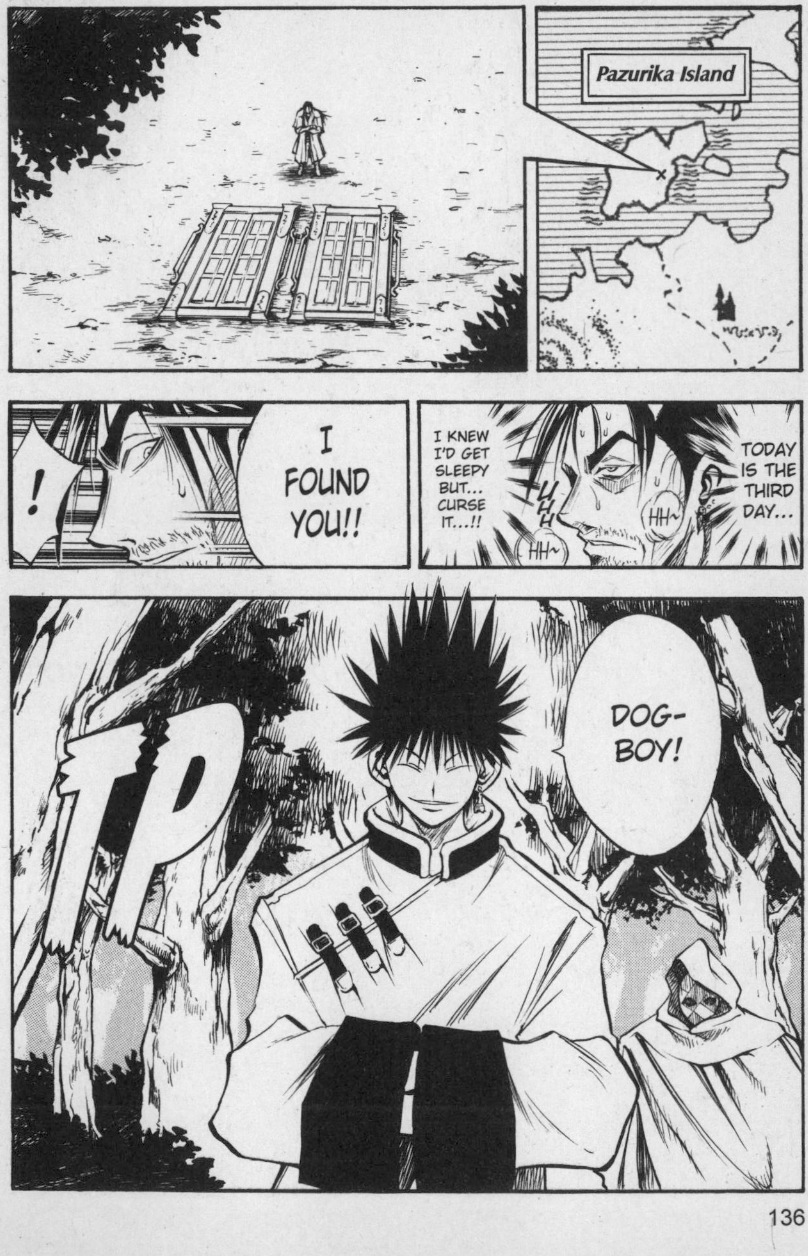
Pazurika Island
TODAY IS THE THIRD DAY...
I KNEW I'D GET SLEEPY BUT... CURSE IT...!!
UHH
HH~
HH~
I FOUND YOU!!
!
DOG-BOY!
TP

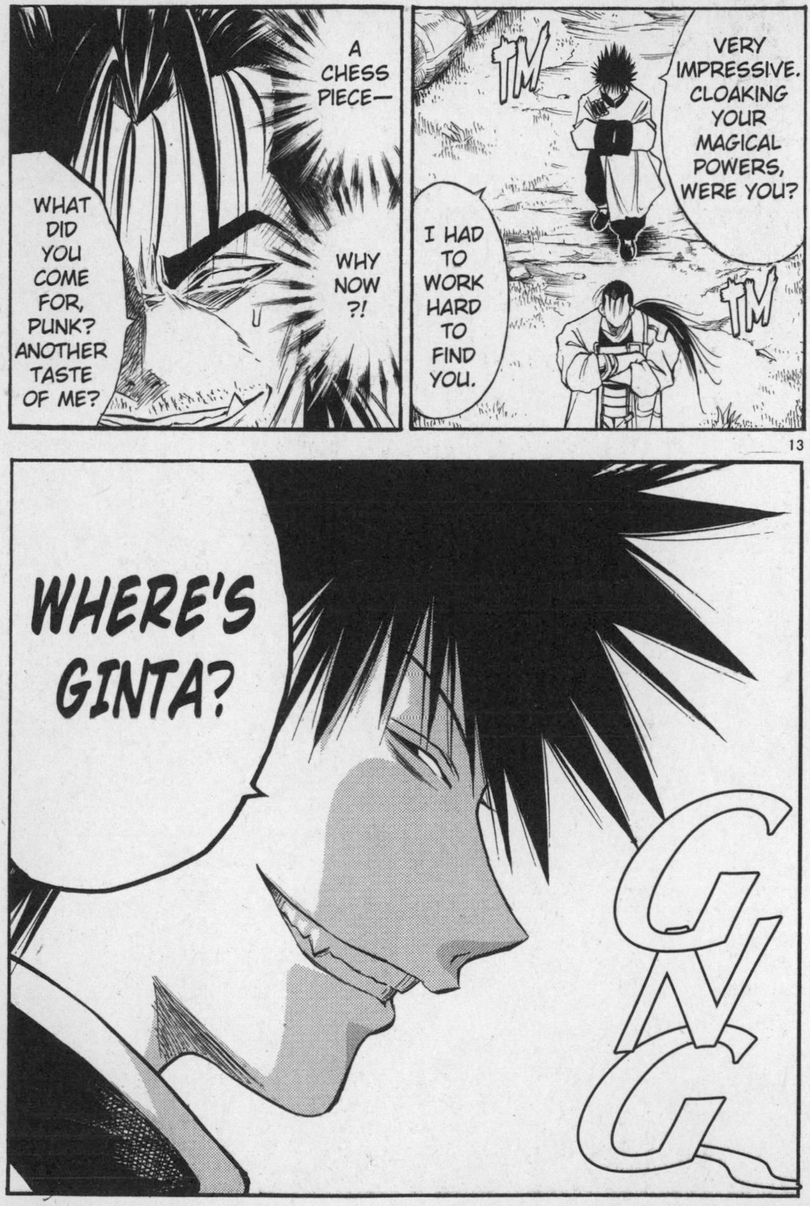
VERY IMPRESSIVE. CLOAKING YOUR MAGICAL POWERS, WERE YOU?
TM
I HAD TO WORK HARD TO FIND YOU.
TM
A CHESS PIECE—
WHY NOW ?!
WHAT DID YOU COME FOR, PUNK? ANOTHER TASTE OF ME?
WHERE'S GINTA?
GNG

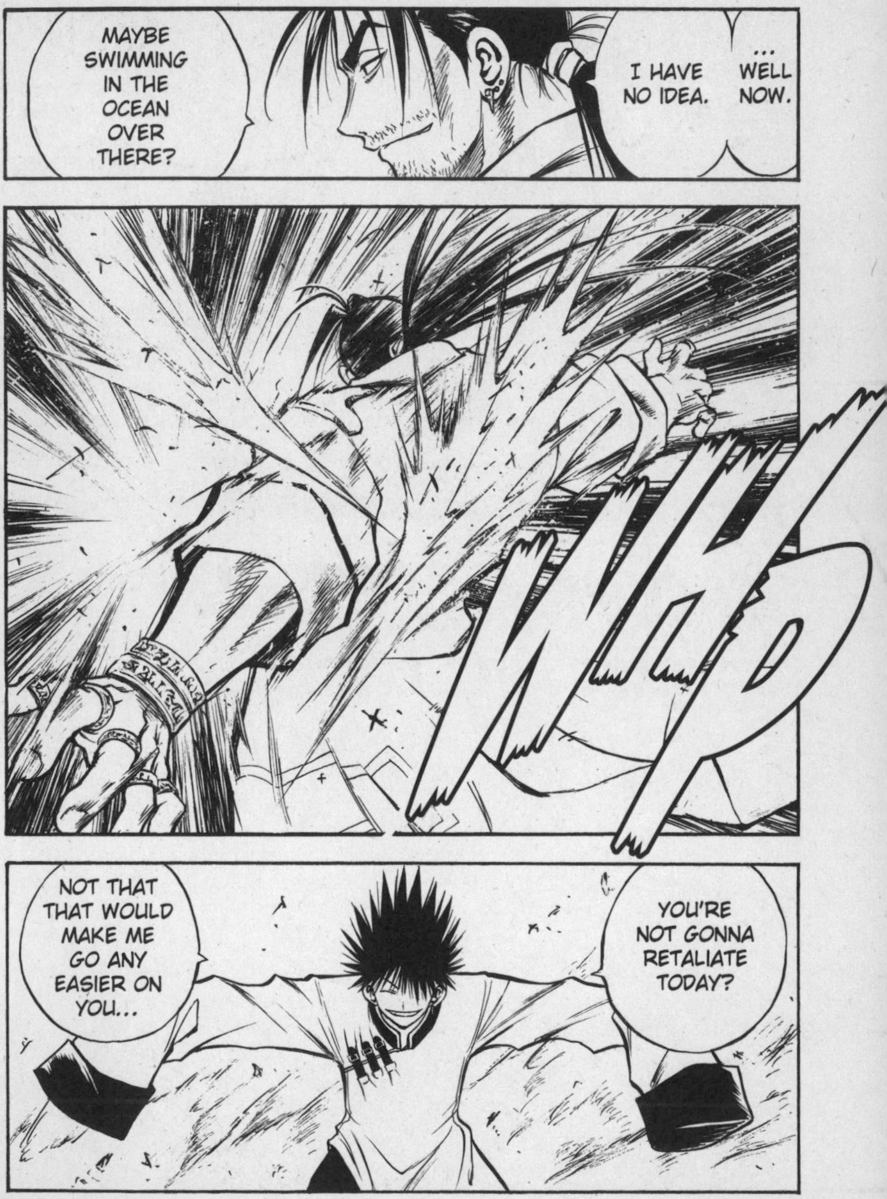

... WELL NOW.
I HAVE NO IDEA.
MAYBE SWIMMING IN THE OCEAN OVER THERE?
WHIP
YOU'RE NOT GONNA RETALIATE TODAY?
NOT THAT THAT WOULD MAKE ME GO ANY EASIER ON YOU...

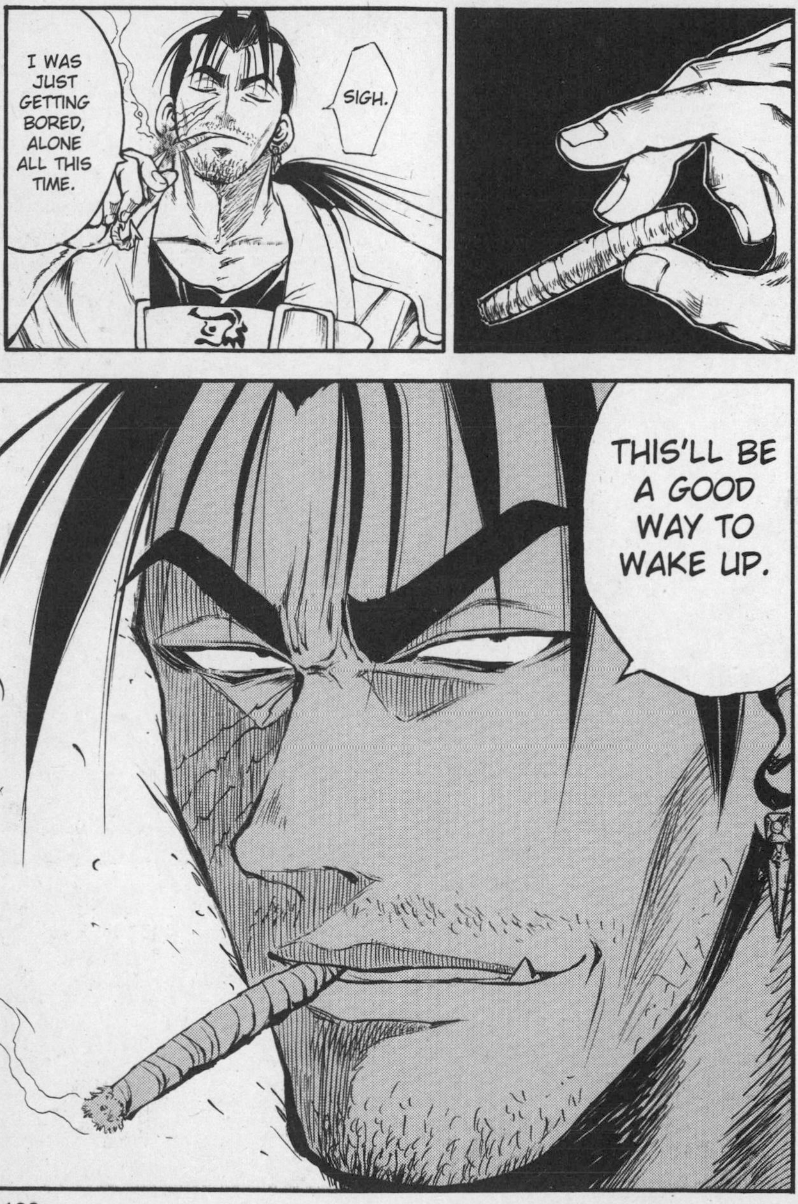
SIGH.
I WAS JUST GETTING BORED, ALONE ALL THIS TIME.
THIS'LL BE A GOOD WAY TO WAKE UP.

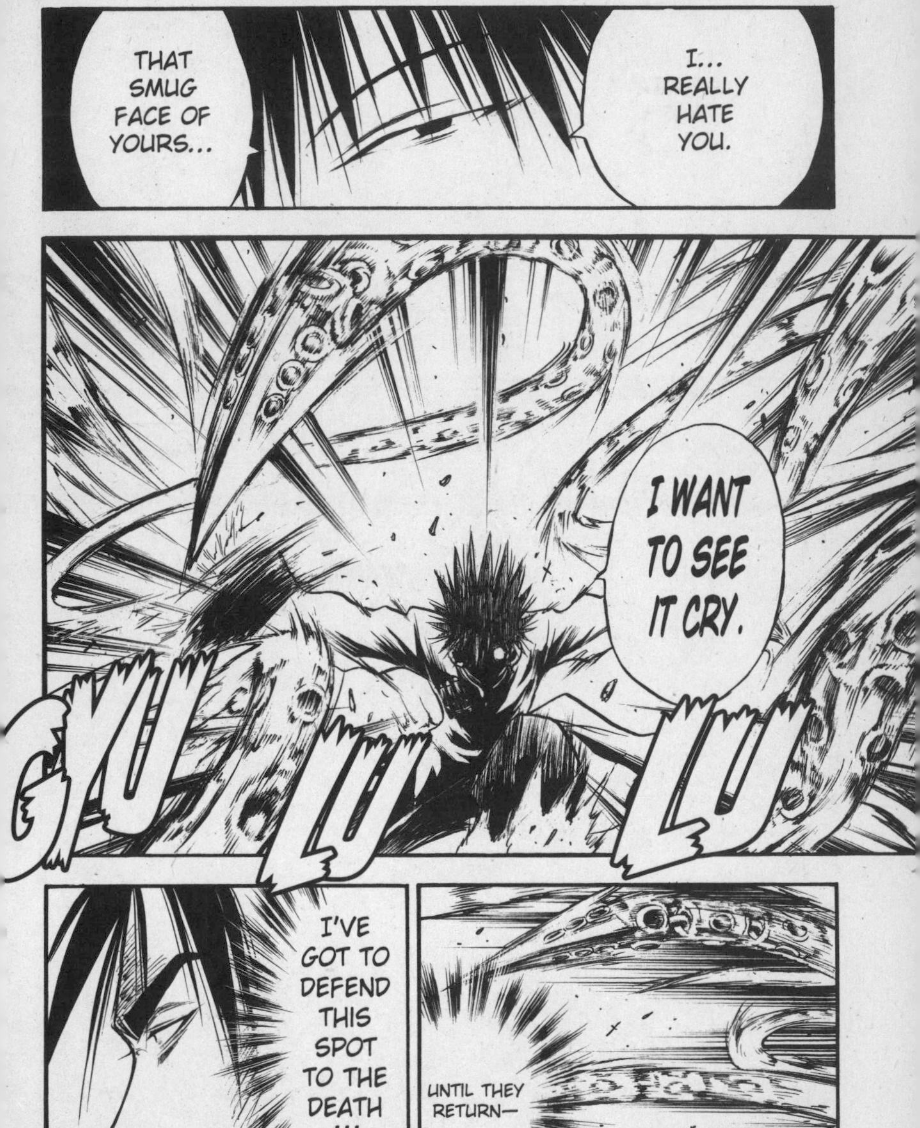
I... REALLY HATE YOU.
THAT SMUG FACE OF YOURS...
I WANT TO SEE IT CRY.
GYU LU LU
UNTIL THEY RETURN—
I'VE GOT TO DEFEND THIS SPOT TO THE DEATH !!!

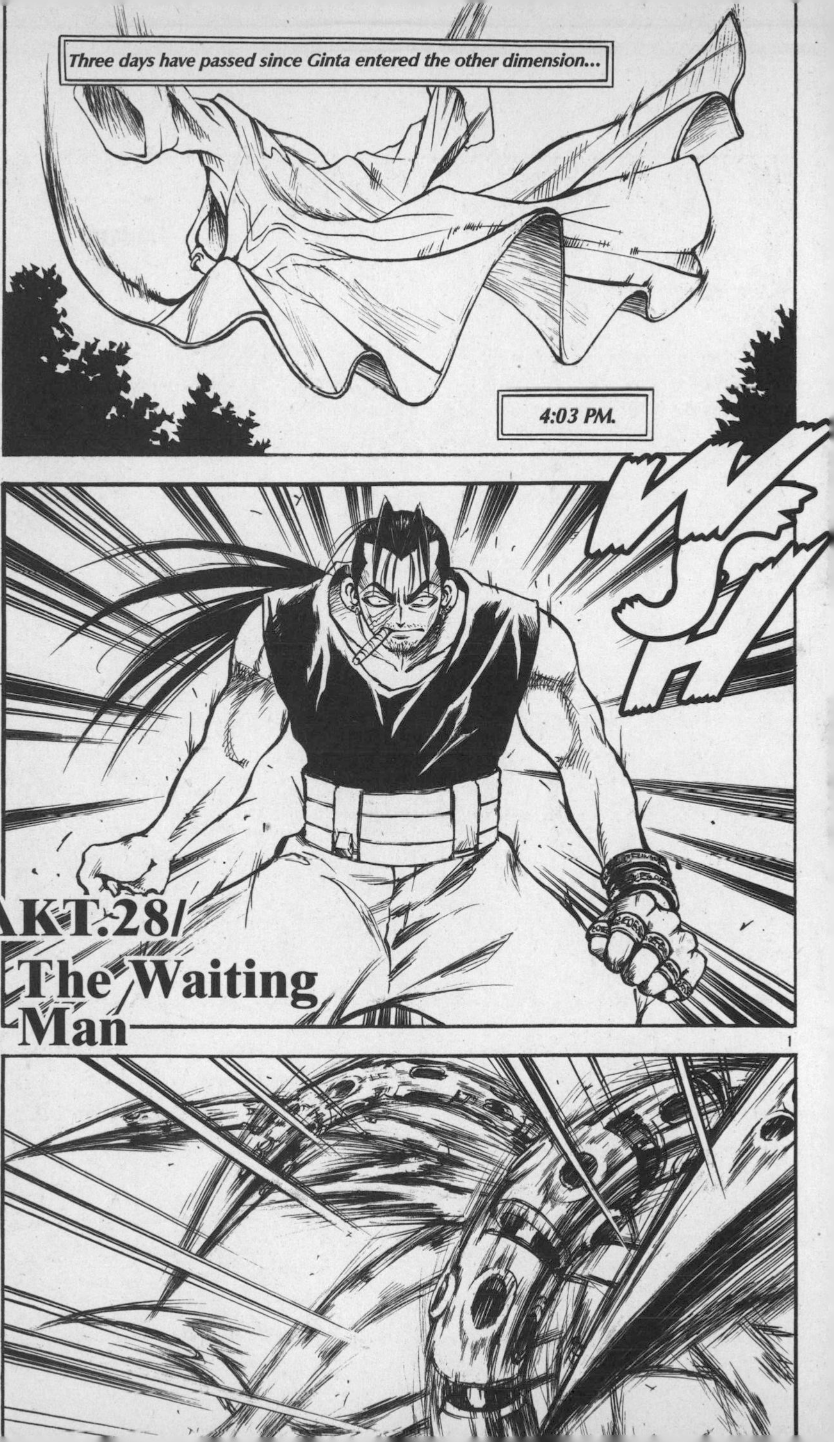
Three days have passed since Ginta entered the other dimension...
4:03 PM.
WSH

AKT.28/ The Waiting Man

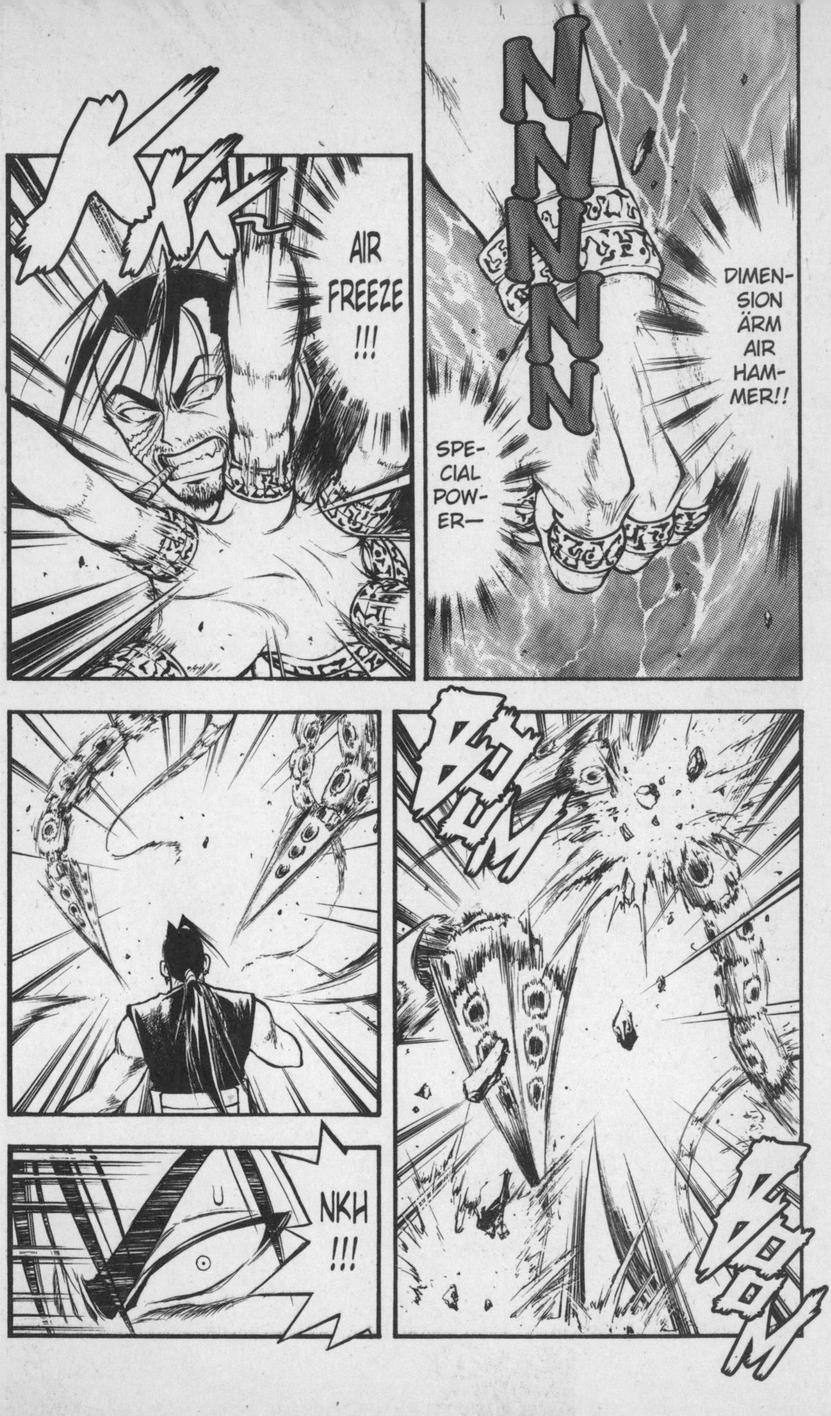
NNNNN
SPECIAL POWER—
DIMENSION ÄRM AIR HAMMER!!
AIR FREEZE!!!
BOOM
BOOOM
NKH!!!

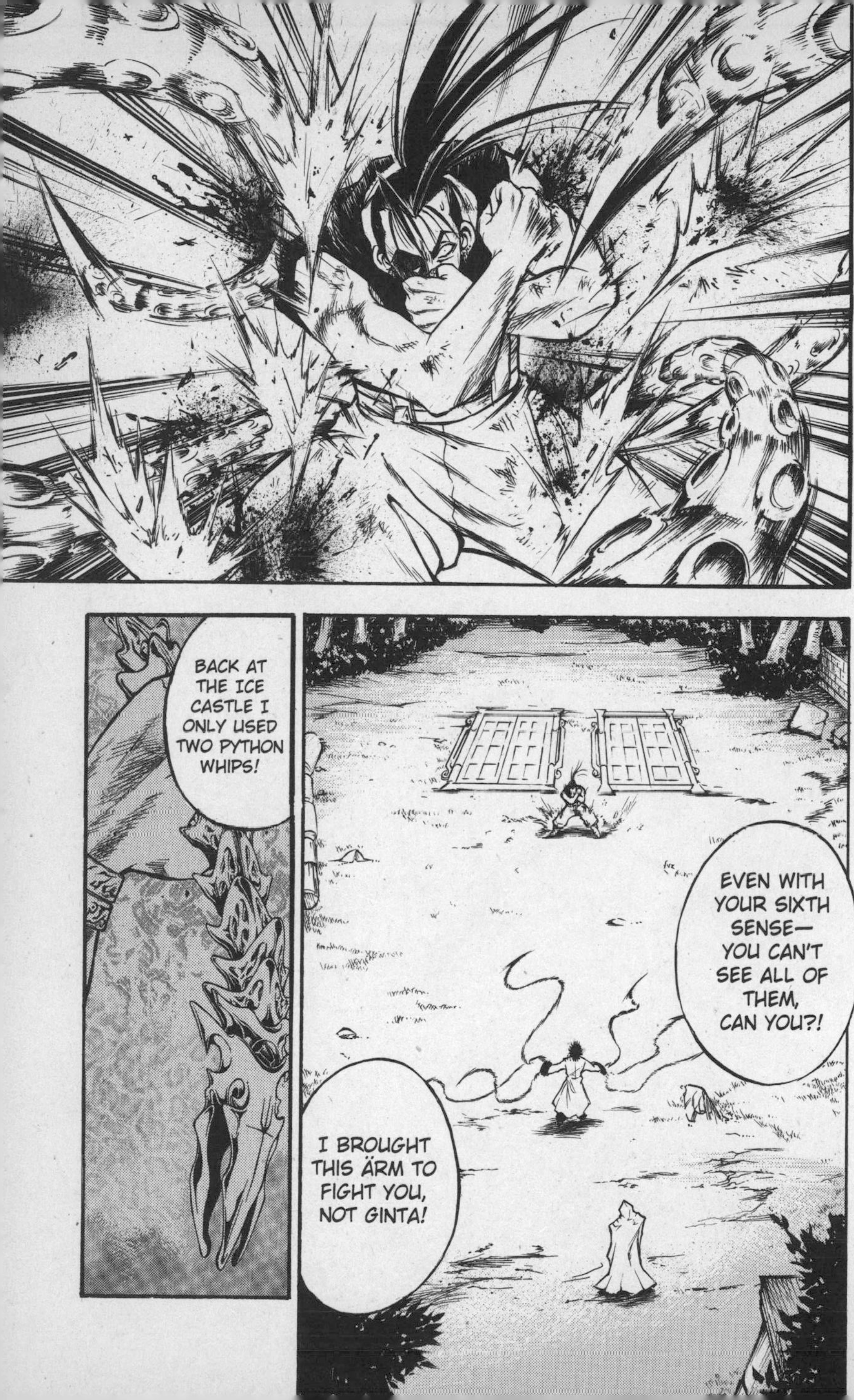
EVEN WITH YOUR SIXTH SENSE— YOU CAN'T SEE ALL OF THEM, CAN YOU?!
I BROUGHT THIS ÄRM TO FIGHT YOU, NOT GINTA!
BACK AT THE ICE CASTLE I ONLY USED TWO PYTHON WHIPS!

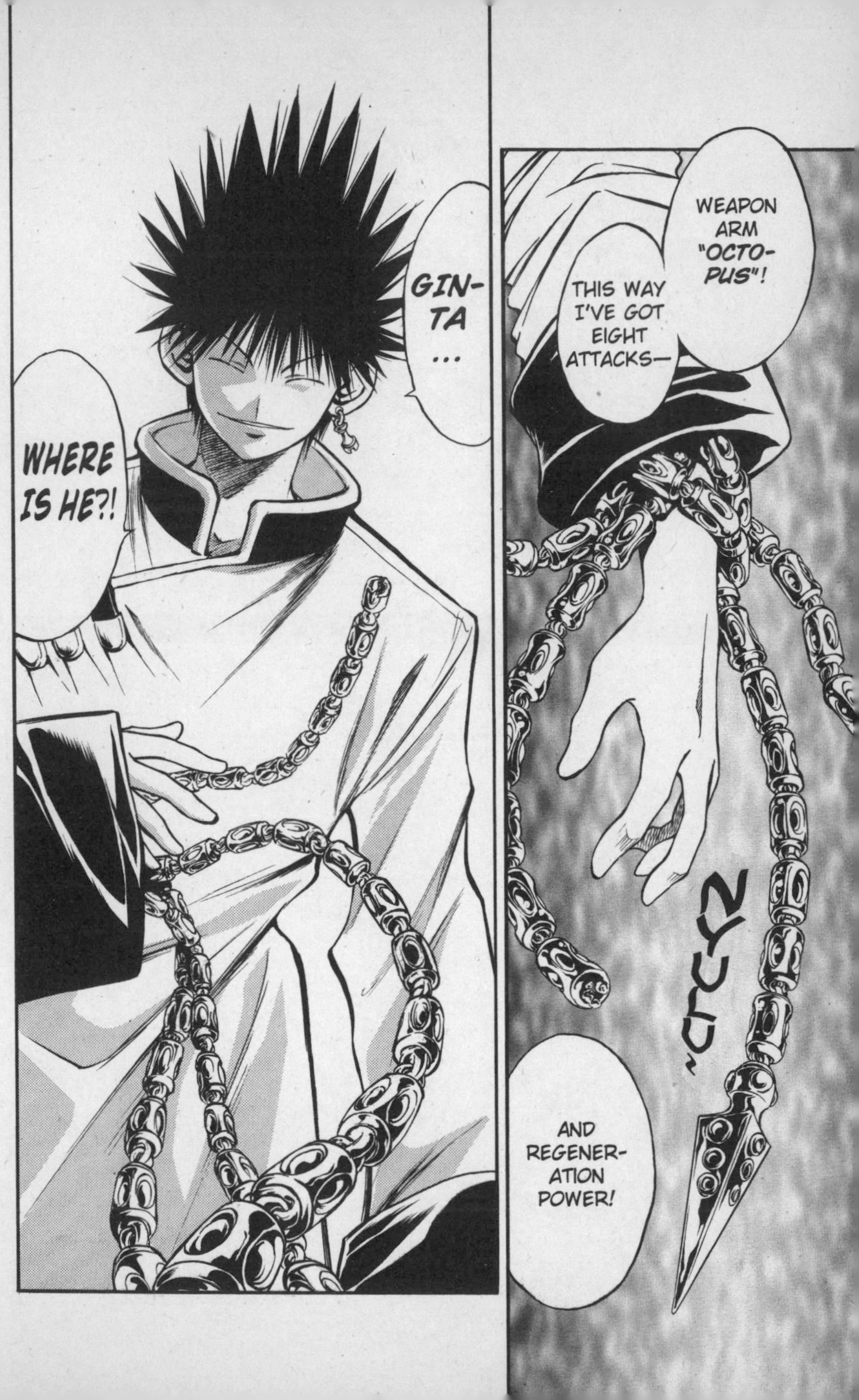
WEAPON ARM "OCTO-PUS"!
THIS WAY I'VE GOT EIGHT ATTACKS—
NYUU
AND REGENER-ATION POWER!
GIN-TA ...
WHERE IS HE?!

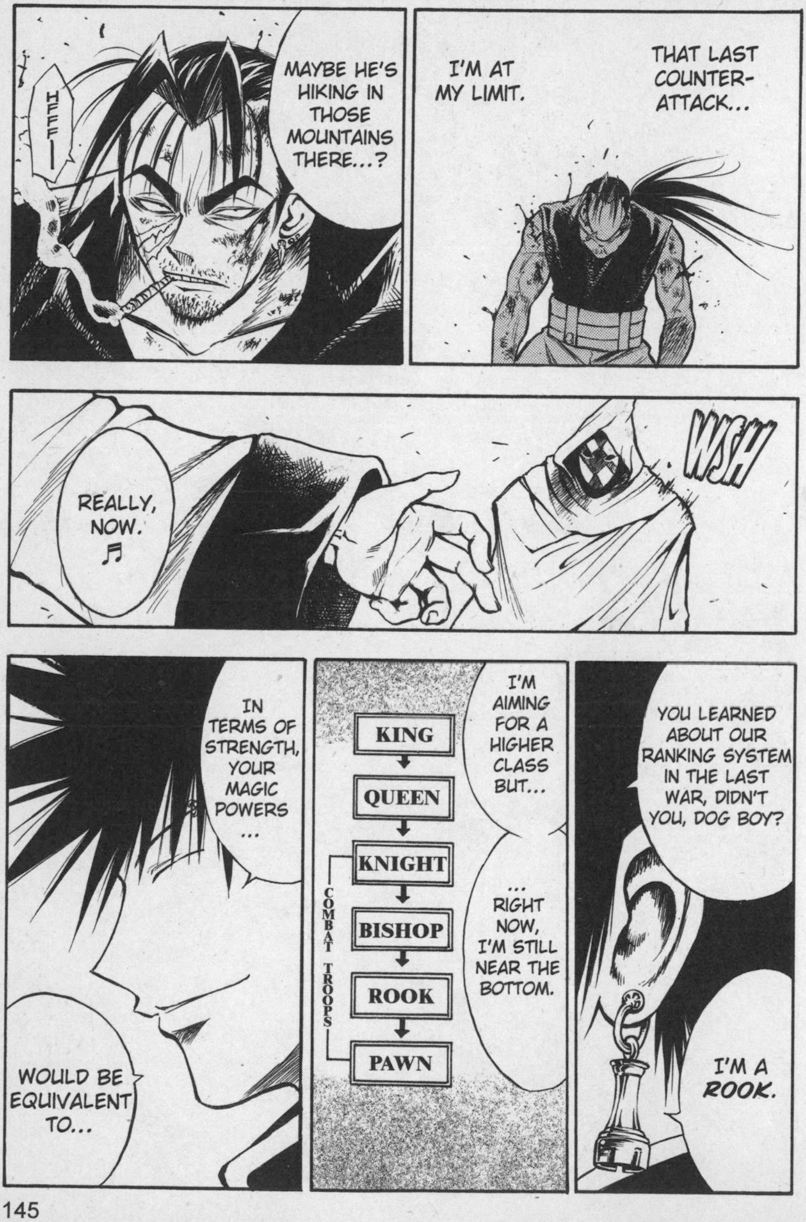
THAT LAST COUNTER-ATTACK...
I'M AT MY LIMIT.
MAYBE HE'S HIKING IN THOSE MOUNTAINS THERE...?
HFF!
WSH
REALLY, NOW. ♬
YOU LEARNED ABOUT OUR RANKING SYSTEM IN THE LAST WAR, DIDN'T YOU, DOG BOY?
I'M A *ROOK.*
I'M AIMING FOR A HIGHER CLASS BUT...
... RIGHT NOW, I'M STILL NEAR THE BOTTOM.
KING
QUEEN
KNIGHT
BISHOP
ROOK
PAWN
COMBAT TROOPS
IN TERMS OF STRENGTH, YOUR MAGIC POWERS ...
WOULD BE EQUIVALENT TO...

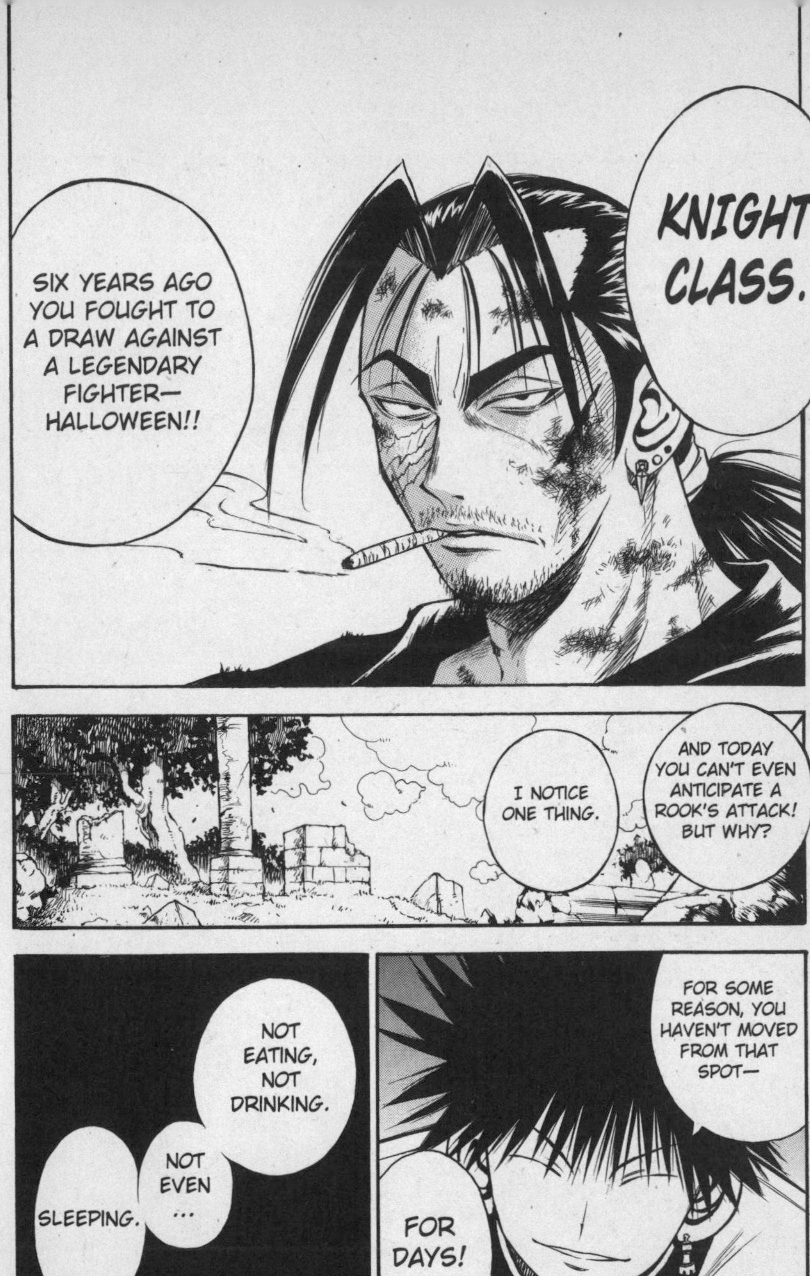
KNIGHT CLASS.
SIX YEARS AGO YOU FOUGHT TO A DRAW AGAINST A LEGENDARY FIGHTER—HALLOWEEN!!
AND TODAY YOU CAN'T EVEN ANTICIPATE A ROOK'S ATTACK! BUT WHY?
I NOTICE ONE THING.
FOR SOME REASON, YOU HAVEN'T MOVED FROM THAT SPOT—
FOR DAYS!
NOT EATING, NOT DRINKING.
NOT EVEN...
SLEEPING.

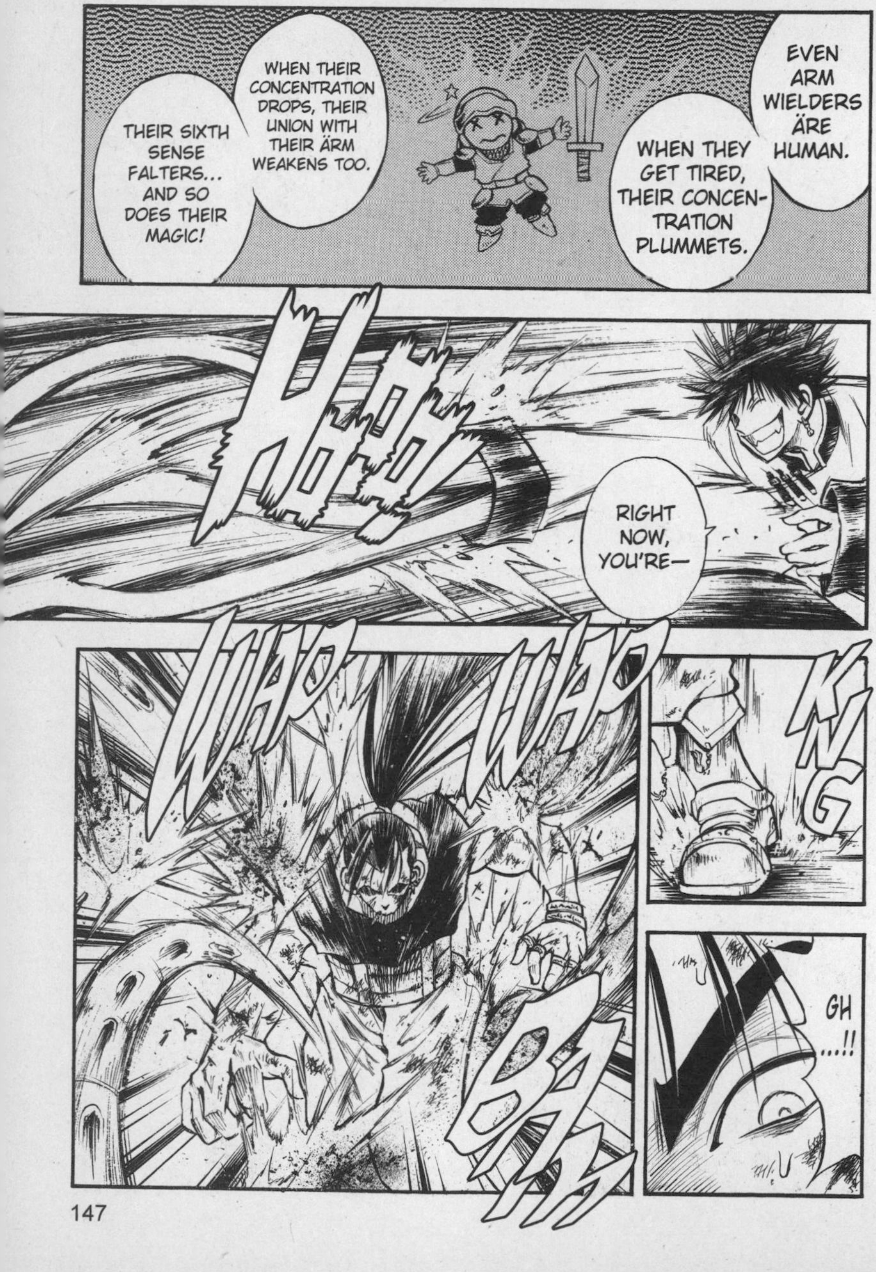
EVEN ARM WIELDERS ÄRE HUMAN.
WHEN THEY GET TIRED, THEIR CONCEN-TRATION PLUMMETS.
WHEN THEIR CONCENTRATION DROPS, THEIR UNION WITH THEIR ÄRM WEAKENS TOO.
THEIR SIXTH SENSE FALTERS... AND SO DOES THEIR MAGIC!
RIGHT NOW, YOU'RE—
GH ...!!
WAP WAP
BAM

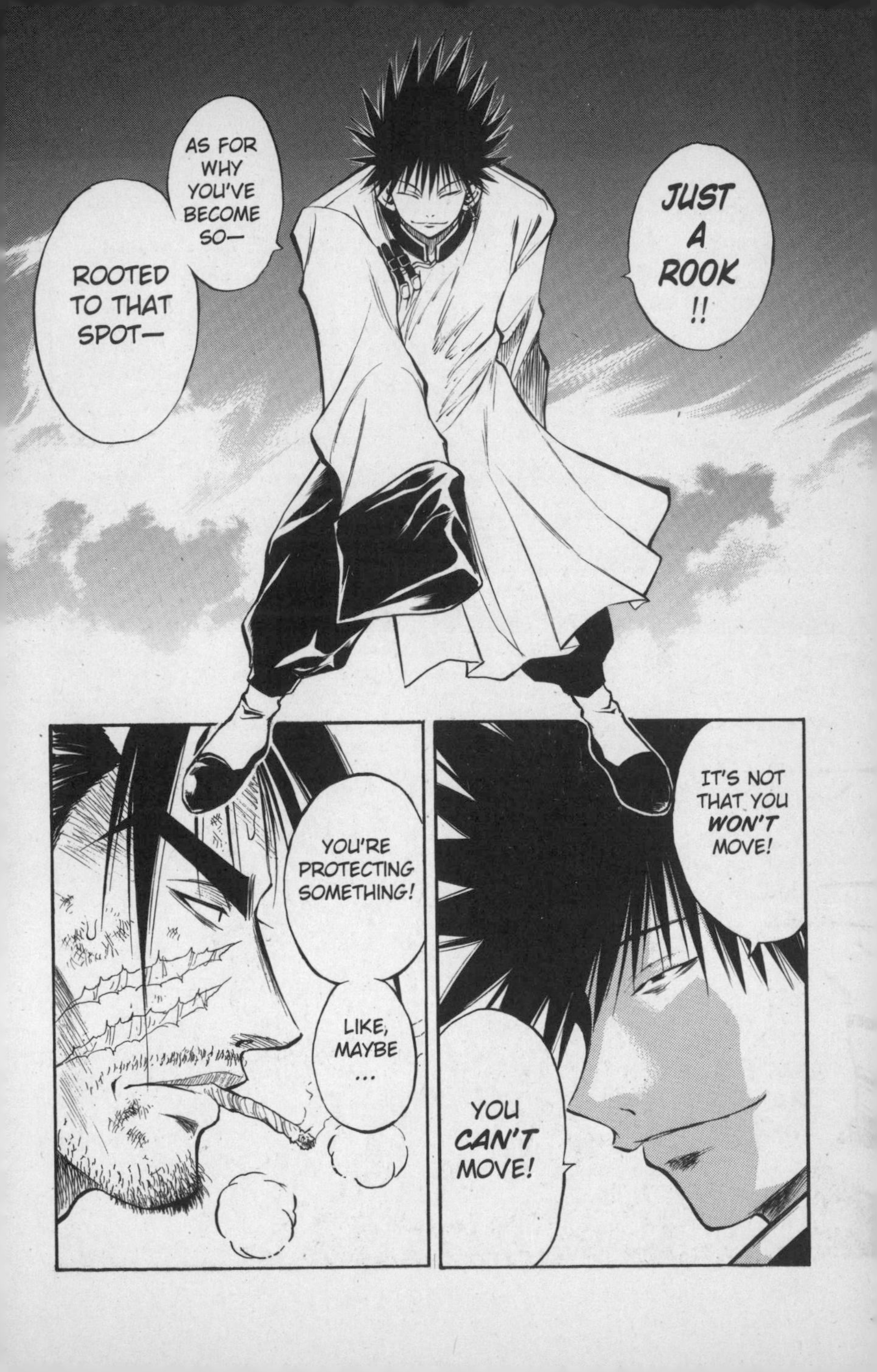
AS FOR WHY YOU'VE BECOME SO—
ROOTED TO THAT SPOT—
JUST A ROOK !!
IT'S NOT THAT YOU *WON'T* MOVE!
YOU *CAN'T* MOVE!
YOU'RE PROTECTING SOMETHING!
LIKE, MAYBE ...

WHAT'S BEHIND YOU THERE—
THOSE DOORS !!!
SH
HEH HEH
RIGHT? ♬
PROUD OF YOURSELF? EVEN A MONKEY COULD FIGURE THAT OUT!
SO WHY DON'T YOU TRY AND OPEN THEM?!
THAT IS... IF YOU CAN BEAT A GUY WHO CAN'T MOVE!!

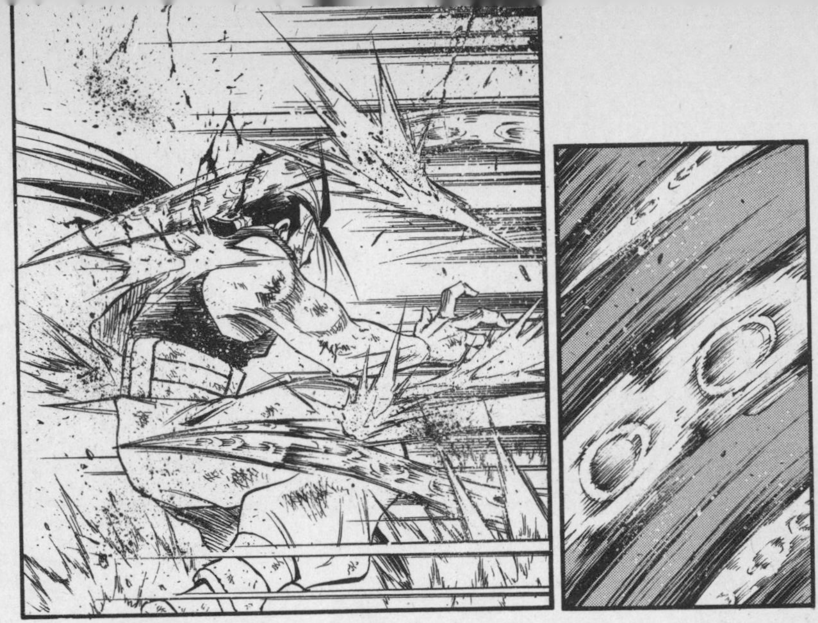

GINTA...

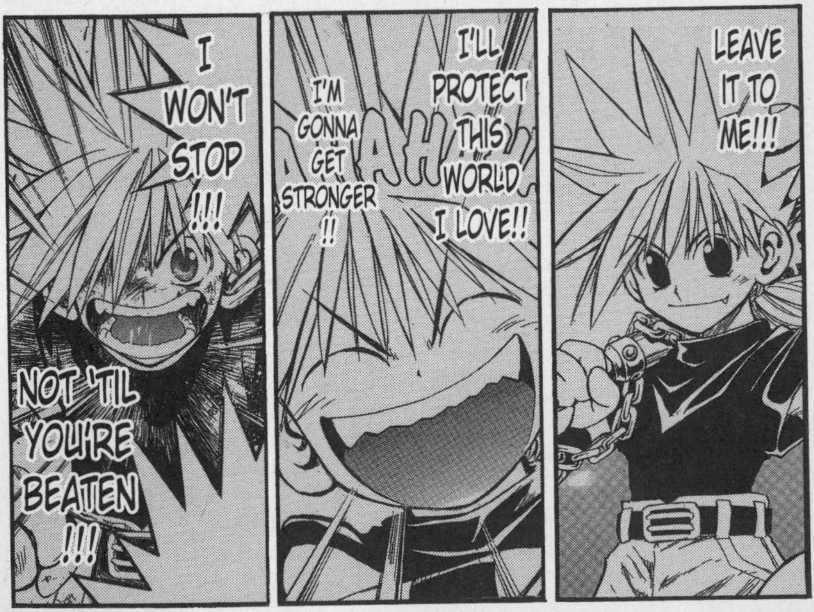

LEAVE IT TO ME!!!
I'LL PROTECT THIS WORLD I LOVE!!
AH
I'M GONNA GET STRONGER!!
I WON'T STOP!!!
NOT 'TIL YOU'RE BEATEN!!!

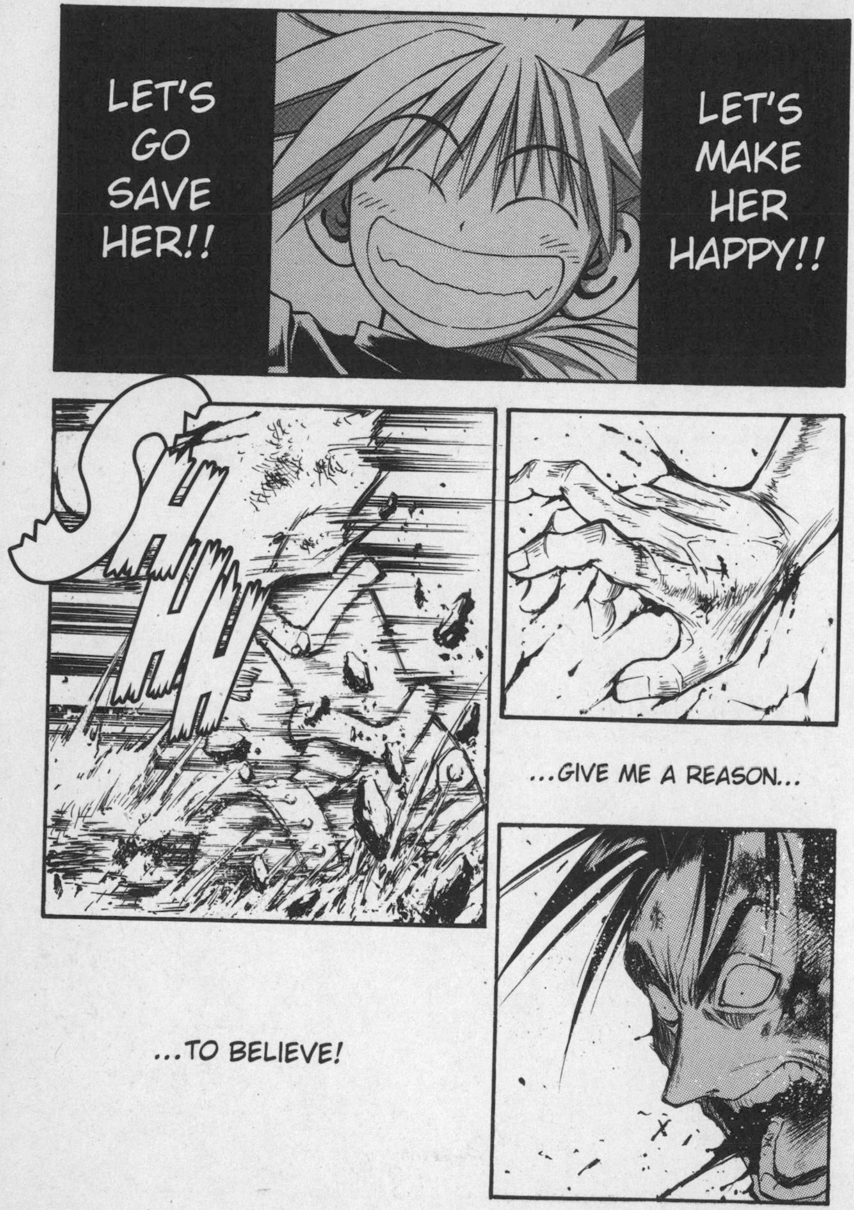
LET'S MAKE HER HAPPY!!
LET'S GO SAVE HER!!
...GIVE ME A REASON...
SHHH
...TO BELIEVE!

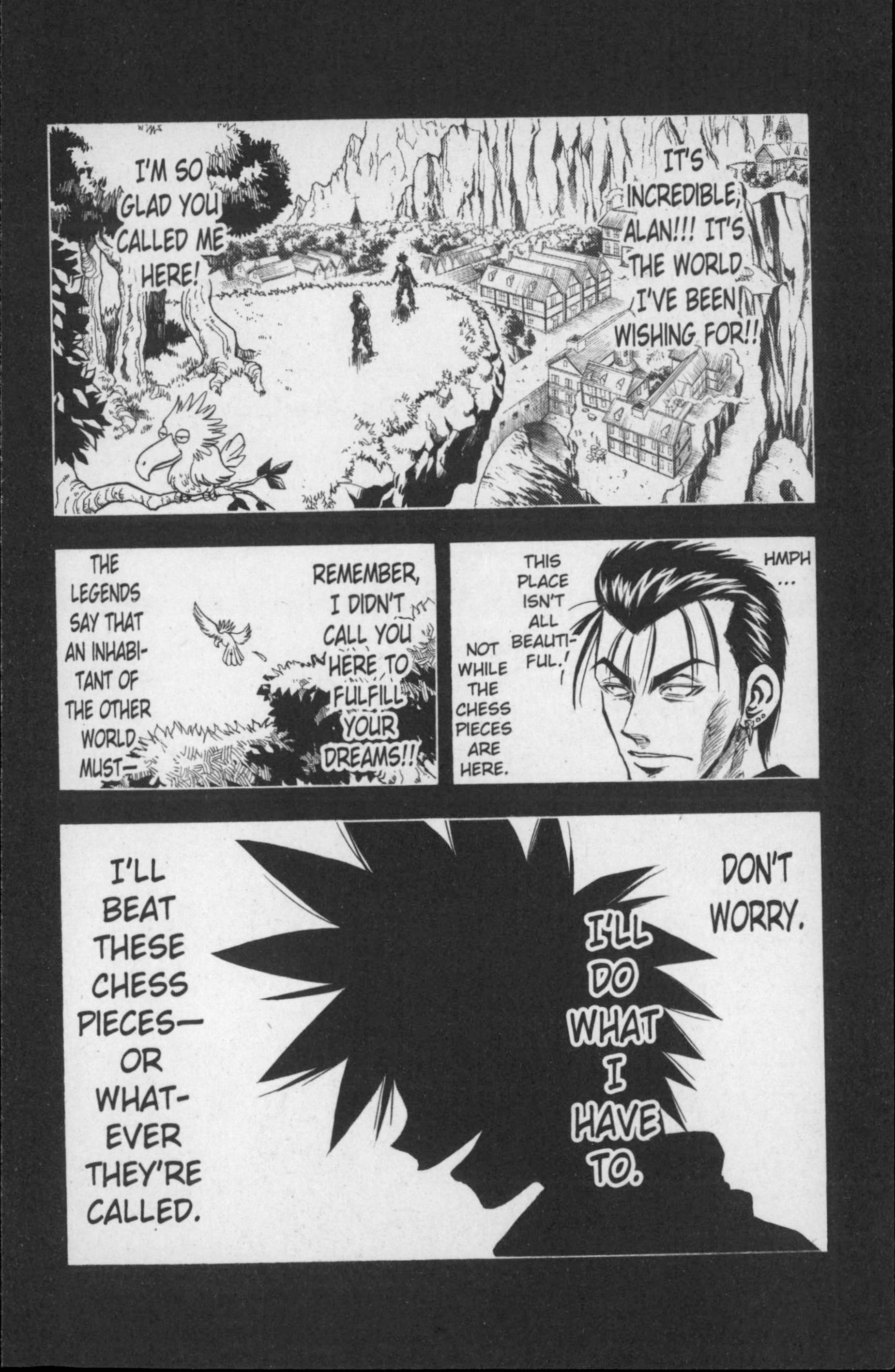
IT'S INCREDIBLE, ALAN!!! IT'S THE WORLD I'VE BEEN WISHING FOR!!
I'M SO GLAD YOU CALLED ME HERE!
HMPH...
THIS PLACE ISN'T ALL BEAUTIFUL.
NOT WHILE THE CHESS PIECES ARE HERE.
REMEMBER, I DIDN'T CALL YOU HERE TO FULFILL YOUR DREAMS!!
THE LEGENDS SAY THAT AN INHABITANT OF THE OTHER WORLD MUST—
DON'T WORRY.
I'LL DO WHAT I HAVE TO.
I'LL BEAT THESE CHESS PIECES— OR WHATEVER THEY'RE CALLED.

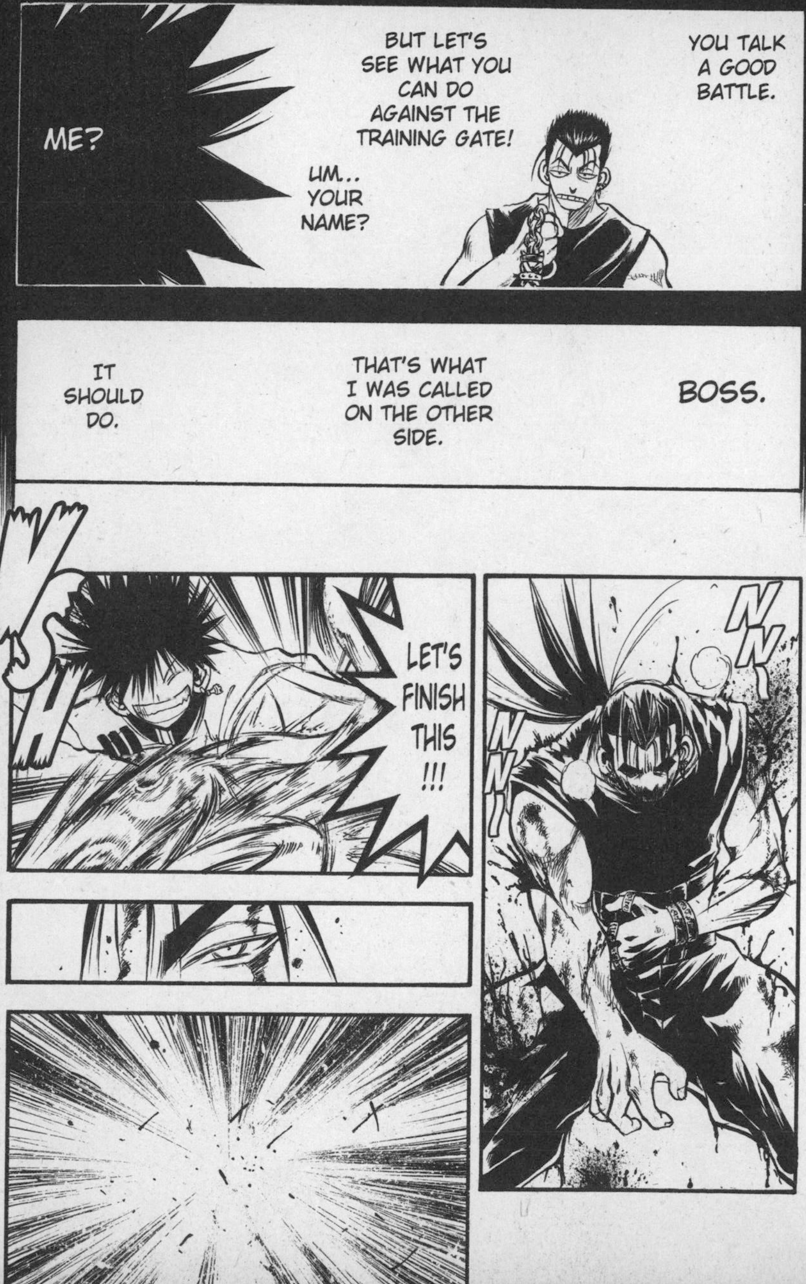
YOU TALK A GOOD BATTLE.
BUT LET'S SEE WHAT YOU CAN DO AGAINST THE TRAINING GATE!
UM... YOUR NAME?
ME?
BOSS.
THAT'S WHAT I WAS CALLED ON THE OTHER SIDE.
IT SHOULD DO.
LET'S FINISH THIS!!!

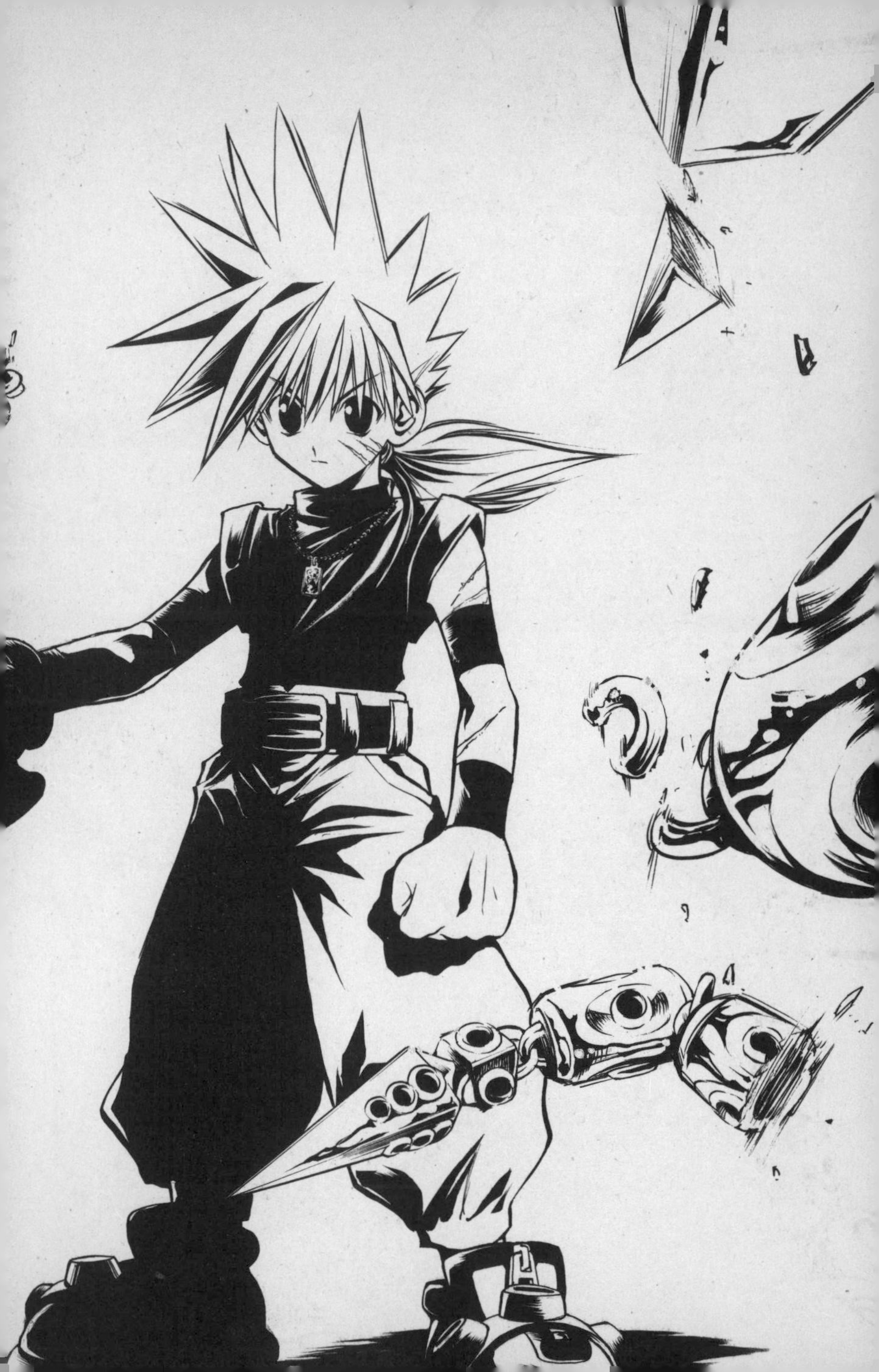

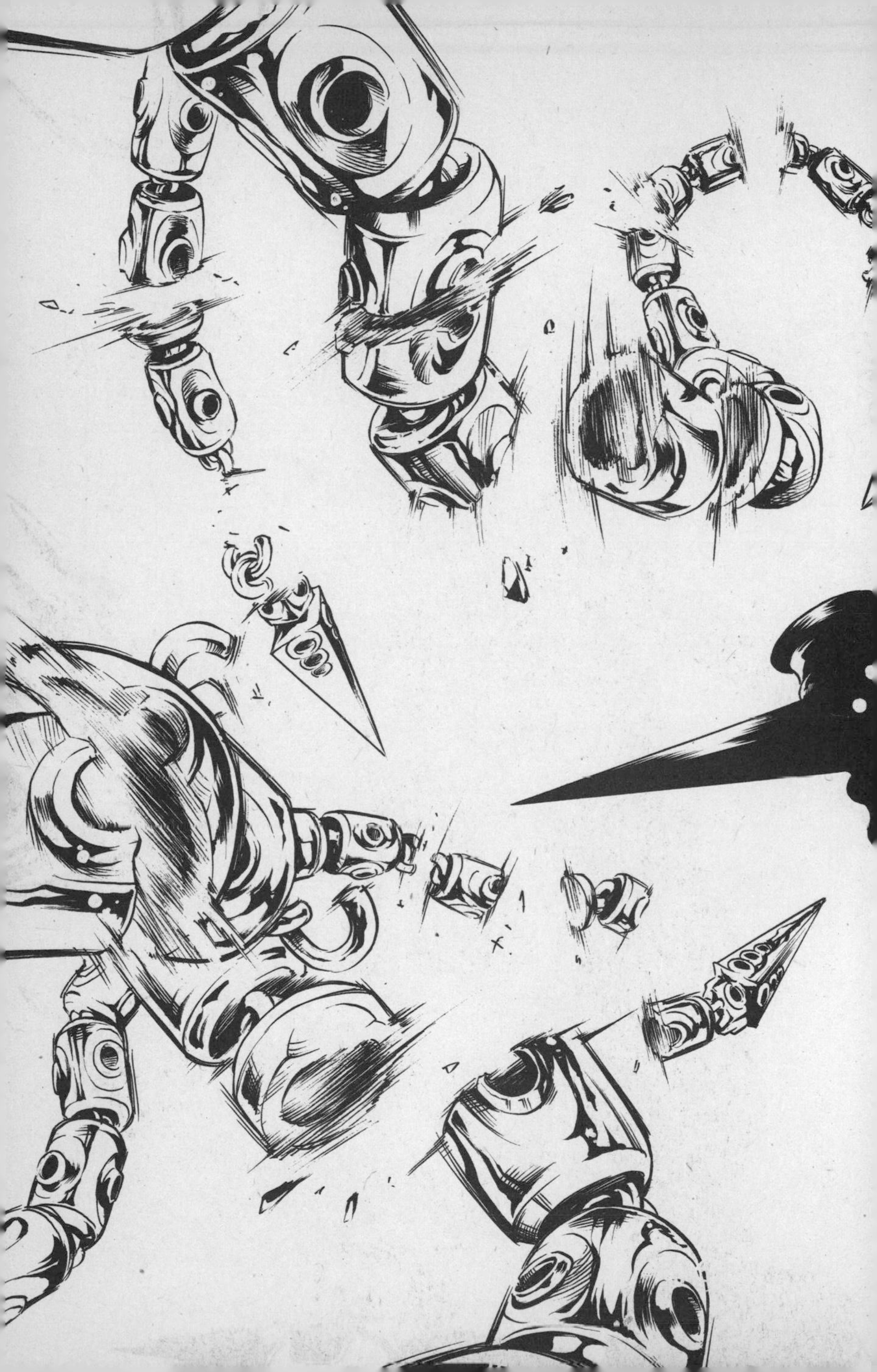

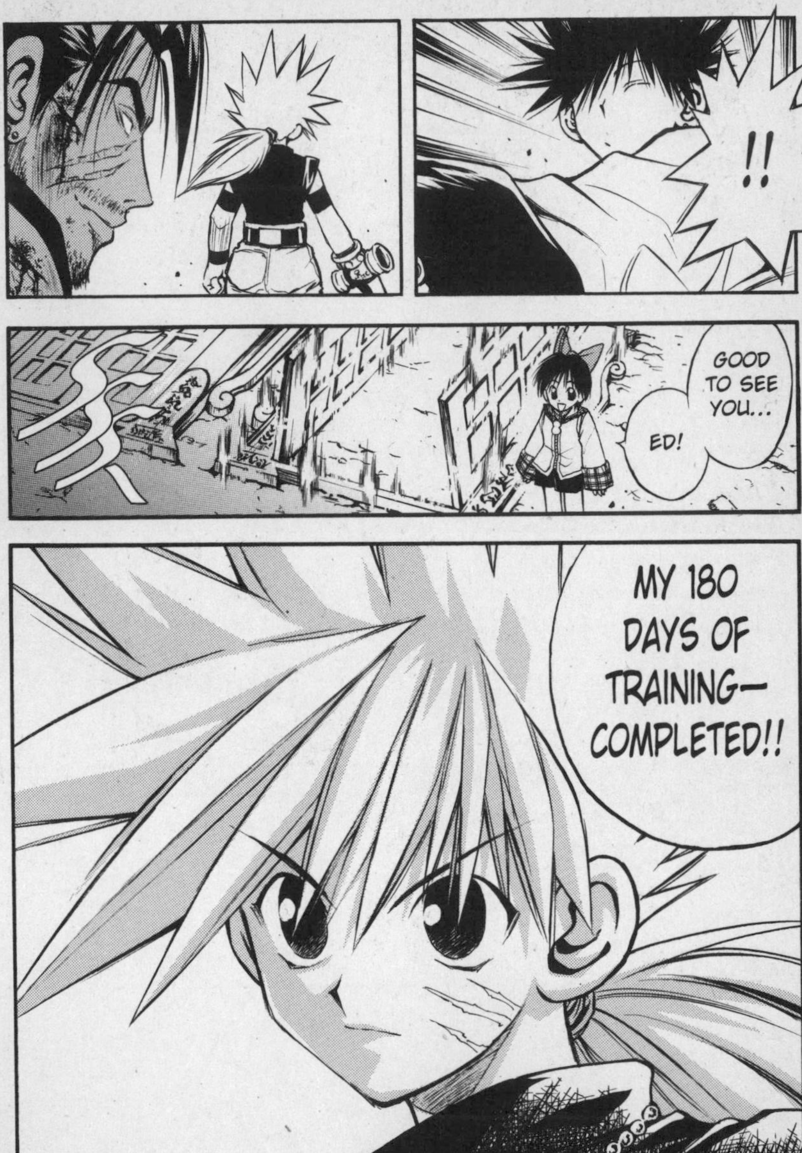
!!
GOOD TO SEE YOU...
ED!
MY 180 DAYS OF TRAINING—COMPLETED!!

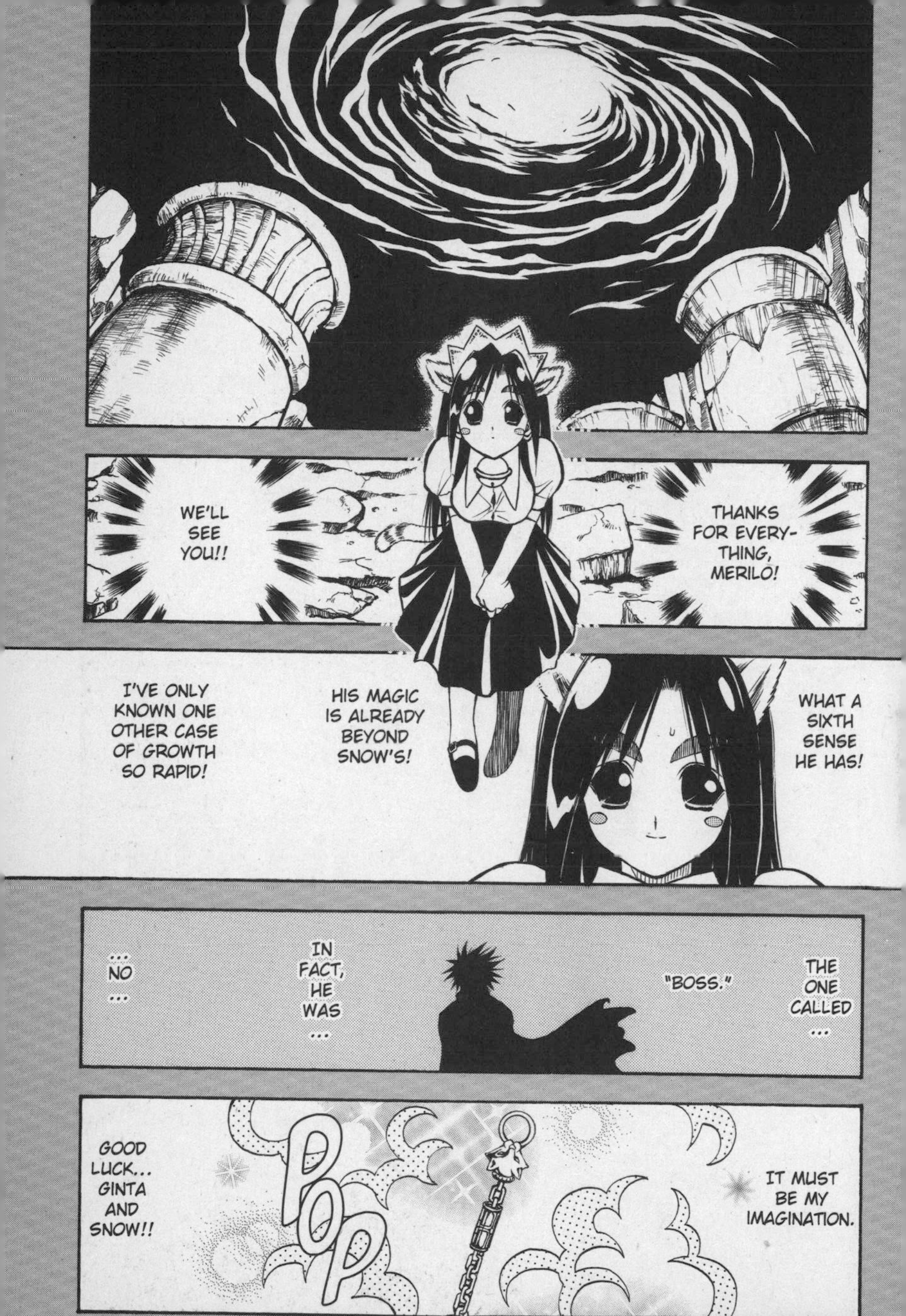
THANKS FOR EVERY-THING, MERILO!
WE'LL SEE YOU!!
WHAT A SIXTH SENSE HE HAS!
HIS MAGIC IS ALREADY BEYOND SNOW'S!
I'VE ONLY KNOWN ONE OTHER CASE OF GROWTH SO RAPID!
THE ONE CALLED ...
"BOSS."
IN FACT, HE WAS ...
... NO ...
IT MUST BE MY IMAGINATION.
POP
GOOD LUCK... GINTA AND SNOW!!

AKT.29/

Ginta vs. Ian

AKT.29/ Ginta vs. Ian

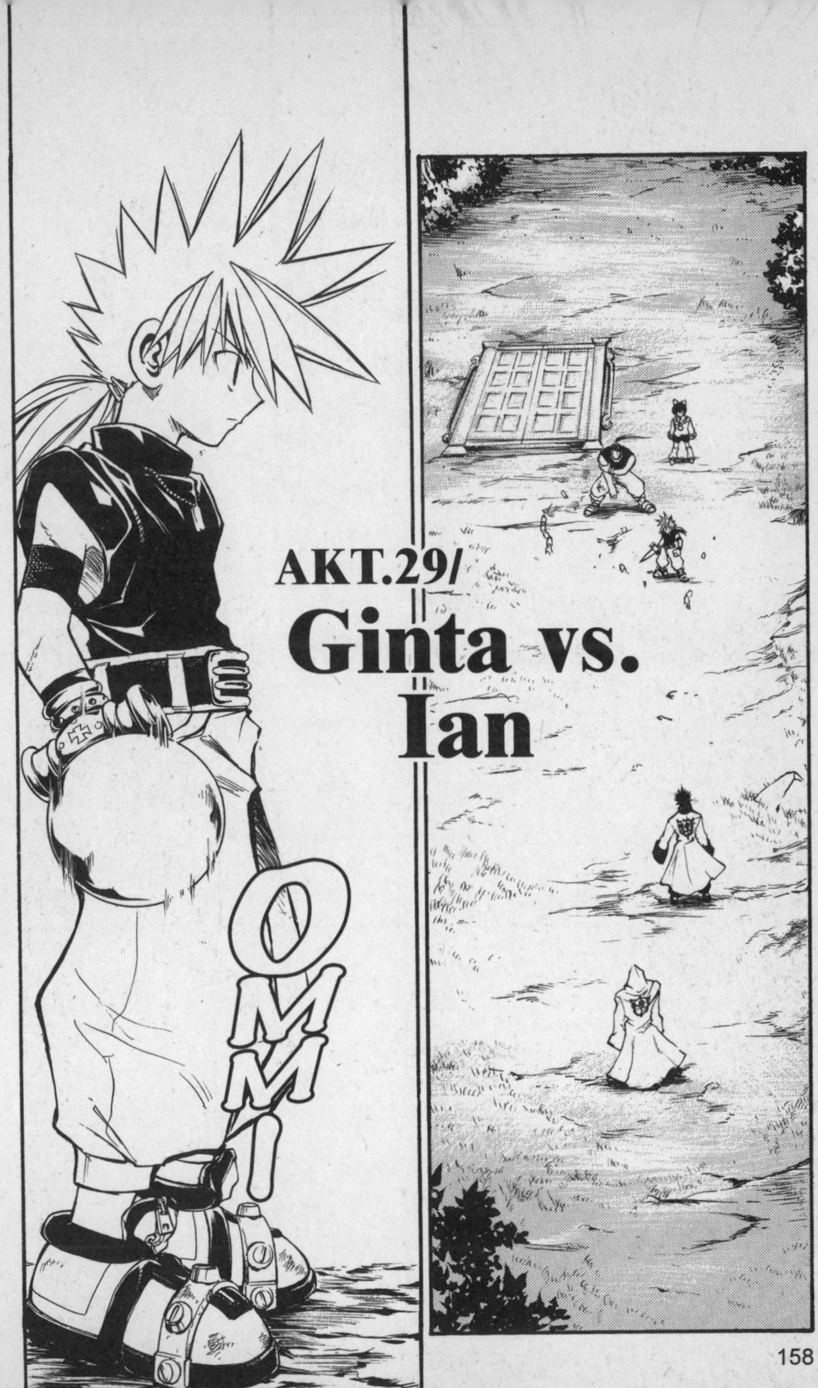
OMM!

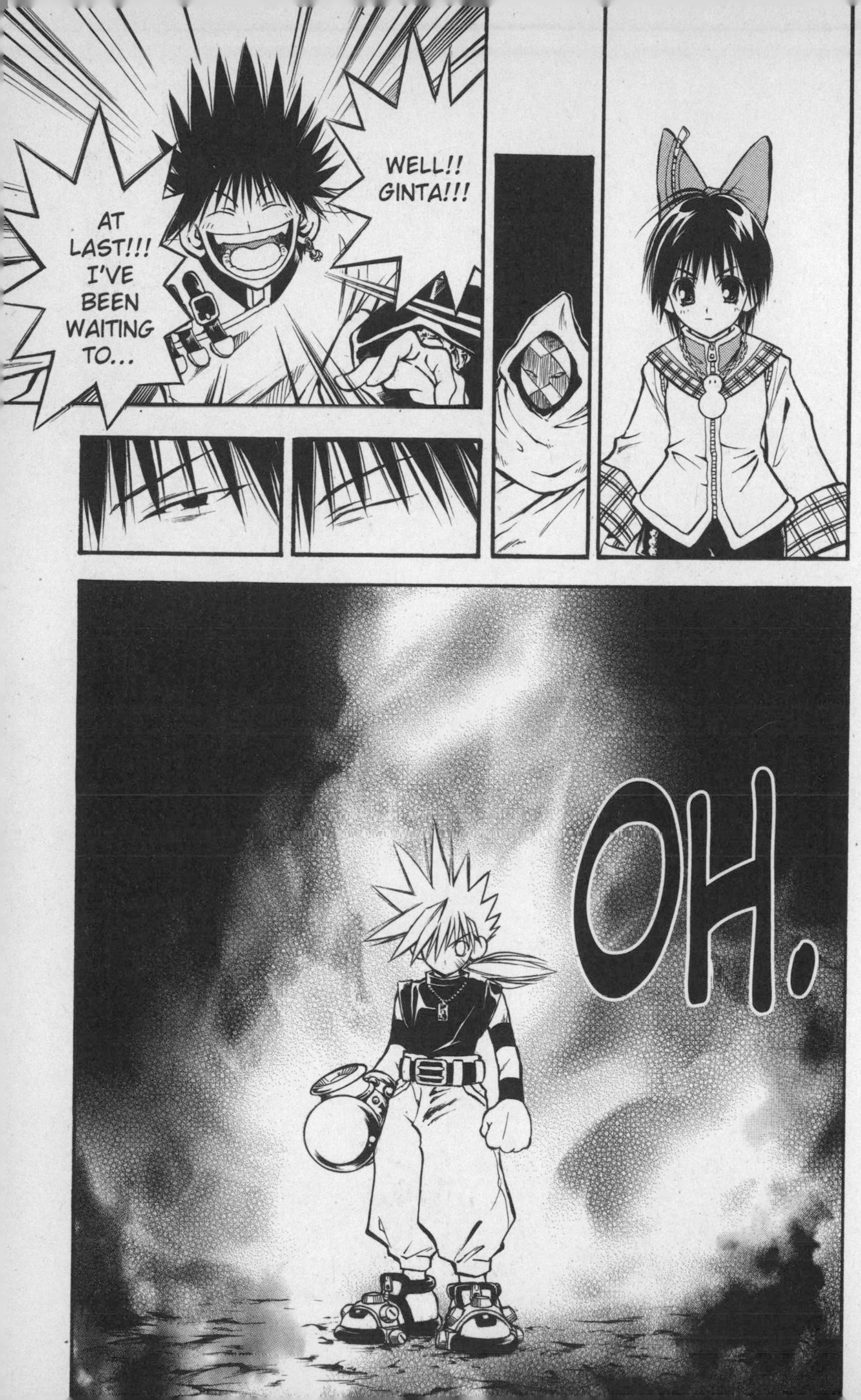
WELL!! GINTA!!!
AT LAST!!! I'VE BEEN WAITING TO...
OH.

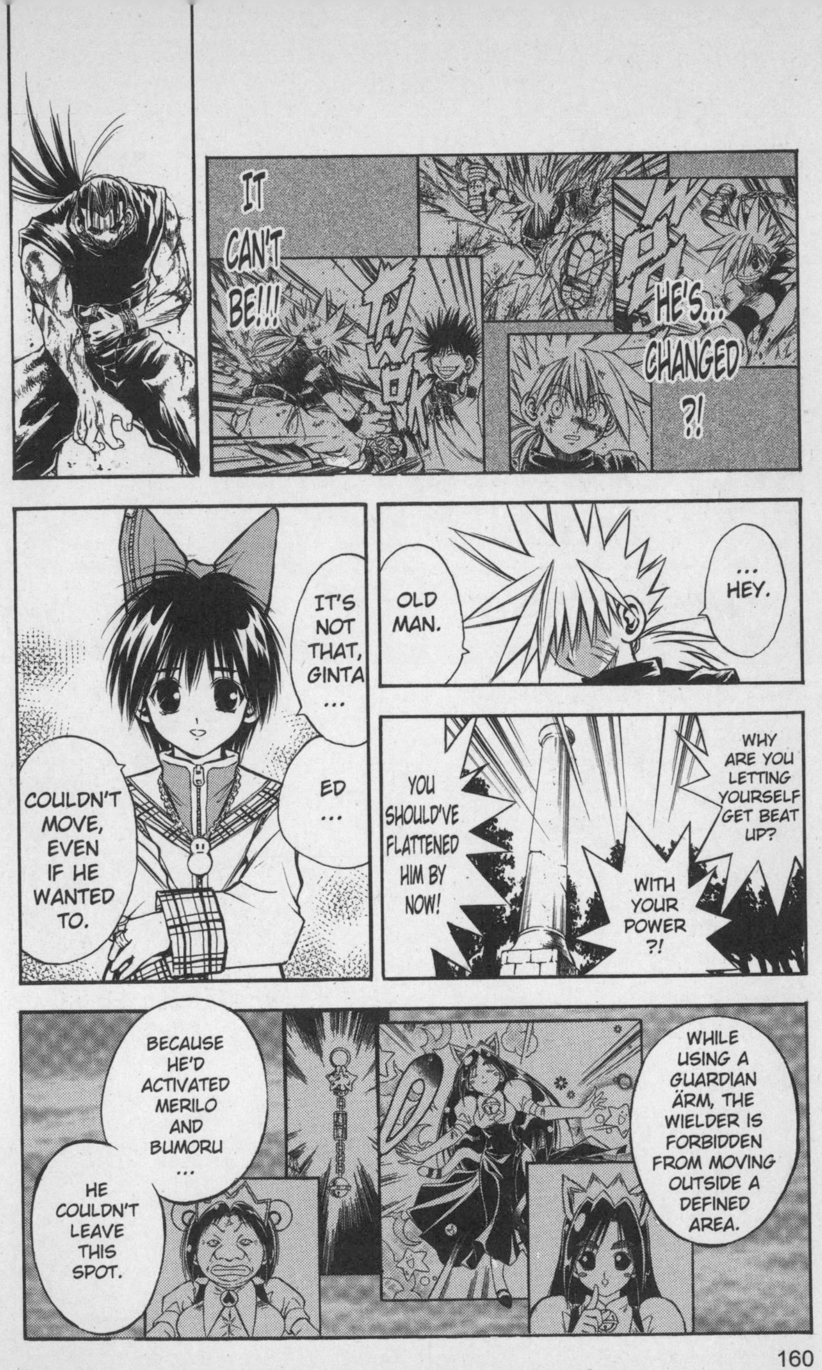
HE'S... CHANGED ?!
IT CAN'T BE!!!
... HEY.
OLD MAN.
WHY ARE YOU LETTING YOURSELF GET BEAT UP?
WITH YOUR POWER ?!
YOU SHOULD'VE FLATTENED HIM BY NOW!
IT'S NOT THAT, GINTA ...
ED ...
COULDN'T MOVE, EVEN IF HE WANTED TO.
WHILE USING A GUARDIAN ÄRM, THE WIELDER IS FORBIDDEN FROM MOVING OUTSIDE A DEFINED AREA.
BECAUSE HE'D ACTIVATED MERILO AND BUMORU ...
HE COULDN'T LEAVE THIS SPOT.

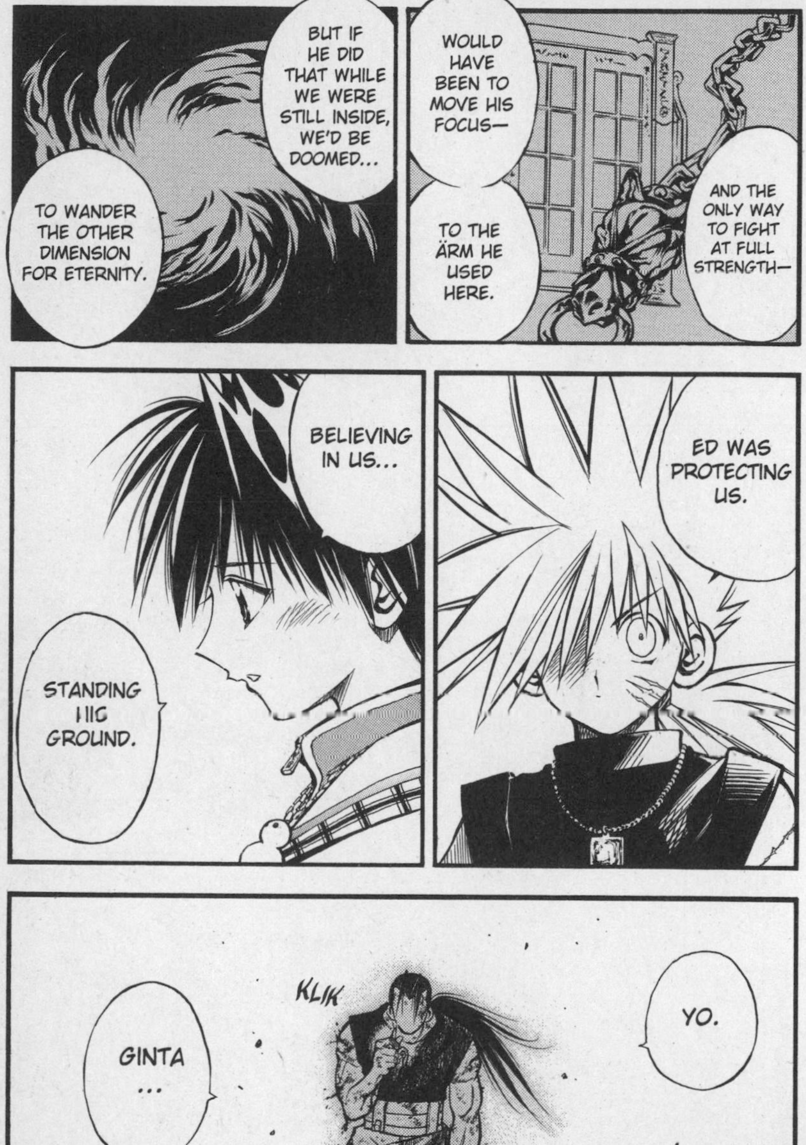
AND THE ONLY WAY TO FIGHT AT FULL STRENGTH—
WOULD HAVE BEEN TO MOVE HIS FOCUS—
TO THE ÄRM HE USED HERE.
BUT IF HE DID THAT WHILE WE WERE STILL INSIDE, WE'D BE DOOMED...
TO WANDER THE OTHER DIMENSION FOR ETERNITY.
ED WAS PROTECTING US.
BELIEVING IN US...
STANDING HIS GROUND.
YO.
KLIK
GINTA ...

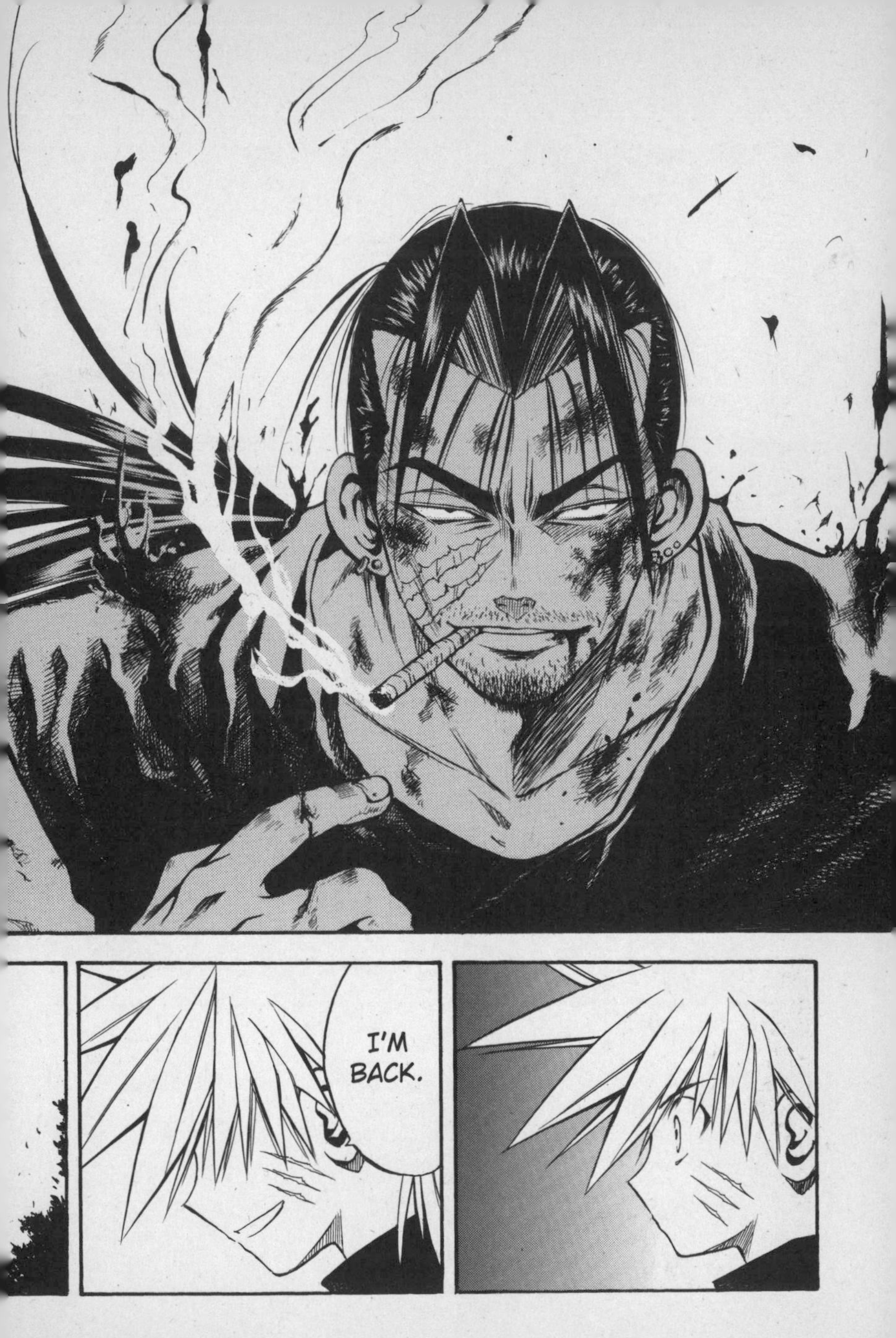
I'M BACK.

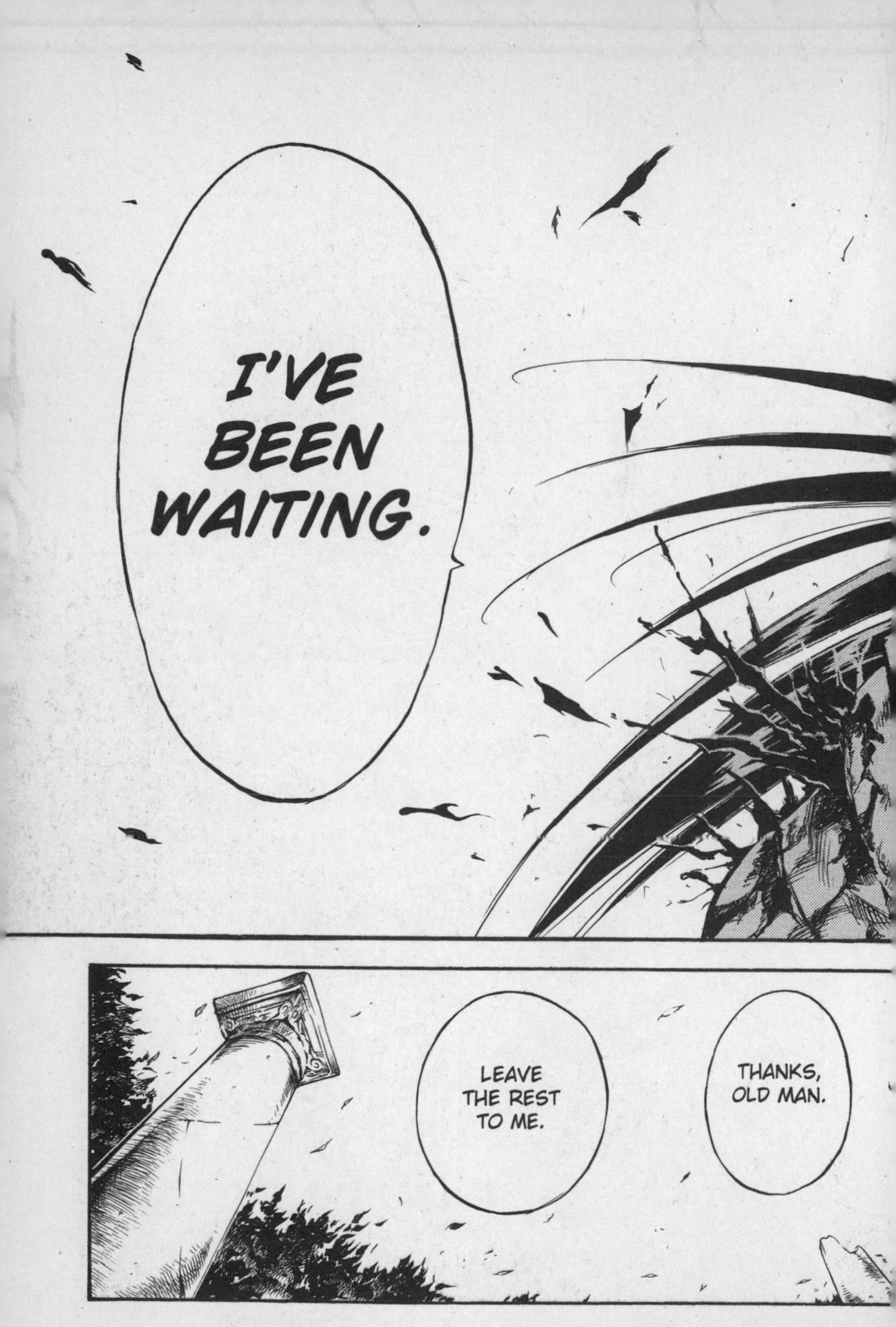
I'VE BEEN WAITING.
THANKS, OLD MAN.
LEAVE THE REST TO ME.

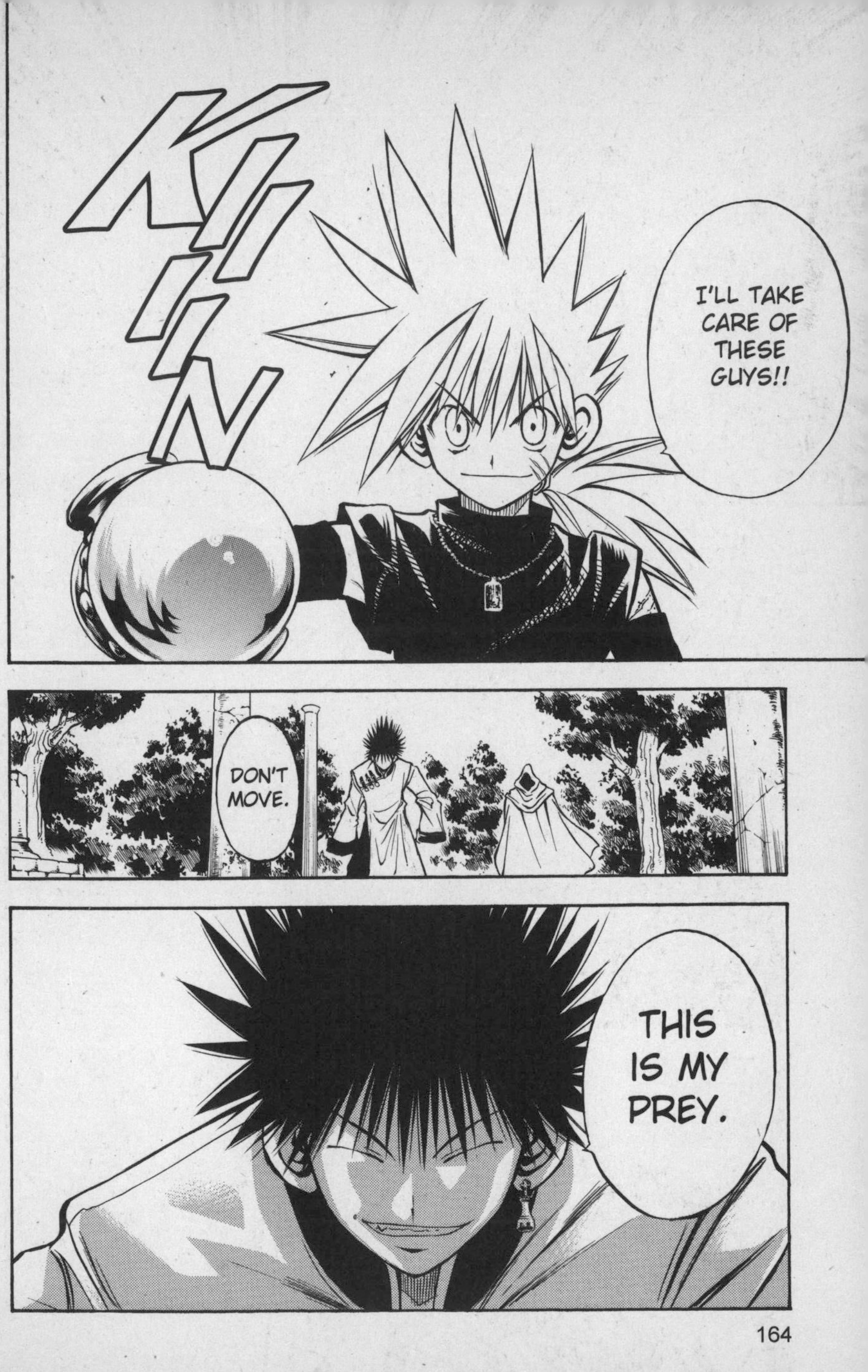
I'LL TAKE CARE OF THESE GUYS!!
KIIIN
DON'T MOVE.
THIS IS MY PREY.

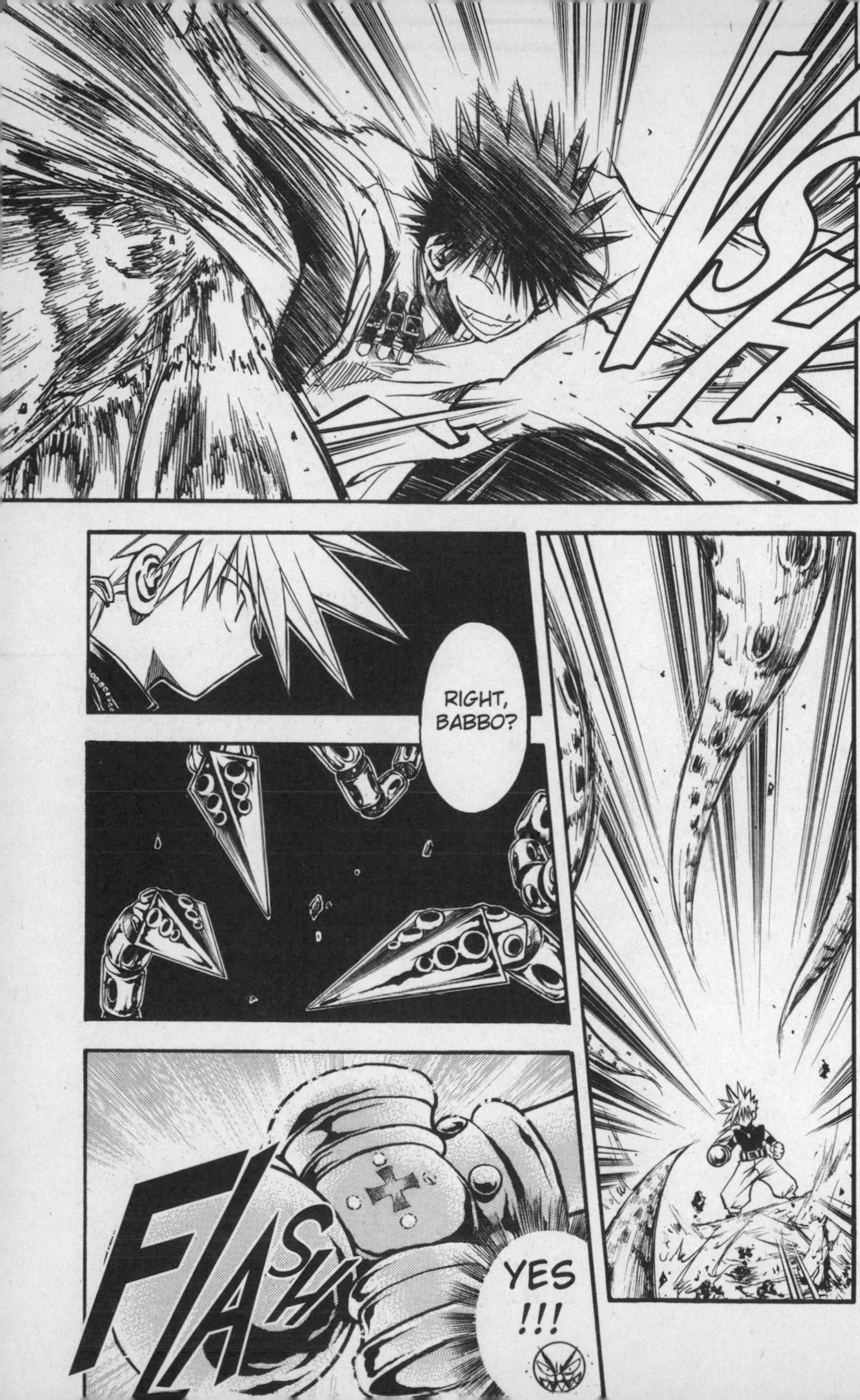
RIGHT, BABBO?
FASH
YES !!!

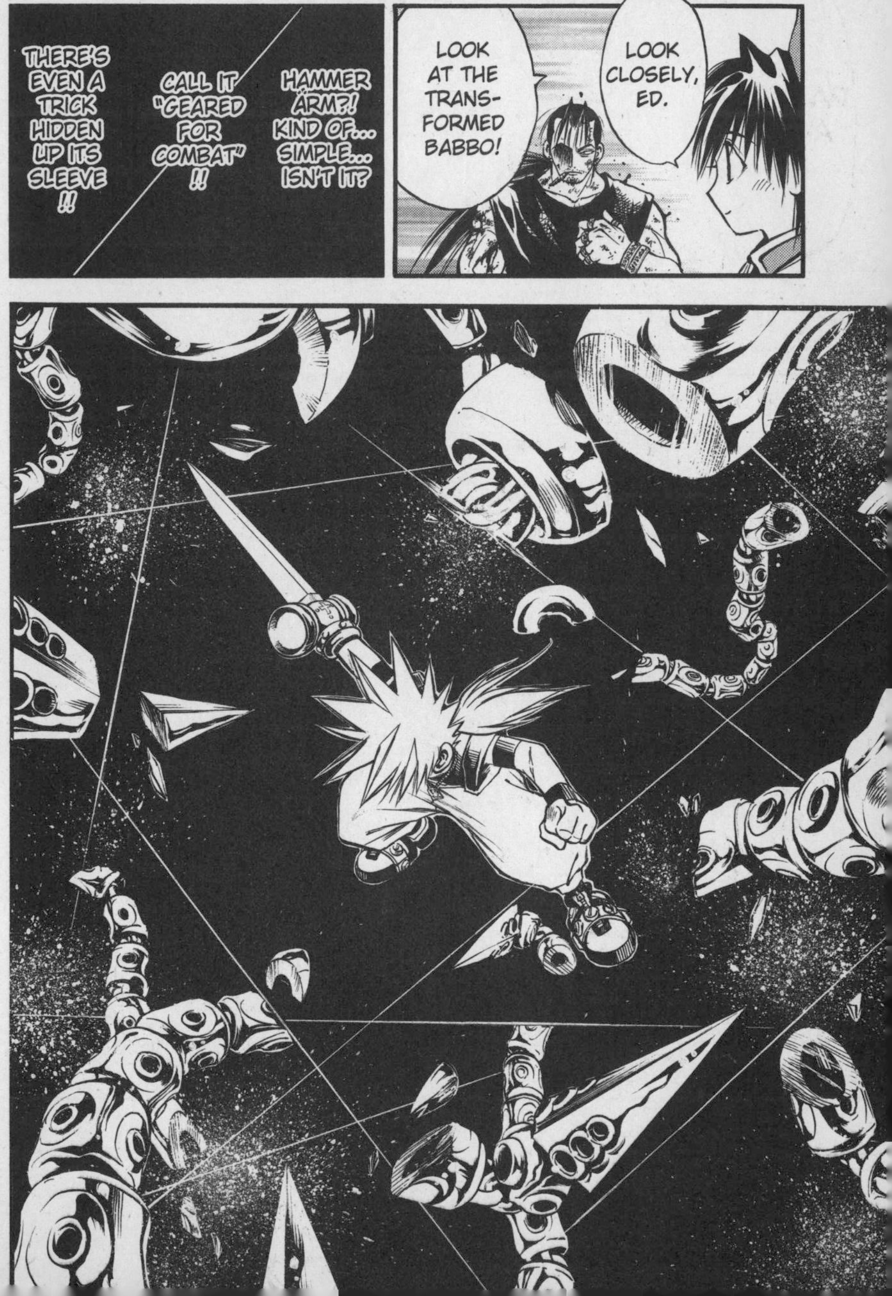

LOOK CLOSELY, ED.
LOOK AT THE TRANS-FORMED BABBO!
HAMMER ARM?! KIND OF... SIMPLE... ISN'T IT?
CALL IT "GEARED FOR COMBAT"!!
THERE'S EVEN A TRICK HIDDEN UP ITS SLEEVE!!

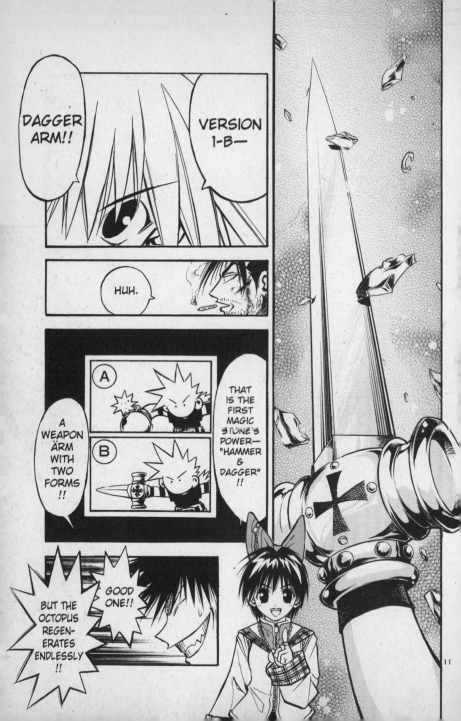

DAGGER ARM!!

VERSION 1-B—

HUH.

A
B

A WEAPON ARM WITH TWO FORMS!!

THAT IS THE FIRST MAGIC STONE'S POWER— "HAMMER & DAGGER"!!

BUT THE OCTOPUS REGENERATES ENDLESSLY!!

GOOD ONE!!

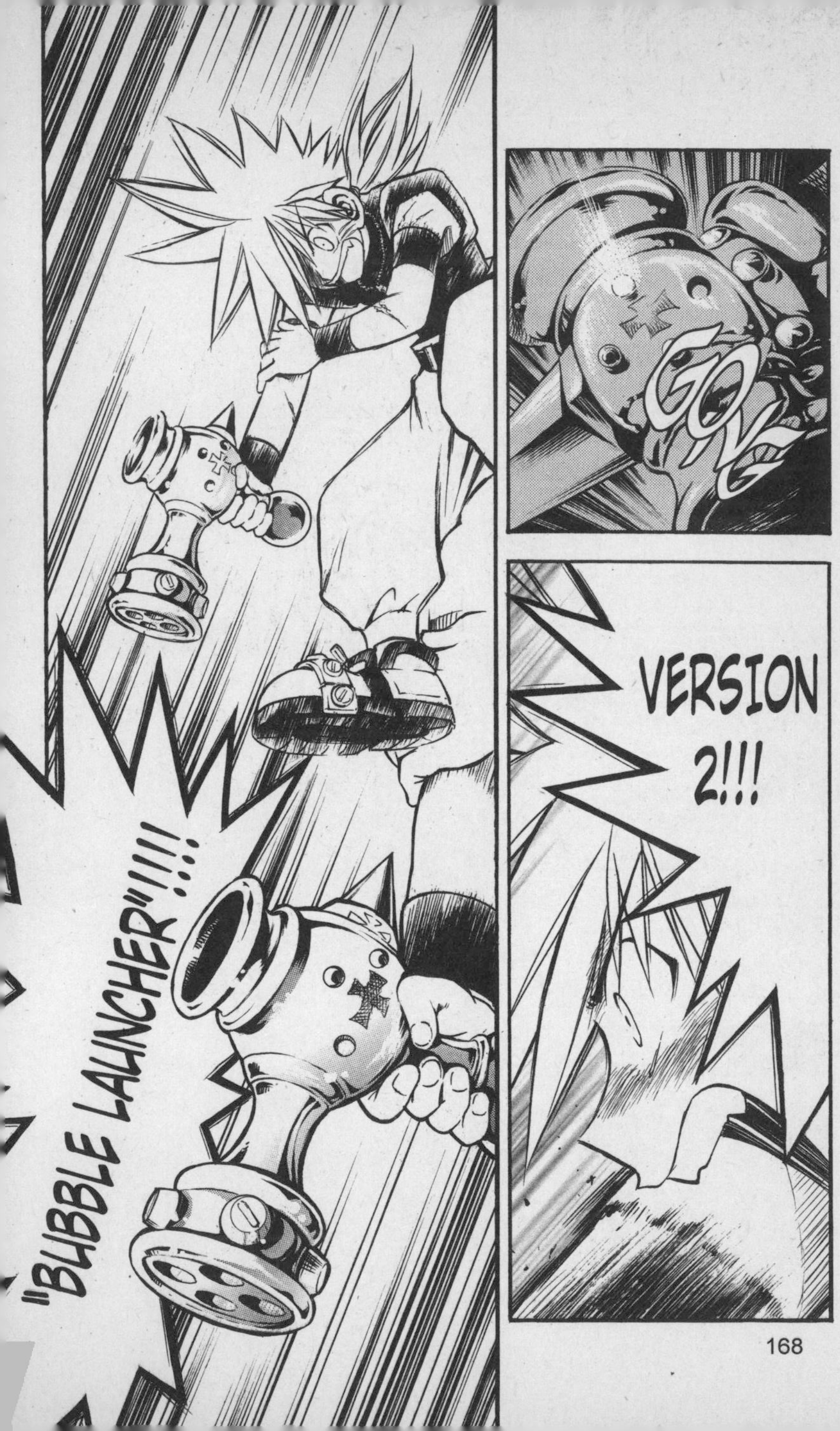
GONG
VERSION 2!!!
"BUBBLE LAUNCHER"!!!!!

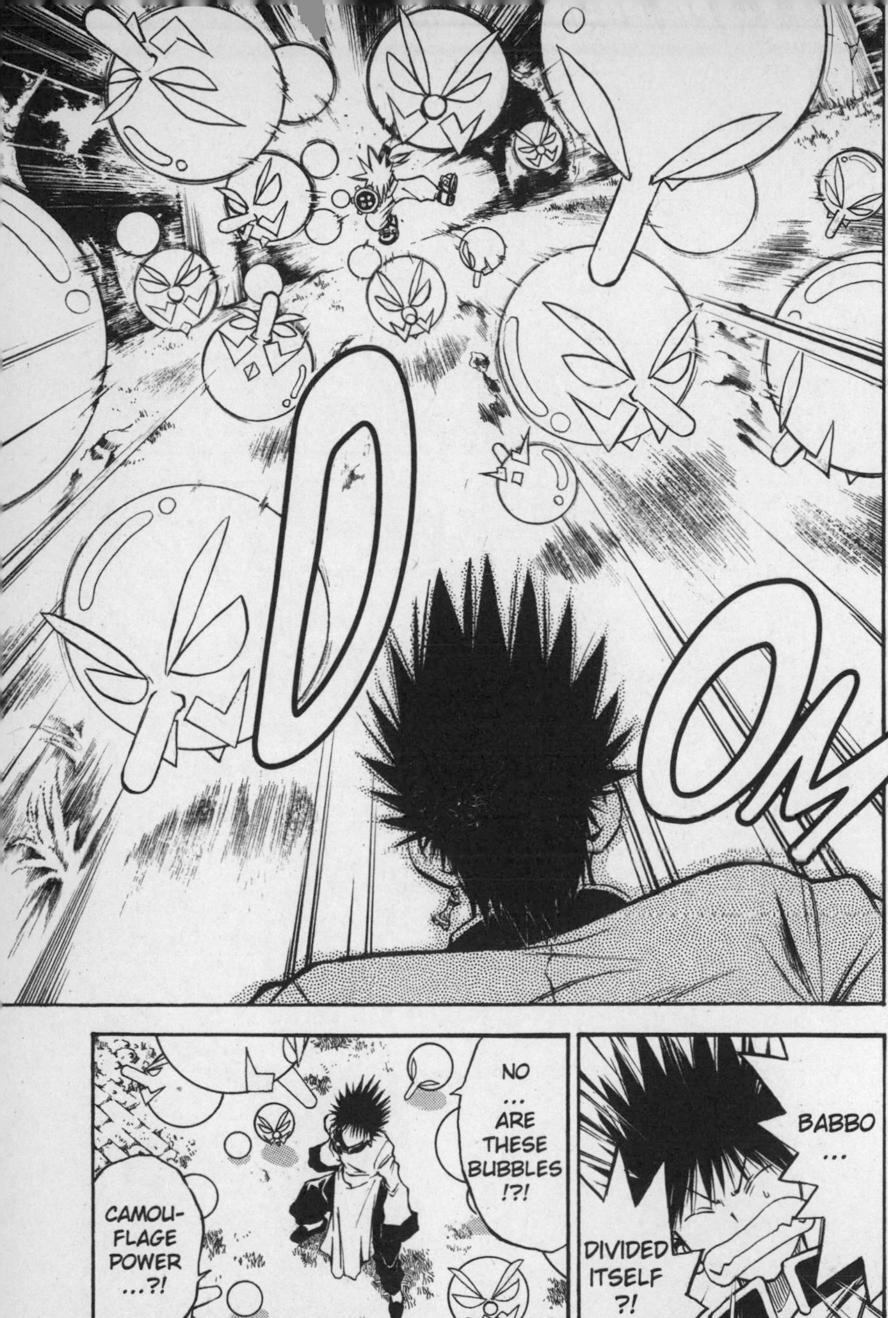
BABBO ...
DIVIDED ITSELF ?!
NO ... ARE THESE BUBBLES !?!
CAMOUFLAGE POWER ...?!

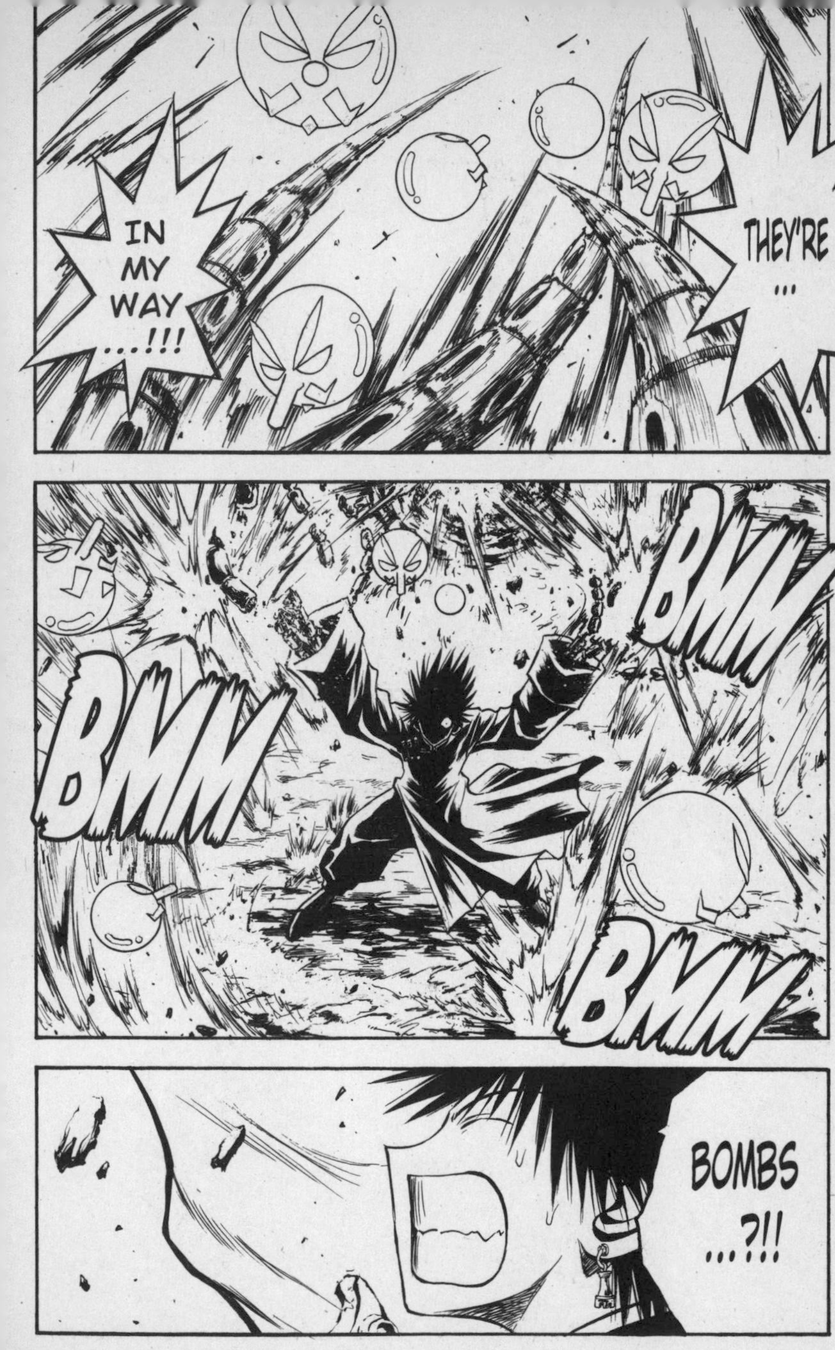
THEY'RE ...
IN MY WAY ...!!!
BMM
BMM
BMM
BOMBS ...?!!

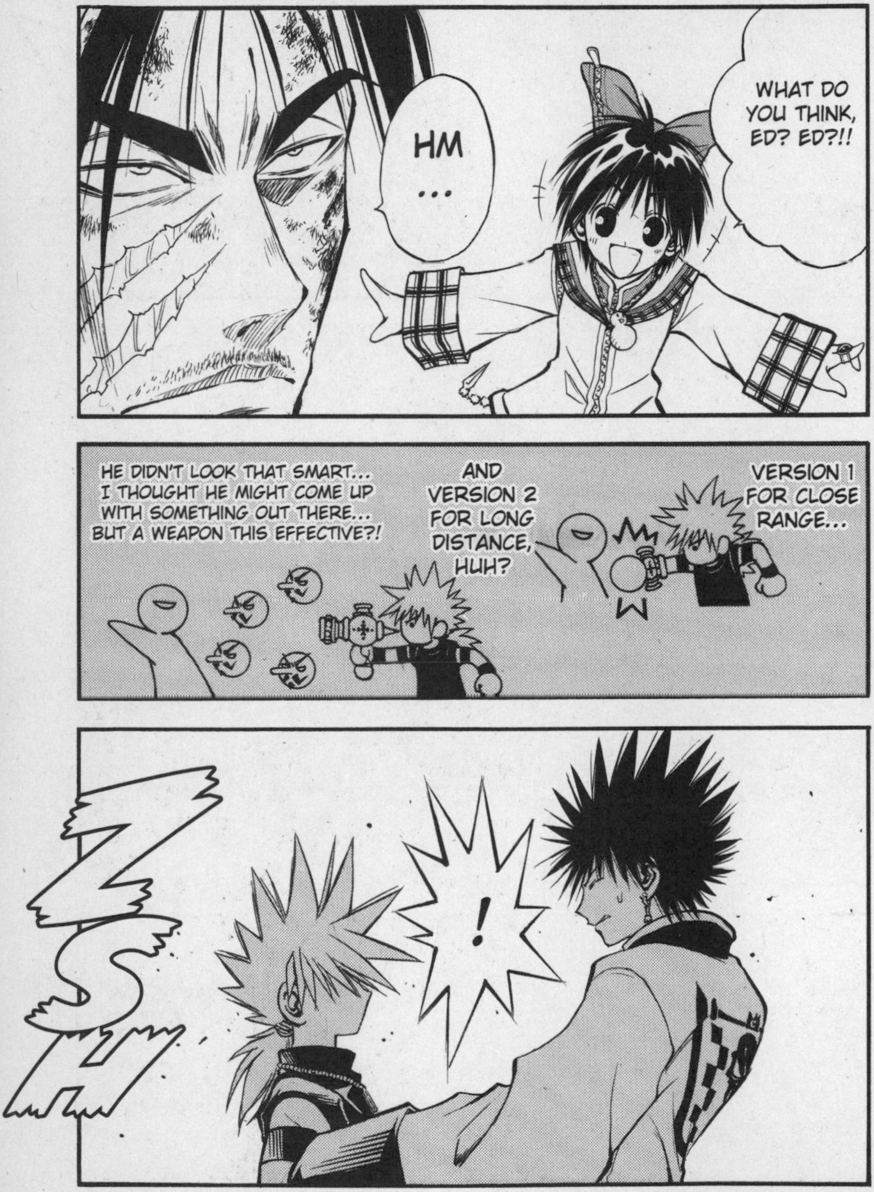
WHAT DO YOU THINK, ED? ED?!!
HM ...
VERSION 1 FOR CLOSE RANGE...
AND VERSION 2 FOR LONG DISTANCE, HUH?
HE DIDN'T LOOK THAT SMART... I THOUGHT HE MIGHT COME UP WITH SOMETHING OUT THERE... BUT A WEAPON THIS EFFECTIVE?!
!
ZSH

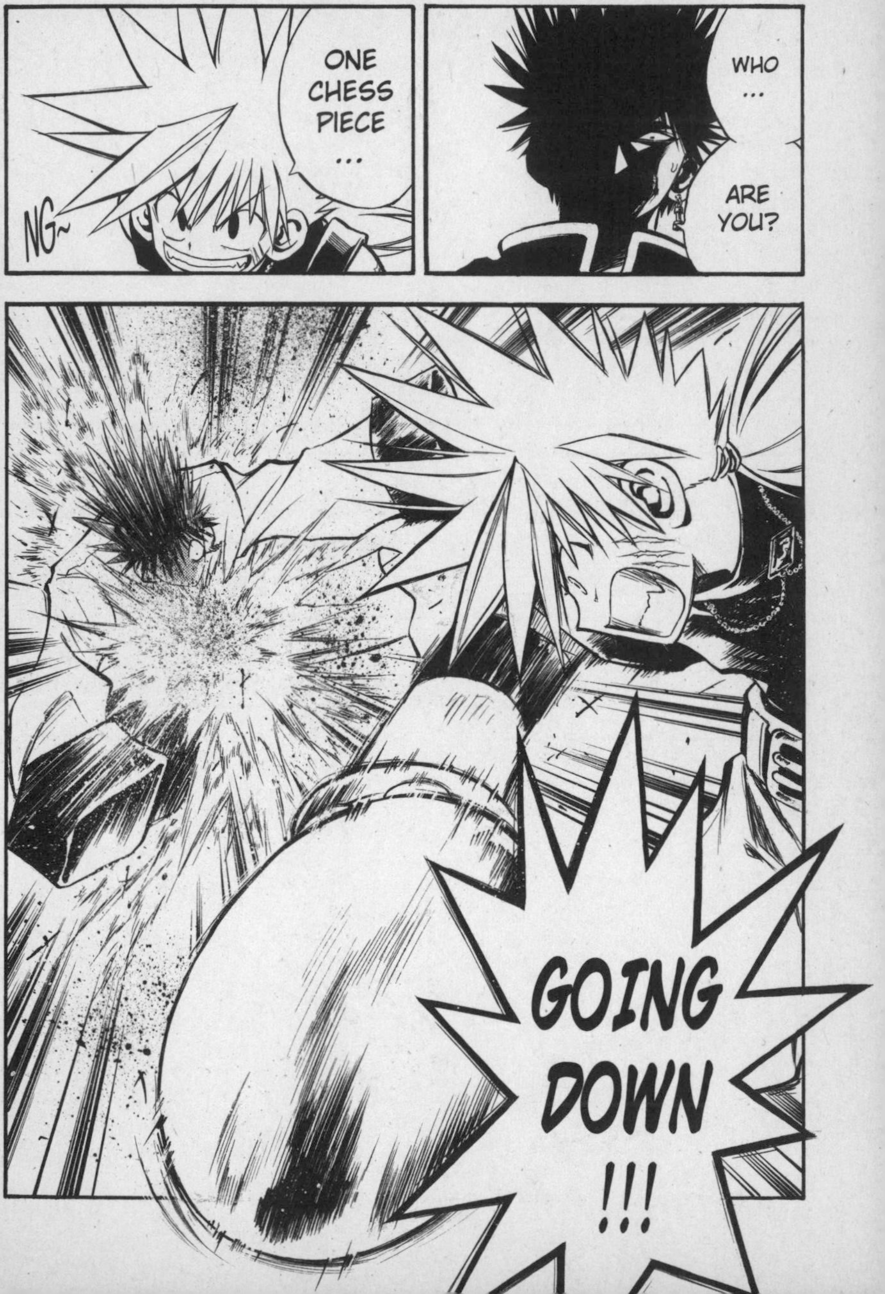
WHO ... ARE YOU?
ONE CHESS PIECE ...
NG~
GOING DOWN !!!

AKT.30/Training's End

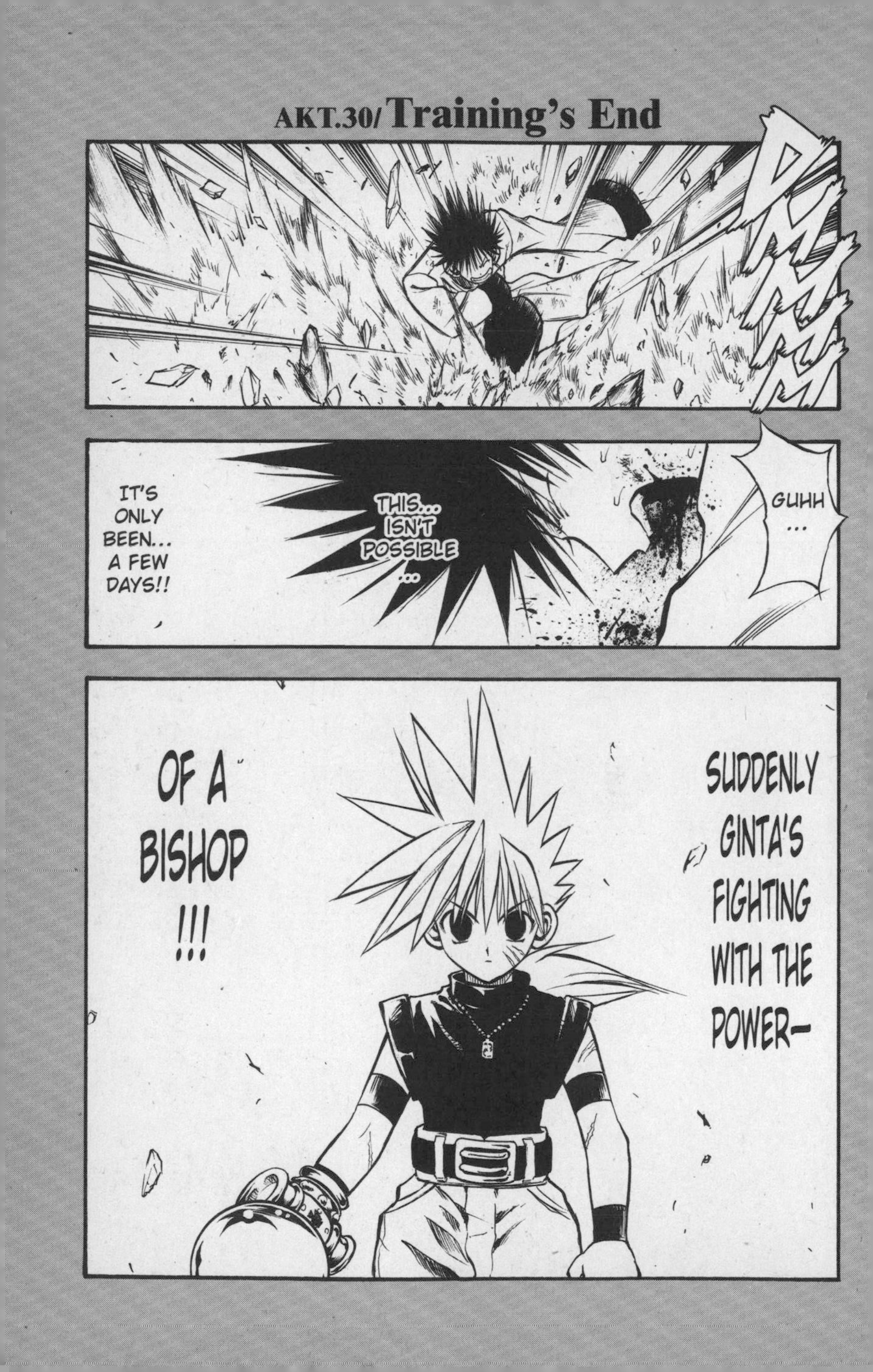
GUHH ...
THIS... ISN'T POSSIBLE ...
IT'S ONLY BEEN... A FEW DAYS!!
SUDDENLY GINTA'S FIGHTING WITH THE POWER–
OF A BISHOP !!!

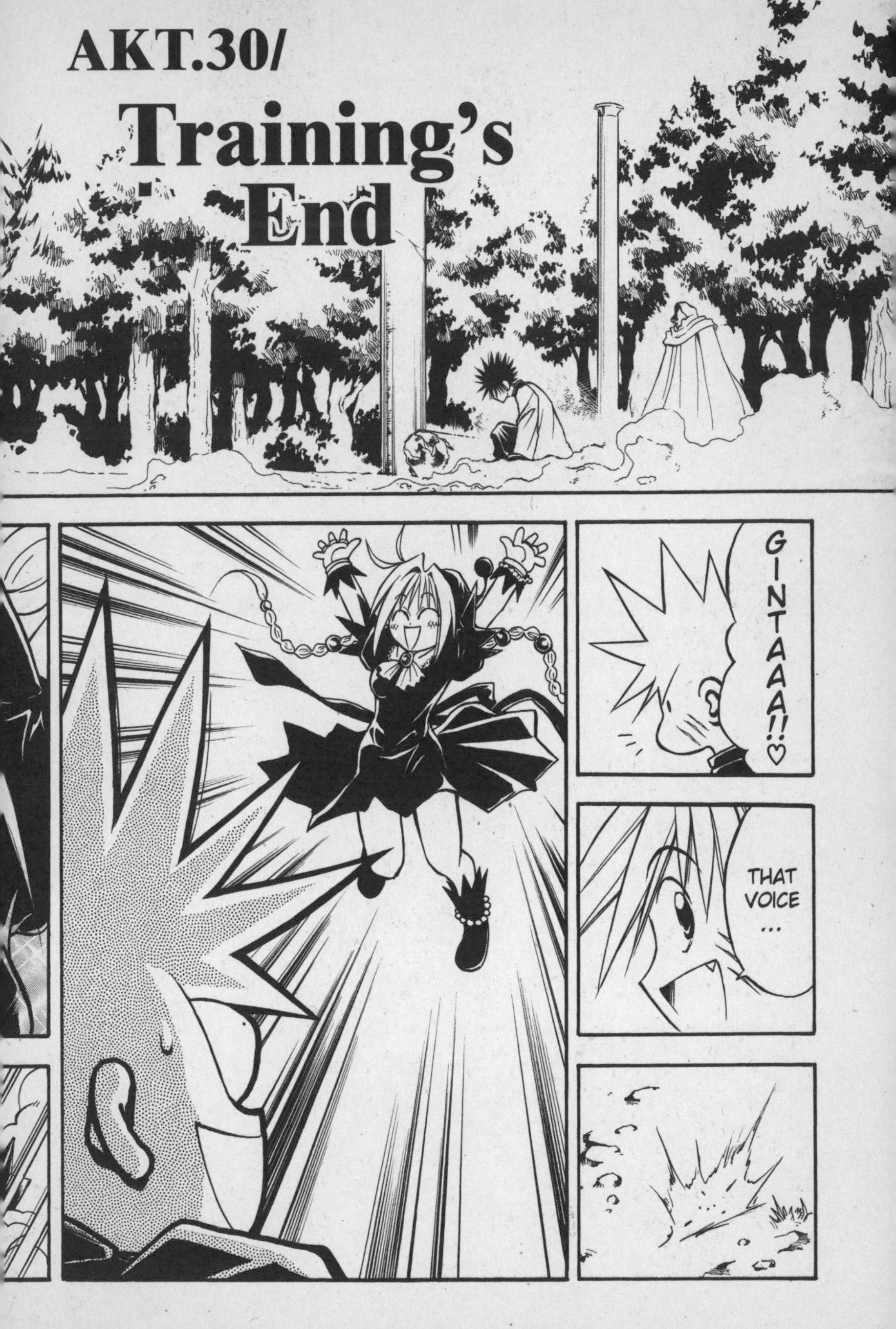
AKT.30/
Training's End
GINTAAA!!♡
THAT VOICE ...

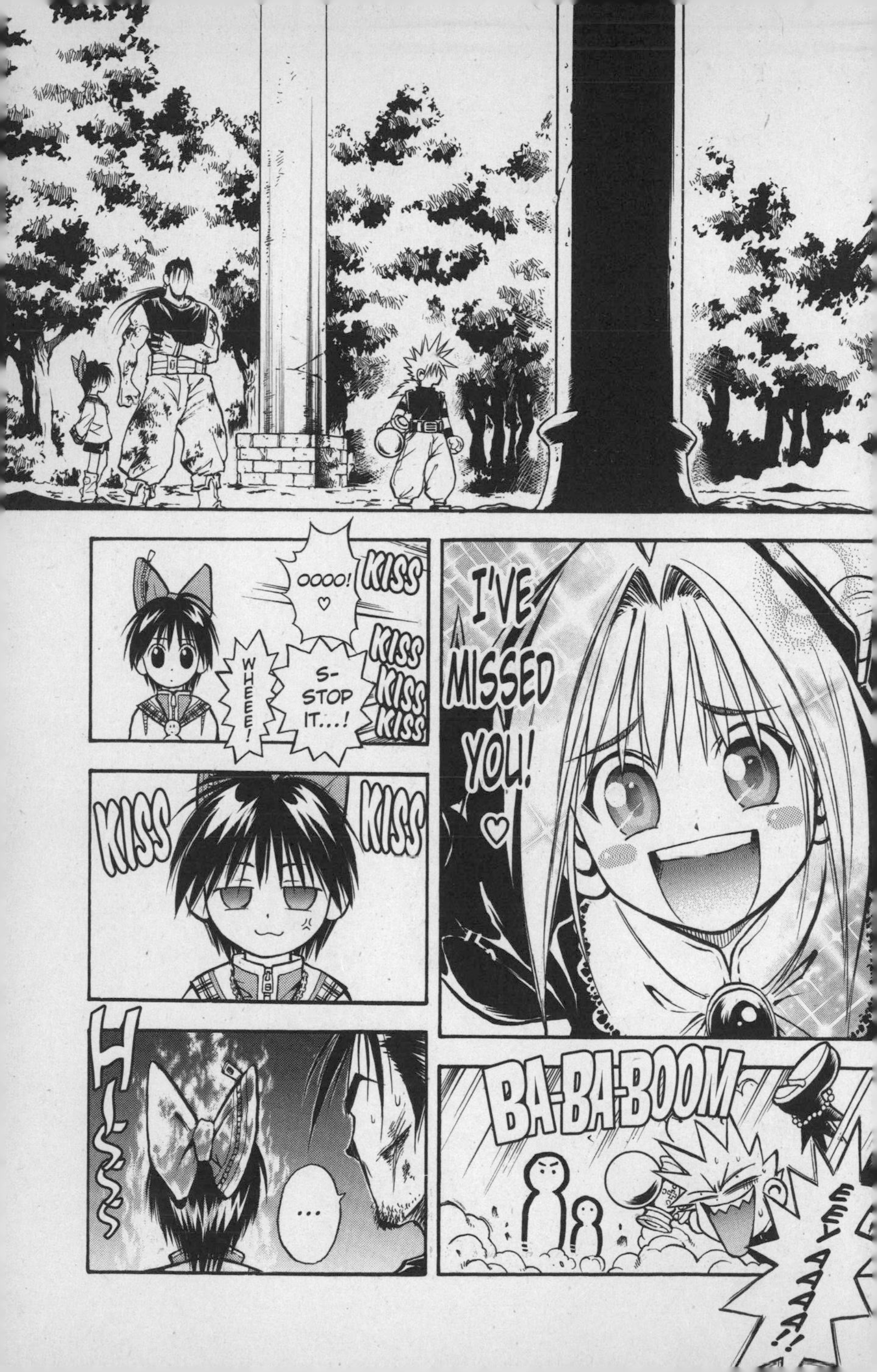
I'VE MISSED YOU! ♥
OOOO! ♥
KISS
KISS KISS KISS
S-STOP IT...!
WHEEE!
KISS
KISS
BA-BA-BOOM
EEYAAAAA!!
...
H-sss

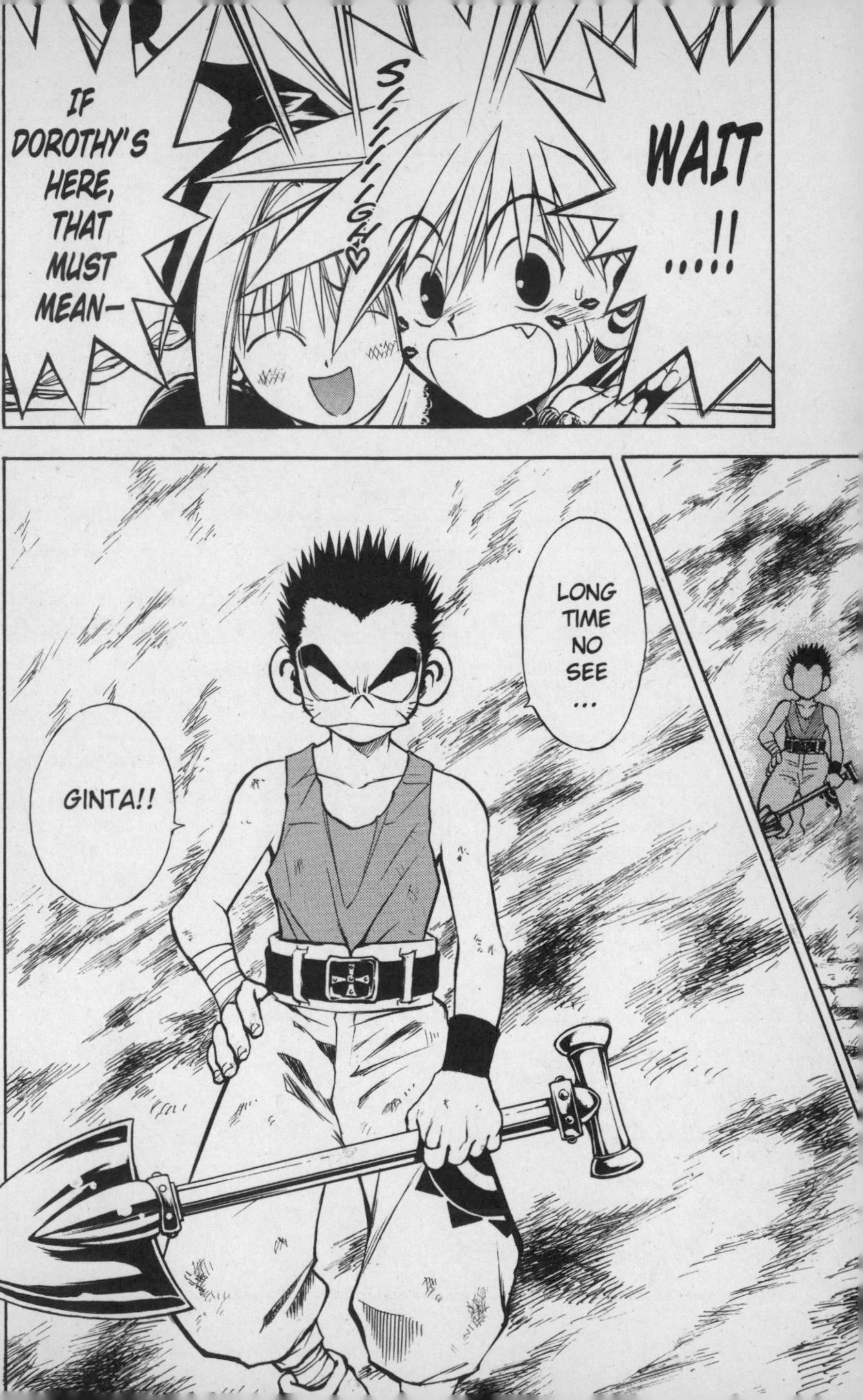
WAIT ...!!
SIIIIIGH♡
IF DOROTHY'S HERE, THAT MUST MEAN—
LONG TIME NO SEE ...
GINTA!!

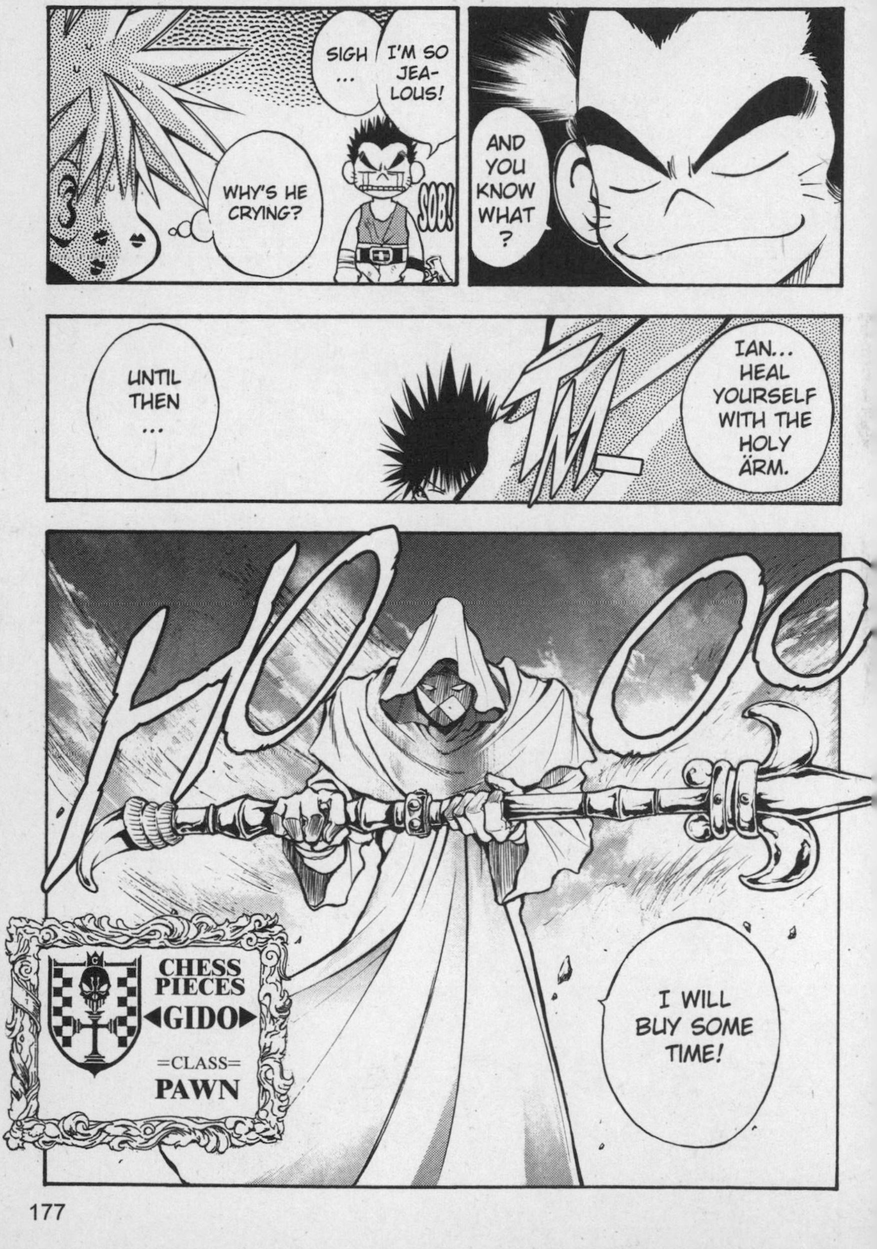
AND YOU KNOW WHAT?
I'M SO JEA-LOUS!
SIGH...
SOB!
WHY'S HE CRYING?
IAN... HEAL YOURSELF WITH THE HOLY ÄRM.
TM-
UNTIL THEN...
HOOOO
I WILL BUY SOME TIME!
CHESS PIECES
◀GIDO▶
=CLASS=
PAWN

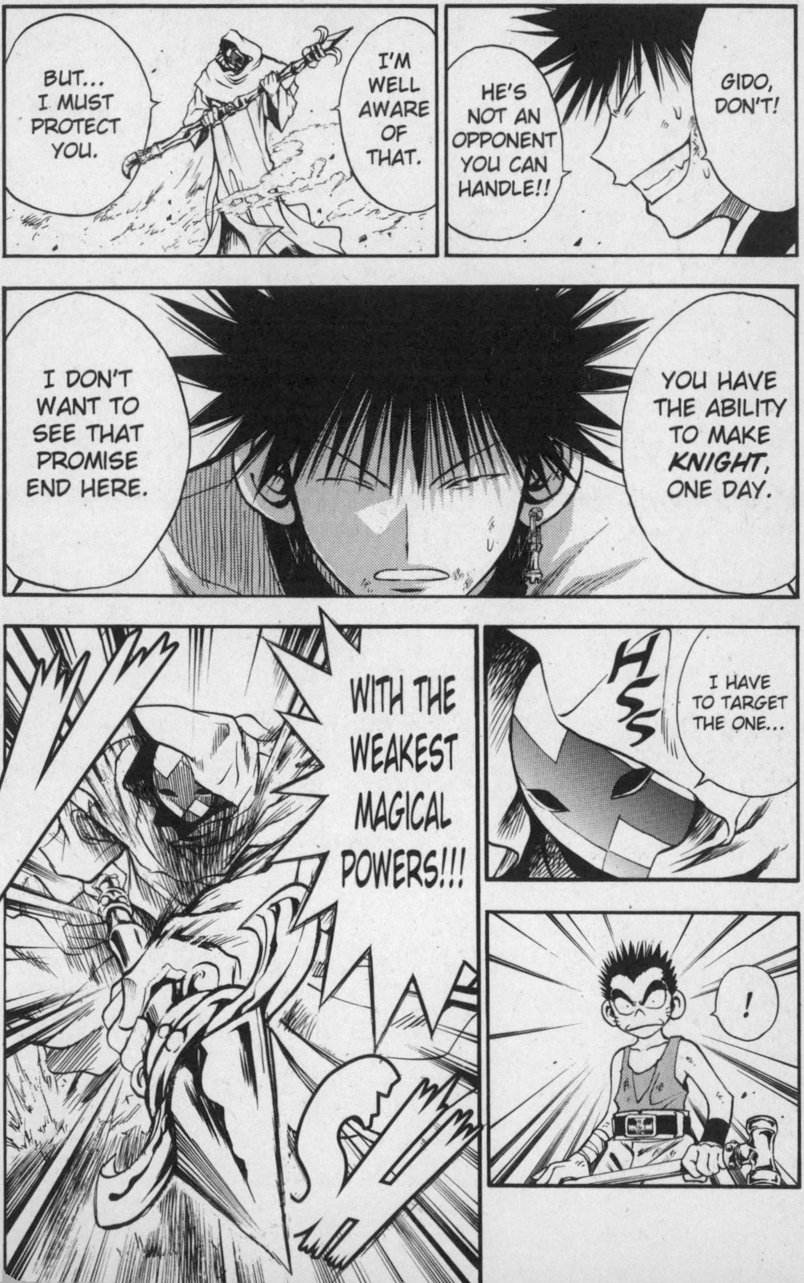
GIDO, DON'T!
HE'S NOT AN OPPONENT YOU CAN HANDLE!!
I'M WELL AWARE OF THAT.
BUT... I MUST PROTECT YOU.
YOU HAVE THE ABILITY TO MAKE *KNIGHT*, ONE DAY.
I DON'T WANT TO SEE THAT PROMISE END HERE.
I HAVE TO TARGET THE ONE...
HSS
!
WITH THE WEAKEST MAGICAL POWERS!!!

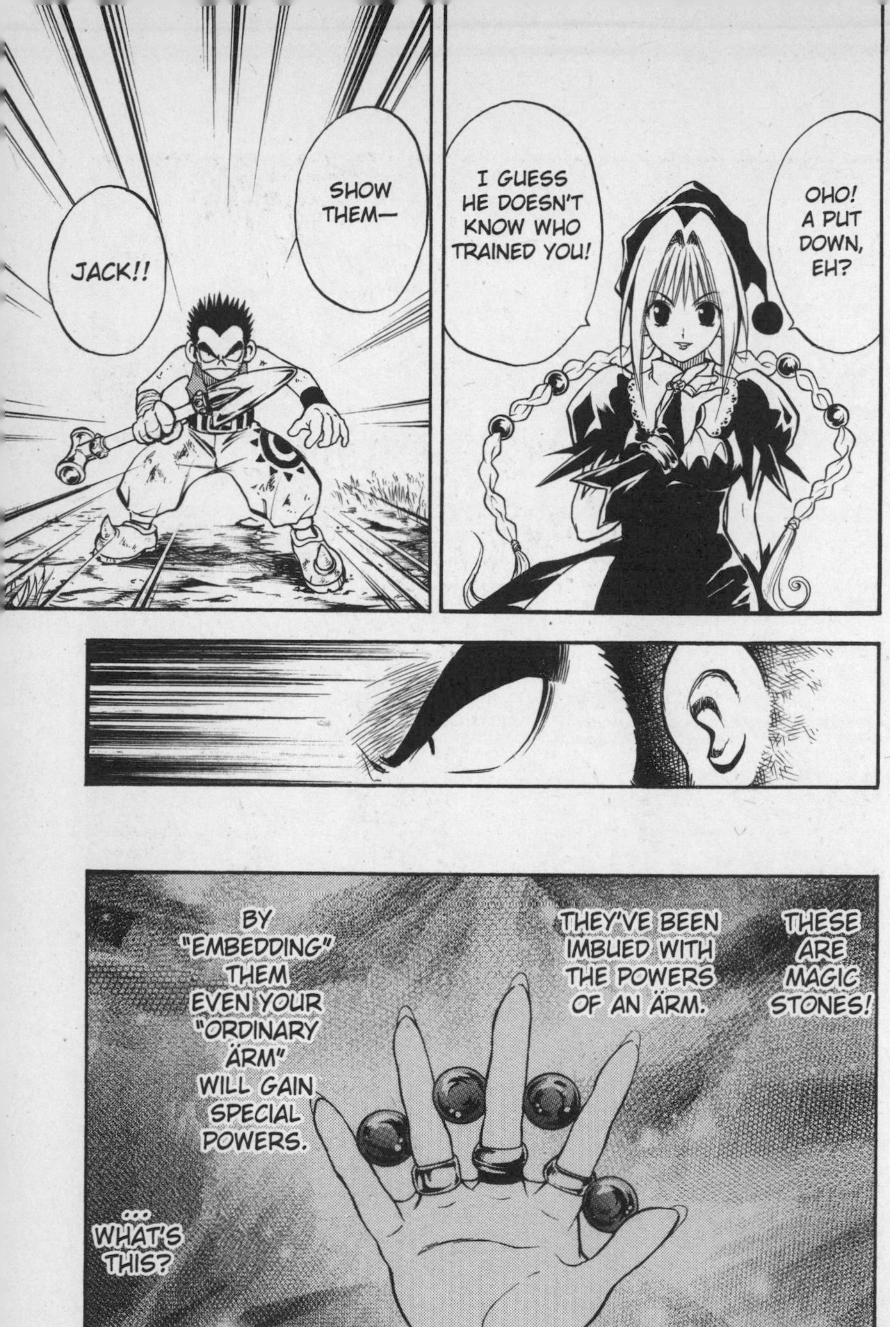
OHO! A PUT DOWN, EH?
I GUESS HE DOESN'T KNOW WHO TRAINED YOU!
SHOW THEM—
JACK!!
THESE ARE MAGIC STONES!
THEY'VE BEEN IMBUED WITH THE POWERS OF AN ÄRM.
BY "EMBEDDING" THEM EVEN YOUR "ORDINARY ÄRM" WILL GAIN SPECIAL POWERS.
...WHAT'S THIS?

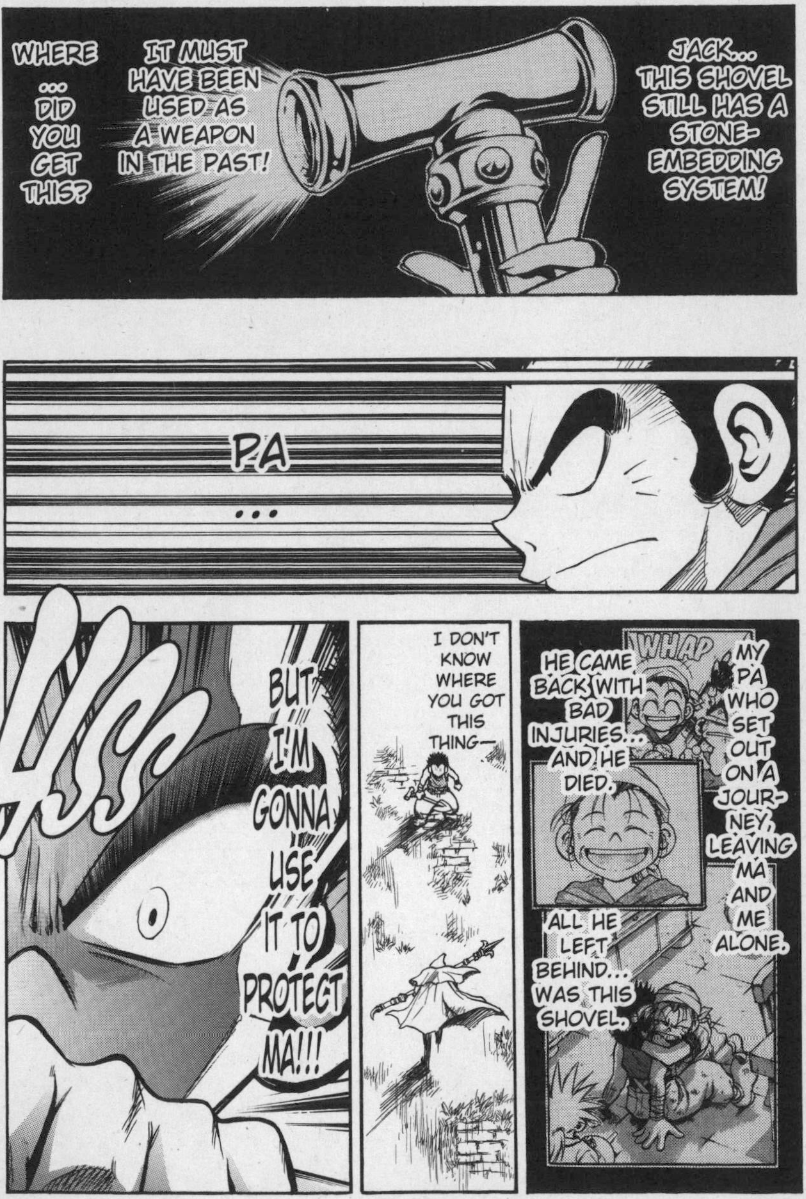
JACK... THIS SHOVEL STILL HAS A STONE-EMBEDDING SYSTEM!
IT MUST HAVE BEEN USED AS A WEAPON IN THE PAST!
WHERE ... DID YOU GET THIS?
PA ...
MY PA WHO SET OUT ON A JOURNEY, LEAVING MA AND ME ALONE.
WHAP
HE CAME BACK WITH BAD INJURIES... AND HE DIED.
ALL HE LEFT BEHIND... WAS THIS SHOVEL.
I DON'T KNOW WHERE YOU GOT THIS THING—
BUT I'M GONNA USE IT TO PROTECT MA!!!
HSS

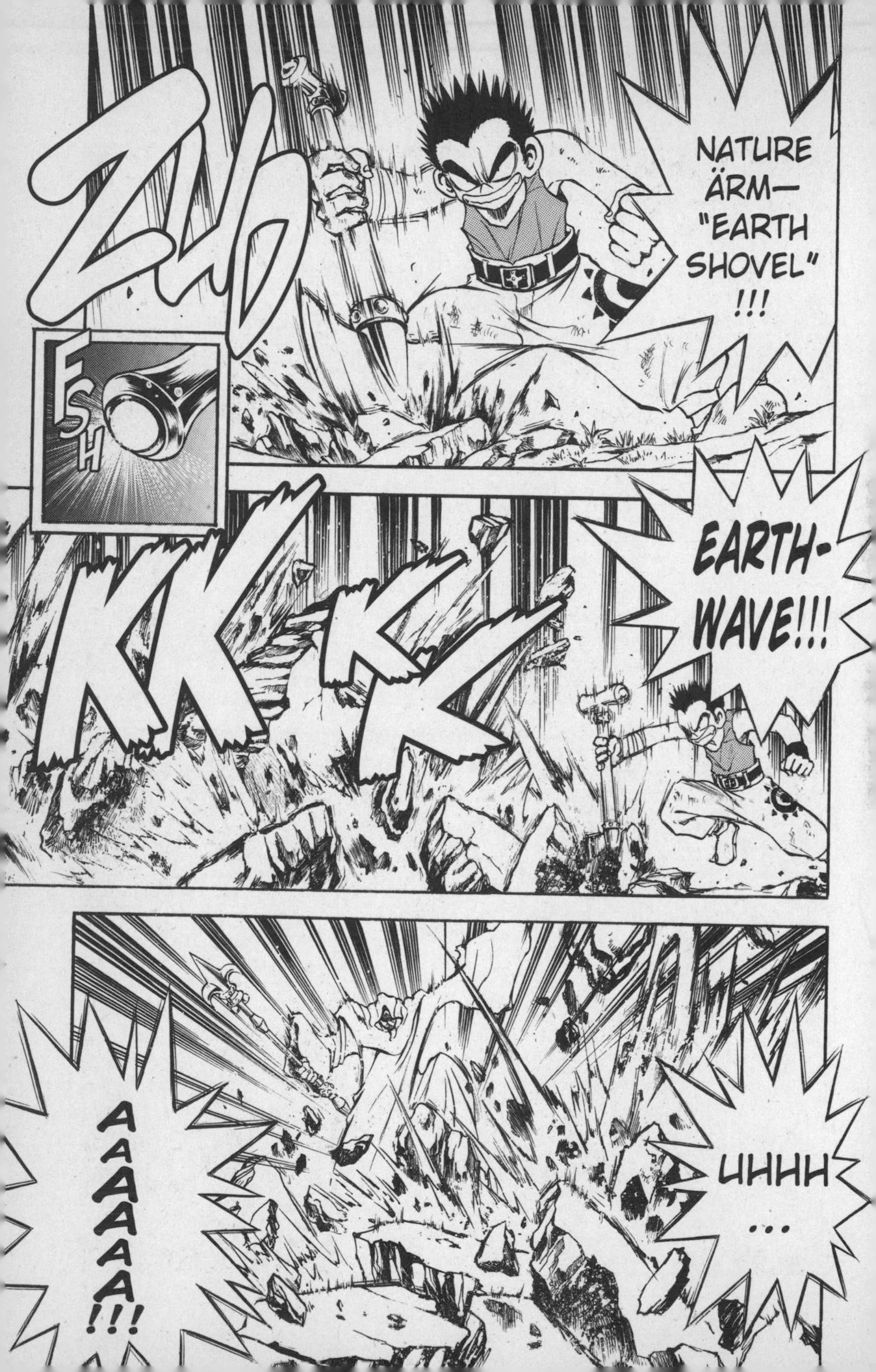
NATURE ÄRM— "EARTH SHOVEL" !!!
FSH
EARTH-WAVE!!!
KKK
UHHH ...
AAAAAAA!!!

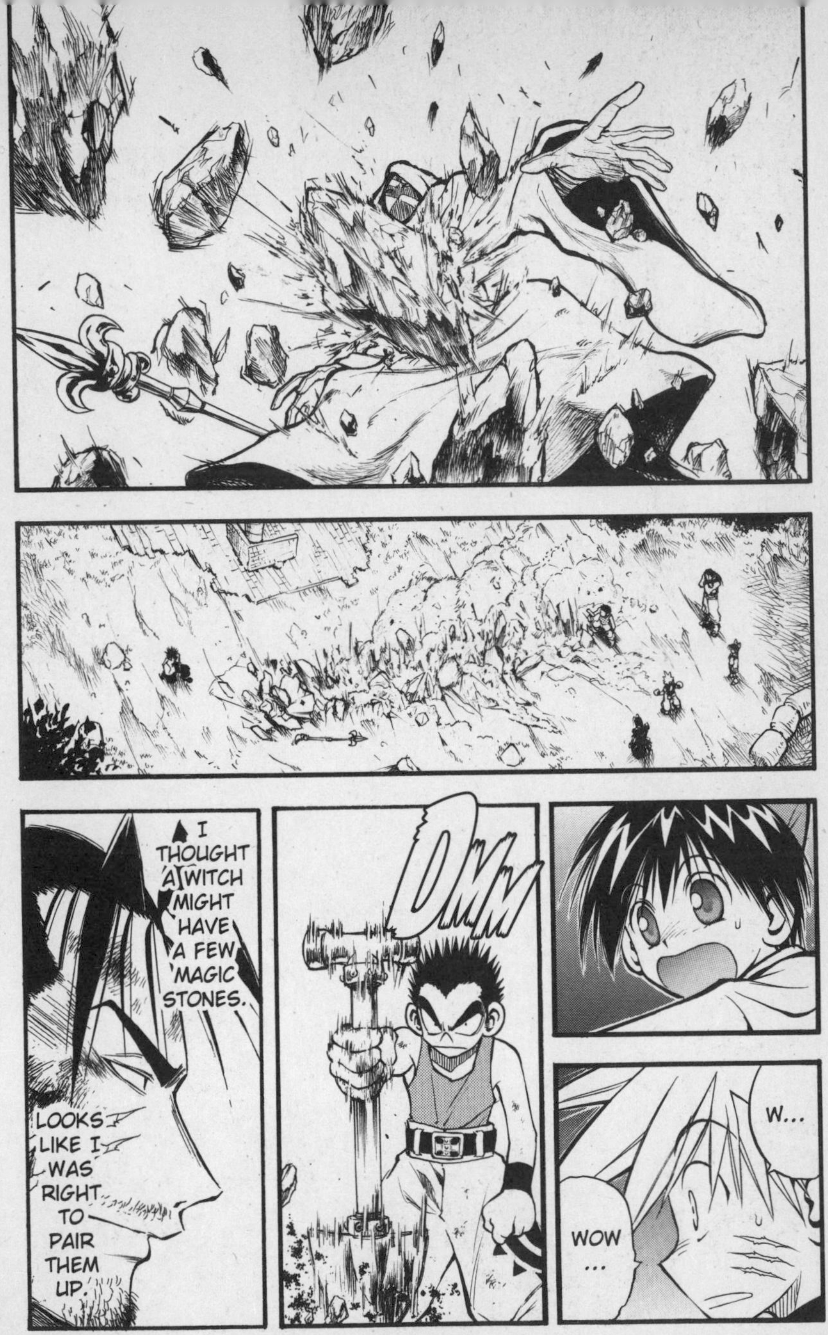
W...
WOW ...
DMM
I THOUGHT A WITCH MIGHT HAVE A FEW MAGIC STONES.
LOOKS LIKE I WAS RIGHT TO PAIR THEM UP.

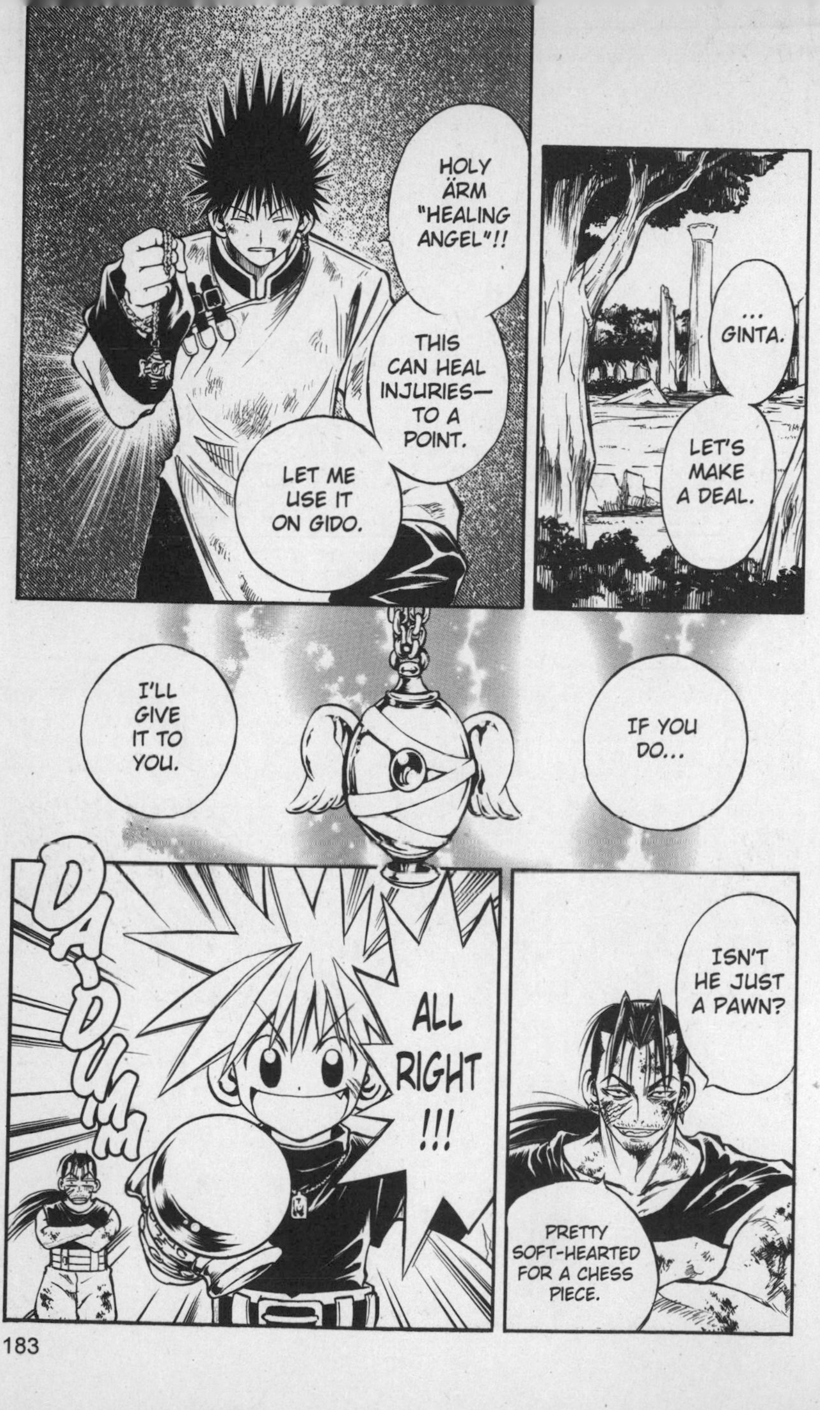
...GINTA.
LET'S MAKE A DEAL.
HOLY ÄRM "HEALING ANGEL"!!
THIS CAN HEAL INJURIES— TO A POINT.
LET ME USE IT ON GIDO.
IF YOU DO...
I'LL GIVE IT TO YOU.
ISN'T HE JUST A PAWN?
PRETTY SOFT-HEARTED FOR A CHESS PIECE.
DADUMM
ALL RIGHT !!!

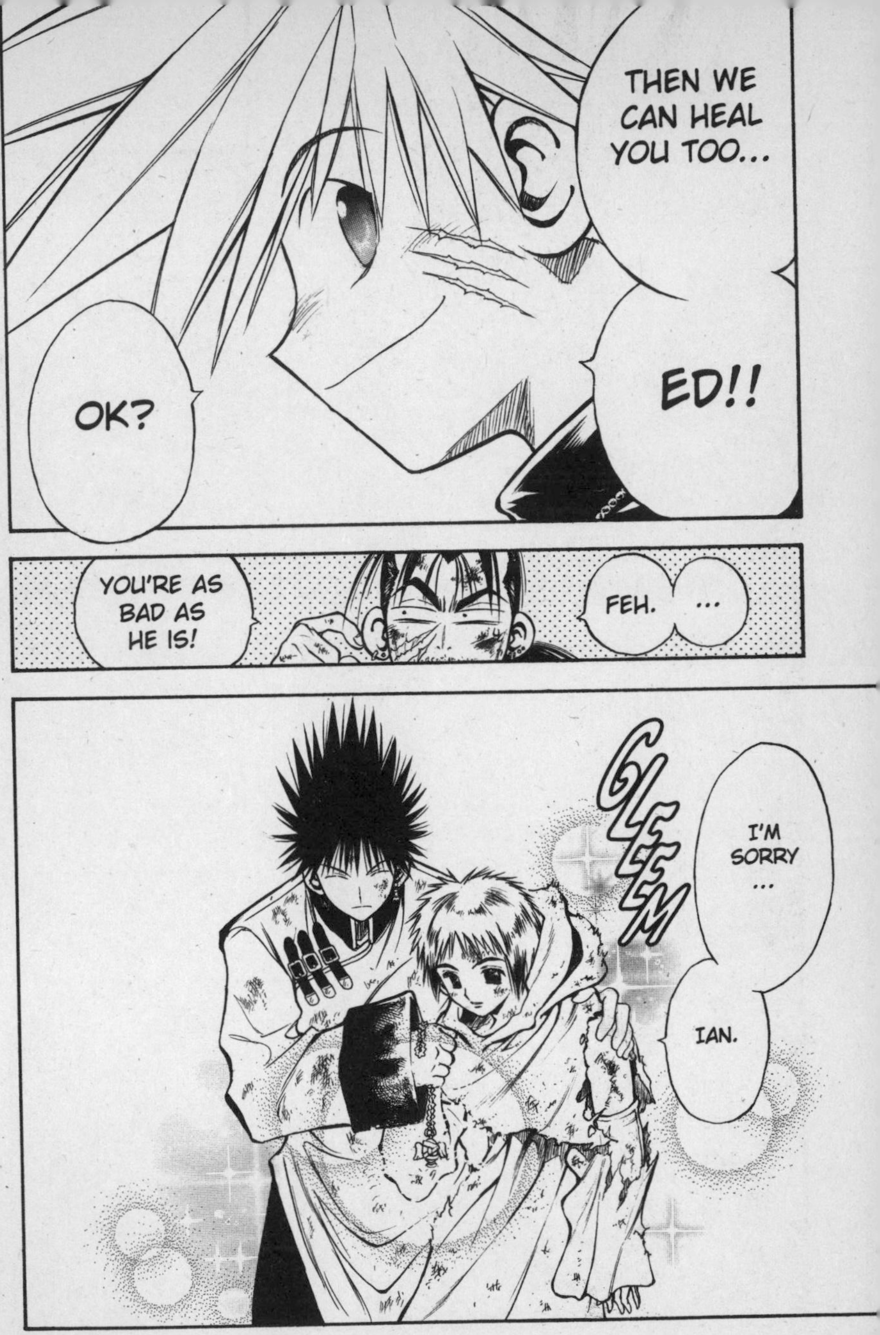
THEN WE CAN HEAL YOU TOO...
OK?
ED!!
...
FEH.
YOU'RE AS BAD AS HE IS!
GLEEM
I'M SORRY ...
IAN.

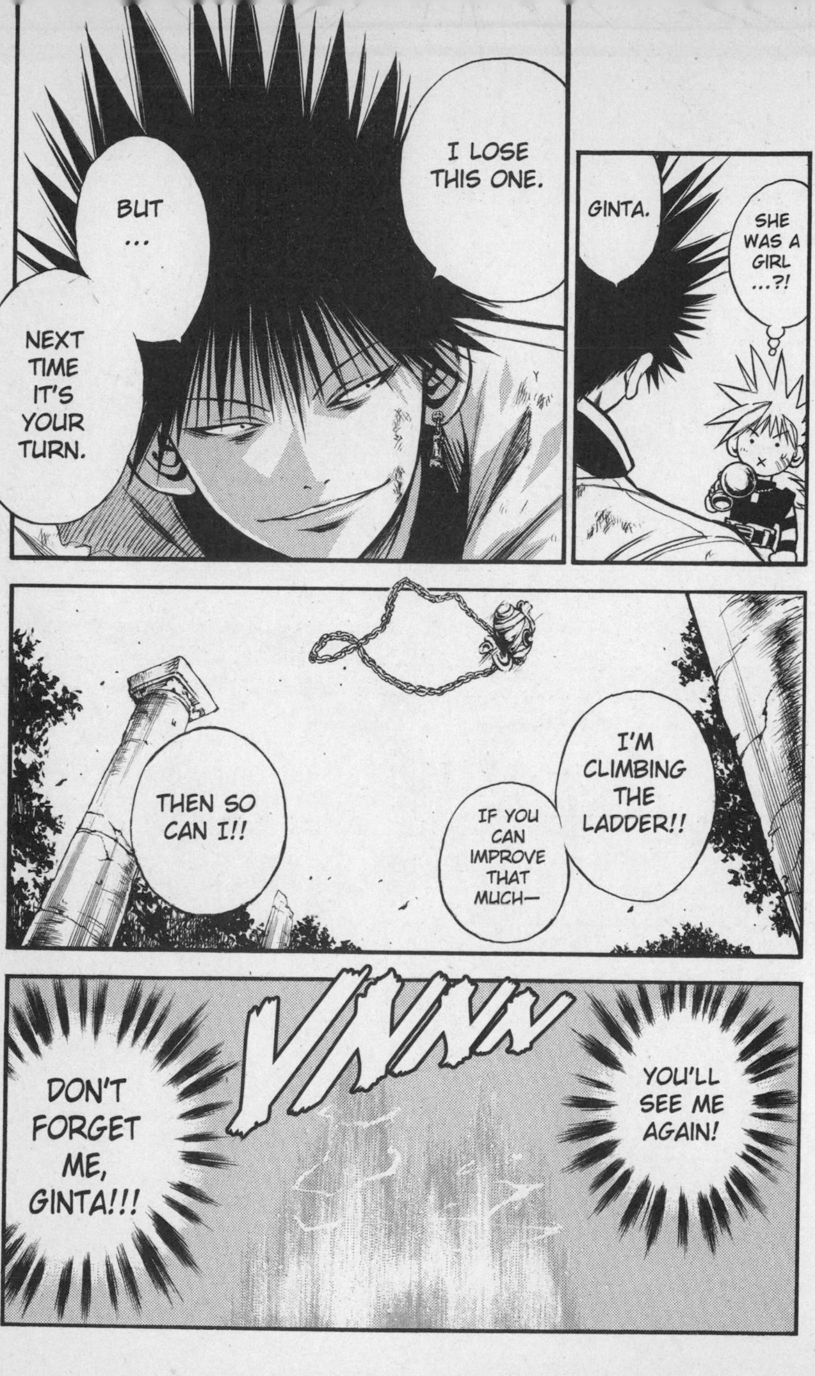
GINTA.
SHE WAS A GIRL ...?!
I LOSE THIS ONE.
BUT ...
NEXT TIME IT'S YOUR TURN.
I'M CLIMBING THE LADDER!!
IF YOU CAN IMPROVE THAT MUCH—
THEN SO CAN I!!
VNNN
YOU'LL SEE ME AGAIN!
DON'T FORGET ME, GINTA!!!

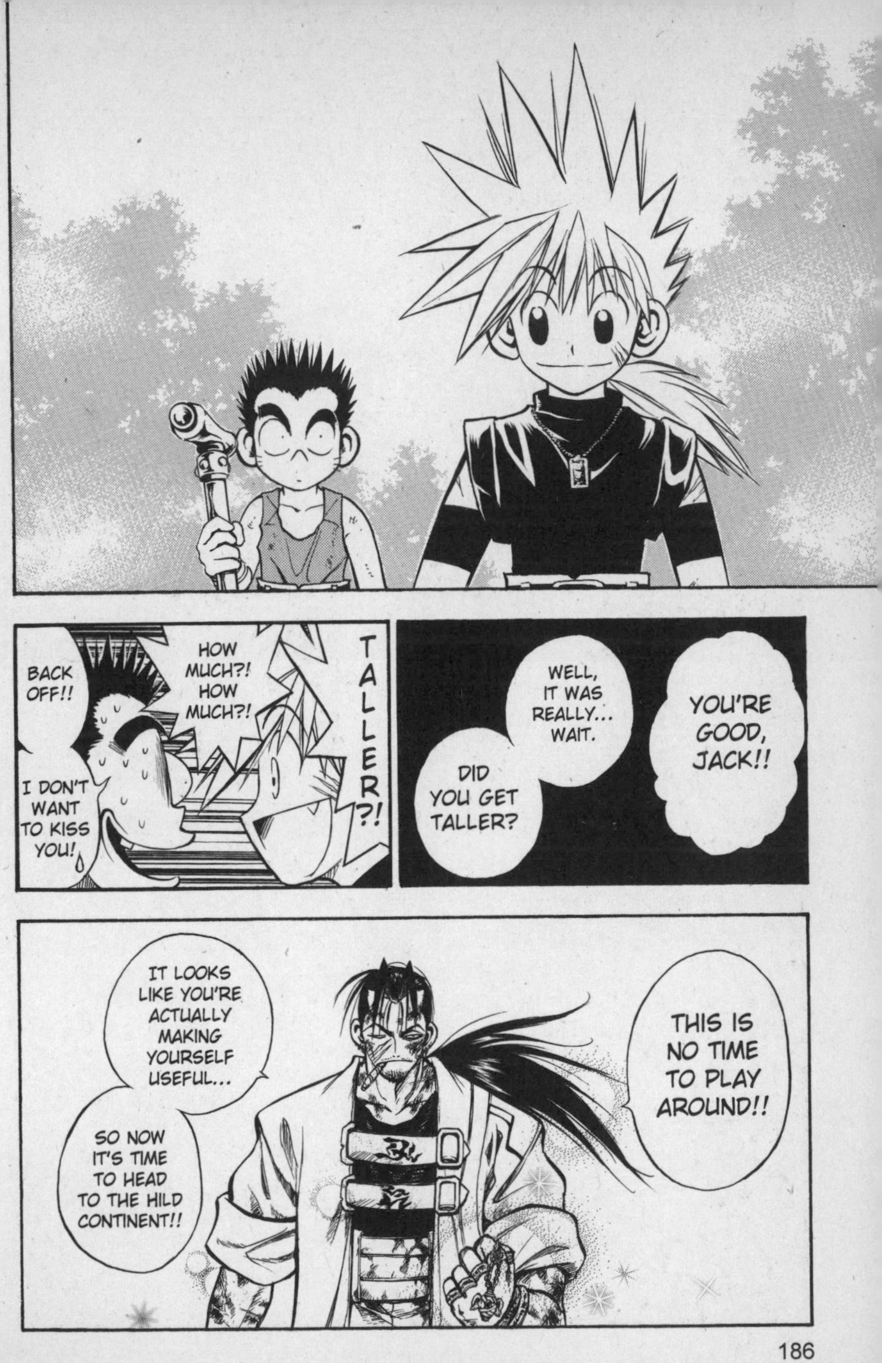
YOU'RE GOOD, JACK!!
WELL, IT WAS REALLY... WAIT.
DID YOU GET TALLER?
TALLER?!
HOW MUCH?! HOW MUCH?!
BACK OFF!!
I DON'T WANT TO KISS YOU!
THIS IS NO TIME TO PLAY AROUND!!
IT LOOKS LIKE YOU'RE ACTUALLY MAKING YOURSELF USEFUL...
SO NOW IT'S TIME TO HEAD TO THE HILD CONTINENT!!

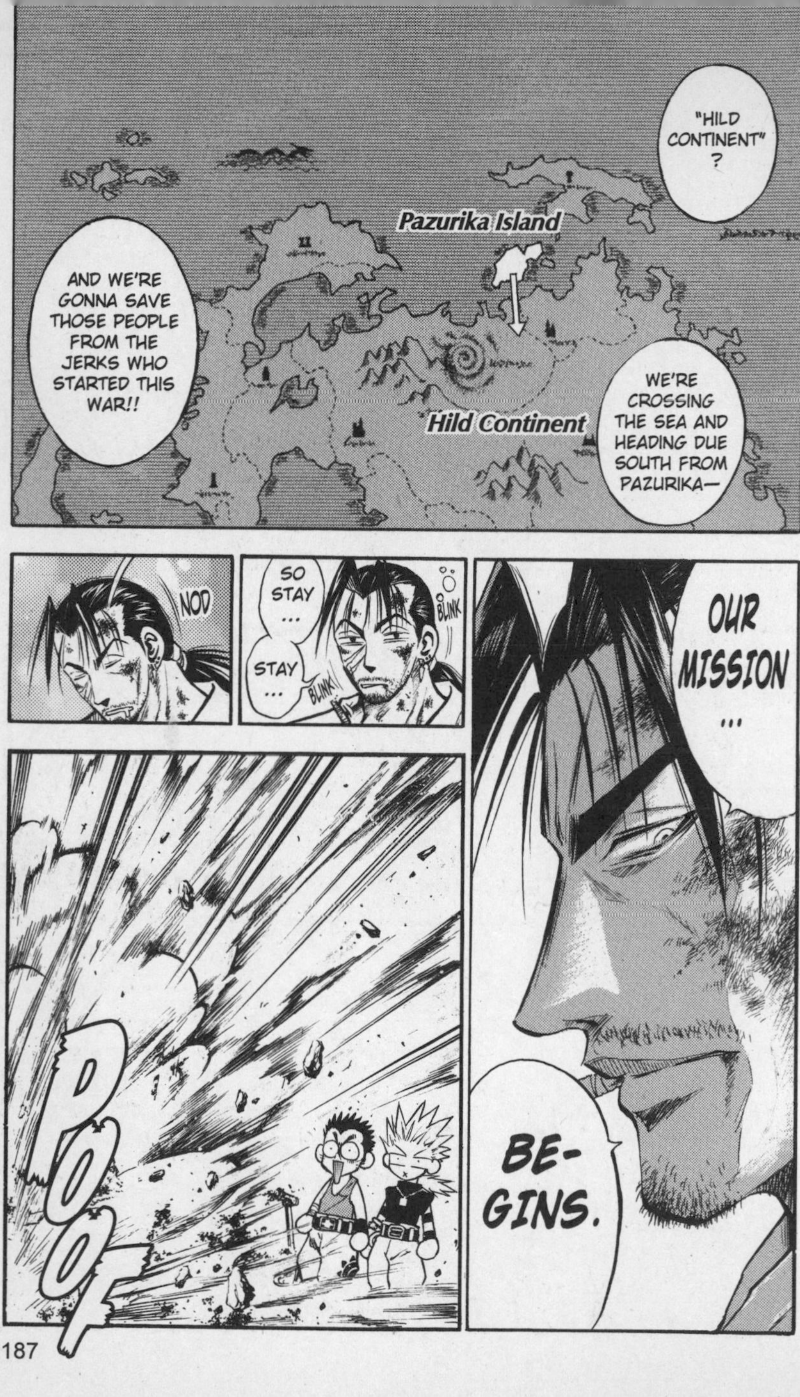
"HILD CONTINENT" ?
Pazurika Island
Hild Continent
WE'RE CROSSING THE SEA AND HEADING DUE SOUTH FROM PAZURIKA—
AND WE'RE GONNA SAVE THOSE PEOPLE FROM THE JERKS WHO STARTED THIS WAR!!
OUR MISSION ...
BE-GINS.
BLINK
SO STAY ...
STAY ...
BLINK
NOD
DOOF

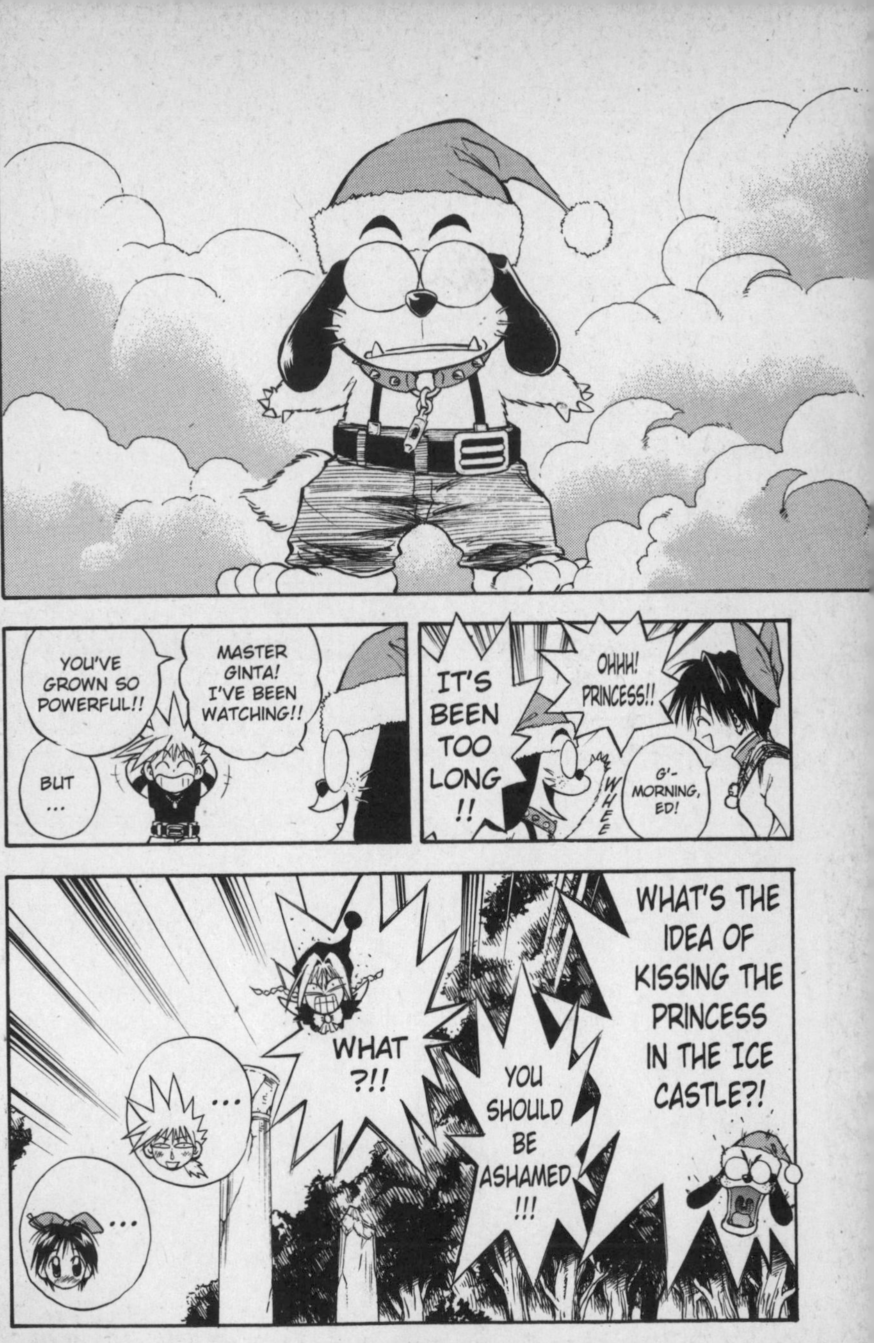

OHHH! PRINCESS!!
IT'S BEEN TOO LONG!!
WHEE
G'-MORNING, ED!
MASTER GINTA! I'VE BEEN WATCHING!!
YOU'VE GROWN SO POWERFUL!!
BUT ...
WHAT'S THE IDEA OF KISSING THE PRINCESS IN THE ICE CASTLE?!
YOU SHOULD BE ASHAMED!!!
WHAT ?!!
...
...

THE EXCITEMENT BUILDS...

MÄR

MÄRCHEN AWAKENS ROMANCE

Find them for the princess... and for Mär Heaven...

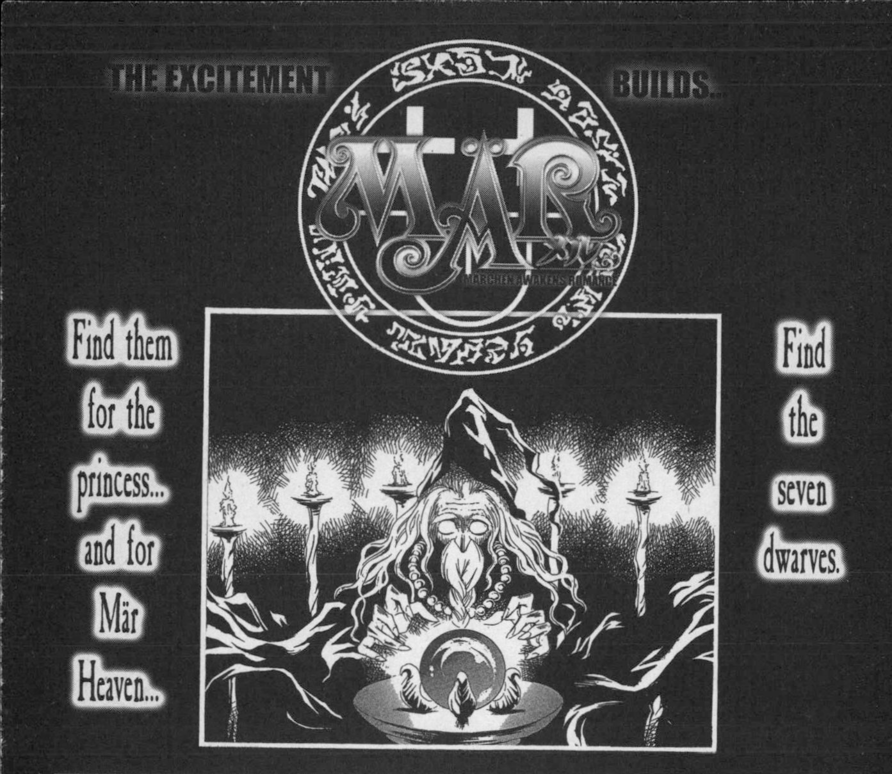

Find the seven dwarves.

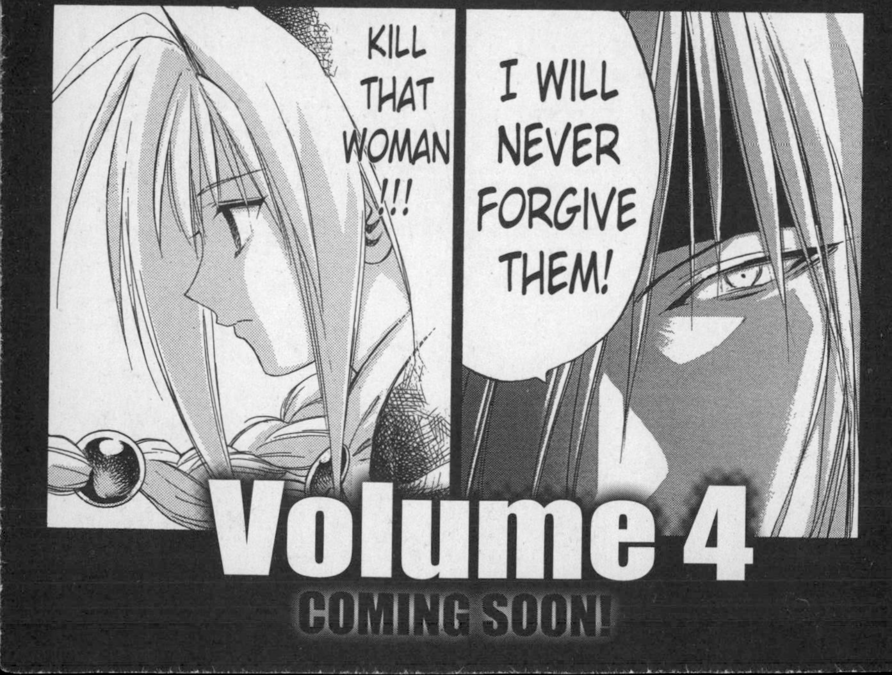
I WILL NEVER FORGIVE THEM!
KILL THAT WOMAN!!!

Volume 4

COMING SOON!

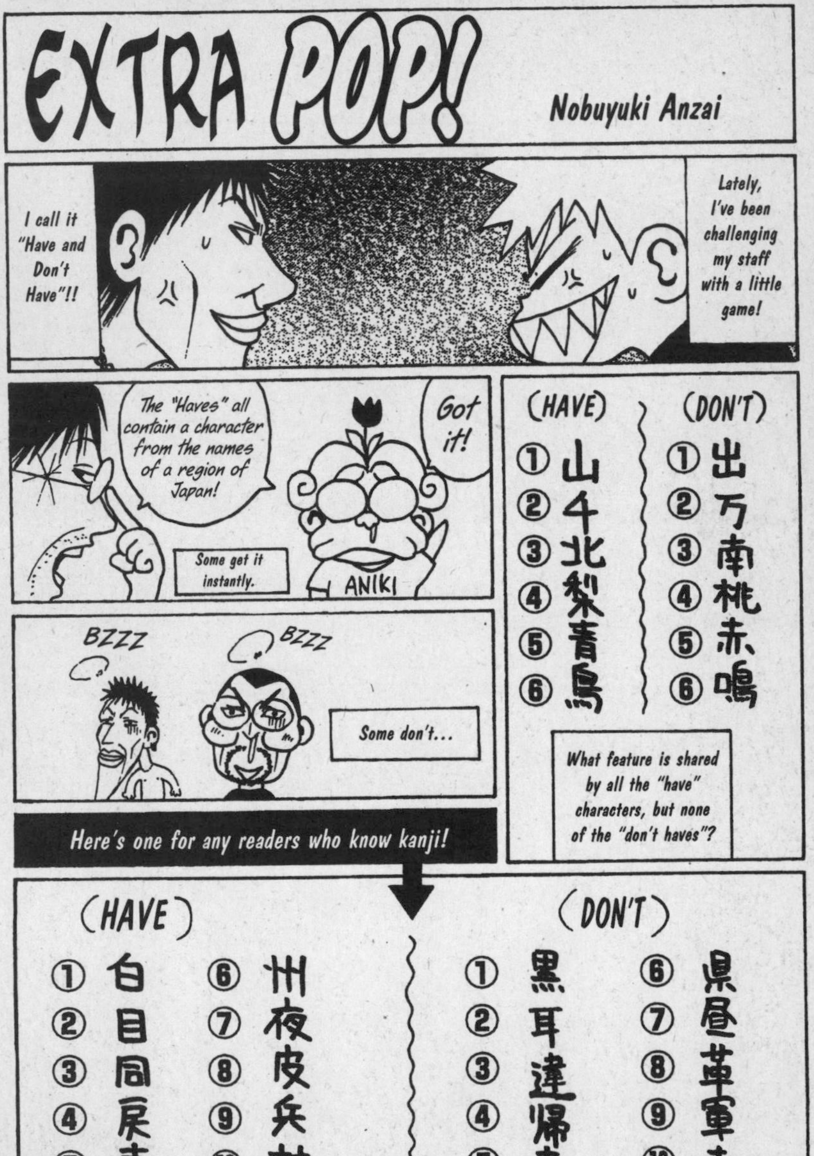
EXTRA POP!
Nobuyuki Anzai
Lately, I've been challenging my staff with a little game!
I call it "Have and Don't Have"!!
(HAVE)
① 山
② 午
③ 北
④ 梨
⑤ 青
⑥ 鳥
(DON'T)
① 出
② 万
③ 南
④ 桃
⑤ 赤
⑥ 鳴
What feature is shared by all the "have" characters, but none of the "don't haves"?
Got it!
The "Haves" all contain a character from the names of a region of Japan!
ANIKI
Some get it instantly.
BZZZ
BZZZ
Some don't...
Here's one for any readers who know kanji!
(HAVE)
① 白
② 目
③ 同
④ 戻
⑤ 青
⑥ 州
⑦ 夜
⑧ 皮
⑨ 兵
⑩ 林
(DON'T)
① 黒
② 耳
③ 達
④ 帰
⑤ 赤
⑥ 県
⑦ 昼
⑧ 革
⑨ 軍
⑩ 森

Author's Message:

Drawing by Koichiro Hishino (sub-chief)

NOBUYUKI ANZAI
安西信行
PRESENTS

For those of you who have gotten this book in your hands,
For those of you who sent fan letters,
For those of you who cheer us on,
I have not lost sight of feeling a great sense of appreciation.

Question & Answer Corner.

Q: When is your birthday?
A: I was born August 19th, 1972. I'm 31 years old (in 2003). An old geezer.

Q: Who are your favorite characters in Mär?
A: Dorothy and Ed (human).

MÄR

Vol. 3
Story and Art by Nobuyuki Anzai

English Adaptation/Gerard Jones
Translation/Kaori Inoue
Touch-up Art & Lettering/James Gaubatz
Design/Izumi Evers
Editor/Kit Fox and Pancha Diaz

Managing Editor/Annette Roman
Director of Production/Noboru Watanabe
Vice President of Publishing/Alvin Lu
Sr. Director of Acquisitions/Rika Inouye
Vice President of Sales & Marketing/Liza Coppola
Publisher/Hyoe Narita

Printed in Canada

Published by VIZ Media, LLC
P.O. Box 77010
San Francisco, CA 94107

10 9 8 7 6 5 4 3 2 1
First printing, August 2005

www.viz.com
store.viz.com

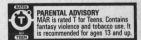

PARENTAL ADVISORY
MAR is rated T for Teens. Contains
fantasy violence and tobacco use. It
is recommended for ages 13 and up.

EDITOR'S RECOMMENDATIONS

If you enjoyed this volume of

MÄR
MÄRCHEN AWAKENS ROMANCE

then here's some more manga you might be interested in.

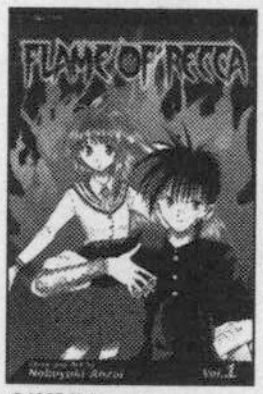
FLAME OF RECCA
Nobuyuki Anzai
Vol.1
©1995 Nobuyuki ANZAI/Shogakukan Inc.

Flame of Recca by Nobuyuki Anzai: Get ready for some red-hot ninja action as Recca Hanabishi uses his fire magic to pummel punks, bullies, and demons alike. While you're at it, don't forget to check out the animated version of *Flame of Recca* too!

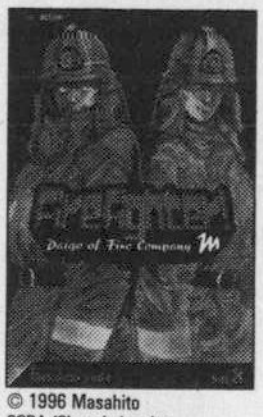
Firefighter!
Daigo of Fire Company M
© 1996 Masahito SODA/Shogakukan Inc.

Firefighter! Daigo of Fire Company M by Masahito Soda: Daigo Asahina has been imbued with the burning desire to save lives, but his highly unorthodox rescue tactics do anything *but* please his higher-ups. Is Daigo destined to become the greatest firefighter of all time? Probably.

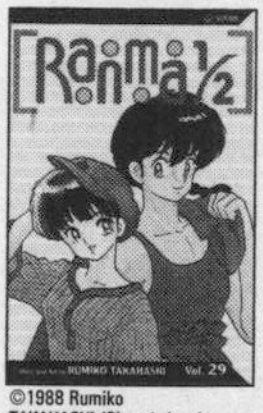
Ranma 1/2
RUMIKO TAKAHASHI
Vol. 29
©1988 Rumiko TAKAHASHI/Shogakukan Inc.

Ranma 1/2 by Rumiko Takahashi: This classic gender-bending action-comedy has become one of the benchmarks by which all other manga are measured. Internationally hailed and beloved by many, this tale of a boy-who-becomes-a-girl mixes martial arts action, romance, and slapstick comedy into a manga that can't be beat. Don't forget the animated version either!

MIDORI DAYS™
Talk About a Right Hook!
I ♥ SEIJI
ONLY $9.99!
Midori Days 1
Kazurou Inoue
MIDORI DAYS
Story and art by Kazurou Inoue
Vol. 1
Seiji is the toughest 17-year-old in town, feared for his deadly "devil's right hand." One day, he wakes up to discover his "devil's right hand" has turned into... a miniature gal named Midori!? What's worse is that Midori is a real girl who's always had a crush on Seiji, and her desperate wish to be connected to him has somehow really, really come true!
Get your hands on the graphic novels—buy yours at store.viz.com today!
viz media
www.viz.com
© 2004 Kazurou Inoue/Shogakukan, Inc.

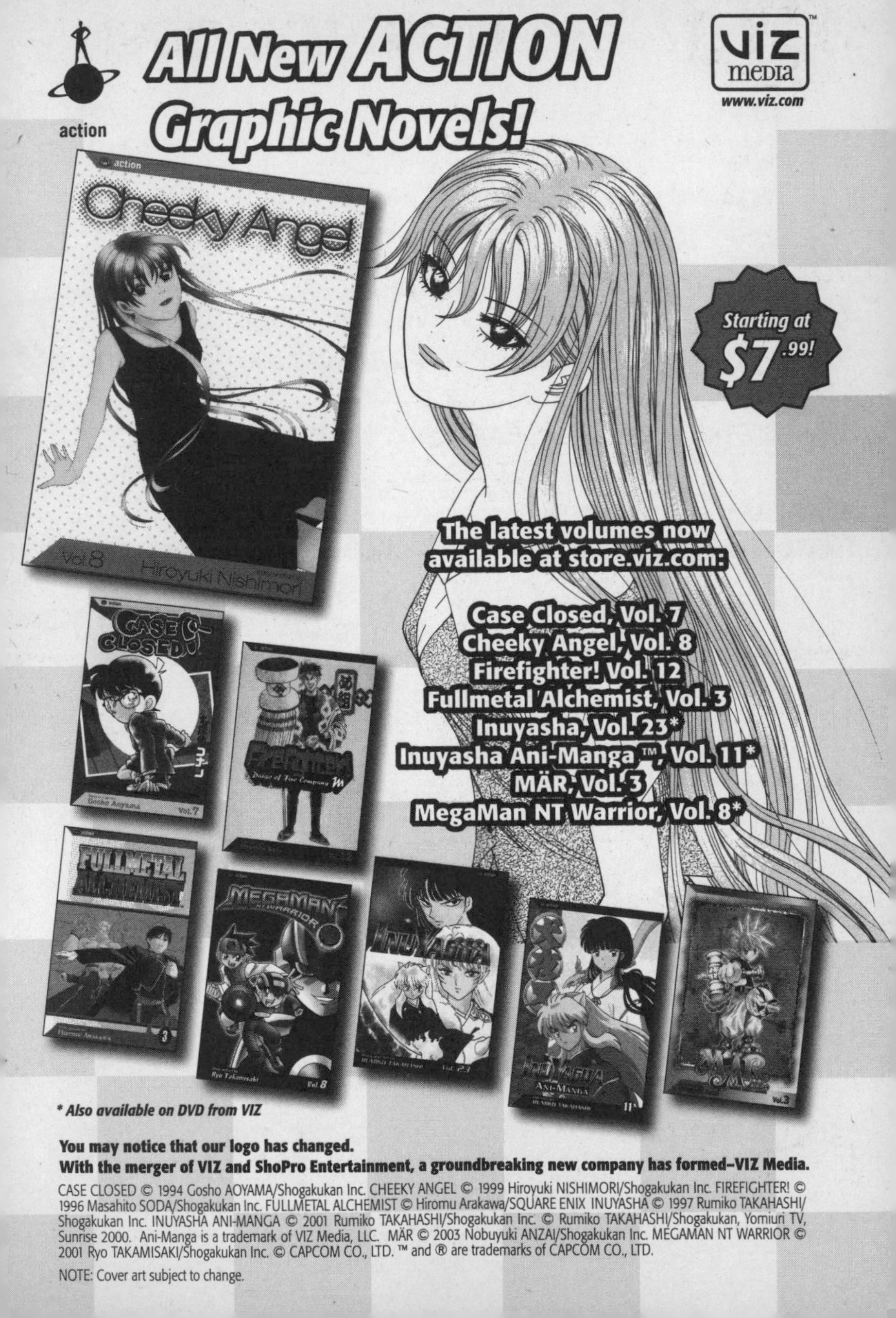

LOVE MANGA? LET US KNOW!

☐ Please do NOT send me information about VIZ Media products, news and events, special offers, or other information.

☐ Please do NOT send me information from VIZ Media's trusted business partners.

Name: _____

Address: _____

City: _____ **State:** _____ **Zip:** _____

E-mail: _____

☐ Male ☐ Female **Date of Birth** (mm/dd/yyyy): ___ / ___ / _____ (Under 13? Parental consent required)

What race/ethnicity do you consider yourself? (check all that apply)

☐ White/Caucasian   ☐ Black/African American   ☐ Hispanic/Latino

☐ Asian/Pacific Islander   ☐ Native American/Alaskan Native   ☐ Other: _____

What VIZ title(s) did you purchase? (indicate title(s) purchased) _____

_____

What other VIZ titles do you own? _____

_____

Reason for purchase: (check all that apply)

☐ Special offer   ☐ Favorite title / author / artist / genre

☐ Gift   ☐ Recommendation   ☐ Collection

☐ Read excerpt in VIZ manga sampler   ☐ Other _____

Where did you make your purchase? (please check one)

☐ Comic store   ☐ Bookstore   ☐ Grocery Store

☐ Convention   ☐ Newsstand   ☐ Video Game Store

☐ Online (site:_____)   ☐ Other _____

How many manga titles have you purchased in the last year? How many were VIZ titles?
(please check one from each column)

MANGA
☐ None
☐ 1 – 4
☐ 5 – 10
☐ 11+

VIZ
☐ None
☐ 1 – 4
☐ 5 – 10
☐ 11+

How much influence do special promotions and gifts-with-purchase have on the titles you buy?
(please circle, with 5 being great influence and 1 being none)

1   2   3   4   5

Do you purchase every volume of your favorite series?

☐ Yes! Gotta have 'em as my own   ☐ No. Please explain: _____

What kind of manga storylines do you most enjoy? (check all that apply)

☐ Action / Adventure   ☐ Science Fiction   ☐ Horror
☐ Comedy   ☐ Romance (shojo)   ☐ Fantasy (shojo)
☐ Fighting   ☐ Sports   ☐ Historical
☐ Artistic / Alternative   ☐ Other_____

If you watch the anime or play a video or TCG game from a series, how likely are you to buy the manga? (please circle, with 5 being very likely and 1 being unlikely)

1   2   3   4   5

If unlikely, please explain: _____

Who are your favorite authors / artists? _____

_____

What titles would like you translated and sold in English? _____

_____

THANK YOU! Please send the completed form to:

viz
media

NJW Research
42 Catharine Street
Poughkeepsie, NY 12601